LEADING AMERICAN
MEN OF SCIENCE

SR Scholarly Resources Inc.
Wilmington, Delaware • London

SCHOLARLY RESOURCES, INC.
Wilmington, Delaware • London

Reprint edition published in 1973
First published in 1910 by Henry Holt and Company,
    New York

Reprinted from the Collection of
Duke University Library

Library of Congress Catalog Card Number: 72-94315
ISBN: 0-8420-1674-0

Manufactured in the United States of America

Rumford.

𝕭iographies of 𝕷eading 𝕬mericans

Edited by W. P. TRENT

LEADING AMERICAN MEN OF SCIENCE

EDITED BY

DAVID STARR JORDAN

President of Stanford University

WITH SEVENTEEN PORTRAITS

NEW YORK

HENRY HOLT AND COMPANY

1910

CONTENTS [1]

[1] The lives are arranged, not chronologically by date of birth, but by median date.

v

PORTRAITS

LEADING AMERICAN MEN OF SCIENCE

EDITOR'S PREFACE

AT the death of Simon Newcomb, it was stated in one of our journals that he had left "a record wholly blameless and wholly salutary, whose work added to the only permanent wealth of nations." In this view is found the key-note of the present volume. In the extension and coördination of human experience, in the widening of the boundaries of knowledge and in the attainment of greater exactness in the details, is found the only permanent wealth of nations. All this constitutes the subject-matter of science, and in science we find the basis for the development of the finest of fine arts, that of human conduct. As we understand better the universe around us, our relations to others and to ourselves, the behavior of our race becomes rationalized. It becomes possible for us to keep ourselves clean, and to make ourselves open-minded, friendly and God-fearing. In the achievements of science, therefore, we may properly find the only permanent wealth of nations. It is the only wealth which is superior to fire and flood, the only wealth beyond the reach of entanglements of political intrigue, or the wanton ravages of war.

To the men who have widened the boundaries of human knowledge, we owe a debt which we can repay only by a friendly remembrance of the work these men have done. We owe them our gratitude for their successes, and their mistakes call on us only for our sympathy. No one knows their struggles or their achievements so well as those who have followed them over the same paths.

In this fact the present volume finds its reason for being. Mr. Henry Holt, whom we may without offense call "our beloved publisher," first planned this book. It was his desire that it should contain short and sympathetic biographies of fifteen leaders in American science, each one written by a man in some degree

3

known as a disciple.   The subjects of these sketches should all be
chosen from the list of those no longer living.   While no one can
say which of all these is greatest, the fifteen should be chosen from
among the great.   Benjamin Franklin, whose name comes to the
front at the first, was omitted, as his biography was already provided for in another volume in the same series.   Simon Newcomb
and William Keith Brooks, men with undisputed place in the
first rank, were added, as they passed from earth while the volume was nearing completion.

At the request of Mr. Holt, the present writer, as a labor of love,
undertook the compilation of these records.   He is responsible
for the choice of subjects, and for the choice of authors, but the
pressure of work forced him to stop at that point, and to place
the editorial work in the more competent hands of Dr. Edwin E.
Slosson, with whom all further responsibility in this volume rests.

But before laying down his pen, a few general considerations
rise to his attention.

This volume constitutes a part of the scientific record of the
republic for a hundred years.   It is the history of struggles in a
new country, without great libraries, great museums or great universities.   It represents self-help and self-reliance to a greater degree than would be shown in a parallel volume in any other land.
It shows the rise of observation and of knowledge derived from
travel, before that arising from experiment, or that deduced by
analytical reasoning.   It shows the early charm of "the land where
nature is rich, while tools and appliances are few, while of traditions there are none."   With this, no doubt, is associated the charm
of loveableness, characteristic of so many of these men, who
studied nature because they loved her.   With all this, too, theirs
were uneventful lives, as we measure life in the stress of modern
industrial development.   Leaving aside Benjamin Thompson,
whose history was wholly unique, nothing startling happened to
any one of them.   None of them gained or lost great wealth.
None of them was elected to the Senate; none of them led embat-
tled hosts to victory, and none took part in any form of public
melodrama which would make his name known in the theaters

or on the streets. Agassiz, always picturesque and always intensely alive, could not be said to have had a commonplace career, for everything in life was to him a marvel. The wonderful was ever close to his open-eyed enthusiasm, and the fresh-laid egg of a snapping turtle recalled the whole succession in a world of eternal life. Another picturesque figure was Audubon, artist and gentleman, in his velvet hunting coat sketching the birds of the American wilderness.

But the rest lived quietly and worked quietly and saw truth. Theirs were happy lives, for the most part very happy, and their record is the register of "the permanent wealth" of our nation.

Another feature we may note in these men is their willingness for public service. The justification of science, is, after all, the help it can give men towards better ordered lives. It was the dream of Professor Baird that there should arise in Washington a great body or bureau of coöperative science, that in this democracy there should be maintained a body of wise men, keen-eyed men who should accomplish by working together what none of them could do separately, and the result of their combined efforts should be always at the service of the bureaus of administration. Thus from the Smithsonian Institution, Henry, Baird, Goode, Langley, arose the National Museum, the Fish Commission; and in similar fashion arose the Marine Hospital Service, the Bureau of Forestry, and the other bureaus of investigation in the Department of Agriculture. But Baird was not alone in giving his great powers freely to the public service. Many other have recognized the fact that pure science and applied science are not different in nature or function, and often science is strengthened and dignified when it is tested by placing it in action.

In going over the lives of these men, we notice that for the most part each one followed his natural bent in devoting himself to science. Love of his work, the pulsation of personal enthusiasm, is perhaps the greatest single asset a man of science can have. Nothing but love of the work could lead a man to take up a scientific career in the pioneer days of the republic, and these days have not yet passed. Men without enthusiasm can be trained to see, to record and to think, but the fine glow of the missionary spirit is not with these.

And this fine glow enabled many of these men to become great teachers. To be a great teacher is in part a matter of tempera-ment, though that power may lie with a silent and reserved man, like Brooks, as well as with the eloquent and visibly sympathetic ways of Agassiz. Some few, though teachers, lacked the teach-ing spirit; Gibbs for example was a lonely thinker, unknown to students and colleagues, the author of books no one in his genera-tion was ready to read.

The crowning privilege of the great teacher lies in the heredity of his inspiration, his power to found a school of greatness among younger men who have caught his enthusiasm and his methods. Such series are well recognized in American science. I once heard Agassiz say: "I lived for four years under Dr. Döllinger's roof, and my scientific training goes back to him and to him alone." The descendants of Agassiz are well traceable in American sci-ence. There is scarcely a worker in biology and geology of the older generation who was not in some degree at some time a pupil of Agassiz. It is now nearly forty years since Agassiz died, and the youngest of those of us who knew him are now coming also to the age of sixty, the age when a man is set in his ways and can learn nothing new.

In his Autobiography, Darwin, who never spared himself, deplores the fact that with increasing knowledge (and a long period of nervous invalidism) his mind had suffered a partial atrophy, and his interest in literature, even the best, had largely failed him. From this unfortunate fact, frankly expressed, the lesson has been drawn wearisomely that one should shun too much devotion to science, under penalty of esthetic and spiritual barrenness. It is clear from the frequent references in these biographies to artistic taste and skill, that Darwin's experience was individual, and doubt-less in some degree pathological. These men for the most part found science a source of mental freshening. They lost no human interest which they had ever possessed. In witness of this fact, we see another of our great men of science, Shaler, a life-long boy, writing off-hand Elizabethan drama, of a degree of merit not surpassed by any who have written the like since the days of the great dramatists themselves.

We find again in the well-ordered lives of most of these men of real greatness, no warrant for the notion that the "superman" will rise superior to the canons of common morality and common decency. They loved their wives, they cherished their families, they never figured in problem plays. The one or two exceptions which the acute historian may discover only serve to emphasize the rule that with sound brains go sound morals.

To compare these men with a like number of like men in England, Germany or France, would be a problem too difficult to be treated here. We are accustomed to hearing our real greatness underrated, while the petty incidents of new world life have been subjects of much cheap boasting. In brief, I believe that these names deserve to stand with the highest in their generation, and that no nation could require a better record than theirs. Germany has more men of scientific eminence for her population. England has fewer. But the greatest of England are in no way less than the greatest of Germany. Social conditions and legal requirements drive students of all grades and of all professions in Germany to the Universities. The fees of many doctors call strong men to the University, when such men in England or in America would be occupied in other ways. German professors supported by fees may teach or study as they like. Once chosen to a professorship the rest depends on their choice. American professors paid directly for teaching, largely with public funds, and never by the fees of their students, must perforce teach. As our universities are organized, half *gymnasium*, half university, the ideal of research can be present with but few of them; actual achievement in investigation with still fewer. Yet, taking the field at large, I cannot sympathize with those who find little to praise in American science. In the fields cultivated in the closet and the library, Germany is preëminent, for she has many closets and many libraries. In the fields which carry men into the open—topographical geology; paleontology; geographical distribution; faunology;

taxonomy, Germany has some of the greatest of names, but her great names are few beside those of the United States. If our besetting sin is lack of intensity, as befits the breadth and length of our continent, that of Germany is myopia, as befits a man whose universe is limited to the field of his microscope. There are many reasons which call the German from business life to the University, and many reasons why science is the well-paid agent of manufacture. With us there are many reasons which call a man away from the classroom, and the intervals between classes still constitute our period for research.

Yet for all these deficiencies we shall find our remedies, and these remedies in time will be potent. The roll of our scientific men to-day shows a worthy succession to the long line from Rumford to Brooks. With all defects in American education, there is no falling off in ability nor in enthusiasm, nor in facility for contact with things as they are. We may be therefore confident that the volume of this series, which shall cover the twentieth instead of the nineteenth century, will show great names, great achievements and great personalities, worthy to rank with the best of these, our fathers in science, and such names, too, in ever increasing numbers, even as proportioned to our wealth and our population.

DAVID STARR JORDAN.

BENJAMIN THOMPSON, COUNT RUMFORD

PHYSICIST

1753–1814

By Edwin E. Slosson

The life of a scholar is apt to be a quiet one, externally devoid of dramatic incidents and sudden changes of fortune, but there is material enough to satisfy a writer of historical romances in the life of the poor New England boy who became, in England, cavalry colonel, Under Secretary of State and Sir Benjamin Thompson; in Bavaria, Count Rumford of the Holy Roman Empire, Privy Councilor, Minister of War, Chief of Police and Chamberlain to the Elector Palatine; in Paris, husband of a *femme savante* of a French Salon; and who died alone and friendless in the city where he had been honored by Napoleon while living, and was eulogized by Cuvier when dead. The name of the New England town which persecuted him as a traitor he made known and honored throughout the world; he left his fortune to the country he fought. England owes to him the Royal Institution, as we owe our similar Smithsonian Institution to an Englishman. In Munich he had a monument erected in his honor while yet alive for his philanthropic work, and was lampooned by the press of London for doing the same work there. As an intellectual free lance he did service in as many different realms of science as he did military service in different countries. He laid the first foundation of the greatest generalization the human mind has yet conceived, the law of the conservation of energy, and he explained the construction of coffee-pots. He was in action and thought a paradoxical philosopher.

Benjamin Thompson was born March 25, 1753, at Woburn, Mass., in the farmhouse of his grandfather Ebenezer Thompson. The house is still standing, preserved as a museum by the Rumford Historical Association. He was a descendant of James Thompson who came to New England with Governor Winthrop in 1630, and was one of the first settlers of Woburn.

A few months after his birth his father died at the age of 26, thus leaving him to the care of his mother and grandfather. Just three years after the birth of Benjamin his mother married Josiah Pierce, Jr., of Woburn, who received from his guardian an allowance of two shillings and fivepence per week until the boy was seven years old. To the apparent misfortune of thus being deprived at an early age of both paternal care and patrimony he owed his European career. As he said in later years to his friend, Professor Pictet of Geneva:

"If the death of my father had not, contrary to the order of nature, preceded that of my grandfather who gave all his property to my uncle, his second son, I should have lived and died an American husbandman. It was a circumstance purely accidental, which, while I was an infant, decided my destiny in attracting my attention to the object of science. The father of one of my companions, a very respectable minister, and, besides, very enlightened (by name Barnard), gave me his friendship, and of his own prompting, undertook to instruct me. He taught me algebra, geometry, astronomy and even the higher mathematics. Before the age of fourteen, I had made sufficient progress in this class of studies to be able, without his aid and even without his knowledge, to calculate and trace correctly the elements of a solar eclipse. We observed it together, and my computation was correct within four seconds. I shall never forget the intense pleasure which this success afforded me, nor the praises which it drew from him. I had been destined for trade, but after a short trial, my thirst for knowledge became inextinguishable, and I would not apply myself to anything but my favorite objects of study."

This account of his early education confirms the legends of his birthplace that the young Benjamin Thompson was somewhat indifferent to the routine duties of the farm and the shop and inclined to devote a larger proportion of his time to scientific experi-

ments and diversions in mathematics than his guardians and
employers thought proper in an apprentice. But in spite of the
variety of his pursuits, he seems to have done his work well and
to have made good use of what schooling he could get. His
teacher at Woburn was John Fowle, a graduate of Harvard College in 1747.

In the year 1766 he was apprenticed to John Appleton of
Salem, an importer of British goods and retailer of general mer-
chandise. It was here he was brought under the influence of the
Rev. Thomas Barnard, minister of the First Church of Salem, and
a man of unusual scholarship and ability. Thompson's accounts
and letters at this time show him to be accurate, orderly and skilful in the use of the pen. He engraved a book-plate for himself
with a very elaborate heraldic device combining, in the common
symbolism of the day, an all-seeing eye, a ship, books, square and
compass, sword and a couchant lion. His friend Baldwin writes
of him:

"He employed as much of his time, as he could by any means
steal from the duties of his station, to amuse himself with study
and little, ingenious, mechanical recreations, and would be more
frequently found with a penknife, file and gimlet under the counter, than with his pen and account books in the counting room."

Benjamin Thompson was no exception to the old saying that
no man ever became a great physicist who did not attempt to
invent a machine for perpetual motion in his youth, for he walked
one night from Salem to Woburn to show Baldwin a contrivance
of wheels and levers which he thought would solve the problem
of perpetual motion.

While he was at Salem the news of the repeal of the Stamp Act
was received, but young Thompson took less interest in its effect
upon the importation business in which he was engaged than he
did in the opportunity of making some chemical experiments
with materials furnished at the expense of the public. But in
grinding together the ingredients of the powder for his home-
made rockets, the mixture exploded, severely burning his face
and breast and temporarily destroying his sight. This accident

did not discourage him, for throughout his life he retained an interest in explosives to which, both in England and Bavaria, he devoted much attention. His letters to his most intimate friend, Loammi Baldwin, afterwards colonel in the Revolutionary Army and engineer of the Middlesex Canal, indicate the extent and diversity of his scientific curiosity.

WOBURN, Aug. 14, 1769.
"MR. LOAMMI BALDWIN,
"Sir: Please to give me Direction of the Rays of Light from a Luminous Body to an Opake and the Reflection from the Opake Body to another equally Dense and Opake; viz. the Direction of the Rays of the Luminous Body to that of the Opake and the direction of rays by reflection to the other Opake Body.
"Yours, etc.,
"BENJAMIN THOMPSON.

"N. B.—From the Sun to the Earth Reflected to the Moon at an angle of 40 degrees."

In 1769 Thompson was apprenticed as clerk to Hopestill Capen, a dry goods dealer in Boston, but his employer having entered into the boycott of British goods, he had little to do and in a few months returned to his house in Woburn where "he was received by his acquaintances with unwelcome pity, as an unfortunate young man, who could not fix his mind on any regular employment, and would never be able to support himself, or afford any consolation to his friends."

His stay in Boston, although short, was utilized in acquiring some of the accomplishments which afterwards proved of so much use to him in the courts of Europe. He took lessons in French every evening, except Sunday, practiced drawing and engraving, played on the violin, rehearsed plays and exercised with the back sword. At the Boston Massacre, March 5, 1770, he is said to have been in the midst of the crowd, sword in hand, eager for an attack upon the British troops which a few years later he was to lead against his own countrymen.

Freed from imprisonment in the shop, Thompson, now seventeen, spent the next two years in the study of medicine and natural philosophy, and in teaching school at Wilmington and Bradford. The program of daily duties that he drew up for himself is so characteristic of the methodical and industrious disposition of his whole life as to be worth quoting;

"From eleven to six, Sleep. Get up at six o'clock and wash my hands and face. From six to eight, exercise one half and study one half. From eight till ten, Breakfast, attend Prayers, etc. From ten to twelve, Study all the time. From twelve to one, Dine, etc. From one to four, study constantly. From four to five, Relieve my mind by some diversion or Exercise. From five till Bedtime, follow what my inclination leads me to; whether it be to go abroad, or stay at home and read either Anatomy, Physic or Chemistry, or any other book I want to Peruse."

He later obtained by the influence of some Boston friends the privilege of attending the lectures of Professor Winthrop on experimental philosophy at Harvard College, and every day he and his friend Baldwin walked eight miles from Woburn to Cambridge, and on their return repeated the experiments in mechanics and electricity with apparatus of their own construction. That the two boys were not so completely absorbed in abstract science as to be oblivious to the attractions of the road is proved by their discovery on a hillside farm in Medford of an apple-tree bearing fruit of superior quality, which was afterwards cultivated by Colonel Baldwin, introduced by Count Rumford into Europe and is still known as the "Baldwin apple."

How much Count Rumford appreciated the help he got from Harvard College is shown by his bequeathing to that institution the reversion of his whole estate, to found a professorship "to teach the utility of the physical and mathematical sciences for the improvement of the useful arts, and for the extension of the industry, prosperity, happiness and well being of Society."   Dr. Jacob Bigelow was first elected to the Rumford Professorship in 1816. His successors have been Daniel Treadwell, Eben Horsford, Walcott Gibbs, and John Trowbridge.

The Rumford Fund for the support of this professorship now amounts to $56,368.73.

Thompson's third attempt at school teaching resulted in a decided change of fortune, for he was called to a town which was to give him a name, a wife and a fortune, the town now known as Concord, New Hampshire, but which had been incorporated in 1733 as Rumford, Essex County, Massachusetts. Here again we may, with advantage, quote his own words as reported by Pictet:

"I was then launched at the right time upon a world which was almost strange to me, and I was obliged to form the habit of thinking and acting for myself and of depending on myself for a livelihood. My ideas were not yet fixed; one project succeeded another and perhaps I should have acquired a habit of indecision and inconstancy, perhaps I should have been poor and unhappy all my life, if a woman had not loved me—if she had not given me a subsistence; a home and an independent fortune. I married, or rather was married at the age of nineteen. I espoused the widow of a Col. Rolfe, daughter of the Rev. Mr. Walker, a highly respectable minister and one of the first settlers of Rumford."

Sarah Walker had married at the age of thirty Colonel Benjamin Rolfe, twice her age, one of the richest and most important men of the country, who had died two years later, leaving her with one son, afterwards Colonel Paul Rolfe. Since she was some thirteen years older than Benjamin Thompson, and so far above the penniless school teacher in social position, it is probable that, as he intimates, she took the initiative in the affair and exercised the privilege of a princess towards a lover of low degree. She took him to Boston before their marriage in the chaise of the late husband (noted in Concord history as the first carriage brought into the place) and gave him an opportunity of indulging for the first time his fondness for fine clothes, for his outfit included a scarlet coat. They drove back through the villlage of Woburn, and stopping at his mother's door, she came out and exclaimed: "Why, Ben, my child, how could you go and spend your whole winter's wages in this way?"

Their wedding tour was taken in the fall of 1772 to Portsmouth near which was a grand military review of the Second Provincial Regiment of New Hampshire. Thompson's fine appearance on horseback as one of the spectators attracted the attention of

Governor Wentworth. His wife introduced him to the governor, and he made such a favorable impression by his readiness in conversation and wide information that he was soon after appointed a major in the regiment. Nothing could have been more suited to Thompson's ambitions, but it brought misfortune upon him in two ways; it offended the other officers that a youth of nineteen, without military experience, should have been thus placed over them, and the marked favor shown him by the governor caused him to be suspected by the patriots as a tool of the Royalists. It was in fact this spite and suspicion that drove him from America.

Young Thompson entered into his new *rôle* of landed proprietor with his usual zeal and energy, introducing new seeds imported from London, and taking an active part in the politics and development of the colony. He broached a scheme for the survey of the White Mountains to Governor Wentworth who not only approved it, but offered to accompany the expedition in person. But it was never carried out, for already more serious affairs were on foot. Thompson's growing popularity with the governor, and his own undeniably aristocratic tendencies combined to render him a suspect by the ardent patriots of the vicinity. In the summer of 1774 he was summoned before the patriotic committee to answer to the charge of "being unfriendly to the cause of liberty," the chief complaint being that he was in correspondence with General Gage in Boston and had returned to him four deserters. He made a satisfactory explanation of his conduct and sentiments and was discharged, but the suspicions were not removed from the minds of his enemies, and since formal and semi-legal proceedings had failed, they resorted to violence. One November night a mob surrounded the Rolfe mansion and demanded Major Thompson, but he, receiving an intimation of the attack and knowing the impossibility of proving his innocence to an impassioned mob, had borrowed a horse and $20 from his brother-in-law and escaped to Woburn. He wrote to the Rev. Walker, his father-in-law, that he "never did, nor, let my treatment be what it will, ever will do any action that may have the most distant tendency to injure the true interests of this my native country." It is quite conceivable, however, that his definition of "true interests" may have differed even at this time, from that of the ardent bands of Tory-hunters then scouring the country.

On May 16, 1775, he was again arrested "upon suspicion of being inimical to the liberties of this country" and was kept in prison for two weeks, when he was formally acquitted by the "Committee of Correspondence for the Town of Woburn" with the verdict that they "do not find that the said Thompson in any one instance has shown a Disposition unfriendly to American Liberty, but that his general behavior has evinced the direct contrary."

He tried to get an appointment in the Continental Army and secured an interview with Washington, but the New Hampshire officers over whom he had been promoted exerted too powerful an influence against him. Nevertheless, during his stay at Woburn he made himself as useful as he was allowed to in the organization of the army. In company with Major Baldwin he inspected the fortifications on Bunker Hill and he spent some time drilling the troops and designing uniforms.

But finding it impossible to secure a position in the American army, and equally impossible, at least for one of his adventurous disposition, to remain neutral and idle in such stirring times, he decided to seek in the British army the military career he coveted and, nearly a year after he had been driven from his home in Concord, he left Woburn for Boston. Here he was received with a welcome from the British very strongly in contrast to the coldness of his countrymen, and, in spite of his youth and inexperience, he soon rose into the confidence of the authorities. Upon the evacuation of Boston he was sent to England to convey the news, and so severed his connection with his native land. He never saw his wife again; the daughter whom he left as an infant twice visited him in Europe when a grown woman.

His early biographers put themselves to much trouble to explain and apologize for his action in thus siding with the enemies of his country, but now, when the descendants of the Loyalists show no less pride in their ancestry than the Sons of the Revolution, we can see the situation in fairer perspective, and, although we may disapprove of his decision and regret the loss to America of another Franklin, we must realize that it was fortunate both for Thompson and the world that his peculiar genius found in Europe a field for its development that America could not have afforded.

On leaving America he wrote to his father-in-law, the Rev. Walker of Concord:

"Though I foresee and realize the distress, poverty and wretchedness that must unavoidably attend my Pilgrimage in unknown lands, destitute of fortune, friends, and acquaintances, yet all these evils appear to me more tolerable than the treatment which I met with from the hands of mine ungrateful countrymen."

If this really represents Benjamin Thompson's anticipations on going to England, it cannot be said that he displayed his usual foresight, for he rapidly rose to a position of wealth, power and esteem there. The government was suffering severely from lack of information on conditions in America. Sir George Germain, the Colonial Secretary of State, in their first interview recognized the knowledge and ability of this young man of twenty-three, and gave him a place in the Colonial Office, admitting him as a member of his own household.

Science was never to Thompson a mental divertisement, but was always intimately associated with his daily duties. Since he was now engaged in improving the military efficiency of the army, he devoted his attention to the study of the action of gunpowder, "to determine the most advantageous situation for the vent in fire-arms, and to measure the velocities of bullets and the recoil under various circumstances. I had hopes, also, of being able to find out the velocity of the inflammation of gunpowder, and to measure its force more accurately than had hitherto been done."

He persistently attacked by every means in his power the problems of explosives which Nobel, Abel, Berthelot, and Kellner have in recent years more successfully studied, chiefly along the lines indicated by him and, in part, using his apparatus. He laid the foundation of the science of interior ballistics by an attempt to measure the explosive force of the gases produced by the explosion of gunpowder, inventing a machine which has ever since been known as "the Rumford Apparatus." This consisted of a small steel mortar mounted vertically upon a bed of solid masonry. The $\frac{1}{4}$ inch bore was closed by a steel hemisphere upon which weights were placed and these increased until they were no longer lifted by the force of the gunpowder exploded. To avoid loss of energy by the escape of gases through the vent, the powder was ignited by applying a red-hot iron ball to the lower end. He gradually increased the charge of powder, until an 8,000 pound cannon had to be used as a weight to counterbalance the force of the explosion, and then the barrel of the apparatus burst into halves. His numerical results were too high, but it was almost a century before better figures were obtained.

Rumford's earlier experiments in England were mostly directed to the problems of external ballistics, especially to the determination of the velocity of the projectile under different charges and kinds of powders and methods of firing. For this purpose he first made use of the ballistic pendulum invented by Robins. The bullet was fired into a wooden target backed with iron and suspended so as to swing back freely when struck. By measuring the chord of the arc of its swing and knowing its weight and that of the bullet, the velocity of the bullet could be calculated.

Rumford improved upon this by measuring the momentum of the gun as well as the equal momentum of the bullet by suspending the gun itself as a pendulum by two cords. This not only gave another series of figures as a check to the former, but it was more accurate, because the movement of a large mass at low velocity can be more easily measured than of a small mass at high velocity.

In his later experiments in Munich he discarded the pendulum target and measured the velocity of the ball solely by the recoil of the gun, experimenting with brass cannon as large as twelve-pounders, in a building which he had erected for the purpose. He was never content with laboratory experiments, and to continue his investigations on gunpowder, he volunteered to go on a cruise of the British fleet under Sir Charles Hardy, in 1779. As no enemy was encountered, he persuaded his friends among the captains "to make a number of experiments, and particularly by firing a greater number of bullets at once from their heavy guns than had ever been done before, and observing the distances at which they-fell in the sea . . . which gave me much new light relative to the action of fired gunpowder."

On this cruise also he devised a simpler and more systematic code of marine signals than that in use. Another result of this three months' cruise was the plan of a swift copper-sheathed frigate.

When, on account of overwork, his health failed and he went to Bath to recuperate, he made a series of experiments on cohesion. These experiments introduced him to Sir Joseph Banks, President of the Royal Society, with whom he was afterwards associated in founding the Royal Institution, and in 1779 he was elected a Fellow of the Royal Society.

Thompson rose rapidly in the Colonial Office, where he became Secretary for Georgia, inspector of all the clothing sent to America, and Under Secretary of State. About the time of the fall of his patron, Lord Germain, on account of the surrender of Cornwallis, he returned to a military career, and was made Lieutenant-Colonel of the King's American Dragoons, a regiment of cavalry which he was to recruit on Long Island. His ship, however, was driven by storms to Charleston, South Carolina, where he reorganized the remains of the royal army under Colonel Leslie, and conducted a successful cavalry raid against Marion's Brigade.

In the spring he arrived at Long Island, and by August 1, 1782, he got the King's American Dragoons in shape to be inspected in their camp about three miles east of Flushing by Prince William Henry, Duke of Clarence, the third son of the King, and afterwards King William the Fourth. The royal cause was, however, hopeless, and the troops under Colonel Thompson did nothing during the year but exasperate the patriots among whom they were quartered. The inhabitants of Long Island preserved for more than one generation the memory of their depredations, especially the destruction of a church and burying-ground in the construction of a fort near Huntington, where the tombstones were used for ovens and stamped the bread with their inscriptions.

Upon his return to England after the disbandment of the British forces, Thompson was made Colonel on half-pay for life, but there was no chance to make use of his military talents in the British service. Accordingly he determined to seek his fortune elsewhere and September 17, 1783, embarked at Dover for the continent. Upon the same boat happened to be Henry Laurens, a former President of the American Congress, recently released from the Tower, and the historian Gibbon who in his letters complains that the three spirited horses of "Mr. Secretary, Colonel, Admiral, Philosopher Thompson," added to the distress of the Channel passage.

He intended to go to Vienna to volunteer in the Austrian army against the Turks, but a curious chance diverted him to Bavaria where he spent much of his life and rose to the highest attainable position. Here again, as in New Hampshire, he owed the beginning of his good fortune to his handsome appearance on horseback at a military parade. At Strasburg, Prince Maximilian of Deux-Ponts, afterwards Elector and King of Bavaria, but then major-general in the French service, while reviewing the troops noticed among the spectators an officer in a foreign uniform, mounted on a fine English horse, and spoke to him. When Thompson told him that he came from serving in the American war, the Prince replied that some of the French officers in his suite must have fought against him, pointing to the French officers who had been in the American Army at Yorktown. Becoming interested in his conversation, the Prince invited Colonel Thompson to dine with him and to meet his late foes. At the table maps were produced and they discussed the campaign until late, and the talk was resumed on the following day. The Prince was so taken with him that he gave him a cordial letter to his uncle, the Elector Palatine, Reigning Duke of Bavaria. He spent five days in Munich with the Elector who offered him such inducements to establish himself in Bavaria that, after visiting Vienna and finding that there was to be no war against the Turks, he returned to England to get the permission necessary for a British officer to enter a foreign service. George the Third not only granted this, but also conferred upon him the honor of knighthood on February 23, 1784.

Karl Theodor, Elector Palatine, had, by succeeding to Bavaria, become the greatest prince in Germany, except the Emperor and the King of Prussia. Sir Benjamin Thompson entered his service as general aide-de-camp and colonel of a calvary regiment. He was assigned a palace in Munich with a military staff and servants.

For eleven years he served the Elector in a great variety of capacities, military and civil, and carried on scientific work in lines suggested by his occupations. Honors, titles and decorations to which he was not indifferent, he received in abundance from rulers and academies of science. The laws of Bavaria did not permit a foreigner to receive one of the orders of that country, but, at the request of the Elector, the King of Poland in 1786 conferred upon him the Order of St. Stanislaus. Two years later he was made major-general and Privy Councilor and Minister of War of Bavaria. In 1791 the Elector made him a Count of the Holy Roman Empire with the Order of the White Eagle. He chose as his new name, Rumford, from the New Hampshire town which he had entered as a poor schoolmaster and left as a political refugee.

The city of Munich was not ungrateful for what Count Rumford did there. While he was in England the people erected a monument in his honor in the park still known as "the English Garden," which he had reclaimed from a waste hunting-ground and made into a public pleasure resort. The inscription reads:

"To Him who rooted out the most scandalous of public evils, Idleness and Mendicity; who gave to the poor help, occupation and morals, and to the youth of the Fatherland so many schools of culture. Go, Passer-by, try to emulate him in thought and deed, and us in gratitude."

A bronze statue of Count Rumford was erected in Munich by King Maximilian II and a replica of it costing $7,500 has been placed in his birthplace, Woburn, Mass., bearing an inscription by President Eliot of Harvard.

Rumford found the Bavarian army most deficient in the two arms in which he was especially interested, cavalry and artillery, and he set himself to remedy the former by establishing a veterinary school and introducing improved breeds of horses; and to develope the artillery service he built a foundry at Munich where guns were constructed according to his designs, based upon careful experimentation. He adopted the method of casting both brass and iron cannon solid and boring them afterwards, and it was while superintending this operation that he made the observations which led to his greatest discoveries, that heat is not a material substance but a mode of motion, and that there is a definite quantitative relation between mechanical work and heat. The "Inquiry Concerning the Source of the Heat which is Generated by Friction" is one of the shortest of his scientific papers, but it would be hard to match it in all scientific literature for originality of conception, importance of matter, completeness of experimental demonstration and clearness of expression. Tyndall quotes it in his *Heat as a Mode of Motion* with the remark: "Rumford in this memoir annihilates the material theory of heat. Nothing more powerful on the subject has since been written."

The dominant theory of the time was that heat was a fluid substance, which was called caloric, held in the pores of bodies and squeezed out like water from a sponge, when they were hammered or rubbed. Rumford was led to question this by observing the large amount of heat continuously generated by friction in the boring of his cannon. If, he reasoned, heat is a substance that has been squeezed out of the metal, then the powder produced by the boring must have less heat in it than the original solid metal, and therefore would require more heat to raise it to a given temperature. Accordingly, he tested the specific heat of a piece of the gun-metal and an equal weight of the borings with his calorimeter, and found that equal amounts of heat raised them to the same temperature. This experiment was not absolutely conclusive, for it still could be argued that, although their thermal capacity was the same at the same temperature, they might have possessed different quantities of heat.

Rumford's next step was to determine how much heat was produced by a certain amount of friction. If he had been content with mere qualitative results, the world would have had to wait longer for the law of the conservation of energy, but he had the passion of the true scientist to express everything possible in definite figures, even if it was nothing more than the cost of pea-soup or the loss of heat from a tea-kettle.

The apparatus he used for the determination of this most important constant of nature, the relation of heat to work, was a brass six-pounder mounted for boring. Into the short cylinder of metal left on the end of the cannon in the process of casting a hole 3.7 inches in diameter was bored to a depth of 7.2 inches. Against the bottom of the hole a blunt iron borer was held by a pressure of 10,000 pounds and the gun was turned on its axis by horse-power. A thermometer, wrapped in flannel, thrust into the hole rose to 130 °F. after 960 revolutions. The weight of the dust produced by the borer was found to be only 833 grains Troy, yet according to the caloric theory this small amount of metal must have had enough heat squeezed out of it to raise the 113 pounds of gun-metal 70 °F.!

Next he fitted a box containing 18¾ pounds of water around the cylinder, and in two hours and a half the water boiled.

"It would be difficult to describe the surprise and astonishment expressed in the countenances of the bystanders, on seeing so large a quantity of cold water heated, and actually made to boil without any fire. Though there was, in fact, nothing that could justly be considered as surprising in this event, yet I acknowledge fairly that it afforded me a degree of childish pleasure, which, were I ambitious of the reputation of a *grave philosopher*, I ought most certainly rather to hide than to discover."

He then determined by experiment how much heat was given off in burning wax candles, and calculated that it would require 4.8 ounces of wax to heat the water and the metal to the same extent.

"From the result of these computations it appears, that the quantity of heat produced equably, or in a continual stream (if I may use that expression) by the friction" in this experiment was greater than that produced by the continuous burning of nine wax candles each ¾ inches in diameter.

Finally Rumford takes the great step of connecting the heat and mechanical work, by calculating the power used in turning the borer and producing the heat by friction. The relation between these two forces of energy, or the dynamical equivalent of heat, he determined as 847 foot-pounds, that is, the work done by raising one pound weight 847 feet will, if converted into heat, raise the temperature of one pound of water one degree Fahrenheit. Considering when it was done, and the crudity of the apparatus, this is an astonishingly accurate result, for it is only about 10% above the figure now accepted, 779. Forty-two years elapsed before it was more accurately determined by Joule as 772 foot-pounds. It is now called the joule, although it might well bear the name of the rumford instead.

As an example of the way Count Rumford sums up his evidence and draws from his experiments a clear and logical conclusion, the closing paragraphs of this historic paper are here given. It will be noted that his language is so simple and direct that the most unscientific reader can follow his demonstration of the new theory.

"By meditating on the results of all these experiments we are naturally brought to that great question which has so often been the subject of speculation among philosophers; namely,—What is Heat? Is there any such thing as an *igneous* fluid? Is there anything that can with propriety be called caloric?

"We have seen that a very considerable quantity of Heat may be excited by the friction of two metallic surfaces, and given off in a constant stream or flux *in all directions* without interruption or intermission, and without any signs of diminution or exhaustion.

"From whence came the Heat which was continually given off in this manner in the foregoing experiments? Was it furnished by the small particles of metal detached from the larger solid masses on their being rubbed together? This, as we have already seen, could not possibly have been the case.

"Was it furnished by the air? This could not have been the case; for, in three of the experiments, the machinery being kept immersed in water, the access of the air of the atmosphere was completely prevented.

"Was it furnished by the water which surrounded the machinery? That this could not have been the case is evident: first, because this water was continually *receiving Heat* from the machinery and could not at the same time be *giving to* and *receiving Heat from* the same body; and, secondly, because there was no chemical decomposition of any part of this water. Had any such decomposition taken place (which, indeed, could not reasonably have been expected), one of its component elastic fluids (most probably inflammable air) [hydrogen] must at the same time have been set at liberty, and, in making its escape into the atmosphere, would have been detected; but, though I frequently examined the water to see if any air-bubbles rose up through it, and had even made preparations to examine them, if any should appear, I could perceive none; nor was there any sign of decomposition of any kind whatever, or other chemical process, going on in the water.

"Is it possible that the Heat could have been supplied by means of the iron bar to the end of which the blunt steel borer was fixed? or by the small neck of gun-metal by which the hollow cylinder was united to the cannon? These suppositions appear more improbable even than either of those before mentioned; for Heat was continually going off, or *out of the machinery* by both these passages, during the whole time the experiment lasted.

"And, in reasoning on this subject, we must not forget to consider that most remarkable circumstance, that the source of the Heat generated by friction, in these experiments, appeared evidently to be *inexhaustible*.

"It is hardly necessary to add, that anything which any *insulated* body, or system of bodies, can continue to furnish *without limitation*, cannot possibly be a *material substance;* and it appears to me to be extremely difficult, if not quite impossible, to form any distinct idea of anything capable of being excited and communicated in the manner the Heat was excited and communicated in these experiments, except it be *motion*."

One more surprising instance of scientific insight this brief paper contains. He not only connects heat, light, chemical action and mechanical movement together as capable of being converted into one another, but boldly extends the generalization to animal life. Since the horse turned the cannon, the strength of a horse can be made to produce heat without fire, light, combustion or chemical decomposition, and this heat, he characteristically suggests, "could be used to cook victual if desired." But this method of producing heat would be disadvantageous, "for more Heat might be obtained by using the fodder necessary for the support of a horse as fuel." The complete demonstration of this suggestion that an animal can be considered simply as one form of heat engine was only given within the last few years by Professor Atwater, by his experiments with a calorimeter large enough for a man to live in.

Count Rumford possessed in a high degree the combination which, unfortunately for the world, is somewhat rare, of executive ability and love of science. Whatever practical work he was engaged in, he at once sought to determine its philosophic principles, and, these discovered, to apply them to the task at hand. His mind turned with marvelous rapidity from the formulation of a natural law to its application to daily life, and *vice versa*. Almost all his published papers show this peculiarity. They usually begin by telling of some trivial incident or accident which directed his attention to the want of information on the subject, then he describes his experiments, quantitative as far as possible, and gives the theory to which they led him, closing the paper with a long and varied list of speculative deductions and possible applications. We may take up any of his essays on heat with the expectation of finding in it somewhere a reference to the needs of the poor, a proof of the beneficence of the Creator and directions for cooking soup, and we shall not be disappointed. His scientific papers make, therefore, very lively reading, even for unscientific readers, on account of their wealth of topics and allusions, their clear style and their portrayal of the personal characteristics of an interesting man. He would be a very dull person and extremely limited in his tastes who could turn over the pages of the four volumes of his work, published by the American Academy of Arts and Science, without soon finding something that would attract his attention and give him helpful ideas.

Because the occupations and experiences of Count Rumford's life were remarkably varied, and his mind was incessantly engaged in philosophic thought concerning them, his name is found among the founders of an astonishingly large number of branches of pure applied science. No one can write the history of the development of our knowledge of heat, light, radiation, convection, cohesion, ballistics, cooking, fireplaces, buildings, clothing, traction, bathing, hospitals, barracks, glaciers, meteorology, conservation of energy, gravitation, theory of colors, or lamps, without mentioning Count Rumford.

The popularity which Count Rumford's essays obtained was in part due to their literary style. They are clear, logical and direct, although in places too rhetorical for modern taste. He is careful to give the exact figures and observations on which he bases his conclusions, so his results can be checked and recalculated by using the more accurate figures that have been obtained since.

A good experiment accurately described never loses its value by lapse of time. Count Rumford's own opinion as to the importance of literary style in scientific work is given in these words:

"Too much pains cannot be taken by those who write books to render their ideas clear, and their language concise and easy to be understood. *Hours* spent by an author in saving *minutes* and even *seconds* to his readers, is time well employed."

Count Rumford could have found no situation better suited to his talents and tastes than this in Bavaria. Here he could play his favorite rôle of benevolent despot to his heart's content. The army was corrupt and inefficient; the country was poor, wasted by war and neglect, the cities swarmed with beggars; schools were lacking; there were more convents than factories, and industry was not in high repute. It is remarkable that so bigoted a ruler as the Elector Karl Theodor should have placed such confidence and power in the hands of an avowed Protestant and a scientist, and that so conservative a community should have allowed a foreigner to carry out radical reforms requiring the coöperation and good-will of large numbers of people, but Rumford had in a marked degree the happy faculty of winning the confidence of both superiors and subordinates. Reformers with both zeal and tact, such as he possessed, are not common in any field of endeavor.

Rumford's first work with the army was to rid it of "graft." The officers sold outfits to the recruits on credit, and ran them each year deeper in debt, for the allowance for food and clothing was insufficient, while the resulting bickering and bargaining between officer and soldier were destructive of discipline.

Rumford's first criticism was that the officer had too much to do with his men. An officer should not be at once commandant, trustee and merchant in his company. Next, that "it is not only unwise but also in a certain sense cruel to put honest men in a position in which their passions can be excited by opportunity and example." He saw, too, that the soldiers kept in idleness in barracks degenerated, and when they were quartered in farmers' houses they were such a terror to the country that the people paid them to stay away. The soldier despised the citizen, and the citizen hated the soldier.

To obviate this, Rumford determined to make the soldier a citizen and to put him in a condition where he would contribute to the wealth and welfare of the country instead of being a drain upon it.

To do this, Count Rumford increased the pay and privileges of the soldiers, improved the quarters, and cut out from their drill all obsolete and dispensable portions. Schools were established in all the regiments for instructing the soldiers and their children in reading, writing and arithmetic, and all books and materials were furnished gratis. With his characteristic economy, he provided that the paper used in the schools should be afterwards made into cartridges, so it cost nothing. The soldiers were employed in such public works as draining marshes, building dykes and making roads; the military bands, that he introduced, playing for them while they worked. Military gardens were provided, and each soldier on enlistment was given a plot of ground, to remain in his possession as long as he cultivated it and kept it free from weeds; seeds and garden utensils being furnished free. Rumford justifies this on the ground that skill in the use of the shovel for intrenching can be obtained by digging in the garden. They were permitted to sell the products, and received pay for all their work. Rumford's military gardens anticipated our Agricultural Experiment Stations, for by means of them he introduced new varieties of crops throughout the country. When a soldier went home on a furlough, he took with him a collection of garden seeds and a few potatoes, and in this way Rumford did for Bavaria what Parmentier did for France.

Idleness and waste were the two great evils against which Count Rumford fought all his life. A beggar and a lazy soldier were his especial detestations. Having put the soldiers at productive work, Rumford next attacked the problem of poverty, led not so much, perhaps, from sentimental love of his fellow-men as by his innate hatred of waste, whether of time or property. A very large proportion of the population of Bavaria at that time was given to begging. Even along the highways in the country almost every person one met on foot held out his hand for alms, and in the cities professional beggars invaded the churches and houses, and besieged the people in the street, exposing loathsome sores, and exciting sympathy by means of maimed and ill-used children. Each beggar had his particular beat or district, and vacancies were eagerly sought for and fought for. Out of a population of 60,000 in Munich, Rumford found 2,600 beggars and indigent persons. This mendicancy and the lying, stealing, vice and abuse of children resulting from it Rumford laid to the injudicious dispensation of alms, due to a false ideal of charity. Instead of punishment or moral suasion he recommended the improvement of conditions, first, by providing food and employment for every man, woman and child. Only when this is done can the penalties against vagrancy be enforced.

Accordingly, he began by establishing a House of Industry in Munich, and, then, by the aid of soldiers "rounded up" all the beggars in the city, and brought them to the large and handsome building provided for them. Here they were given such work as

they could do, for which they received a warm dinner and pay-
ment. Everything possible was done for their comfort and convenience. The workrooms were well ventilated and lighted, and
pains were taken to give the edifice an air of elegance as well as of
neatness and cleanliness. In the passage leading to the paved
court was an inscription in letters of gold upon a black ground
"*No alms will be received here.*" Count Rumford gives his theory
of philanthropy in the following words:

"When precepts fail, habits may sometimes be successful. To
make vicious and abandoned people happy, it has generally been
supposed, first, to make them virtuous. But why not reverse this
order! Why not make them first *happy*, and then virtuous! If
happiness and virtue be *inseparable*, the end will be as certainly
obtained by the one method as by the other; and it is most undoubtedly much easier to contribute to the happiness and comfort of persons in a state of poverty and misery than by admoni-
tions and punishment to reform their morals."

The House of Industry was chiefly devoted to the manufacture
of clothing for the army and for sale; from the cording and spin-
ning of flax, hemp, cotton and wool to the finished garment; and
work of a sort suited to his capacity was found for every one, from
the aged and infirm to the youngest.

Especial attention was given to training the children in habits
of industry. Even with them Rumford carried out his plan of
avoiding the use of force. Every child was given his dinner and
his three kreutzers a day, whether he worked or not, but the children who refused to work were compelled to sit on a bench and
watch their companions working, until they cried for something
to do. Then they were given light spinning-wheels, and promoted
and publicly rewarded as they became more skilful. Twice a day
they attended school in the same building.

The financial success of the House of Industry was largely due
to the system of keeping accounts devised by Rumford, very
much like those now in use in modern manufactories. "Lead us
not into temptation" was a verse of Scripture the inspiration of
which he never doubted, and he was strongly of the opinion that

the best way to keep men honest was to give them no chance to be dishonest. Every piece of yarn transferred from one room to another, every loaf of stale bread collected from the bakers had to be duly recorded on printed blanks. In his recommendations for all charitable work he emphatically insists upon strict book-keeping and publicity of accounts. All cases of relief were to be listed alphabetically.

In his plans for systematic, impersonal, non-patronizing and business-like assistance to self-support, Count Rumford antici-pated the organized charities of a hundred years later, but in the tact with which he secured the coöperation of the whole com-munity, including the authorities of army, church and state, prominent citizens of the middle classes, and the poor themselves, he has had, unfortunately, few imitators. In five years he practi-cally abolished beggary in Bavaria, and converted many of the former mendicants into industrious and self-respecting people. He took less pride in his decorations and titles than in telling that when he was dangerously sick in Munich, he was awakened by hearing the confused noise of the prayers of a multitude of people who were passing in the street, and was told that it was the poor of Munich who were going to the church to put up public prayers for him, "a private person, a stranger, a Protestant."

Rumford was able to carry out his plan of providing free dinners to all who needed them by turning his inventive genius to the subject of cooking, and making the first scientific study of cheap and nutritious diet and the economical management of heat. His specialty was a rich soup made of peas and barley, into which he afterwards introduced potatoes, surreptitiously, because of the popular prejudice against them. The secret of its preparation lay in cooking for over four hours at a low temperature, and by his skilful contrivances in the kitchen three women did the cook-ing for a thousand persons. A pound and a half of soup, with seven ounces of rye bread cost only one cent. He shows what a great loss of heat occurs in cooking by the ordinary methods, which unfortunately are still in use. In particular he objected to rapid boiling which, as he says, cannot raise the temperature above the boiling-point, but uses more than five times as much heat as is necessary to heat the same quantity of water from the freezing-point, and at the same time destroys the taste by carrying off the volatile flavors. His cooking was done in closed vessels, covered with wood or some other non-conducting material, to prevent the radiation of heat, in fact constructed on the same principle as the calorimeter he employed for scientific research. All these lessons Mr. Edward Atkinson and others have been vainly trying to teach us in recent years. The "fireless cooker" now coming into use is a belated application of Rumford's idea.

To obviate the great waste of heat in roasting on a spit before an open fire, he invented the sheet iron oven known as the "Rumford roaster." A dripping-pan filled with water prevented the decomposition of the fat by the high temperature, and the flues were arranged so that a blast of hot air could be passed over the meat to brown it when it was cooked.

In 1795, after eleven years in Munich, Rumford returned to England for the purpose of publishing his essays on heat and its utilization, and on public institutions for the poor. He was then at the height of his renown as scientist and philanthropist, and was everywhere received with great honor. In England and Ireland he assisted in the establishment of soup-kitchens and work-houses, and introduced into public institutions his system of heating and cooking by steam. Models of his fireplaces, stoves and cooking utensils were placed on exhibition for workmen to copy, for he always refused to take out patents on his inventions. He writes that at this time he "had not less than five hundred smoking chimneys on my hands" in public and private buildings, many of them chronic and thought incurable. The great waste of heat in the old-fashioned fireplace shocked his economical nature, and he studied the scientific principles involved, in order to check the excessive consumption of fuel, increase the radiation in the room, and prevent loss of fuel in the smoke. He proved the best possible proportions for the chimney recess of the open fireplace to be that the width of the back should equal the depth from front to back and that the width of the front should be three times the width of the back, a rule which is followed to this day. By making the angle of the sides of the fireplace 45°, the greatest possible amount of heat was reflected into the room. He recommended the use of fire-clay instead of metal and of clay fire-balls to insure complete combustion and increase the radiating surface. Refuse coal-dust was made into briquettes. His chief improvement consisted in the reduction of the size of the chimney throat and in rounding off the edge of the chimney breast. Since a room is warmed from the walls, and not by radiant heat passing through the air, this work involved a study of the radiating power of different surfaces and materials, and proceeding from the fact smoke is pushed up, not drawn up the chimney, he was led to make extensive investigations in the theory of ventilation.

As it was hopeless to make the open fireplace an economical heater, he turned his attention to the construction of cooking ranges and to the utilization of waste heat of smoke and steam. In the Bavarian House of Industry he passed the smoke from the cooking ranges through copper pipes in a wooden cask, and used it for cooking his pea-soup. From his experience he calculated that the private kitchen expends ten times as much fuel as the public kitchen.

The progress of the century since then has been along the lines indicated by Rumford. The range has been instituted for the fireplace, closed and jacketed vessels are employed for cooking, steam-pipes are used for heating buildings, and the utilization of waste heat has become a factor of recognized importance in factory management. The first range built in this country in conformity with Rumford's principle was constructed under the direction of Professor John Kemp of Columbia College in 1798.

The question of suitable covering for steam-pipes used for heating rooms required for its solution a knowledge of radiation from different surfaces, and in this field Rumford did some excellent original work. In these experiments he used two cylindrical vessels of thin sheet brass filled with warm water and covered with whatever coating or covering he wished to test. To determine which radiated heat the faster, he constructed a "thermoscope" or differential thermometer, consisting of a closed glass tube with the bulbs at each end turned up. In the middle was a drop of colored alcohol which moved in one direction or the other when the bulbs were unequally heated. When he held a cylinder filled with warm water and blackened on the bottom over one bulb, and a cylinder with water at the same temperature and bright on the bottom over the other, the drop of alcohol moved instantly away from the blackened surface, showing that it emitted heat more rapidly at the same temperature. By moving the cylinder back and forth until the drop remained at rest, their relative distances gave data for calculating their relative radiating power. All metals, he found, gave off heat at the same rate, and he asks: "Does not this afford a strong presumption that heat is in all cases excited and communicated by means of radiations, or *undulations*, as I should rather choose to call them?"

His theory of heat is so clearly expressed and anticipates in so many respects our modern ideas, that it is worth quoting as an example of the use of the scientific imagination.

"No reasonable objection against this hypothesis (of the incessant motions of the constituent particles of all bodies) founded on a supposition that there is not room sufficient for these motions, can be advanced; for we have abundant reason to conclude that if there be in fact any indivisible solid particles of matter (which, however, is very problematical) these particles must be so extremely small, compared to the spaces they occupy, that there must be ample room for all kinds of motion among them.

"And whatever the nature or directions of these internal motions may be, among the constituent particles of a solid body, as long as these constituent particles, in their motions, do not break loose from the systems to which they belong (and to which they are attached by gravitation) and run wild in the vast void by which each system is bounded (which, as long as the known laws of nature exist, is no doubt impossible) the form or external appearance of a solid cannot be sensibly changed by them.

"But if the motions of the constituent particles of any solid body be either increased or diminished, in consequence of the actions or radiations of other distant bodies, this event could not happen without producing some visible change in the solid body.

"If the motions of its constituent particles were *diminished* by these radiations, it seems reasonable to conclude that their elongations would become less, and consequently that the volume of the body would be contracted; but if the motions of these particles were increased, we might conclude, *a priori*, that the volume of the body would be expanded.

"We have not sufficient data to enable us to form distinct ideas of the nature of the change which takes place when a solid body is melted; but as fusion is occasioned by heat, that is to say, by an augmentation (from without) of that action which occasions expansion, if expansion be occasioned by an increase of the motions of the constituent particles of the body, it is, no doubt, a certain additional increase of those motions which causes the form of the body to be changed, and from a solid to become a fluid substance.

"As long as the constituent particles of a solid body which are at the surface of that body do not, in their motions, *pass by each other*, the body must necessarily retain its form or shape, however rapid those motions or vibrations may be; but as soon as the motion of these particles is so augmented that they can no longer be restrained or retained within these limits, the regular distribution of the particles which they required in crystallization is gradually destroyed, and the particles so detached from the solid mass form new and independent systems, and become a liquid substance.

"Whatever may be the figures of the orbits which the particles of a liquid describe, the mean distances of those particles from each other remain nearly the same as when they constituted a solid, as appears by the small change of specific gravity which takes place when a solid is melted and becomes a liquid; and on a supposition that their motions are regulated by the same laws which regulate the solar system, it is evident that the additional motion they must necessarily acquire, in order to their taking the fluid form, cannot be lost, but must continue to reside in the liquid, and must again make its appearance when the liquid changes its form and becomes a solid.

"It is well known that a certain quantity of *heat* is required to melt a solid, which quantity disappears or remains *latent in* the liquid produced in that process, and that the same quantity of heat reappears when this liquid is congealed and becomes a solid body."

From this disquisition on molecular physics he at once draws the practical conclusion that a saucepan ought to be smoked on the bottom and bright on the sides in order to absorb and retain the greatest amount of heat. Stoves ought not be polished, but are better rusted. Steam-pipes used for heating rooms should be painted or covered with paper.

He then considers the question of why negroes are black and arctic animals white, and goes so far in these speculations as to lose sight of his own experiments which proved that color made no practical difference in the radiation and absorption of heat.

"All I will venture to say on the subject is, that were I called to inhabit a very hot country, nothing should prevent me from making the experiment of blackening my skin, or at least wearing a black shirt in the shade and especially at night, in order to find out, if by those means, I could not continue to make myself more comfortable."

Nothing in fact did prevent him, not the criticisms of his friends, the remonstrances of his wife or the jeers of the street gamins, from wearing a complete suit of white clothes from hat to shoes, on Paris streets as a demonstration of their superiority over black clothing.

Rumford says he considers his researches on clothing "by far the most fortunate and the most important I ever made," because they contribute to health and comfort of life. With this practical object in view, he devoted many years to experiments on the propagations of heat through solids, liquids and gases, and attained very clear ideas of the three ways in which heat travels, by direct radiation, by conduction from particle to particle, and by convection or currents of heated particles. These experiments were made by thermometers with the bulb sealed into the center of a large glass bulb. The space between the outer bulb and the thermometer of two of these instruments being filled with the substances to be compared, they were taken from boiling water and plunged into ice-cold water or *vice versa*, and the rate of change of the thermometer noted. In this way he determined that moist air is a better conductor of heat than dry. Thus he explains "why the thermometer is not always a just measure of the apparent or sensible heat of the atmosphere," and why colds prevail during autumnal rains and spring thaws, and why it is so dangerous to sleep in damp beds and live in damp houses, and he takes occasion, as usual, to pay a few compliments to Divine Providence for so arranging it that cold air shall contain less moisture than warm.

He exhausted the air from the space surrounding the thermometer in one of these double-walled apparatus by fastening the bulb on the upper end of a barometer tube, and discovered that through such a Torricellian vacuum heat passes with greater difficulty than through the air. It was by means of this double-walled vacuum apparatus, silvered on the internal surfaces as recommended by Rumford, to prevent the radiation of heat, that Professor Dewar a hundred years later was enabled to experiment with liquified air and hydrogen in the Royal Institution which Rumford founded. Bottles, jacketed with a vacuum as Rumford suggested, are now in use to provide automobilists with hot and cold drinks.

In the same way he tested the relative conductivity for heat of a layer of fur, wool, silk, cotton, linen and many other substances, and found that heat does not pass from particle to particle of the air (conduction), but by currents (convection), and that such fibrous bodies as cloth and fur are poor conductors of heat, because the air in their interstices is prevented from circulating. Recent researches on adsorption have proved that he was right in the importance he attached to the "cast" or layer of air which is held so firmly to the surface of the fibers that it is very difficult to remove. He applies the principle he had discovered in the explanation of why bears and wolves have thicker fur on their backs than on their bellies, and how the snow protects the ground.

By exposing dry cloths, fur and down on china plates in a damp cellar and then reweighing them, he determined the quality of moisture they absorbed from the atmosphere, and, finding that wool absorbed most, he determined to wear flannel next to the skin in all seasons and climates; a deduction of doubtful validity.

The important researches he conducted on convection owed their origin to the fact that he was brought up in "the Great Pie Belt." Like other New England boys he was much struck with the length of time it took for an apple-pie to get cool enough to eat.

"and I never burnt my mouth with them, or saw others meet with the same misfortune, without endeavoring, but in vain, to find out some way of accounting in a satisfactory manner for this surprising phenomenon."

Having in later life burnt his mouth, this time on a spoonful of thick rice soup with which he was feeding himself while watching an experiment, he determined to settle the question. Accordingly he made some apple-sauce, and filling with it the jacket of his double-walled thermometer, he found that it required twice as many seconds to cool as when the jacket was filled with water. Next he evaporated the apple-sauce, dried the fiber and found that apple-sauce was 98 per cent water. So small an amount of solid matter could not interfere with the transmission of heat through the water, except by hindering the circulation of the water. He deduces from this that the reason why animals and plants do not more easily freeze during the winter is because sap and animal fluids are thick and viscid, and also are prevented from circulating freely by the cell walls. By heating a glass cylinder (test-tube) containing a powder suspended in water, he was able to see the warm currents ascending on one side and the cold currents descending on the other, and to demonstrate that heat is not conducted in liquids equally in all directions as it is in solids, but by rising currents due to the expansion of the liquid by heat. He found to his surprise that he was able to boil water in the upper part of the tube while holding the lower part in his hand, and that a cake of ice fastened at the bottom of the tube filled with boiling water required hours to melt, while one at the top melted in a few minutes. From these and many similar experiments he was led to the conclusions that air, water and all fluids are non-conductors of heat, and that heat cannot be propagated downwards in liquids as long as they continue to be condensed by cold.

He shows that life on this globe would be impossible if it were not for the fact that water by cooling from about 40° F. to 32° F. expands instead of contracts, for if ice were heavier than water it would sink to the bottom, and all lakes would be frozen solid and not melted during the summer.

"It does not appear to me that there is anything which human sagacity can fathom within the wide-extended bounds of the visible creation which affords a more striking or more palpable proof of the wisdom of the Creator, and of the special care he has taken in the general arrangement of the universe to preserve life, than this wonderful contrivance,"

that water forms the only exception to the universal law that all bodies are condensed by cold.

"If, among barbarous nations, *the fear of a God* and the practice of religious duties tend to soften savage dispositions and to prepare the mind for all those sweet enjoyments which result from peace, order, industry, and friendly intercourse, *a belief in the existence of a Supreme Intelligence*, who rules and governs the universe with wisdom and goodness, is not less essential to the happiness of those who, by cultivating their mental powers, *have learned to know how little can be known*."

This sentence, from its style and mode of thought, its unconscious arrogance and ostentatious modesty, is so characteristic of its age that it could be dated with considerable certainty, even if found on a loose leaf. The more thorough study of the nature of the last hundred years has shown that the conception of the "Great Architect of the Universe" given in the natural theology of that day must be either abandoned as inadequate or enlarged to a more comprehensive ideal of creative wisdom. Rumford is, of course, wrong in thinking that water is the only exception to the general rule that heat expands and cold contracts. Bismuth, cast-iron, type-metal and most alloys expand on solidifying, and this also is of benefit to mankind, for without this property it would be impossible to make good castings.

During the year Rumford spent in England he gave $5,000 to the Royal Society of London, and a like sum to the American Academy of Arts and Sciences, the interest to be given every two years as a premium to the person who made the most important discovery or useful improvement on heat or light, "as shall tend most to promote the good of mankind." The Rumford Medal of the Royal Society has been regularly awarded every two years to the most distinguished scientists of Europe and America, beginning in 1802 with Rumford himself. The American Academy, on the contrary, found the plan "absolutely impracticable" and, for forty-three years during which very great progress was made in the knowledge of light and heat, and especially in such practical applications as improved stoves and lamps which Rumford especially favored, no award was made. The fund by 1829 had grown so large that the courts were called upon to allow the money to be expended for the promotion of science in other ways, such as lectures, books and apparatus. Count Rumford seems to have changed his mind as to the value of this method of promoting the advancement of science, for when he founded the Royal Institution a few years later he expressly prohibited all premiums and rewards. The Rumford Fund of the American Academy now amounts to $58,722, and gives an annual income of more than half the original gift, which is expended for the furtherance of researches in heat and light.

Before leaving England in 1797 Count Rumford was joined by his daughter whom he had left an infant in America twenty-two years before. His wife had died five years before at the age of fifty-two. Many of the letters of his daughter are printed in Ellis's *Life of Count Rumford*, and give an interesting picture of society at the Bavarian court as seen by the New England girl, as well as a self-revelation of the transformation of Sally Thompson into Sarah, Countess of Rumford. She expected to find her father dark in complexion, for her childish impressions had been formed from the only portrait her mother had of him, a silhouette profile. Her mother had told her that he had "carroty" hair, whereas she found it "a very pretty color." He had bright blue eyes and a sweet smile. Dr. Young of the Royal Institution says, "in person he was above middle size, of a dignified and pleasing expression of countenance and a mildness in his manner and tone of voice." In disposition, however, he was authoritative and dictatorial. Always a brilliant conversationalist, he was inclined in his later years to monopolize the table talk, and he made himself unpopular by promptly correcting, from his wide experience and remarkable memory, any misstatements of detail made by a member of the company. He spoke English, French, German, Spanish and Italian fluently, and published scientific papers in the three first-named languages. He was punctilious in etiquette, nice in dress and fond of titles and decorations. Throughout his life he was unduly popular with the ladies.

In early life he practiced music and he sketched his own inventions, but had no taste for painting, sculpture or poetry. He took pleasure in landscape gardening, but knew nothing of botany. His favorite games were billiards and chess, but he rarely played the latter because his feet became like ice. He was very abstemious in eating, partly from theory, partly on account of his poor health. He never drank anything but water.

In spite of a tendency toward display and a liking for elegance in housing and habit, he was very careful in his expenditures and strict in his accounts. He allowed no object to remain out of place after he had used it, and he was never late to an appointment. Cuvier in his eulogy says he worshiped "order as a sort of subordinate deity, regulator of this lower world." "He permitted himself nothing superfluous, not a step, not a word; and he intrepreted the word 'superfluous' in its strictest sense."

Count Rumford on his return to Munich with his daughter after a year in England found himself placed in a position of great responsibility and difficulty. By the defection of Prussia the burden of resistance to the victorious armies of the French republic had been thrown upon the Austrians who were unable to make a stand against the advance of Moreau. A week after his arrival the Elector fled from Munich and took refuge in Saxony, leaving Count Rumford at the head of the Council of Regency. After their defeat at Friedberg, the Austrians under Latour retreated to Munich, closely followed by the French, and demanded admittance to the city. This Rumford refused to grant, and when General Moreau arrived with the French army, he also kept them out of the city by the promise of supplies and the withdrawal of the Bavarian contingent. Since Count Rumford was now in command of the Bavarian troops crowded into the city and camped in the public places, he improved the opportunity to introduce regimental cooking stoves made of sheet copper and fire-brick, similar to those now used in military campaigns.

When Moreau retreated the Elector returned, and Rumford was rewarded for his services in this emergency by being placed at the head of the Department of General Police, and soon after by being appointed Minister Plenipotentiary from Bavaria to Great Britain. He thus left Munich for London, but the British Government held that it was altogether impossible to receive as the representative of a foreign Power, even of so close an ally as Bavaria, one who was a British subject, a former member of the State Department and still on the pay-roll of the British army.

He was unwilling to return to Bavaria where his patron, the Elector Palatine, Karl Theodor, on account of his age (75) and weakness of character was no longer able to protect him against the intrigues and envy of the Bavarian officers, and where the unsettled state of the country was not favorable to scientific pursuits. He decided therefore to remain in England in an unofficial capacity, and purchased a villa in Brompton Row, Knightsbridge, near London, which he fitted up in accordance with his own ideas of ventilation and heating. Double walls and windows prevented the escape of heat, and the space between the glass partitions was filled with plants; the decorations were harmoniously arranged according to Newton's theory of complementary colors; folding beds economized space, and the cooking was done in the dining-room, without annoyance from odor or heat.

At this time Count Rumford contemplated a visit to America, and even proposed to purchase an estate near Cambridge and settle down in his native country. In spite of his active service in the British army, he had retained the friendship and esteem of Colonel Baldwin and other prominent men in the United States. He had been elected honorary member of the American Academy of Arts and Sciences and of the Massachusetts Historical Society, and his Essays, published in this country, had made him well known. He now transmitted to the President of the United States through Rufus King, American Minister to England, his

plans for an American Military Academy like the one he had
founded in Bavaria, and a model of a field-piece of his own invention. This resulted in an offer from the War Department, authorized by President John Adams, of appointment as Superintendent
of the American Military Academy about to be established, and
also as Inspector-General of the Artillery of the United States,
with suitable rank and emoluments.

But at the time this offer was received Rumford was too much
engrossed with a new project in England to accept it. For two
years, except when he was sick, he worked night and day with all
his energy to found "a public institution for diffusing the knowledge and facilitating the general introduction of useful mechanical
inventions and improvements, and for teaching, by courses of
philosophical lectures and experiments, the application of science
to the common purposes of life."

The Royal Institution remains the chief monument to the memory of Rumford, for thanks to his excellent plan and organization, and to the men of unusual ability who have occupied positions in it, there have emanated from it many of the most important discoveries in science of the past century, and it has done
more for the advancement of knowledge than the old and richly
endowed universities of Oxford and Cambridge.

Count Rumford succeeded in interesting all classes, from court-
iers to mechanics, in his project. He secured a very large number
of "proprietors" at fifty guineas or more, and annual subscribers
at three guineas, including many nobles, prelates, members of
Parliament, ladies and scientific men, and in 1800 the Institution
received the royal approval.

A suitable building was constructed, containing a lecture
theater, a museum of models and inventions, a chemical laboratory,
a library and a conversation room, an experimental kitchen, a
printing plant for publishing the *Journal*, and workshops for
making apparatus. Board and lodging were to be provided for
some twenty young men to study mechanics, and apprentices
were to be admitted free to the gallery of the lecture room.
Rumford, always on his guard against "graft," made elaborate

rules against any rewards or prizes for inventions made in the Institution, and against any exercise of favoritism by the authorities.

In some respects the Royal Institution departed from Rumford's intentions as soon as he relinquished his somewhat despotic control. He obviously had in mind a sort of technological school and laboratory for inventing useful appliances, and testing them for the benefit of the public according to the idea thus expressed in his Prospectus:

"It is an undoubtable truth that the successive improvements in the condition of man, from a state of ignorance and barbarism to that of the highest cultivation and refinement, are usually effected by the aid of machinery in procuring the necessaries, the comforts and the elegancies of life; and that the preëminence of any people in civilization is, and ought ever to be, estimated by the state of industry and mechanical improvement among them."

When Rumford left England the instruction in mechanics was quietly dropped, because it was thought that teaching science to the lower classes had a dangerous political tendency. The stone staircase leading to the mechanics' gallery was torn down, the culinary contrivances and the models were put away, and the workmen discharged. For a time the Royal Institution seemed likely to degenerate into a mere fashionable lecture course for "a number of silly women and dilettante philosophers."

The Royal Institution owes its survival and success to the fact that it has always contained one or two determined investigators, and that they were given a free hand. Rumford rightly prided himself on his choice of Humphry Davy, then twenty-three years old, as assistant lecturer in chemistry, at a salary of $500 a year, room, coals and candles and a folding bed from the model room being provided for his accommodation. Five years later in the laboratory of the Royal Institution, Davy decomposed the fixed alkalies by the electric current, and obtained from them the new metals, sodium and potassium. Faraday, then twenty-one, attended four lectures of Sir Humphry Davy, wrote out his notes, illustrated them by sketches of the apparatus, and sent them in to the lecturer, in this way securing a position in the Royal Institution, where he discovered that a current of electricity could be generated by passing a wire in front of a magnet, which is the essential principle of all our dynamos and motors. The Royal Institution also gave to Dalton, Tyndall and Dewar the opportunity to carry on their researches. Dr. Thomas Young, the discoverer of the wave theory of light, was chosen by Rumford for the lecturer on physics. If, then, the Royal Institution has failed to carry out some of Rumford's plans for applied science, the discoveries which have been made in the field in which he was equally interested have resulted in greater benefits to mankind than even his imagination could conceive. Were he living now, he would not find reason to deplore, as he often did, the conservatism of manufacturers and the delay in the application of scientific discoveries to practical purposes, although he might still argue, as he used to do, that the promotion of invention by commerical and selfish motives is wasteful and unsystematic.

Although Count Rumford's genius eminently fitted him for planning and promoting the establishment of such institutions, his temperament was not such as to enable him to work well as one of a number of managers who all regarded themselves entitled to as much consideration and authority as himself. His dictatorial manner and fondness for having his own way caused some friction in the conduct of affairs. His health was poor, and his sensitive nature was excessively irritated by the savage attacks of the reviewers and satirists of the time upon his scientific and philanthropic work. The Royal Institution was ridiculed as an attempt to make science fashionable, and his efforts in behalf of the poor were attacked on two different grounds, by the radicals as an attempt to squeeze down the poor to a lower standard of life by feeding them on such stuff as Indian corn and potatoes; and, on the other hand, by aristocrats, because it was dangerous to society to instil into the minds of the lower classes ideas above their station. It was thought to be a degradation of science to apply it to such ignoble purposes as stoves and pots. Peter Pindar, for example, writes:

"Knight of the dish-clout, whereso'er I walk,
I hear thee, Rumford, all the kitchen talk:
Note of melodious cadence on my ear,
Loud echoes, 'Rumford' here and 'Rumford' there.
Lo! every parlor, drawingroom, I see,
Boasts of thy stoves, and talks of naught but thee."

After two years in his quiet villa in Brompton Row his visits
to the continent became longer and more frequent, as he looked
about for a new field of activity. Besides his offer from America,
he had an invitation from the Czar of Russia to enter his service,
and the new Elector of Bavaria, afterwards made king by Napoleon, showed him some favor and increased his pension. But
Paris drew him the strongest, chiefly by two attractions, Napoleon
and Madame Lavoisier. At a meeting of the French Institute in
1801 he sat near the First Consul, while Volta read his paper on
his galvanic pile, which was discussed by Napoleon with great
clearness and force. When Rumford was presented to him,
Napoleon said he knew him by reputation, and that the French
nation had adopted some of his inventions. Immediately after
this interview he received an invitation to dine with Napoleon, as
the only stranger present. Rumford was later elected a member of
the French Institute, on the same date as Jefferson, President of
the United States, and he contributed to it many important papers.

He had become intimately acquainted with Madame Lavoisier
while traveling in Switzerland, and, since she was handsome,
rich, clever in conversation and interested in science, he had reason to suppose that she would make a desirable wife. She was
the daughter of Mr. Paulze, a contractor of the finances under the
old régime. At fourteen she had been married to the chemist
Lavoisier, then twice her age, and she assisted him in the laboratory, in translating and in drawing the illustrations for his great
Traité de Chimie. When the Revolution broke out Lavoisier was
arrested at the instigation of Marat, whose essay on fire he had
contemptuously criticized. When brought before the revolutionary
tribunal in 1793 Lavoisier begged for a few more days of life, in
order to see the outcome of a chemical experiment on which he

was engaged, but Coffinhal, vice-president of the tribunal, declared that "the Republic has no use for savants," and so he was guillotined.

Count Rumford was married to Madame Lavoisier in 1805, and set up a handsome establishment in the center of Paris. But neither party found the other agreeable to live with, as they were both too independent and differed decidedly in their tastes. Madame Rumford was fond of lavish entertainments and elaborate dinners, while the Count ate little and drank less, and detested idle conversation. Probably De Candolle's analysis of their temperaments will say all that it is necessary about their marital unhappiness.

"Rumford was cold, calm, obstinate, egotistic, prodigiously occupied with the material element of life and the very smallest inventions of detail. He wanted his chimneys, lamps, coffee-pots, windows, made after a certain pattern, and he contradicted his wife a thousand times a day about the household management. Madame Rumford was a woman of resolute wilful character. Her spirit was high, her soul strong and her character masculine."

And one scene from their married life narrated in the Count's own words in a letter to his daughter Sarah will be sufficient to explain why they separated:

"A large party had been invited I neither liked nor approved of, and invited for the sole purpose of vexing me. Our house being in the center of the garden, walled around, with iron gates, I put on my hat, walked down to the porter's lodge and gave him orders, on his peril, not to let anyone in. Besides, I took away the keys. Madame came down, and when the company arrived she talked with them,—she on one side, they on the other of the high brick wall. After that she goes and pours boiling water on some of my beautiful flowers!"

Four years of such life were enough; they parted and lived happily ever after. Madame Lavoisier de Rumford kept her coterie of distinguished people about her until the day of her death at the age of seventy-eight, when with her perished the last of the eighteenth century salons. Count Rumford retired to a villa in

Auteuil, a suburb of Paris, where he spent the remaining five years of his life in peace and quiet, dividing his time between his laboratory and his garden with its fifty varieties of roses, gradually becoming more isolated from society, and retaining only few friends, among whom were Lagrange and Cuvier. His daughter Sarah joined him for a time, but was not with him when he died.

His scientific researches in Paris were largely devoted to light, and in this field his discoveries were of great importance and practical value. In order to get the arithmetical results for which he always strove, it was necessary to find a method of measuring the relative intensity of different sources of light, and for this purpose he invented what is known as the Rumford photometer. In this the standard lamp and the one to be compared with it are so placed that the two shadows cast by an opaque rod upon a screen side by side are of equal intensity, then the relative brightness of the lights are inversely as the squares of their distances from the screen. He had an assistant move the lamps lest he should be led into the temptation to distort his observations in accordance with his theory. Since he found that the same weight of wax or oil burned under different conditions gave off very different amounts of light, he came to the conclusion that light cannot be of the chemical products of combustions, but was a wave motion in the ether due to the heating of solid particles in the flame. Finding how small was the light compared, with what might be obtained from the fuel, he experimented on wicks, air-holes, polyflame burners, chimneys, etc., until he had constructed fourteen different kinds of lamps. According to the Paris wits, one of these gave so powerful a light that a man carrying it in the street was so blinded by it that he could not find his way home, but wandered in the Bois de Boulogne all night.

He anticipated the impressionist artists in the discovery of blue shadows, and, by a series of very skilful experiments, he showed that whenever shadows were cast by two lights of different colors, the shadows were of the complementary color, one real and the other imaginary. Each color called up in the mind its companion which, when combined with it, produced a pure white.

He calls attention to the value of such studies for artists, house furnishers and "ladies choosing ribbons," and suggests entertainments of color harmonies, like musical concerts. Rumford also experimented on the chemical effects produced by light, such as the deposition of a film of metallic gold and silver on a ribbon or slip of ivory which had been dipped in a solution of their salts; a reaction which forms the basis of modern photography.

His researches on heat and light were based upon determinations of the heat of combustion of the fuel used by means of an ingeniously devised calorimeter. In this the products of combustion are drawn through a worm immersed in a known quantity of water and the increase in the temperature of the water determined by a thermometer immersed in it. By having the water at the beginning of the experiment about as much cooler than the room as it was warmer at the end, one of the chief sources of error, that of loss of heat to the air, was practically eliminated: a method still in use. With this apparatus, which has only recently been superseded by the bomb calorimeter using compressed oxygen, he determined with remarkable accuracy the heat of burning alcohol, hydrogen, carbon and many kinds of wood, coal, oil and wax. From a determination of the heat of combustion of wood and of charcoal made from it, he deduced the fact that the gas lost in making charcoal is the most valuable part of the fuel.

In looking over Count Rumford's papers after a hundred years of scientific work has been done in the fields where he was a pioneer, one is forcibly struck by his selection of what were the most important problems to be solved. This is shown, for example, in the interest he took in the inconspicuous phenomena of surface tension, and his study of the pellicle covering the surface of water, which supports a globule of mercury as in a pocket, and gives footing to water-spiders. He clearly shows the importance of this in movements of sap in the trees and of the fluids of the animals; a line of investigation that just now is proving extremely fruitful in physics and physiology.

While in Paris he experimented on the proper construction of wagon wheels, and invented a dynamometer by which the pull of the horse was registered by the needle of a spring-balance. **Having** ascertained in this way that broad tires reduced the traction power, he adopted them for his carriage notwithstanding the jeers of the street crowds.

Count Rumford died in Auteuil August 21, 1814, in his sixty-second year. Baron Cuvier, Permanent Secretary of the French Institute, and his intimate friend, pronounced the eulogy before the Institute, coupling his name with that of another recently deceased member, Parmentier, who introduced the potato into France. Both savants, he says, were defenders of the human race against its two greatest enemies, hunger and cold; both these enemies are to be fought with the same weapon, the proper use of carbon compounds. The physicist who invents an economical fireplace is as though he had added acres of wood; the botanist who brings a new edible plant virtually increases the arable land. In laboring for the poor, Count Rumford was rewarded by his greatest discoveries, so Fontenelle's remark could be applied to him that "he had taken the same road to Heaven and to the Academy."

ALEXANDER WILSON

ORNITHOLOGIST

1766–1813

BY WITMER STONE

ALEXANDER WILSON has been termed "the father of American Ornithology," and not without reason. He was not the pioneer writer upon American birds as Catesby, Forster and others preceded him by many years, but to him we are indebted for the first comprehensive work on the birds of our country at large, and the first work which merited the title that he bestowed upon it, *American Ornithology.*

Wilson's *Ornithology* was not a scientific work so far as matters of anatomy and taxonomy were concerned. Indeed, knowledge of these subjects was not very far advanced at that day and our author had given them little attention. His aim was to picture each bird as accurately as his skill permitted both with brush and pen and to include in his text, backgrounds and sidelights upon its life and haunts drawn from his travels and rambles through wood and field.

Love of nature always predominates over technique and this spirit of the *Ornithology* seems to have pervaded much of our subsequent ornithological literature to a great extent. Possibly the nature of the study is to some degree responsible, but this early work seems to have set a style which has been followed in the volumes that have succeeded it.

Wilson's character is in no small degree reflected in his work. He was not a scientific man in the modern sense, not a closet naturalist, but a poet who loved nature for herself and he took up the study of ornithology not as science but because the beauty of the birds and the melody of their songs appealed to him.

51

He later recognized the importance of scientific accuracy and bibliographic research, but this came as a secondary result of the line of work upon which he had set out, and was not a primary interest with him. His *Ornithology* was born in the woods not in the museum or library.

Wilson was doubtless acquainted with the birds of his native country and knew them by name just as he knew the thistle, the heather and the bracken, for upon landing in America one of his first comments was upon the strange birds and shrubs that surrounded him, but there is no evidence that he had any early inclination toward the study of birds except as they formed a part of nature which was ever dear to him.

Every lover of nature seems to have within him more or less latent talent for art, poetry and natural history, and circumstances largely determine which of the three comes most prominently to the surface. In Wilson, poetry first filled his mind and became the aim of his life, but his talent in this direction was not sufficiently great to earn him conspicuous notoriety and it was as a chronicler of nature that he became famous though he did not enter upon this rôle until the last decade of his life.

Alexander Wilson was born in the Seedhills of Paisley in Renfrewshire, Scotland, July 6, 1766, the son of Alexander Wilson and Mary McNab. The early death of his mother may have had some effect upon his after life as it is said that she intended that he should study for the ministry. However this may be his father and stepmother seem to have done as much for him as their poverty and the large size of their family permitted. He attended the Paisley grammar school and learned to read and write, but was compelled in later life to make up for many deficiencies which had they been supplied at the proper time would have aided him greatly in his life's work.

While a small boy he was engaged for a short time, at least, as a cattle herd on the farm of Bakerfield, but when only thirteen years of age became apprenticed to his brother-in-law, William Duncan, to learn the "art of weaving" which was the occupation of nearly all of his friends and relatives.

Even at this time Wilson was writing verses and his mind was ever turning to the outdoor life which was dear to his heart and in comparison with which the loom was a sorry bondage. As the only visible means of earning a living he continued weaving until 1789 when he joined his brother-in-law in a tour of eastern Scotland as a peddler. This undertaking was prompted by his love of tramping and his restlessness under uncongenial confinement; not by any love or ability for trading, for that he did not possess. While gratifying his taste for outdoor life he was by no means benefited financially by the change. However, he gave full rein to his poetical ambition, and with his characteristic impetuosity he soon had visions of publishing his volume of verses and sharing in the notoriety that had just greeted the issue of Burns' first poems. Wilson was evidently acquainted with Burns as some of his verses show and entertained a very high opinion of him. To what extent Burns' success may have influenced him or his style is hard to say, but one of the best of Wilson's productions published anonymously was attributed to the "plowman," doubtless to the author's great gratification.

Wilson reached the height of his practical ambition in 1790 when he published a volume of his poetical writings. It was, however, an indifferent production and failed to bring him the renown that he coveted. In 1792 he was back at the loom but as before despondent and unhappy and in sore straits financially. He continued to publish occasional poems in the local papers and now and then indulged in sarcastic verses on certain civil authorities and other self-important personages. This practice finally brought him face to face with libel charges, resulting in fines and imprisonment.

Upon his release, consumed with bitterness and more despondent than ever he resolved to leave his native country and try his fortune in America. Accordingly, accompanied by his nephew, William Duncan, he sailed from Belfast on May 23, 1794, and reached the mouth of Delaware bay on the 11th of July.

Impatient to be once more ashore they landed at New Castle, Delaware, "happy as mortals could be" and went on foot to

Wilmington and thence to Philadelphia through virgin forest most of the way, past log cabins, and occasional farms. "On the way," Wilson writes to his parents, "I did not observe one bird such as those in Scotland but all much richer in color . . . some red birds, several of which I shot for our curiosity." This quotation is worthy of note as it shows an early interest in birds and an appreciation of the difference in the avi-fauna of the two countries. At the same time we find no further mention of birds in his correspondence for many years.

The two weavers found no opening for men of their trade in Philadelphia and seem to have been compelled to accept any kind of employment that was offered. Wilson, always of a delicate constitution and unfitted for hard labor, succeeded in securing a school first at Frankford and later at Milestown, a short distance north of the city. The requisites of the country schoolmaster were not very severe at this time, and as Wilson wrote a good hand and had always been a reader his education, in spite of early short-comings, was apparently fully equal to the calls made upon it. With the idea of advancing in this profession he seems to have been constantly endeavoring to improve himself in mathematics and other studies in which he recognized himself as deficient.

His particular friend at this period of his life was Charles Orr, a writing master in Philadelphia and a man of studious nature with whom Wilson maintained an active correspondence. His letters of September, 1800, show that he had been forced to relinquish his school on account of ill health, but at the earnest request of the trustees agreed to try it again. "I was attached to the children and to the people," he wrote, "and if they would allow me one week more to ramble about, I would once more engage, though I should die in their service. My request was immediately acceded to, and I am once more the dominie of Milestown school." Later he writes, "I have begun the old way again and have about thirty scholars. I study none and take my morning and evening ramble regularly. Do you spend any of your leisure hours with the puzzling chaps, algebra and trigonometry, etc., or are you wholly absorbed in the study of mechanics? You must write me particu-

larly. I think I shall take a ride 15 or 20 miles on Saturday. I find riding agrees better with me than any other exercise. I always feel cheerful after it, and can eat confoundedly. Have you made any new discoveries in the Heaven above, or the earth beneath, with your telescope or microscope?"

At this time his nephew had moved to Ovid, Cayuga county, New York, where they had purchased a tract of land and begun to farm. Other members of his family came hither from Scotland and it seems to have been Wilson's intention to join them though he afterwards abandoned the idea.

In 1801 Wilson left Milestown and obtained a school at Bloomfield, N. J., where he remained about a year. He seems to have had little trouble in securing positions. School-teachers, were, to be sure, scarce and salaries small, as he complained bitterly with respect to his Bloomfield engagement where the people "paid their minister 250 pounds a year for preaching twice a week and their teacher 40 dollars a quarter for the most spirit-sinking, laborious work, six, I may say twelve times weekly."

Wilson, however, seems to have possessed the requisites of a teacher in no small degree; he was both a disciplinarian and an instructor and succeeded in his main object, that of imparting knowledge to his pupils. He also seems to have gained the respect and good-will of the people among whom he established himself so that they were loath to have him leave them. In describing his Bloomfield school he writes: "The schoolhouse in which I teach is situated at the extremity of a spacious level plain of sand thinly covered with grass. In the centre of this plain stands a newly erected stone meeting-house, 80 feet by 60, which forms a striking contrast with my sanctum sanctorum, which has been framed of logs some 100 years ago, and looks like an old sentry box. The scholars have been accustomed to great liberties by their former teacher. They used to put stones in his pocket, etc., etc. I was told that the people did not like to have their children punished, but I began with such a system of terror as soon established my authority most effectually. I succeed in teaching them to read and I care for none of their objections."

Wilson became involved in a love affair while at Milestown, which did not end happily for him, and his sensitive nature ever subject to fits of despondency became more than ever affected during his stay at Bloomfield where he was surrounded by strangers. He proposed to his friend Orr that they open a school somewhere under their joint management; he even thought of turning his back upon his adopted country and returning to the shores of Caledonia, and meanwhile he consoled himself in his solitude with writing poems.

In February, 1802, he moved again, this time to take charge of the school at Gray's Ferry just outside the city of Philadelphia. He had evidently not recovered from his despondency, as he writes, "I shall recommence that painful profession once more with the same gloomy sullen resignation that a prisoner re-enters his dungeon or a malefactor mounts the scaffold; fate urges him, necessity me. The present pedagogue is a noisy, outrageous fat old captain of a ship, who has taught these ten years in different places. You may hear him bawling 300 yards off. The boys seem to pay as little regard to it as ducks to the rumbling of a stream under them. I shall have many difficulties to overcome in establishing my own rules and authority. But perseverance overcometh all things."

Little did Wilson suspect that this last move would prove the turning-point of his life and raise him from oblivion to fame though not in the field in which he had always imagined that his genius lay.

Amid the green fields and the budding woods of early spring he forgot his troubles and his spirits rose again with their characteristic impetuosity. Poetry as usual was his resource: "My harp is new strung," he writes, "and my soul glows with more ardour than ever to emulate those immortal bards who have gone before me . . . my heart swells, my soul rises to an elevation I cannot express."

But poetry was soon to take second place in his consideration.

Close to Gray's Ferry lay the homestead of the Bartrams, a curious old stone mansion surrounded by the historic botanical garden the pride of the famous old botanist, John Bartram. Here there were living at this time the two sons of the original proprietor, John and William Bartram. The latter, then a man, of sixty-one years of age, was a botanist of perhaps quite as much ability as his father, while he also possessed a hoard of knowledge on general natural history equalled by but few men of his time. He had traveled when a young man through Georgia, Carolina and Florida and published a report on his travels. Being exceedingly modest, however, he never sought fame by further publications, though he generously aided all who came to him for assistance and advice and shared with them his store of knowledge.

Between Bartram and Wilson a close intimacy immediately sprang up, and the association with the venerable naturalist and the atmosphere which prevaded the botanic garden soon kindled into flame the latent interest in birds which up to that time had been dominated by the spirit of poetry.

Ornithology was almost as much a hobby with Bartram as botany, and he had published in his *Travels* a list of the birds of eastern North America, consequently he gave every encouragement to the development of this taste in his young friend.

The meagerness and inaccuracy of the literature of American ornithology, and the obvious need of science for the knowledge that he felt he could supply strongly appealed to Wilson, while the recreation from his confining school duties which the pursuit of this study would afford him, was an additional allurement.

In 1803 he writes to a friend, "I have had many pursuits since I left Scotland . . . and I am now about to make a collection of all our finest birds."

The first essential in natural history research in those days was the preparation of drawings of the objects studied, and Wilson being by no means an artist born set about the laborious task of learning to draw. Night after night he worked patiently with brush and pencil in his efforts to produce satisfactory pictures of the birds which he shot. Alexander Lawson, the engraver, gave him instruction and Miss Nancy Bartram, a niece of the naturalist, also helped him. Wilson never attained much artistic ability, but his sole object, the production of faithful bird portraits, he did accomplish and in a style superior to any work published up to that time and to many that came after.

Some of his first efforts he sent to Bartram with the following explanation: "The duties of my profession will not admit me to apply to this study with the assiduity and perseverance I could wish. Chief part of what I do is sketched by candle-light, and for this I am obliged to sacrifice the pleasures of social life, and the agreeable moments which I might enjoy in company with you and your amiable friend. I shall be happy if what I have done merits your approbation." To Lawson he writes about this time, "Six days in one week I have no more time than just to swallow my meals and return to my *Sanctum Sanctorum*. Five days of the following week are occupied in the same routine of *pedagoguing* matters; and the other two are sacrificed to that itch for drawing, which I caught from your honorable self. I am most earnestly bent on pursuing my plan of making a collection of all the birds in this part of North America. Now I don't want you to throw cold water, as Shakespeare says, on this notion, Quixotic as it may appear. I have been so long accustomed to the building of airy castles and brain windmills, that it has become one of my earthly comforts, a sort of a rough bone, that amuses me when sated with the dull drudgery of life."

Quoting again from his letters as the best record we have of his progress, we find him writing to Bartram in March, 1804:

" I send for your amusement a few attempts at some of our indigenous birds, hoping that your good nature will excuse their deficiencies, while you point them out to me. I am almost ashamed to send you these drawings, but I know your generous disposition will induce you to encourage one in whom you perceive a sincere and eager wish to do well. They were chiefly colored by candle light.

"I have now got my collection of native birds considerably enlarged; and shall endeavour, if possible, to obtain all the smaller ones this summer. Be pleased to mark on the drawings, with a pencil, the name of each bird, as, except three or four, I do not know them. I shall be extremely obliged to you for every hint that will assist me in this agreeable amusement. . . . I declare that the face of an owl, and the back of a lark, have put me to a nonplus; and if Miss Nancy will be so obliging as to try her hand on the last mentioned, I will furnish her with one in good order, and will copy her drawing with the greatest pleasure; having spent almost a week on two different ones, and afterwards destroyed them both, and got nearly in the slough of despond."

The next two years passed rapidly at Gray's Ferry. Wilson concentrated his attention upon the collecting and drawing of birds, while his leisure moments were spent in the company of his friend and adviser, for whom his love and esteem were constantly increasing. "I confess," he writes, "that I was always an enthusiast in my admiration of the rural scenery of Nature; but since your example and encouragement have set me to attempt to imitate her productions, I see new beauties in every bird, plant, or flower I contemplate; and find my ideas of the incomprehensible First Cause still more exalted, the more minutely I examine His work." And again regarding some more drawings sent to Bartram, "Criticise these, my dear friend, without fear of offending me—this will instruct, but not discourage me. For there is not among all our naturalists one who knows so well what they are, and how they ought to be represented. In the mean time accept of my best wishes for your happiness—wishes as sincere as ever one human being breathed for another. To your advice and encouraging encomiums I am indebted for these few specimens, and for all that will follow. They may yet tell posterity that I was honored with your friendship, and that to your inspiration they owe their existance."

Meanwhile the school went on and the scholars became interested in gratifying their master's tastes. "I have had live crows, hawks and owls,—oppossums, squirrels, snakes, and lizards," writes Wilson, "so that my room has sometimes reminded me of Noah's ark; but Noah had a wife in one corner of it, and in this particular our parallel does not altogether tally. I receive every subject of natural history that is brought to me and though they do not march into my ark from all quarters, as they did that of

our great ancestor, yet I find means, by the distribution of a few
five-penny *bits*, to make them find the way fast enough. A boy,
not long ago, brought me a large basket full of crows. I expect
his next load will be bull-frogs, if I don't soon issue orders to the
contrary."

The winter of 1804–05 was very severe and the suffering was
great. Many scholars were unable to continue in attendance at
Wilson's school-house and he was in such financial straits that he
was forced to propose giving up his position. The trustees, however, would not hear of it and immediately raised sufficient funds
to retain his services.

In October, 1804, Wilson took a journey mainly on foot to visit
his nephew at Ovid, continuing to Niagara Falls and returning
to Gray's Ferry in December. This trip inspired his last lengthy
poem, which was separately published as *The Foresters* being in
fact a narrative of the trip in verse. The varied scenery also
stirred up the old spirit of restlessness, and he wrote to Bartram
of the advisability of becoming a traveler "to commence some
more extensive expedition, where scenes and subjects entirely new,
and generally unknown, might reward my curiosity; and where
perhaps my humble acquisitions might add something to the store
of knowledge." He also asked how he might best acquire a
knowledge of botany and mineralogy.

Whatever Bartram's advice may have been Wilson seems to
have continued his study of scientific literature with redoubled
vigor. His letters at this time contain comments and criticisms
on current publications which indicate a considerable breadth of
knowledge, and early in the following year he was appointed
assistant editor of *Rees's New Cyclopaedia*, then being published
by Bradford and Company of Philadelphia. He received a "generous salary" of $900 per year and was at last freed from the
drudgery of his school, though for a time at least his work was
more confining and necessitated his residence in the heart of the
city which he thoroughly detested.

Almost from the time Wilson set foot on American soil he became strongly attached to the country, and his letters to friends at

home constantly boast of the resources and possibilities of the States. President Jefferson commanded his deep respect and admiration, especially on account of his scientific attainments, and to him he seems to have looked for some assistance in the prosecution of his ornithological studies. He sent him with much diffidence drawings of two birds which he had secured on his journey to Niagara and received a very appreciative letter from the president. Encouraged by this Wilson wrote again just before receiving his editorial appointment and applied for a position on the expedition then being fitted out by the government under Captain Nicolas Pike to explore the sources of the Arkansas River; no attention, however, was paid to his application.

The idea of publishing the results of his bird studies seems to have taken definite shape in Wilson's mind toward the end of the year 1805, and he at that time was making attempts at etching on copper. Catesby for economy's sake etched his own plates, and Wilson being no better situated financially probably saw no other way to reproduce his drawings. His first efforts which Ord tells us were plates one and two of the *Ornithology* were sent to Bartram on November 29, 1805, and January 4, 1806, the latter one accompanied by the following note: "Mr. Wilson's affectionate compliments to Mr. Bartram; and sends for his amusement and correction another proof of his *Birds of the United States*. The coloring being chiefly done last night, must soften criticism a little. Will be thankful for my friend's advice and correction." In the letter to President Jefferson above alluded to, he clearly states his purpose of publishing as he says, "Having been engaged, these several years, in collecting materials and finishing drawings from Nature, with the design of publishing a new Ornithology of the United States of America, so deficient are the works of Catesby, Edwards, and other Europeans, I have traversed the greater part of our northern and eastern districts; and have collected many birds undescribed by these naturalists. Upwards of one hundred drawings are completed, and two plates in folio already engraved."

By April, 1807, the propectus was ready, and apparently dissatisfied with his own efforts he had engaged Alexander Lawson to etch the plates. The remuneration could not have been great and the profits were lessened by the labor that was necessary to bring the plates up to the author's ideal. In fact Lawson told Ord that he found frequently his reward did not amount to more than fifty cents a day, but he was so anxious to encourage his friend that he made no complaint and his work was in a great measure a labor of love. In planning for the publication Wilson no doubt derived great benefits from his association with Bradford and Company and it was of course this house which was to issue the work.

In the autumn of 1808, with a sample copy of volume one, he started upon a personal canvass of the country for the two-hundred and fifty subscribers which were considered necessary before the publication could be seriously prosecuted, the subscription price being $120. Traveling by stage and on foot he visited Princeton, New York, New Haven, Boston and Portland Maine, and returned by way of Dartmouth College and Albany, stopping at all the smaller towns on the way where possible subscribers might be found.

His success was varied; scientific men of means subscribed as did many prominent citizens interested in the advancement of literature and science. Many others, however, while lavish in praise of his beautiful pictures were appalled at the price and still others seemed to totally lack appreciation of the merits of his work. Governor Tompkins of New York, afterwards Vice-President of the United States, said, "I would not give a hundred dollars for all the birds you intend to describe, even had I them alive."

Such rebuffs must have been hard to bear, but Wilson had plenty of pluck and his letters home while avoiding any mention of his success are full of descriptions of the places he visited. Every spot of historic interest inspired him with respect. He visited Bunker Hill with a feeling of veneration and was surprised that the people living in the vicinity did not seem to share it.

Upon his return to Philadelphia Wilson set out almost immediately upon a southern tour, visiting Washington, Charleston, and

Savannah, in which latter city he succeeded in bringing the total of his subscription list up to the requisite two hundred and fifty; "having," to quote his own words, "visited all the towns within one hundred miles of the Atlantic from Maine to Georgia and done as much for this bantling book of mine as ever author did for any progeny of his brain." His experience in the south was much like that in the north. "In Annapolis," he writes, "I passed my book through both Houses of the Legislature; the wise men of Maryland stared and gaped, from bench to bench; but having never heard of such a thing as one hundred and twenty dollars for a book, the ayes for subscribing were none."

In Charleston he found such "listlessness and want of energy" that he could get no one to draw him up a list of likely subscribers and "was obliged to walk the streets and pick out those houses, which, from their appearance indicated wealth and taste in the occupants, and introduce myself." However, his task was accomplished, and flushed with success he embarked for Philadelphia in March, 1809, ready to push the publication of his volumes with all possible haste.

Wilson's canvassing trips were profitable in other ways than the securing of subscribers. His scientific acquaintances had hitherto been mainly limited to Philadelphia or to such visitors as he met at Bartram's hospitable mansion. He knew Thomas Say, George Ord, Benjamin S. Barton, and the Peales, while he had met Michaux and Muhlenberg, the botanists. Now, however, in every town he sought out those interested in Natural History. As he himself put it: "Whatever may be the result of these matters, [subscriptions] I shall not sit down with folded hands. . . . I am fixing correspondents in every corner of these northern regions, like so many pickets and outposts, so that scarcely a wren or tit shall be able to pass along, from New York to Canada, but I shall get intelligence of it. . . ."

Notable among his new acquaintances was Abbott of Georgia, famous for his publication on the insects of his native state. With him he arranged for the forwarding of such southern birds as he was personally unable to secure as well as any that were in Abbott's estimation new to science. These Wilson agreed to pay for through his agent in Savannah.

In January, 1810, the second volume of the *Ornithology* appeared, and shortly afterward Wilson started westward to explore the ornithological *terra incognita* that lay beyond the Alleghanies. He had for some years realized the necessity of exploring this country as he supposed there were many birds to be found there which never came east of the mountains. In 1805 he had arranged such an excursion in company with Bartram, but the failing health of the venerable botanist finally compelled him to relinquish all thought of going, while Wilson, after failing to receive an appointment upon the government expedition, also abandoned the project as he realized that his finances would not warrant such an undertaking. Now, however, the expedition was imperative both on account of the probable scientific results and the possible subscribers to be obtained in the towns of the Ohio and Mississippi Valleys.

His route lay from Pittsburg down the Ohio, which he traversed in a rowboat, as far as Louisville. There he sold his skiff to a man who wondered at its curious Indian (!) name "The Ornithologist," and set out on foot to Lexington and Nashville. He visited the Mammoth Cave and sent to the editor of the *Portfolio* in Philadelphia letters containing a careful description of this and other interesting points that he passed on his journey.

Before leaving Nashville he wrote to a friend, "Nine hundred miles distant from you sits Wilson, the hunter of birds' nests and sparrows, just preparing to enter on a wilderness of 780 miles,— most of it in the territory of Indians,—*alone*, but in good spirits, and expecting to have every pocket crammed with skins of new and extraordinary birds before he reaches the City of New Orleans."

The territory of Mississippi through which Wilson traveled alone on horseback was then mainly populated by the semicivilized Indian tribes which were afterwards transported to the present Indian Territory and he met but few white men. The route was exceedingly difficult, being through dense forests and "most execrable swamps." On the seventeenth day he reached Natchez and from there followed the Mississippi River to New Orleans.

Here he secured a substantial addition to his subscription list and sailed for Philadelphia, well satisfied with his trip. He skirted but did not touch the peninsula of Florida, a land which had he but known it would have yielded him more novelties than that which he had just traversed.

During the years 1811 and 1812 Wilson seems to have lived almost continuously at Bartram's, which was always such a congenial home to him, and meanwhile the publication advanced rapidly.

After the fifth volume was completed in 1812 he went again to New England to visit his agents and look after his subscribers. Upon his return he devoted himself to the water birds which he had previously somewhat neglected and made a number of excursions across the state of New Jersey to Egg Harbor, then a great resort for sea birds of various kinds. Upon these trips he was accompanied by his friend Ord then about thirty years of age, afterwards president of the Academy of Natural Sciences of Philadelphia.

About this time Wilson began to reap the rewards of his labors,— financial reward there was apparently none, since the expense so far had fully equalled the receipts,—but his merit was gaining recognition.

He was elected a member of the American Society of Artists in 1812 and of the American Philosophical Society and the recently formed Academy of Natural Sciences in the following year.

During the summer of 1813 owing to the difficulty of procuring colorists for the plates he attended personally to much of this work and overtaxed himself. His whole energy seems to have been directed toward the finishing of his work. In July he writes, "My eighth volume is now in the press and will be published in November. One more volume will complete the whole." His constitution, however, which had always demanded plenty of outdoor exercise could not stand this constant application and when shortly after this he was stricken with an attack of dysentery, he lacked the requisite strength to resist the disease and after only a few days illness he died on August 23, 1813.

The premature close of such a career was lamentable. With fame just within his grasp and possibilities of various kinds before him, it is difficult to say what Wilson would have accomplished had he been permitted to round out his life.

His friend Ord completed the *Ornithology* from the fragments left by the author, probably as faithfully and as nearly in accord with Wilson's ideas as it could have been done, and later published several reprints. The revised editions and further popularization of the work, and a work on North American mammals, all of which Wilson had in mind, could, however, be executed by no other hand. Furthermore the existence of an ornithologist of such pre-eminent ability must have exerted a decided influence upon the subsequent development of scientific work in America and it is impossible to say what effect his later work might have had upon the productions of those who succeeded him.

The character of Alexander Wilson, the man, may be read in the outline of his life and the history of his work, but his friend Ord has given us a sketch of his personality:

" Wilson was possessed of the nicest sense of honor. In all his dealings he was not only scrupulously just but highly generous. His veneration for truth was exemplary. His disposition was social and affectionate. His benevolence was extensive. He was remarkably temperate in eating and drinking, his love of study and retirement preserving him from the contaminating influence of the convivial circle. But as no one is perfect, Wilson in a small degree partook of the weakness of humanity. He was of the *genus irritabile*, and was obstinate in opinion. It ever gave him pleasure to acknowledge error, when the conviction resulted from his own judgment alone, but he could not endure to be told of his mistakes. Hence his associates had to be sparing of their criticisms, through a fear of forfeiting his friendship. With almost all his friends he had occasionally, arising from a collision of opinion, some slight misunderstanding, which was soon passed over, leaving no disagreeable impression. But an act of disrespect he could ill brook, and a wilful injury he would seldom forgive.

"In his person he was of a middle stature, of a thin habit of body; his cheek bones projected, and his eyes, though hollow, displayed considerable vivacity and intelligence; his complexion was sallow, his mein thoughtful; his features were coarse, and there was a dash of vulgarity in his physiognomy, which struck the observer at the first view, but which failed to impress one on acquaintance. His walk was quick when travelling, so much so that it was difficult for a companion to keep pace with him; but when in the forests, in pursuit of birds, he was deliberate and attentive—he was, as it were, all eyes and all ears. Such was Alexander Wilson."

So far as we can learn no one differed from the above estimate of the man except Audubon who charges him with failure to acknowledge information that he gave him and with publishing a copy of one of his drawings without credit. These claims were not made until after Wilson was dead and are so at variance with his character as depicted by others that they would seem scarcely worthy of notice were it not that so much has been made of them both by Audubon and his biographers. Audubon at several points in his ornithological writings makes sarcastic remarks about Wilson, and there is every reason to believe that he was much embittered at his failure to secure a publisher for his work in Philadelphia and New York owing to the field being filled by that of Wilson. His relations with Ord and other of Wilson's supporters, moreover, were not friendly, and these facts doubtless had much to do with his attacks. The meeting between the two ornithologists took place at Louisville in March, 1810, when Wilson was seeking birds and subscribers on his western tour. They were quite unknown to each other even by name or reputation. Audubon at the time was only thirty years of age and had no reputation except among his immediate friends. He had made a number of drawings of birds, but had no thought of publishing them. He accompanied Wilson upon a day's hunting during his stay in Louisville as Wilson himself states, but the latter doubtless never thought of crediting Audubon with such observations as they may have made, when in each other's company. As to the drawings, all that Wilson made on this part of his trip were lost, and there is absolutely no reason to doubt his statement that he secured the small-headed Flycatcher as he described, inasmuch as Ord immediately published the fact that he was with Wilson when he shot the bird and Lawson stated that he had the specimen before him when engraving Wilson's plates. Audubon's memory seems to have been at fault in this instance, and his hostility to Ord doubtless inspired this and other reflections on Wilson, as elsewhere he speaks of him with great kindness.

Wilson entered upon the production of his *Ornithology* with no motive other than the desire to benefit science, and he expressed no expectations of great financial profit or sensational notoriety. He expended upon the work all the money that he had and was eventually compelled to resign his position as editor of the *Encyclopædia* so engrossing were the demands of his own publication. At the time the second volume was about ready for the press he wrote to Bartram: "I assure you my dear friend that this undertaking has involved me in many difficulties and expenses which I never dreamed of and I have never yet received one cent from it. I am therefore a volunteer in the cause of Natural History impelled by nobler views than those of money." In the preface to the fifth volume, too, he says: "The publication of an original work of this kind in this country has been attended with difficulties, great, and it must be confessed sometimes discouraging to the author whose only reward hitherto has been the favorable opinion of his fellow citizens and the pleasure of the pursuit." There is no evidence that circumstances had altered at the time of his death, and though he speaks with satisfaction of the approval of his friends, his reward even in this line had scarcely begun to reach him when his labors were so suddenly terminated.

In forming our estimate of the value to science of Wilson's work we naturally compare it with that of other ornithologists. Compared with his predecessors, his chief merit is originality. He had no model upon which to build his *Ornithology* and was indeed familiar with only the works of Catesby, Latham, Turton, Edwards and Bartram, and the obvious errors which pervade most of these drove him to rely only upon Nature herself for his facts. He broke boldly away from all the fables and hearsay reports that fill the pages of the early writers and described only such birds as he had himself seen and such characteristics of habit as he was personally familiar with or which he had first hand from reliable observers.

Thus relying wholly upon his own resources he produced a treatise which at once placed American Ornithology upon a firm basis, and upon the foundation thus laid each subsequent writer from Audubon and Nuttall on, has simply added his portion toward the completed structure. The first writer upon a fauna is in a different position from any of those who come after, and can hardly be fairly compared with them since they have all had his work as a guide.

In the case of Alexander Wilson we find him most frequently compared with Audubon, since their works were of essentially the same compass. From an artistic standpoint Audubon's work is far superior; he was preëminently an artist, both by birth and education, while Wilson made no pretensions to art; but as a scientific work so far as the country covered by Wilson is concerned it added but little to Wilson's accounts, and this in spite of the fact that the latter's bird studies covered but ten years, while Audubon had devoted thirty years to the study before he began publication. Indeed, to the present day but twenty-three indigenous land birds from east of the Alleghanies and north of Florida have been added to Wilson's list.

To give some idea of the rank of Wilson's work with the scientific publications of the time we may quote Baron Cuvier to the effect that "he has treated of American birds better than those of Europe have yet been treated." The impetus that such a work, produced in America and by the support of American subscribers must have given to American science is hard to estimate, as is also the attention which it must have directed toward America as a country which not only possessed a rich fauna and flora but which gave promise of producing men thoroughly capable of making known its riches to the scientific world and among the van of this assemblage stands Alexander Wilson, a Scotchman by birth but an American in his interests and sympathies.

John J. Audubon

JOHN JAMES AUDUBON

ORNITHOLOGIST

1780–1851

By Witmer Stone

Probably no name is more nearly synonymous with the study of birds than that of Audubon, and no ornithologist is more widely known. In science and literature as well as in other fields notoriety is due either to the personality of the man or to the work which he has accomplished, while in certain cases both contribute to his fame. Audubon is a striking example of this, and the aid that he gave to the development of American Ornithology rests quite as much upon his striking personality and the unique character of his bird portraits as upon the actual scientific value of the labors that he performed.

We cannot, therefore, form an estimate of his relative position in the world of science without a careful consideration of Audubon the man as well as of Audubon the ornithologist.

Unfortunately no one who knew him well has given us a careful review of his life and character and consequently we are compelled to fall back upon an autobiography covering his early life, written for his children and upon his journals for the history of his later achievements.

It seems somewhat characteristic of the man that he does not state when he was born and such mentions as he makes of his age are at variance, so that his granddaughter states in her sketch of his life "he may have been born anywhere between 1772 and 1783"; the usually accepted date is, however, May 5, 1780.

His father, Jean Audubon, an admiral in the French navy, was a man of wide experience. He rose entirely through his own exertions, having shipped on a fishing vessel at the age of twelve and later commanded trading vessels until entering the service of his country. He prospered, too, and finally became possessed of estates in France and Santo Domingo, besides a farm in Pennsylvania. On one of his excursions from his Santo Domingo estates to Louisiana, then a French territory, the elder Audubon married a lady of Spanish descent who became the mother of the ornithologist. Returning to Santo Domingo soon after his birth, the mother perished in the negro uprising on the island while the father and infant son escaped and made their way back to France. In a few years the father was married again to Anne Moynette.

Under the care of his stepmother young Audubon seems to have enjoyed every pleasure that youth could wish; she "was desirous," he writes, "that I should be brought up to live and die like a gentleman, thinking that fine clothes and filled pockets were the only requisites needful to attain this end. She therefore completely spoiled me, hid my faults, boasted to every one of my youthful merits and more than all frequently said in my presence that I was the handsomest boy in France. All my wishes and idle notions were at once gratified so far as actually to give me *carte blanche* at all the confectionary shops in the town and also of the village of Coneron when during the summer we lived, as it were, in the country."

Audubon's father having himself suffered from lack of educational advantages realized the importance of their cultivation on the part of his son whom he destined for the navy. School, however, had no attractions for the boy. He says: "I studied drawing, geography, mathematics, fencing, etc., as well as music for which I had considerable talent. I had a good fencing master and a first rate teacher of the violin, mathematics was hard dull work, I thought; geography pleased me more. . . . My mother suffered me to do much as I pleased and it was not to be wondered at that instead of applying closely to my studies I preferred associating with boys of my own age and disposition who were more fond of going in search of birds' nests, fishing, or shooting, than of better studies."

The mania for rambling about the country and collecting curiosities seemed to increase, and upon the return of his father from a cruise abroad, Audubon was taken under his personal care. Studies now became more obligatory, but without any marked increase of interest upon his part or any lessening of his love of outdoor life. At this period of his life he states that he had made some drawings of French birds but apparently without any thought or interest in ornithology, and simply because they appealed to him as subjects upon which to exercise his artistic skill.

When somewhat over seventeen years of age Audubon was sent to America to look after the Pennsylvania estate at Mill Grove on the Perkiomen not far from its juncture with the Schuylkill. His father it seems despaired of making a student of him or of interesting him in the career that he had planned for him and thinking him old enough to enter seriously upon life intrusted him with the responsibility of his American property.

Audubon experienced a severe attack of sickness upon reaching New York and after his recovery was temporarily the guest of his father's agent, Miers Fisher, a Philadelphia Quaker, whose tastes it may be imagined were totally different from those of the gay young Frenchman—in fact to quote Audubon "he was opposed to music of all description, as well as to dancing, could not bear me to carry a gun or fishing rod and indeed condoned most of my amusements."

After a short period of restless toleration of his uncongenial surroundings Audubon was established as his own master on the Mill Grove estate. Here, surrounded by nature, he indulged to his heart's content all the pleasures that he so enjoyed. He describes himself at this time as "extremely extravagant." "I had no vices," he says, "it is true, neither had I any high aims. I was ever fond of shooting, fishing and riding on horse-back; the raising of fowls of every sort was one of my hobbies, and to reach the maximum of my desires in those different things filled every one of my thoughts. I was ridiculously fond of dress. To have seen me going shooting in black satin small clothes, or breeches, with silk stockings, and the finest ruffled shirt Philadelphia could afford, was, as I now realize, an absurd spectacle but it was one of my many foibles and I cannot conceal it. I purchased the best horses in the country, and rode well, and felt proud of it; my guns and fishing tackle were equally good, always expensive and richly ornamented, often with silver. Indeed, though in America, I cut as many foolish pranks as a young dandy in Bond Street or Piccadilly."

Audubon spent much of his time with brush and pencil and many of his drawings at Mill Grove were of birds, which continued to attract his attention, although he had apparently no more scientific interest in them than when a boy in France, and it was their portraiture that chiefly concerned him.

After a short time the elder Audubon sent over from France as a partner and partial guardian a man by the name of Da Costa who soon managed to get the control of affairs at Mill Grove almost entirely into his own hands and proved to be such a rascal that Audubon was forced to seek the aid of friends in order to obtain passage to France, to inform his father of the true character of the man under whose authority he had been placed. Having secured the discharge of the objectionable guardian he remained for two years with his parents "in the very lap of comfort" shooting and drawing zoölogical subjects, especially birds. A matter of much moment which was also settled during his visit to France was the approval of his proposed marriage to Miss Lucy Bakewell, the daughter of a neighbor at Mill Grove, to whom he had become deeply attached.

Audubon returned to America in 1806 in company with Ferdinand Rozier whom his father had selected as his future business partner.

A brief mercantile experience in the office of Miss Bakewell's uncle gave Audubon "some smattering of business" as he terms it, which his future father-in-law thought very important, if he contemplated the support of a wife, but which Audubon found very uncongenial. This over and impatient to seek his fortune he was married on April 8, 1808, and set out from Mill Grove accompanied by his wife and his business partner and provided with a stock of goods with which to establish a general store in the west. Louisville, Ky., was his objective point, having been much impressed with the opportunities offered by the town when on a brief visit some two years before.

The party journeyed across to Pittsburg and down the Ohio by boat and saw only success and prosperity for the future in that great country, the development of which was only just beginning.

The business prospered, as Audubon says, "when I attended to it," "but birds were birds then as now and my thoughts were ever and anon turning toward them as the objects of my greatest delight. I shot, I drew, I looked on nature only; my days were happy beyond human conception and beyond this I really cared not . . . and I could not bear to give the attention required by my business."

While Rozier was content behind the counter Audubon made the necessary trips to New York and Philadelphia for fresh supplies of goods, and the varied scenery of river and mountain and the birds and other wild tenants of the forests of Ohio and Pennsylvania rendered these trips periods of constant delight.

In 1810 longing for wilder surroundings the business was removed to Henderson, Ky., one hundred and twenty-five miles down the Ohio, and here it was the same old story; Rozier conducted the store and Audubon spent his time hunting and fishing and in this way gratified his tastes while he also contributed not a little to the support of the family. But business at Henderson was not very prosperous and another move was made, this time to St. Genevieve, a French settlement on the Mississippi. Here Audubon became very discontented while Rozier was delighted, the people being congenial to him and the business prosperous. The outcome of it was that Audubon sold out all his interests to his partner on April 11, 1811, and journeyed back across the prairie to Henderson where he had left his wife and child, happy in his freedom from all business cares, and sanguine as he always was when the immediate future was provided for.

Two incidents of this early business career deserve mention.

While at Louisville in March, 1810, there walked into the store one day Alexander Wilson, then on a canvassing trip through the west. Audubon saw for the first time a volume of the *American Ornithology* and in return showed to Wilson his own drawings of birds. What were the feelings of the two men? who can tell? Wilson made very little mention of the meeting in his diary, while Audubon years later made charges of plagiarism against Wilson which seem not to accord with the facts and make a disagreeable incident in the history of American ornithology. It would be interesting to know what part this chance interview with Wilson and the sight of his book played in the ultimate determination of Audubon to publish his own drawings. Up to this time he certainly seems to have entertained no such idea.

An equally important incident, although it came to nothing, was Audubon's application for a position on the Lewis and Clark expedition. It is hard to suggest what influence the presence of a man of his attainments would have had upon the scientific results of this historic exploration.

Besides Audubon's association with Rozier he was also a partner in the business of his brother-in-law, Thomas W. Bakewell, at New Orleans and about this time this venture failed, thus reducing Audubon's means materially. He now determined upon a journey back to Pennsylvania and traveled on horseback through Tennessee and Georgia and thence north to his old home. Here he found that his Mill Grove property had been sold by his father-in-law and upon receiving the sum that had been realized he returned to Henderson and again engaged in business. For the time he prospered, but he had no judgment in commerical affairs; new partners and new ventures were rapidly followed by new misfortunes and before long everything had to be relinquished to the creditors of the company and Audubon was left penniless. "Without a dollar in the world," he says, "bereft of all revenues beyond my own personal talents and acquirements, I left my dear log house, my delightful garden and orchards, with that heaviest of burdens, a heavy heart, and turned my face toward Louisville. This was the saddest of all my journeys,—the only time in my life when the Wild Turkeys that so often crossed my path, and the thousands of lesser birds that enlivened the woods and the prairies all looked like enemies, and I turned my eyes from them, as if I could have wished that they had never existed."

This financial calamity seems to mark the turning point in Audubon's career for although prosperity did not come to him for some years he was at once forced through necessity to make use of his real talents instead of engaging in business for which he had neither taste nor ability. He began to draw portraits in black chalk and succeeded so well that he soon gained great popularity and was enabled to settle in Louisville.

One possession with which both Audubon and his wife were endowed and the value of which can hardly be estimated was a charming personality; everywhere they made friends, not merely acquaintances but friends who were only too glad to render them every assistance in their power, and in the period of adversity which came to them during the years 1818 and 1819, and at other times later on, they owed not a little to the generosity of their friends.

The year 1818 found the family in Cincinnati where Audubon was engaged at the museum in stuffing birds, an occupation which he continued for only six months owing to the failure of the authorities to furnish him the promised remuneration. He now fell back upon his pencil and gave lessons in drawing, while he was actually forced to depend to some extent upon his gun to supply his table.

A sedentary life had no attractions for Audubon and he could never remain long in one place without experiencing the restless desire to be again roaming the forest and sooner or later he succumbed. So now after a couple of years he determined on a trip southward to New Orleans. His wife was established with kind friends in Cincinnati and was supporting herself in part by teaching. In such sympathy was she with his undertakings and with such confidence in his ultimate success in anything he attempted that she was ever willing to sacrifice personal comforts rather than prove an obstacle to his plans.

As has already been stated, Audubon had always been interested in drawing birds. His early efforts represented the birds suspended as dead game, but later he depicted them in life-like attitudes. Ever since coming west he had been drawing every variety of bird that he came across and had accumulated quite a collection. Just when he conceived the idea of publishing these drawings it is hard to say; he himself states that it was not until he met Charles Bonaparte in Philadelphia in 1824, but there is reason to think that he had the publication in mind before this time. However this may be he made this trip to New Orleans primarily with the idea of adding to his collection the many new varieties of birds that he felt sure must exist in the swamps and cane-brakes of the south and in the state which was ever dear to him as his birthplace.

Reaching New Orleans in the winter of 1820-21 he spent a whole year in rambling about the country and drawing the birds that he procured, while he supported himself by drawing portraits. The next year he was joined by his family and gave lessons in drawing while he and his wife filled positions as tutors both at New Orleans and Natchez. In this period, too, Audubon made his first attempt at painting in oils, being instructed by a traveling portrait painter, one John Stein.

In January, 1823, the family were forced to separate for a time, Mrs. Audubon going with her younger son John to live on the plantation of a Mrs. Percy at Bayou Sara where she was to act as governess to her small daughter. Audubon and his son Victor traveled about the country for a time with the artist Stein, supporting themselves by painting portraits, but at the approach of winter established themselves at Shipping Port, Ky., where Victor entered the counting-house of his uncle Mr. Berthond.

March, 1824, marks a critical point in Audubon's life. In this month he made a journey to Philadelphia taking with him his drawings of birds and there for the first time introduced them to the scientific world, and seriously discussed the possibility and best method of securing their publication. He could hardly have come to a less sympathetic community. Philadelphia had been Wilson's home and his memory was still fresh in the minds of the scientific men; a continuation and a new edition of his *Ornithology* were at that very time being published and it is not surprising that another aspirant to ornithological fame should be looked upon by many with rather small favor. Furthermore, the difficulties that Wilson had encountered in publishing his work were well known and the far greater size of Audubon's plates made their publication seem well-nigh impossible even to those who were entirely in sympathy with the undertaking. It is not surprising that Audubon, full of enthusiasm and lacking in experience, was much disheartened. But this visit in spite of its discouragements was of vast benefit to the artist-naturalist. He made the acquaintance of Charles Lucien Bonaparte, Edward Harris, Richard Harlan, George Ord, Charles A. LeSueur and other members of the Academy of Natural Sciences, several of whom became his close friends. Harris, especially, proved not only a friend but on many occasions a benefactor both to Audubon and to his wife. He was a wealthy and generous man and an ornithologist of no mean ability, and the admiration that he felt for Audubon and the unselfish interest in the successful outcome of his undertaking have seldom been paralleled. Ord on the contrary became one of Audubon's bitterest enemies. He had been the close friend of Alexander Wilson, and was at the time of Audubon's visit to Philadelphia publishing another edition of the *American Ornithology*, so that the prospect of a work so much more elaborate as Audubon's promised to be no doubt aroused his jealousy. At the same time Ord's criticism seems to have been sincere. We must remember, that Audubon was at this time in no sense a scientific man, but an artist with a strong love of nature and with a temperament derived perhaps from his French ancestry, which impressed his writings and perhaps his speech with a somewhat careless exaggeration of style that did not at all appeal to Ord who was of the exact closet-naturalist type. Audubon loathed the science of the museums and his knowledge of birds was what he derived from close association with them in the forest. It is therefore little to be wondered that Ord while he may have conceded Audubon's artistic talents, resented his reception as an "ornithologist" as the term was then understood. Indeed, John Cassin who was of much the same school as Ord says of Audubon upon meeting him many years later, "I do not particularly admire him, he is no naturalist,—positively not by nature, but an artist, no reasonable doubt of it! [1] "

It was in art circles that Audubon profited most during the five months that he remained in Philadelphia. He took lessons from Thomas Sully and saw much of Rembrandt Peale for both of whom he had a high regard.

Passing on to New York he was much more enthusiastically received but got no more encouragement in the project that he had in view than he did in Philadelphia, and thoroughly convinced of the impossibility of publishing his plates in America, he determined to abandon the attempt until his resources would permit of his going to Europe.

Returning to Bayou Sara after a trip along the great lakes he set about painting and giving lessons in drawing, music and dancing and endeavored by every means in his power to raise money. His success was phenomenal and his wife contributing her savings to his fund, he was enabled to realize his hopes and sailed from New Orleans April 26, 1826, with his precious paintings.

He spent just three years in England and Scotland and accomplished much. His striking personality and the size and orginality of his bird paintings attracted wide attention. He exhibited them at various places and realized considerable profit from the admission fees, while he sold a large number of oil paintings and so managed to support himself. After some difficulty he arranged for the engraving and coloring of the sample plates and secured enough subscribers to warrant the continuation of the work.

Mr. Lizars of Edinburgh, the engraver of the plates for *Selby's British Birds* engraved the first plates of Audubon's work, but the main portion of them was done by Havell of London. By the close of the year 1830, one hundred plates had been issued. They were elephant folio, about three by two and a half feet, large enough to allow of the presentation of all the birds natural size, and with

[1] Letter to Spencer F. Baird.

each a branch or spray of some tree or plant. Five plates formed a "part" and there was no text save the name of the bird and plant.

Audubon made friends everywhere as he had done in America and there was wide-spread interest in the success of his publication as well as wonder at his undertaking such an enormous task.

He says, "My success in Edinburgh borders on the miraculous. I am fêted, feasted, elected honorary member of societies, making money by my exhibition and my paintings. It is Mr. Audubon here and Mr. Audubon there and I can only hope that Mr. Audubon will not be made a conceited fool at last." He met all the prominent scientific men of England and Scotland as well as many other celebrities, such as Sir Walter Scott and Sir Thomas Lawrence, while during a brief canvassing trip to France in 1828 he made the acquaintance of Cuvier, Geoffroy St.-Hilaire and many other savants as well as the Duc d'Orléans.

While admirers were plentiful, subscribers as usual were scarce; hard to get and harder still to keep, and the ornithologist was continually reduced to such straits that he was forced to paint pictures and sell them at the shops in order to meet the cost of his publication.

Returning to America in the spring of 1829 he spent a year in collecting and painting such birds as he had not already procured, passing most of his time in Pennsylvania and New Jersey. Upon the approach of winter he joined his wife in Louisiana and the following April sailed with her for England.

He returned to America twice more during the publication of the work to procure additional material, one visit lasting from August, 1831, to April, 1834, and the other from July, 1836, to the following summer.

During the first period he visited Florida, New Brunswick and Labrador and spent considerable time with his friend Rev. John Bachman at Charleston, S. C., whom he first met in October, 1831, and who later became related through the marriage of his daughters to Audubon's sons.

On his second trip besides stopping with Bachman he visited

the Gulf of Mexico in company with Edward Harris, cruising along the coast as far as Galveston, Texas.

Victor Audubon was sent to England to superintend the publication of the work during his father's absence in October, 1832, and under his direction it went steadily on. The letter press was begun in October, 1830, under the title of the *Ornithological Biography* and kept pace with the issue of the plates so that the two were finished at nearly the same time, the last volume of the letter press in 1839 and the last fascicle of plates, the eighty-seventh, on June 30, 1838.

The great work completed, the family had no particular object in remaining longer in England and toward the close of 1839 they all returned to New York. While Audubon had most friendly feelings toward England and Scotland as it was there that the publication of his work was made possible, he nevertheless always looked upon America as his country and his home.

The family at last in comfortable circumstances purchased an estate known now as Audubon Park, and included within the city limits of New York, but at that time far removed from the city and surrounded by woodland except where it stretched down to the sandy shore of the Hudson. Here Audubon and his wife, his sons [1] and their families lived together and carried on the publication of the other works which bear the name of the great naturalist. Both sons inherited their father's artistic ability and upon them devolved a large part of the work.

First there was published an octavo edition of the plates accompanied by the original letter press but all arranged in systematic order. This was followed by the great work on the *Quadrupeds of America* which was prepared in conjunction with Bachman.

Before the preparations for this work were fairly under way the old spirit of unrest which had characterized the whole life of the naturalist again made its appearance. It seemed as if he could not settle down, he longed to penetrate the wilds of the far west where his mind's eye saw endless new birds and quadrupeds. He had procured from John K. Townsend, a Philadelphian orni-

[1] Both had been left widowers and had married again.

thologist who crossed the continent in 1834, many new birds which were figured in various volumes of his great work and he had always longed to see for himself some of the feathered inhabitants of the wonderful country that stretched away beyond the Mississippi. So in 1843, overcoming the scruples of his friends and relatives who thought him too old for such an extended journey, he started via St. Louis and up the Missouri, on one of the American Fur Company's boats for Ft. Union on the eastern boundary of the present state of Montana. His friend Harris accompanied him and acted as general financial manager of the expedition. John G. Bell, the taxidermist, Isaac Sprague and Lewis Squires made up the party.

Spencer F. Baird, afterward secretary of the Smithsonian Institution, but then a young man, had recently become acquainted with Audubon and was asked to accompany him but decided not to go.

The expedition was eminently successful and many specimens of birds and quadrupeds were secured.

In 1846, Audubon began to show signs of physical failure. Dr. Brewer says of him at this time, "The patriarch had greatly changed since I had last seen him. He wore his hair longer and it now hung down in locks of snowy whiteness on his shoulders. His once piercing gray eyes, though still bright, had already begun to fail him. He could no longer paint with his wonted accuracy, and had at last most reluctantly been forced to surrender to his sons the task of completing the illustrations to the *Quadrupeds of North America*. Surrounded by his large family, including his devoted wife, his two sons with their wives and a troop of grandchildren, his enjoyments of life seemed to leave him little to desire. . . . A pleasanter scene, or a more interesting household it has never been the writer's good fortune to witness."

His son John Woodhouse did the remaining plates of the Quadrupeds, while Bachman wrote a large portion and edited all of the text of the work.

By 1848, the mind of the ornithologist had failed. He experienced no period of invalidism, but during the next three years his strength gradually ebbed away until on January 27, 1851, when surrounded by his family his eventful life came peacefully to an end.

It will be seen that Audubon's contribution to science is practically embodied in the *Birds of America* and the *Ornithological Biography ;* the *Quadrupeds* being only a joint production, with Bachman as the chief scientific contributor. Futhermore, the two works, the former all plates, the latter all text, represent the two sides of the man or rather his two consuming interests.

From the outset his main thought seems to have been the publication of his paintings, the characterization of the new species being of secondary consideration. He tells us in his journal how Bonaparte looking over his drawings picked out the species that were new to science and penciled suitable names on them urging Audubon to publish them at once in some journal so that he should ensure credit for his discoveries, but the suggestion availed nothing and he says in another connection, "I do not claim any merit for these discoveries and should have liked as well that the objects of them had been previously known as this would have saved some unbelievers the trouble of searching for them in books and the disappointment of finding them actually new. I assure you that I should have less pleasure in presenting to the scientific world a new bird the knowledge of whose habits I do not possess, than in describing the habits of one long since discovered."

Therefore to his mind the first task was the publication of the plates, the work of Audubon, the artist. These plates constitute as has been said the "greatest tribute ever paid by art to science." In their size they stand unique among natural history illustrations, while their style is striking, original and quite different from anything that had previously been produced, but in the desire for action, the birds are sometimes placed in what are certainly unusual if not as Dr. Coues has said, anatomically impossible attitudes.

The biographies comprising the work of Audubon "the naturalist," are on the same plan as those of Wilson, but Audubon was a more fluent writer and seemed able to arouse the sympathy of his reader with the experiences that he relates, while the more or less irrelevant matter which he often incorporates into the biographies as well as the "episodes," which are interpolated through the volumes add largely to their fascination.

The relative merit of the texts of Wilson and Audubon, so far as they portray the habits and life history of the birds will doubtless always be a matter of personal opinion.

Audubon's far larger experience renders many of his sketches more exhaustive than Wilson's, while the far greater number of reliable correspondents which he was enabled to avail himself of tended to the same end. At the same time there are occasionally inconsistencies and evidences of handling the subject with a sort of "poetic license," as well as a great deal of personal incident, which to some has appeared uncalled for. Some of Audubon's writings brought forth severe criticism, but usually from men who were so obviously his enemies that their charges carry less weight than they otherwise might.

Preparing his manuscript as he did in the heart of a scientific community, Audubon had constantly impressed upon him the need of accuracy in the strictly technical parts of his work. When describing his travels and the habits of the birds that he encountered he was full of enthusiasm, but for the technical portion he had an avowed dislike. Therefore he determined to secure some one who could attend to this portion of the biographies, and generally supervise his manuscripts. Negotiations with William Swanison failed of results because Swanison insisted upon being recognized as a coauthor, to which Audubon would not agree, and eventually William McGillivray, a Scotch ornithologist, was engaged. Just how much of a hand McGillivray had in the work it is impossible to say, but he doubtless was quite a factor in the preparation of the technical descriptions and the *Synopsis* which was issued after the completion of the great work, and, as Elliot has said, whatever scientific value there is in Audubon's *Biography* is derived largely from McGillivray's coöperation.

Compared with the works of his predecessors, Audubon differed, in including a much larger number of birds with which he was not personally familiar, thus making his work more nearly a complete treatise on the bird life of America than any which had preceded it.   Wilson treated of two hundred and seventy-eight species, of which two hundred and sixty-five are now recognized, while Audubon treated in all five hundred and nine of which four hundred and seventy-three are recognized to-day as belonging to our fauna.   Of those additional to Wilson ninety-three are water birds,[1] and one hundred and seventeen land birds.   Of the latter only forty-six came under his own observation, no less than fifty-one being furnished him by John K. Townsend, the first ornithologist to cross the continent to the shores of the Pacific.

While honored with memberships in many scientific societies, Audubon took no part in their deliberations and felt himself out of place in such assemblages.   He says of a meeting of the Royal Society of London: "The evening was spent at the Royal Society, where as at all Royal Societies, I heard a dull heavy lecture."

As has already been said Audubon was popular with almost every one with whom he came in contact, interesting and vivacious in conversation, a talented musician and above all with every characteristic of the artist strongly marked.   In person he was always strikingly handsome.   In his early prime he says of himself, "I measured five feet ten and a half inches, was of a fair mien, and quite a handsome figure, large dark and rather sunken eyes, light colored eye-brows, aquiline nose, and a fine set of teeth; hair, fine texture and luxuriant, divided and passing down behind each ear in luxuriant ringlets as far as the shoulders."

He continued to wear his hair in this fashion after he reached Edinburgh, nor did he seem to mind the attention that he thus attracted.   Mr. Joseph Coolidge who accompanied Audubon on his Labrador expedition in 1833, gives us a picture of the naturalist, as he knew him, "You had only to meet him to love him," he says, "and when you had conversed with him for a moment, you looked upon him as an old friend, rather than a stranger. . . .   To this day I can see him, a magnificent gray haired man, childlike in his simplicity, kind-hearted, noble-souled, lover of nature and lover of

1 Wilson never completed his work and the water birds are very deficient.

youth, friend of humanity, and one whose religion was the golden rule." His kindness to young ornithologists is again attested by the letters and journal of Spencer F. Baird, who as a student in New York City, saw a great deal of the then venerable naturalist and received much kindly instruction and encouragement from him.

While it has been his reputation as an artist and a student of the habits of birds, that has made the name of Audubon famous, there is one characteristic which we can trace through his whole eventful life, which was primarily responsible for his success and without which he would probably never have achieved notoriety. This was the indomitable courage and preseverance with which he carried out the gigantic publication that had early become established in his mind as his life-work. In spite of hardship, poverty and actual want he persevered until success crowned his efforts. And if, we see here and there exaggeration in his plates or if passages in his writings seen to personify the subjects or to tend toward egotism, we must remember the character of the man, whose pencil was striving to present to us the action and life of the creatures he loved to watch; whose pen could not describe their habits without telling us also of the feelings that arose within him as his mind reverted to the scenes of which he wrote, and who could not help looking upon them as fellow-beings. This was no museum savant but a painter-naturalist, who holds a distinct place in the history of Ornithology.

And of his work we can truly say that no paintings have inspired more men to follow on the path he trod, and no text on bird life has been read with more consuming interest.

B Silliman ~

BENJAMIN SILLIMAN

CHEMIST

1779–1864

By Daniel Coit Gilman

Benjamin Silliman, for fifty years a leader among the scientific men of the United States, has won the grateful remembrance of his countrymen by important services in four distinct fields.

He was an admirable teacher of undergraduates in Yale College, and was an efficient aid in building up every department of that famous institution during his long connection with it.

He was a pioneer in providing advanced instruction for special students of science.

By his lectures delivered in every part of the country, he contributed, in a large degree, to the promotion of a love of science and to the foundation of scientific institutions.

He began and maintained, with much sacrifice, the *American Journal of Science* which has continued for nearly fourscore years and ten to be a leading repository of American science.

An extended memoir of Professor Silliman, including extracts from his correspondence, was prepared and published soon after his death by one of his younger colleagues, Professor George P. Fisher. This work is so complete and is based on such trustworthy papers, that very little, if anything, can be added to it. Moreover, the memoir is so readable that the present writer would not venture upon the preparation of this paper, were it not that younger generations, to whom "Professor Silliman" is a name and but little more, may read a short article while a long biography might deter them. By the permission of Dr. Fisher, free use will be made of his material, for which this general acknowledgment is gratefully made.

I have besides read over afresh the appreciation of Professor A. W. Wright, the affectionate estimate of President Dwight, and the six volumes of *Silliman's Travels*,—three on Europe as seen by him in 1805–06; two on Europe visited forty-five or six years later; and one on Canada in 1810.

For the sake of a personal flavor, may I be allowed to add that during my college course I attended, with my classmates, his lectures on Geology, Mineralogy and Chemistry, and I had also the privilege of being a frequent and informal visitor in his house, where I learned to love and admire his noble qualities, as I enjoyed his fund of anecdotes regarding the men whom he had met and the events of which he had been a witness or in which he had taken part. Hearing Silliman and Kingsley, friends of half a century, cap each other's stories as they sat together in the parlor, after the tea-cups, is a delightful and ineffaceable memory.

I remember him at that time, when he was not far from seventy years old, six feet in height, broad-shouldered, of elastic step, with thin, grayish well-trimmed hair and a smooth chin, never hurried and never worried, entirely self-possessed before an audience, successful in his demonstrations, graceful in his gestures, fluent and sometimes discursive in his speech, loving to hear or to tell appropriate anecdotes, welcomed everywhere in private or in public, a reverent worshiper in the college chapel, where in his turn he conducted prayers, never troubled by religious doubts, an unquestioning believer. While his pecuniary resources could not be called affluent, he was always able to live like a gentleman in constant unostentatious hospitality. Among college professors I have never known one who bore his self-conscious dignity with so much ease and affability, and who extended his courtesies so naturally and so acceptably to superiors, inferiors and equals. Among hoary headed men, I have never seen a finer example of conservatism without senility and of never failing enthusiasm, enriched by experience, always ready for progress, always welcoming new light, alway s encouraging the young and seconding their endeavors.

The ancestry of this eminent man was of the best New England stock. His grandfather, Ebenezer (Yale, 1727), was a Judge of the Superior Court of Connecticut, and the proprietor of a large landed estate in Fairfield. His father, Gold Selleck Silliman, a successful lawyer, who had graduated at Yale in 1752, took an active part in the Revolutionary struggle, and acquired the rank of Brigadier-General in the Connecticut militia. He was engaged in the battles of Long Island, White Plains and Ridgefield, and was charged with the defense of southwestern Connecticut from the incursions of the enemy. So active did he become that a special expedition was sent by Sir Henry Clinton for his arrest, which was effected at midnight, May 11, 1779, at his house on Holland Hill. After military imprisonment for a year, General Silliman was restored to his family. Soon after her husband's arrest, Mrs Silliman retreated, with her eldest child, to a retired settlement, not far away, then called North Stratford, and now Trumbull. Here Benjamin was born, August 8, 1779. When he was eleven years old, his father died, July 21, 1790, in the fifty-ninth year of his age.

The mother traced her descent from John Alden and Priscilla Mullins, of the Mayflower Pilgrims, whose romantic story has been told by the poet Longfellow. She was the daughter of Rev. Joseph Fish, for fifty years a Congregational minister in North Stonington, Conn. Her death occurred in 1818 when her son, at the age of forty years, had acquired distinction.

Both parents were of unusual excellence, well born, but not in affluence, well placed, well connected, well educated, very patriotic and deeply religious.

Until the death of the mother, the home of the Silliman family continued to be in that part of Fairfield known as Holland Hill, some two or three miles from the village. Upon the same lofty ridge, commanding a beautiful view over Long Island Sound and its adjacent coasts, is Greenfield Hill, where Timothy Dwight, afterwards President of Yale College, maintained an academy for the instruction of girls. There are charming glimpses of this rural life. By birth, education and choice, Benjamin and his elder brother, Gold Selleck, were country boys, and adopted the amusements and varieties of exercise which belong peculiarly to the country. Much company resorted to Holland Hill, and near by, the village of Fairfield was the home of many families of refinement and influence, as the names of Thaddeus Burr, Jonathan Sturges and Andrew Eliot suggest. Here a little later, dwelt Roger Minot Sherman.

The first experience of Benjamin Silliman, away from the parental roof, began in New Haven, where he was admitted as a student of Yale College in the autumn of 1792,—then but thirteen years of age, the youngest of the class save one. He had been well fitted for his college course by the minister of Fairfield, Rev. Andrew Eliot, who had graduated at Harvard in 1762. He was a thorough scholar who took delight in imparting to his few pupils a love of the classics, especially of Virgil, but unfortunately, his choice library had been consumed when General Tryon burnt the town of Fairfield in 1779.

Dr. Ezra Stiles was President of the college until 1795 when he was succeeded by Dr. Timothy Dwight. Silliman's reminiscences of this period give amusing illustrations of the conditions under which students grew up at that time.

After taking his degree, in the class of 1796, he had for the next few years the experience of many college graduates,—uncertainty as to his future. He spent some time with his mother, looking after her affairs, taught school for a while in Wethersfield, and began the study of law at New Haven under the guidance of Simeon Baldwin, David Daggett and Charles Chauncey, and was duly admitted to the bar in 1802. While pursuing these studies, he held the office of tutor in Yale College, having received the appointment in 1799 when he had just reached the age of twenty years. An eye-witness,[1] then a student, describes his initiation into the tutorial office thus:— I recall "a fair and portly young man, with thick and long hair, clubbed behind,

[1] Rev. Noah Porter, D.D., of Farmington, Conn.

(*a la mode* George Washington), following President Dwight
up the middle aisle for evening prayer, and taking his seat in a
large square pew at the right of the pulpit.   After prayers, a call
from the President, *Sedete omnes*, brought us all upon our seats,
when Silliman, at a sign from the President, rose and read a
written formula declaring his assent to the Westminster Cate-
chism and the Saybrook platform.   So he was inducted into the
tutorship."   Three years later, in September, 1802, he became a
member of the College church and from that time onward to the
close of his life, there are many proofs of the sincerity of his
Christian experience.

The earliest indication of interest in science on the part of
Silliman, appears to be an essay which he read before the Brothers
in Unity at Yale when he was sixteen years old.   It is a concise
survey of the three kindoms of nature in their fundamental
peculiarities!   Occasionally, like other students, he turned to
verse.   His piece at graduation was a poetical sketch of the condition of European nations, contrasted with the lot of this country,
and when he took his second degree, in 1799, he read a poem on
"Columbia."

Toward the close of his life, Professor Silliman wrote out from
time to time his reminiscences, having chiefly in view (as his
biographer, Dr. Fisher says), that department of instruction in
Yale College with the origin and growth of which he was so
closely connected, and as many of his early letters are also
extant, I can give in his own phrases the story of the introduction
of Chemistry into the curriculum of Yale.

For many years under Clap and Stiles, mathematics and natural philosophy had been taught.   Some apparatus had been
collected and was sacredly guarded in a room always kept closed
except when students or visitors were admitted to it.   This
apartment was in the old "South Middle," which stands in the
present quadrangle fortunately saved as an honored relic of
colonial times; "in the old college, second loft, north east corner,
room No. 56," in Silliman's record.   "There was an air of
mystery about the room," says Silliman and "we entered it with

awe, increasing to admiration after we had seen something of the apparatus and the experiments. There was an air-pump, an electrical machine of the cylinder form, a whirling table, a telescope of medium size, and some of smaller dimensions; a quadrant, a set of models, for illustrating the mechanical powers, a condensing fountain with *jets d'eau*, a theodolite, and a magic lantern—the wonder of Freshmen. These were the principal instruments; they were of considerable value: they served to impart valuable information, and to enlarge the student's knowledge of the material world."

The professor of Mathematics and Natural Philosphy at this time was Josiah Meigs, who afterwards won further distinction as President of the University of Georgia, and still later, as Professor of Experimental Philosophy in Columbian University, Washington. He was a man of great ability and belonged to a family, of which other members have won distinction, among them, Dr. Charles D. Meigs and General M. C. Meigs. His lectures at Yale, during seven years, were delivered from the pulpit of the College Chapel. To him, Silliman attributes his earliest impressions in respect to Chemistry. The lecturer had read Chaptal, Lavoisier and other French writers; from these he occasionally introduced, says his pupil, chemical facts and principles in common with those of Natural Philosophy. Thus, he continues, was created "in my youthful mind a vivid curiosity to know more of the science to which they appertained. Little did I then imagine that Providence held this duty and pleasure in reserve for me."

The turning-point in Silliman's life occurred in 1801. He had been invited to take up his residence in Georgia, under favorable auspices, and while he was considering this proposal, he met President Dwight "one very warm morning in July," as he says, "under the shade of the grand trees in the street in front of the College buildings, when, after the usual salutations, he lingered, and conversation ensued. I felt it to be both a privilege and a duty to ask his advice." "I advise you not to go," was the reply of his chief, "for these reasons among others."

He then proceeded to say that the College had resolved to establish a professorship of Chemistry and Natural History. No American appeared qualified to discharge the duties of the office and there were objections to calling a foreigner. The College had therefore decided to select one of its younger graduates and encourage him to prepare himself for the professorship. He then asked Silliman's consent to have his name presented for appointment. The young lawyer was staggered by this suggestion, but after deliberation, he decided to accept the call. Thus began the career which continued for half a century and exerted a strong influence upon the progress of science throughout the United States.

How should the prospective Professor of Chemistry fit himself for the post to which he was unexpectedly called? Where could he turn for instruction? Whom could he consult? Philadelphia was then the principal seat of science in America; the influence of Franklin and Rittenhouse was still felt. The Medical School had already acquired distinction, and a course of lectures on Chemistry formed a part of its regular courses of instruction. Dr. James Woodhouse was the lecturer, in this subject. Some éclat was given to his instruction by the fact that he had just returned from London where he had been with Sir Humphry Davy. Silliman's picture of the situation is not altogether flattering. The lecture rooms were crowded, there was no assistant, the apparatus was humble, but the experiments were numerous and made a strong impression upon his pupil. Woodhouse seems to have been in advance of his time by ridiculing the idea that the visitation of yellow fever was a visitation of God for the sins of the people.

Among the companions of Silliman was Robert Hare, who had then perfected his invention of the oxyhydrogen blowpipe, and presented the instrument to the Chemical Society of Philadelphia. Silliman worked with Hare and made important suggestions for the improvement of this apparatus. Among the other men of science whom he saw were Dr. Benjamin Rush, Dr. Benjamin Smith Barton, Dr. Caspar Wistar and the illustrious Joseph

Priestley, then living at Northumberland, and not infrequently seen at the hospitable table of Dr. Wistar.

In his transits from New York to Philadelphia, Silliman often stopped in Princeton where he found an inspiring friend in Dr. Maclean whom he speaks of as his earliest master in Chemistry. Although he did not have the opportunity to attend any lectures there, he calls Princeton his "first starting-point" in that science. The young chemist spent a second winter in Philadelphia when he continued to be intimate with Robert Hare, and in the spring returned to New Haven and began to write his lectures. Among the instructions from President Dwight, which Silliman received in Philadelphia was one requesting him to pay some attention, if possible, before his return, to "the analyzing of stones." "The President has received some of the basalts from the Giant's Causeway, and supposes that there is a stone in the neighborhood of this town of a similar nature; he wishes to ascertain the fact."

In the following summer he delivered his first course of lectures upon Chemistry. He had prepared them with a great deal of care, and he afterwards pointed with pride to the names of distinguished men who were members of the class,—John C. Calhoun, Bishop Gadsden, John Pierpont, the poet, and many others. During his absence a subterranean lecture room had been fitted up for his laboratory, but so inconvenient was it, that the young chemist was obliged to get several members of the corporation into the gloomy cavern, fifteen or sixteen feet below the surface of the ground, before they could be persuaded to improve this faulty situation. In this deep-seated laboratory, Silliman worked during fifteen of the best years of his life and he has left particular accounts of the simple apparatus which he possessed. He was much encouraged by a remark of the great Dr. Priestley, namely,

"that with Florence flasks (cleaned by sand and ashes) and plenty of glass tubes, vials, bottles, and corks, a tapering iron rod to be heated and used as a cork borer, and a few live coals with which to bend the tubes, a good variety of apparatus might be fitted up.

Some gun-barrels also, he said, would be of much service; and I had brought from Philadelphia an old blacksmith's furnace, which served for the heating of the iron tubes. He said, moreover, that sand and bran (coarse Indian meal is better), with soap, would make the hands clean, and that there was no sin in dirt."

Not long after the commencement of his duties, the College determined to spend $10,000 in the purchase of books and apparatus. Silliman was intrusted with this responsibility and at the end of March, 1805, sailed for Europe. He had given lectures during the winter at the rate of four in a week, in all "sixty lectures or more, including some notices of Mineralogy." Of his travels in England, Holland and Scotland, a very entertaining narrative was published in 1810. Few books of the time had a wider circulation. Repeated editions were called for, and ten years after the original publication, the book was reissued with additions from the original manuscripts of the author. The introductions which the young man carried with him brought him into acquaintance with many of the most distinguished men of the day. Among others whom he seems to have seen familiarly, may be named Sir Joseph Banks, the President of the Royal Society, Watt, the improver of the steam-engine, then a man of seventy years of age, Mr. Greville whose fine collection of minerals was subsequently added to the British Museum, Dr. Wollaston, the Secretary of the Royal Society, Mr. Cavendish, the distinguished chemist, Rennel the geographer, and many more. He saw something of the Clapham circle, particularly William Wilberforce, Mr. Thornton and Lord Teignmouth. Sir Humphry Davy, then about twenty-five years of age and "of an appearance more youthful than might have been expected from his years," was only in town for a day or two before Silliman's departure, but a brief visit to this great man made a strong impression upon the young American.

After a short journey in Holland and Belgium, of which he has left extended accounts, Silliman proceeded to Edinburgh where he spent the winter of 1805–06. About thirty Americans, most of them from the South, were then enrolled as students, and two of them, afterwards known as the Rev. John Codman, D. D., of Boston, and Professor John Gorham, M. D., of Washington, were his familiar companions. The reader will be disappointed if he turns to the *Travels* for an account of the condition of science or of the methods employed for its promotion. Two pages include all that he has here to say upon this subject, but the deficiencies are fully supplied by the reminiscences afterwards published by his biographer.

The University of Edinburgh in its intellectual activity and in its renown then surpassed any other university in the English-speaking world. The records of its preëminence are abundant. For example, Russell's recent biography of Sidney Smith throws this sidelight upon the state of society not long before the arrival of Silliman.

The University of Edinburgh was then in its days of glory. Dugald Stewart was Professor of Moral Philosophy; John Playfair, of Mathematics; John Hill, of Humanity. The teaching was at once interesting and systematic, the intellectual atmosphere liberal and enterprising. English parents who cared seriously for mental and moral freeedom, such as the Duke of Somerset, the Duke of Bedford, and Lord Lansdowne, sent their sons to Edinburgh instead of Oxford or Cambridge. The University was in close relations with the Bar, then adorned by the great names of Francis Jeffrey, Francis Horner, Henry Brougham, and Walter Scott. While Michael Beach was duly attending the professorial lectures, his tutor was not idle. From Dugald Stewart and Thomas Brown, he acquired the elements of Moral Philosophy. He gratified a lifelong fancy by attending the Clinical Lectures given by Dr. Gregory in the hospitals of Edinburgh, and studied Chemistry under Dr. Black. He amused himself with chemical experiments.

"I mix'd 4 of Holland gin with 8 of olive oil, and stirr'd them well together. I then added 4 of nitric acid. A violent ebullition ensued. Nitrous ether, as I suppos'd, was generated, and in about four hours the oil became perfectly concrete, white and hard as tallow."

The renown of Joseph Black, Professor of Chemistry, who had died in 1799, still shed its luster upon *Auld Reekie*. Many interesting stories are told of this great teacher. "Chemistry," he said, "is not yet a science. We are far from knowing first principles, and we should avoid everything that has the pretensions of a full system." Late in life, Silliman sometimes repeated the following anecdote (which is quoted by Miss Clerke from Ferguson), respecting the death of Professor Black:

"Being at table with his usual fare, some bread, a few prunes, and a measured quantity of milk diluted with water, and having the cup in his hand when the last stroke of the pulse was to be given, he appeared to have set it down on his knees, which were joined together, and in the action expired without spilling a drop, as if an experiment had been purposely made to evince the facility with which he departed."

To Professor John Robison, the colleague of Black, Silliman had brought special introductions. Perhaps at Dr. Maclean's suggestion, Princeton had already conferred upon him an honorary degree. His death occurred before the letter could be presented. It was therefore to the lectures of Professor Thomas Charles Hope, who had been a pupil of Lavoisier, that Silliman resorted. The art of lecturing was then developed to great perfection, and although Dr. Hope gave no teaching in practical chemistry before 1823, he must have been an inspiring and brilliant teacher, performing experiments in the presence of his class in the most skilful manner. His reception of the young American is thus decribed:

"Dr. Hope was a polished gentleman, but a little stately and formal withal. After reading the letter of introduction, he turned to me and said, 'I perceive that I am addressing a brother Professor.' I bowed, a little abashed; a very young man, as I still was (at the age of 26), thus to be recognized as the peer of a renowned veteran in science, the able successor, as he had been the associate, of the distinguished Dr. Black. He proceeded,— 'Now sir, from long experience, I will give you one piece of advice,—that is, never to attempt to give a lecture until you are entirely possessed of your subject, and never to venture on an ex-

periment of whose success you are doubtful.' I bowed respectfully my assent, adding at the same time that I was happy to find
that I had begun right, for I had hitherto endeavored to adopt
the very course which he had presented, and which I should endeavor still to follow. I thought I perceived that something in
his manner indicated that he would have been quite as well
pleased if I had not in some measure anticipated his experience.
He proved himself a model professor, and fully entitled to act as
a mentor."

In the expectation that a medical school would be established
in New Haven, Silliman attended anatomical lectures in Philadelphia, and he did likewise in Edinburgh. Dr. James Gregory
was then chief of the Edinburgh Medical School, the leading
consultant in medicine, and, like his colleague Hope, an admirable
lecturer. To his courses Silliman was naturally attracted. "His
lectures," says his pupil, "were very informal, although not imme-
thodical; if they were written out, he made no use of notes, but
began without exordium, and poured out the rich treasures of his
ardent mind with such crowding rapidity of diction that it was not
always easy to apprehend fully his thoughts, because we could
not distinctly hear all his words. He had many historical and personal anecdotes, some of which have remained with me during the
fifty-two years that have passed since I heard them."

Dr. John Murray, a private lecturer, not connected with the
University, gave instruction to a company of thirty-five or forty
persons in his own house, and in this less formal and more familiar mode of instruction, Silliman found a valuable accessory to the
lectures of Dr. Hope. "Both united," he says, "gave a finish and
completeness that was all I could desire to enable me to resume
my course of instruction at home."

Edinburgh was then the seat of a great scientific battle. Professor Robert Jameson had recently returned from Freiberg where
he was fully imbued with the geological tenets of Werner respecting the agency of water in the phenomena of Geology. Dr.
Murray was a zealous advocate of these Wernerian theories. Dr.
Hope, on the other hand, defended what was called the philosophy
of fire,—and the extended researches of Dr. Hutton. The discus-

sions of these two men afforded a rich entertainment to Silliman
and a wide range of instruction, and his allusions to this igneous
and aqueous controversy formed an interesting chapter in his subsequent American lectures.

The teachers of Silliman were not the only men of mark whom
he met. He describes an interview with Dugald Stewart, then the
pride and ornament of Edinburgh. The conversation turned upon
American literature, for which the philosopher showed but little
appreciation. "When our poems were inquired for," says Silliman, "it was evident that the distinguished men around me had
not heard even the names of our poets, Dwight, Trumbull, Barlow,
Humphreys, and others."

Sir David Brewster, Professor Leslie, the Earl of Buchan
(Washington's correspondent), and Anderson, the editor of the
British Poets, are among others whom he met, but with them his
relations were but brief.

I have given so much space to this Edinburgh chapter, chiefly
because it shows the dawn of instruction in Chemistry, partly also
because of the famous men referred to, and partly because of the
influence exerted upon the young American professor. Looking
back, toward the end of his life, Silliman acknowledges his debt to
Edinburgh in these words: Upon its characteristics "I endeavored to form my professional character, to imitate what I saw and
heard, and afterwards to introduce such improvements as I might
be able to hit upon or invent. It is obvious that, had I rested content with the Philadelphia standard, except what I learned from
my early friend, Robert Hare, the chemistry of Yale College would
have been comparatively an humble affair. In mineralogy, my
opportunities at home had been very limited. As to geology, the
science did not exist among us, except in the minds of a very few
individuals, and instruction was not attainable in any public
institution. In Edinburgh there were learned and eloquent
geologists and lecturers, and ardent and successful explorers; and
in that city the great geological conflict between the Wernerian
and Huttonian schools elicited a high order of talent and rich
resources both in theory and facts."

On his return, Silliman reached New Haven, Sunday, June 1, 1806, and went at once to evening prayers in the College Chapel. His days of tutelage were over and his career as a teacher began. He soon made a comparison between the geological features of New Haven and Edinburgh, and read a paper on this subject before the Connecticut Academy. In the autumn, his lectures began and they continued, practically without interruption, until his final release from official duties.

During this long period, Silliman was identified with Yale College. No one in the faculty attracted more students, no one exerted greater influence beyond the college walls. His lectures were anticipated by successive classes with expectations of pleasure and profit which were never disappointed. In later years, ladies were regularly admitted. The lecturer was always punctual, prepared, fluent and entertaining. He was skilful in the demonstrations which he made before the class. After giving up the subterranean room already referred to, his instructions were given in the old dining-room of the College, a lecture room capable of holding more than a hundred persons, with accessory rooms for preparations. Although this was called a laboratory, its construction and its uses were very different from those now found in well-organized colleges. Silliman was far from being a man of routine. He threw himself, heart and soul, into the varied interests of the College, and, from time to time, engaged in public affairs, as the following narrative will show. It will be more impressive to avoid the chronological order in the treatment of his career, and to discuss, under various headings, his manifold services.

We begin with his characteristics as a teacher of undergraduates.

During fifty years, three men, selected by President Dwight, were closely associated in the administration of Yale College. Jeremiah Day began as Professor of Mathematics and afterwards succeeded to the Presidency. James L. Kingsley, first a Professor of Ancient Languages and Ecclesiastical History, was relieved from these multiplex appointments, one after another, retaining until the close of his life, the professorship of Latin. Silliman began as Professor of Chemistry and Natural History, but Natural History, if that term be regarded as including Zoölogy and Botany, never entered into his field of special study. Mineralogy and Geology were added to Chemistry for a time, and Pharmacy was specified in the catalogues of the Medical School. These three men, very different in their intellectual qualities, supplemented the instruction of each other. Silliman was the attractive lecturer, the college orator, the man who came to the front on all academic occasions. Kingsley was the retired scholar, learned, accurate, ready, masterly as a critic, thorough as a teacher. Day, a wise and judicious administrator, in addition to the duties then commonly assigned to a college president, gave instruction in Moral Philosophy.

Discriminating appreciations of these three men, with characteristic stories, are given in the *Memories of Yale Life and Men*, by the second President Dwight. He quotes from President Woolsey the saying that Silliman, among all the men who lived in New Haven during the century, was the most finished gentleman, not only in external demeanor, but in his character and soul. Dwight says that

"His language and style, his wonderful facility of expression and clearness of statement, and the grace and force of the presentation of his thought were admirably fitted to arrest and hold the attention of his hearers at all times, as well as to impress upon their memory the facts and truths which he brought before them."

Then he adds this amusing story, illustrating the genuine kindliness of the man:

"I well remember one illustrative case, respecting which there had been long-continued deliberation, with the differences of views that were frequently manifest, and the minds of some of the gentlemen were convinced that disciplinary measures were essential. The kindly professor was requested to give the first vote in the decision. He took the College Catalogue which was lying on the table near him, and opening it he said, 'What is the student's name, Mr. President?' 'Jones,' the President replied. 'Ah,' said he, after turning over the pages somewhat carefully, 'Jones of the Junior Class?' 'Yes,' was the reply. 'I notice that he is from Baltimore,' the professor answered; 'when I was lecturing in that city, his father entertained me most hospitably at his house. I think I would treat the young man as leniently as possible.' Jones was not the young man's name, though I have allowed myself to call him so. I do not recall what fate befel him as the result of the vote on that afternoon. I think it not unlikely that I voted on the unfavorable side. Very possibly, that side of the case was the right and reasonable one to take. But it was not a matter of infinite importance, and may well be forgotten after so long a time. There was, however, given to us, on that day, a vision for a moment of the kindly sentiment of a gracious gentleman, which remains with me at this hour, and which I think may, if remembered, have done more of good for all those to whom it was given, than any mistaken vote could have done of injury to the well-being of the academic community."

No better proof can be given of Silliman's inspiring qualities as a teacher than to note on the catalogue of Yale graduates during the first half of the century, the names of those who became investigators and teachers. The most illustrious was James Dwight Dana, who came to Yale attracted by the fame of Silliman. Those who became jurists, divines, statesmen and men of affairs could always be trusted, in their various vocations, to be the friends and promoters of science, and this too at a period when many educated persons regarded science as antagonistic to religion, and many more believed that attention to science would be prejudicial to the Humanities.

As a colleague, Silliman was about as free from defects as a man can be. He was especially distinguished by that consideration for others which led him to appreciate and assist their endeavors, to keep free from jealousy and rivalry, and to think much more of the general good than of personal preferment or the attainment of gratitude or recognition. He was not merely the occupant of a professor's chair, nor was he so absorbed by studies and duties that he was indifferent to the doings of his colleagues and the opportunities of his alma mater.

In the establishment of a cabinet of minerals; the acquisition of the Trumbull gallery; the purchase of the Clark telescope; the foundation of the Medical School; and the initiation of the Sheffield School of Science he is especially to be remembered.

Among the treasures of the Peabody Museum in New Haven are the collections in mineralogy and geology, which were once in the foremost rank and are still among the most extensive and valuable in this country. The contrast is very great between these well-filled cases and drawers, enriched by many contributions, secured by many able investigators, and the meager outfit provided for Silliman. He often told the story that, when he was designated a professor, he put all the minerals belonging to the College in a candle box and took them to Philadelphia to be named by Dr. Adam Seybert. Some purchases were soon afterwards made, and at length an opportunity occurred which Silliman was quick to improve. Colonel George Gibbs, a lover of science, had returned from Europe and was resident in Newport, R. I., where he was often visited by the Yale professor. He had formed an extensive and valuable collection of minerals,—ten thousand or more specimens,—and Silliman persuaded him to place them on public exhibition in Yale College where they remained from 1810 until 1825, attracting great attention. A subscription was then taken up for its purchase, and the collection became the property of the College. Many additions were subsequently secured from Robert Bakewell, William Macclure, Alexander Brongniart (of Paris), and G. A. Mantell.

Fisher tells this characteristic story:

"When Mr. Edward Everett came to New Haven to deliver his discourse upon Washington, he related in a short speech to the college students, an anecdote connected with the purchase of the Gibbs Cabinet. Understanding that this collection was offered for sale, Mr. Everett had suggested to several friends of Harvard that it might be secured for that institution. 'But,' said Mr. Everett, 'they hung fire; and after the bargain was concluded by Mr. Silliman, I observed to him that I hoped the affair would give a useful lesson to our people against delay in such matters.' 'You are welcome,' said Mr. Silliman with a smile, 'to any *moral* benefit to be derived from the matter; we, meanwhile, will get what good we can from the Cabinet.' "

For many years the Trumbull gallery of paintings shared with the cabinet of minerals the interest of visitors to New Haven.

Every stranger was expected to "go to prayers" in the College Chapel, and to visit these two collections.

This is the story of the gallery. The famous painter, Colonel John Trumbull (a son of Jonathan Trumbull, known as Washington's Brother Jonathan), and Silliman had long been friends, and Silliman had married the artist's niece. At the age of seventy-four years, this historical painter,—to whom the country is indebted for priceless portraits of Washington and others of the earliest supporters of the Republic,—confided to Silliman his impecunious circumstances, and referred to his pictures as his chief resource. He intimated his willingness to give them to Yale College in return for a competent annuity for the rest of his life. Silliman, with his quick responsiveness, caught at this remark, reported it at once in New Haven, and initiated the measures by which a gallery was constructed, the pictures placed on the walls, and the annuity secured. Thus in 1830, the college secured these works which are now among the invaluable possessions of the Yale School of the Fine Arts.

With similar tact, Silliman procured from Sheldon Clark, a farmer living in a country town near New Haven, the money requisite for purchasing a telescope, which for many years stood first and best among the astronomical instruments of this country. To Silliman also is credited the impulse given by the Connecticut Academy of Arts and Sciences to the proposal of a geological survey of the State which resulted in the reports of James G. Percival and Charles U. Shepard.

At the beginning of the ninteeenth century, President Dwight had in mind the enlargement of the College, "which then passed not only in name but in spirit from the eighteenth to the nineteenth century." Silliman knew of this purpose, as we have seen, and was governed by it during his courses of study in Philadelphia and Edinburgh. Many years before, Dr. Stiles had drafted the plan of a university, particularly describing law and medical lectures. It is needless to repeat here the annals which have lately been skilfully reproduced by Dr. W. H. Welch. [1] Finally

[1] See his historical address at New Haven, in 1901.

in 1810, largely through the efforts of Dwight and Silliman, the medical institution of Yale College was created by the General Assembly. Silliman was regarded as already a professor in this institution. Four capital men constituted the first faculty,—medical teachers, says Dr. Welch, who could challenge comparison with any similar group in this country. One of them, Dr. Nathan Smith, shed undying glory upon the school. He was far ahead of his time, and his reputation had steadily increased as the medical profession has slowly caught up with him.

Silliman's part in organizing the Sheffield School is less obvious, but at the critical moment, it was of great significance. He was an old man, asking to be released from active duties, but he served as a member of the important committee which, in 1846, recommended the establishment of a department of Philosophy and the Arts in Yale College. Out of this movement soon came the Scientific School, whose early days he watched and favored with more than paternal interest. A memorial, chiefly prepared by Silliman, embodying the outline of a School of Science was presented in 1846 to the College Corporation, and he personally appeared before that august body to urge upon them the necessity of meeting the growing demands of the public in this direction.

During most of his career, Silliman was accustomed to receive in his laboratory assistants and pupils, not a few of whom rose to eminence. I am not aware that any complete list of these aspirants is in existence, but in their teacher's reminiscences, references are made to some of the more distinguished. For nine years he had in his service a bright boy named Foot, who came to him a lad of twelve years old, and who ultimately rose to distinction as a surgeon in the U. S. Army. Then for years he had only hired men, house servants,—"some of them clumsy, heavy-handed men, from whom the glass vessels suffered not a little." After 1821, genuine scholars were enlisted,—among them these whose names I bring together as an indication of the desire, in the early part of the last century, for special advanced instruction, so much in vogue in these later times. [1] The story of Silliman's laboratory

[1] These were among those who acted as his assistants or worked in his

will, one of these days, make a good prelude to the history of university education in this country as distinguished from collegiate.

The term "University Extension" did not come into vogue until long after the career of Silliman was ended,—but many years previous, in the full maturity of his powers, he gave to public audiences long courses of lectures closely akin to those which he was accustomed to give in college. His dignified and courteous manners, fluent delivery, and well-chosen illustrations sustained the reputation which had he acquired as the father of American science. When his theme was chemistry, he performed experiments in the presence of his auditors which always interested and not seldom surprised them. When geology was his subject, the lecture room was hung with colored pictures of the flora and fauna of paleontological periods, with fiery portrayals of volcanic fires, or with quieter but not less impressive views of the glaciers in Switzerland and the basaltic columns of Staffa. He never "posed" as a man of superior or mysterious learning, but he always spoke as an educated gentleman, eager to interest and instruct his hearers. Perhaps the most brilliant of these courses were those in which he inaugurated the lecture system of the Lowell Institute in Boston. In the winter of 1839–40 he gave twenty-four lectures upon geology which were so popular that every lecture was repeated. He had a similar experience in the following winter, when his course in chemistry, including twenty-four lectures, was given to a second audience. In the next two winters, (1841–42 and 1842–43) he delivered two courses on chemistry, and they also were repeated. Professor J. P. Cooke, who followed Silliman many years later, declared that he was led, as a boy, by these lectures to devote himself to science. Hundreds of able lecturers have appeared on this fa-

laboratory: Sherlock J. Andrews, William P. Blake, George T. Bowen, William H. Brewer, George J. Brush, James D. Dana, Chester Dewey, Sereno E. Dwight, Amos Eaton, William C. Fowler, Robert Hare, Edward Hitchcock, Oliver P. Hubbard, T. Sterry Hunt, Edward H. Leffingwell, John P. Norton, Denison Olmsted, Charles H. Porter, Charles H. Rockwell, Charles U. Shepard, Benjamin Silliman, Jr., Benjamin D. Silliman, Mason C. Weld.

mous platform, but only one has spoken so often,—Professor Louis Agassiz,—and he alone equalled Silliman in the presentation of a scientific theme to a public audience.

It appears that he began his career as a public lecturer as early as 1831, when James Brewster of New Haven, a manufacturer of carriages, persuaded Silliman and his colleague Olmsted to give courses of lectures to mechanics and others who could not attend instruction in the day. It is said that this was the first time in our country when college professors went out to lecture to the people upon natural and mechanical science. In following years, we hear of this popular exponent of science in Hartford, Boston, Lowell, New York and Baltimore. Still later, he went to Mobile, New Orleans and Natchez. In 1852 he lectured before the Smithsonian Institution in Washington, and in 1855, when he was seventy-five years old, he acceded to a repeated request and lectured in St. Louis.

Silliman regarded the Lowell lectures as the crowning success of his professional life and this was doubtless true of his appearance in public. His real distinction, however, did not rest on these transient victories, but on his career at home as a professor in Yale College and on his long service in maintaining the *American Journal of Science.*

In these days when scientific periodicals are numerous, and when every branch of investigation has its special journal, it requires some effort of the imagination to appreciate the state of things in the early part of the last century. Three learned societies, the American Academy in Boston, the American Philosophical Society in Philadelphia, and the Connecticut Academy in New Haven, were engaged in the publication of memoirs. The *American Journal of Mineralogy*, edited by Dr. Archibald Bruce in 1810, died in early childhood at the age of one year. As Silliman was traversing Long Island Sound one day, in 1817, he met Colonel George Gibbs who urged upon him the establishment of a new journal of science, "that we might not only secure," he says, " the advantages already gained, but make advances of still more importance." After much consideration and mature advice, Silliman determined to make the attempt. Out of deference to Dr. Bruce, then in declining health, he asked his opinion of the project, which was given at once in favor of the effort, and moreover in approbation of the plan, which included the entire circle of the physical sciences and their applications.

At the Yale Bicentennial Celebration in 1901 there were repeated allusions to the value of this publication, and the words of one of the speakers on that occasion were these:

"Benjamin Silliman showed great sagacity when he perceived, in 1818, the importance of publication, and established, of his own motion, on a plan that is still maintained, a repository of scientific papers, which through its long history has been recognized both in Europe and in the United States, as comprehensive and accurate; a just and sympathetic recorder of original work; a fair critic of domestic and foreign researches; and a constant promoter of experiment and observation. It is an unique history. For more than eighty years this journal has been edited and published by members of a single family,—three generations of them, —with unrequited sacrifices, unquestioned authority, unparalleled success. In the profit and loss account, it appears that the college has never contributed to the financial support, but it has itself gained reputation from the fact that throughout the world of science, Silliman and Dana, successive editors, from volume 1 to volume 162, have been known as members of the Faculty of Yale. I am sure that no periodical, I am not sure that any academy or university in the land, has had as strong an influence upon science as the *American Journal of Science and Arts*."

Professor Joseph Henry has left on record an extended appreciation of the *American Journal*. Its establishment and maintenance, he says,

"Under restricted pecuniary means, was an enterprise which involved an amount of thought and of labor for the expenditure of which the editor has well merited the gratitude not only of his own countrymen, but of the world. It has served not only to awaken a taste for science in this country by keeping its readers continually informed of the discoveries in science wherever it is cultivated; but above all, it has called into the field of original observation and research a corps of efficient laborers, and has furnished a ready means of presenting the results of their labors to the world, through a medium well suited to insure attention and to secure proper acknowledgment for originality and priority. Nor are the results which have been thus evoked few or unimportant, since many of them relate to the objects and phenomena of a vast continent almost entirely unexplored, in which Nature has exhibited some of her operations on a scale of grandeur well calculated to correct the immature deductions from too limited a survey of similar appearances in the Old World. For conducting such a journal, Professor Silliman was admirably well qualified. He occupied a conspicuous position in one of the oldest and most respectable institutions of learning in this country; he was intimately acquainted with the literature of science; was a fluent, clear, and impressive writer, an accurate critic, and above all, a sage and impartial judge."

For an estimate of the scientific work of this remarkable man, I have the pleasure of adding an appreciation by Professor A. W. Dwight, P. D., at one time Professor of Molecular Physics and Chemistry, and afterwards of Experimental Physics in Yale University. His official and personal relation to Silliman qualified him in an exceptional manner for this labor of love.

"While it is doubtless true that Professor Silliman's reputation and influence were more largely due to his remarkable skill as a teacher, and to his brilliant courses of public lectures upon science, the fact should not be overlooked that he showed great activity as an investigator also. One of his earliest scientific publications was an account of the famous meteorite which fell in Weston, Conn., Dec. 14, 1807. In addition to the earlier reports of the fall published by him, which aroused great interest, and were widely copied, he made a chemical analysis of the meteorite, an account of which was communicated to the American Philosophical Society, of Philadelphia, and published in its *Transactions*. It was subsequently republished in the *Memoirs* of the Connecticut Academy of Arts and Sciences, and was finally reprinted in the *American Journal of Science*. This account, which at once attracted attention in scientific circles, was deemed of such interest and importance that it was not only republished in various scientific journals, but was read aloud in the Philosophical Society of London, and also in the French Academy.

"Very early after entering upon his professorship he made many experiments with the blowpipe which had been invented, not long before, by his friend Professor Hare. This apparatus he greatly improved by an arrangement for storing the two gases in separate recipients, and leading them to the burner by separate tubes, so that they were united only at the tip, thus securing for the first time entire safety from explosions. To him is also due the name compound blowpipe by which the instrument was generally known. He continued the work of Hare upon the fusibility of various materials, and added to the list many substances which had hitherto been considered infusible.

"For the more adequate illustration of the principles of electricity he had caused to be constructed a powerful battery of many cells, then often called a deflagrator, by means of which he was enabled to exhibit the phenomena of the voltaic arc with unusual splendor and completeness. It was in the course of experiments with this apparatus that he observed the fusion and volatilization of carbon in the arc, and the transference of the carbon by the current, from the positive pole, where it left a crater-like cavity, to the negative pole, where it built up a kind of stalagmitic accretion, considerably increasing the length of the pole. This result aroused great interest, and, though questioned by some, was fully confirmed by Despretz and others who had repeated his experiments. When the work of Gay-Lussac in obtaining potassium from its hydrate was made known he successfully repeated the experiment, and was doubtless the first person in the United States to obtain the element in the metallic form.

"These researches had met wide recognition and were esteemed as of great interest and permanent value. But though the most important, they constituted but a small proportion of his contributions to science. Numerous articles upon scientific questions were published by him in the *American Journal of Science* and elsewhere. Of these the *Catalogue of Scientific Memoirs,* published by the Royal Society of London, enumerates by title more than sixty, and several more which were published by him in collaboration with others. Many of these contributions were republished abroad, some of them in several different journals.

"Among other professional labors, less strictly in the way of scientific research, but still of value as original investigations, may be mentioned a laborious exploration of the gold mines of Virginia, a study of the coal formations of Pennsylvania, and a scientific examination of the culture and manufacture of sugar.

The latter was undertaken by appointment of the United States Government, and his results were embodied in a voluminous report which was published by the Government.

"These labors exhibit Professor Silliman as possessing the genuine instinct of discovery, the quick recognition of new and interesting facts, and enthusiasm in following them up to novel and important results. That his successes in other directions somewhat overshadowed them does not detract from their permanent value, and it cannot be doubted that, but for the absorption of his energies in his devotion to the duties of a laborious and responsible position, they would have had a much greater development."

These sketches of the services of Silliman which entitle him to the grateful remembrance of his countrymen, will now be supplemented by some further data in respect to his life.

In the autumn of 1819, in company with Mr. Daniel Wadsworth of Hartford, he made a journey to Quebec, and his narrative of previous travels in Europe having been most favorably received by the public, Silliman was naturally led to publish a similar account of his American experiences. This volume is entitled to a memorable place in Americana. It is full of allusions to the physical aspect of the country which was traveled, from Hartford to Albany, through Lake Champlain to Montreal, from Montreal to Quebec, and afterwards down the Connecticut River to Hartford. Historical incidents are constantly introduced, and comments upon the people whom he met. The pencil drawings of Mr. Wadsworth were reproduced for the illustration of the book by an engraver, "a young man of twenty, almost entirely self-taught, whose talents were deserving of encouragement and who had been highly spoken of by the first historical painter in this country." The concluding remark of the author may excite a smile:

"I have said very little of the public houses and accommodations, on the journey. Should this be thought a deficiency, it is easily supplied; for, we found them, almost without exception, so comfortable, quiet, and agreeable, that we had neither occasion, nor inclination to find fault. Great civility, and a disposition to please their guests, were generally conspicuous at the inns; almost everywhere, when we wished it, we found a private parlour and a separate table, and rarely, did we hear any profane or course language, or observe any rude and boisterous deportment."

During the second visit to Europe, just alluded to, Silliman had the opportunity of meeting face to face many of the men with whom, as editor of the *American Journal of Science*, he had corresponded, and he was everywhere received with the consideration which was his due. His enthusiasm in looking for the first time upon Vesuvius and Ætna, and upon the glaciers of Switzerland is charmingly recorded. It is hardly surpassed by the gratification which he had in the society of Sir Charles Lyell and Dr. Mantell in London, and in seeing Milne Edwards, Arago, Brongniart and Cordier in Paris, and in meeting Humboldt, Ritter, the Roses and other savants in Berlin.

This man of science was an intense patriot. Born in the time of the Revolution, the son of a successful leader in the colonial forces, his earliest days made him familiar with the principles, the methods and the men who established our national government. He married into the Trumbull family preëminent not only in Connecticut, but throughout the colonies, for devotion to the cause of liberty, and many important papers came into his possession. He was closely associated during many years with Colonel Trumbull, the aide-de-camp of Washington. When New Haven was in danger of attack in the War of 1812, he was one of those who handled a spade in the construction of batteries upon the harbor side of the New Haven bar. From his earliest manhood he was keenly alive to the evils of slavery, although he did not on that account turn away from friendships with men in the South. As the crisis of the Civil War drew near, he was outspoken for the restriction of slavery, and his support of the Kansas defenders of freedom exposed him to much obloquy. During the war he was an earnest promoter of the Union, fearless and unfaltering. One incident during the Kansas excitement brought him great reproach from sympathizers with the South,—but he was undisturbed by the contumely cast upon him. The story is thus briefly told by Mr. Henry T. Blake:

"In March, 1856, occurred the famous Kansas Rifle meeting in the North Church. It was begun as a semi-religious service held on a week-day evening to bid farewell to a band of citizens who were about going to Kansas as settlers in the interest of freedom. Henry Ward Beecher addressed them, and there was not a thought of presenting them with arms, until it was spontaneously suggested by that noble embodiment of every personal and civic virtue, Prof. Silliman senior. The rifles never did much damage directly to the Border Ruffians, but the fame of the event spread throughout the country. The hint was taken, and the example followed by every emigrant aid society which sent out its party thereafter, with the result that Kansas was saved, and formed an outpost of the utmost importance in the war for the Union."

The domestic life of Silliman was exceptionally happy. He married in 1809 Harriet Trumbull, daughter of the second Governor Trumbull of Connecticut, and their house was the home of simple and refined hospitality where neighbors, students and kindred, as well as strangers of distinction from every part of this country and from Europe, were sure of a welcome. For more than fifty years he dwelt on Hillhouse Avenue, having, for a long period, his son Benjamin as his next door neighbor on the one side, and on the other, his son-in-law James D. Dana.[1] After the death of Mrs. Silliman in 1850, he made a second visit to Europe in company with his son Professor Benjamin Silliman, Jr., and not long after his return, he married Mrs. Sarah McClellan Webb, (a relation of his first wife), of Woodstock, Conn., who survived him.

When he reached the age of seventy years, Silliman tendered his resignation. Similar action was previously taken by President Day and subsequently by Kingsley, Woolsey and the younger

---

[1] The daughters of Professor Silliman were married to John B. Church, Oliver P. Hubbard, James D. Dana and Edward W. Gilman. His son Benjamin was a professor in Yale College from 1846 until his death in 1885. Edward S. Dana, now editor of the *American Journal of Science*, is a grandson of the founder.

Dwight, so that the Psalmist's limit had almost become the usage of Yale College; although to this rule, there have been and there ought to be exceptions. In Silliman's case, the authorities requested him to recede from his purpose and he did so for a brief period. His end came in New Haven, November 24, 1864, in his eighty-sixth year, while his mental faculties were not impaired and his bodily strength scarcely abated.

He was the recipient of many scientific and academic honors, though it was not customary to bestow them as freely in his days as it is in these times, and their enumeration seems trivial compared with the record of his work and the recognition bestowed upon him by distinguished men. Of more value than diplomas are the letters he received from his compeers at home and abroad.

It is generally admitted that no one has ever been connected with Yale College entitled to greater affection and admiration than that bestowed on the one of its faculty who lived to be called the Nestor of American Science. Among the innumerable tributes to his memory, I will select these words of a man of rare ability and discrimination,—Professor Jeffries Wyman, the comparative anatomist, of Harvard University.

"For Professor Silliman's life and character I have a feeling of deep reverence. This is greater than that towards any other person with whom I have come in contact in the relation of a teacher. I prize highly, very highly, what he taught me in science, and the direction he gave to my studies, all unconsciously to himself; but I have no words to express my admiration of the moral dignity of his character and its beneficent influence. After the lapse of a quarter of a century, I find myself often recurring to the teachings and example set before us during the seasons he passed in Boston. His cordial greeting; his dignified, yet often joyous manner; his freedom from bigotry; his earnestness and devotion to the pursuits of knowledge; his readiness to impart his stores of learning; his kindness of heart, and, above all, his great Christian excellence, his peaceful and finished life, have made him to me a model man."

Professor Fisher prefixed to his memoirs some lines of Cowper which were copied again by Dr. Dwight, and with a third repeti-

tion of these appropriate words, I conclude my tribute to one of
the best of men.

> "Peace to the memory of a man of worth,
> A man of letters, and of manners too!
> Of manners sweet as virtue always wears
> When gay good-nature dresses her in smiles.
> He graced a college, in which order yet
> Was sacred; and was honor'd, loved, and wept,
> By more than one conspicuous there."

Joseph Henry

JOSEPH HENRY

PHYSICIST

1797–1878

By Simon Newcomb

THE visitor to the great rotunda of the Congressional Library at Washington will see among the statues which surround it and illustrative of the history of thought one bearing the very simple name of HENRY. The object of the present chapter is to present a brief sketch of the man whose memory is thus honored.

Joseph Henry was the first American after Franklin to reach high eminence as an original investigator in physical science. He was born in Albany, December 17, 1797. It should be remarked that there is some doubt whether the year was not 1799. But the writer has reason to believe the earlier date to be the correct one. Little more is known of his ancestors than that his grandparents were Scotch-Irish and landed in this country about the beginning of the Revolutionary War. Nothing was known of his father which would explain his having had such a son. His mother was a woman of great refinement, intelligence and strength of character, but of a delicate physical constitution. Like the mothers of many other great men, she was of deeply devotional character. She was a Presbyterian of the old-fashioned Scottish stamp and exacted from her children the strictest performance of religious duty.

The educational advantages of young Joseph were no other than those commonly enjoyed by youth born in the same walk of life. At the age of seven years he left his paternal home and went to live with his grandmother at Galway, where he attended the district school for three years. At the age of ten he was placed in a store kept by a Mr. Broderick, and spent part of the day in business duties and part at school. This position he kept until the age of fifteen. During these early years his intellectual qualities were fully displayed, but in a direction totally different from that which they ultimately took. He was slender in person, not vigorous in health, with almost the delicate complexion and features of a girl. His favorite reading was not that of his schoolbooks, nor did it indicate the future field of his activities. His great delight was books of romance. The lounging place of the young villagers of an evening was around the stove in Mr. Broderick's store. Here young Henry, although the slenderest of the group, was the central figure, retailing to those around him the stories which he had read, or which his imagination had suggested. He was of a highly imaginative turn of mind, and seemed to live in the ideal world of fairies.

At the age of fifteen he returned to Albany, and, urged by his imaginative taste, joined a private dramatic company, of which he soon became the leading spirit. There was every prospect of his devoting himself to the stage when, at the age of sixteen, accident turned his mental activities into an entirely different direction. Being detained indoors by a slight indisposition, a friend loaned him a copy of Dr. Gregory's lectures on Experimental Philosophy, Astronomy, and Chemistry. He became intensely interested in the field of thought which this work opened to him. Here in the domain of nature were subjects of investigation more worthy of attention than anything in the ideal world in which his imagination had hitherto roamed. He felt that there was an imagination of the intellectual faculties as well as of the emotions and that the search after truth was even more attractive than the erection of fairy palaces. He determined to make the knowledge of the newly opened domain the great object of his life, without attempting to confine himself to any narrow sphere. Mr. Boyd, noticing his great interest in the book, presented it to him; and it formed one of his cherished possessions as long as he lived. His appreciation of it was expressed in the following memorandum written upon the inside of the cover:

"This book although by no means a profound work, has under Providence exerted a remarkable influence on my life. It accidentally fell into my hands when I was about sixteen years old, and was the first book I ever read with attention. It opened to me a new world of thought and enjoyment; invested things before almost unnoticed, with the highest interest; fixed my mind on the study of nature; and caused me to resolve at the time of reading it, that I would immediately commence to devote my life to the acquisition of knowledge.

"J. H."

His mother's means were, however, too limited to permit of his constant attendance at a school. He began by taking evening lessons from two of the professors in the Albany Academy, his main subjects of study being geometry and mechanics. For a period he was teacher in a country school. He thus gained a small sum which enabled him to enter as a regular student at the Albany Academy where, however, his studies had again to be interrupted. After another brief absence he returned to his school, where he finished his studies when about eighteen years of age. His record was now so good that Dr. Romeyn Beck, the principal of the Academy, recommended him to the position of private tutor in the family of General Stephen Van Rensselaer, the patron, who was also officer of the first board of trustees of the Academy. He found this situation to be a very pleasant one, and was treated with great consideration by the family of Mr. Van Rensselaer. His duties required only his morning hours so that he could devote his entire afternoons to mathematical and physical studies. In the former he went so far as to read the *Mécanique Analytique* of La Grange.

The investigator never works at his best without the aid and encouragement of his fellow-men. This indispensable requirement was afforded to the young scientist by the organization of the Albany Institute in 1824, of which the patron was the first President. Henry at once became an active member of this society. His first paper was read October 30, 1824, on the *Chemical and Mechanical Effects of Steam*. In this paper he gave the results of very ingenious experiments on the temperature of steam escaping from a boiler as measured by a thermometer under various circumstances.

Placing the thermometer in steam-jet at a distance of four inches from the outlet, and then applying more and more heat to the water in the boiler, he found that the steam, instead of being hotter, actually grew cooler the hotter the fire was made.   At the highest pressure the steam at a little greater distance would not scald the hand at all although it would scald it when the pressure was lower.   The explanation was that the great expansion caused by the increased temperature of the steam when it first escaped produced a stronger cooling effect, which more than made up for the higher temperature.   Carrying out the same idea of the production of cold by the rarefaction of air, he published the principles by which to-day ice is manufactured by the condensation and rarefaction of air.   Half a pint of water was poured into a strong copper vessel of a globular form, and having a capacity of five gallons; a tube of one-fourth of an inch caliber, with a number of holes near the lower end, and a stop-cock attached to the other extremity, was firmly screwed into the neck of the vessel; the lower end dipped into the water, but a number of holes were above the surface of the liquid, so that a jet of air mingled with the water might be thrown from the fountain.   The apparatus was then charged with condensed air, by means of a powerful condensing-pump, until the pressure was estimated at nine atmospheres.   During the condensation the vessel became sensibly warm.   After suffering the apparatus to cool down to the temperature of the room, the stop-cock was opened: the air rushed out with great violence, carrying with it a quantity of water, which was instantly converted into snow. After a few seconds, the tube became filled with ice, which almost entirely stopped the current of air.   The neck of the vessel was then partially unscrewed, so as to allow the condensed air to rush out around the sides of the screw: in this state the temperature of the whole interior atmosphere was so much reduced as to freeze the remaining water in the vessel.

His delicate constitution now suffered so much from confinement and study that he accepted an invitation to go on a surveying expedition to the western part of the state. As a result of this expedition he published a topographical sketch of New York which appeared in the *Transactions* of the Albany Institute. It comprised a sketch of the physical geography of the state with especial reference to the newly inaugurated canal system.

In this work his constitution was completely restored, and he returned home with a health and vigor which never failed him during the remainder of his long and arduous life. Soon after his return he was elected Professor of Mathematics in the Albany Academy. Here a new field was opened to him. It is one of the most curious features in the intellectual history of our country that, after producing such a man as Franklin, it found no successor to him in the field of science for half a century after his scientific work was done. There had been without doubt plenty of professors of eminent attainments who amused themselves and instructed their pupils and the public by physical experiments. But in the department of electricity, that in which Franklin took so prominent a position, it may be doubted whether they enunciated a single generalization which will enter into the history of the sciences. This interregnum closes with the researches now commenced by Professor Henry.

That these researches received the attention that they did and led to the author holding so high a place in the estimation of his fellow-men must be regarded as very creditable to the people of Albany at that time, at a period of our history when the question of supposed usefulness was apt to dominate all others. It was then seventy years since Franklin had drawn electricity from the clouds, and fifty years since Volta and Galvani had shown how an electric current could be produced by dropping metals into acid; and what effect such a current had on the legs of a frog. And yet, during these two generations, no one had any idea that these discoveries could ever be put to any practical use, except so far as the destructive agency of lightning could be annihilated by steel-pointed conductors. Under such conditions Henry might well have seemed to his fellows as a man who, though possessing great talents was ready to waste his time in investigating matters of no human interest. But instead of taking this view he received such encouragement and support that he was enabled to continue investigations into the laws of electricity, and to make new discoveries which have since proved to be of great practical importance in the application of that agent. To give a clear idea of a few of these investigations we must recall some of the laws of electricity.

Before Henry's time it was known that, when a wire was wrapped around a piece of iron, and an electric current passed through the wire, the iron instantly became a magnet, attracting every piece of iron in its neighborhood. If the iron was well annealed and soft, it lost its magnetism, and its attraction ceased the moment the current was interrupted. Every one who has seen the Morse telegraph at work knows it is by this property of the electric current that messages are transmitted. Henry's first experiments were devoted to showing how the power of a single battery to produce this effect could be enormously increased by passing more and more coils around the magnet. Carrying forward his experiments he made enormous magnets which held up weights greater than anyone had before supposed a magnet could ever do. With a battery having a single plate of zinc, of half a square foot of surface, he made a magnet lift a weight of 750 pounds,—more than thirty-five times its own weight. In connection with this experiment he showed the difference between the quantity of electricity and its projectile force, a distinction at the base of all modern appliances of electricity.

At Albany in 1831–32 Henry showed for the first time how easily an electric telegraph could be constructed. He ran the wires of an electric circuit several miles in length around one of the upper rooms in the Albany Academy. An electric current was sent around this circuit from a small battery passing in its course through the coils of an electromagnet. A permanent magnet was swung between the poles of this electromagnet in such a way that, when the current was sent through the circuit, a bell was rung. In this way he demonstrated that it was possible to send signals to a distance of many miles by means of an electric current. Acting on his avowed principle that when the scientific investigator had shown a practical result to be possible, there would be plenty of inventors to put the discovery to practical uses, he himself never attempted to do more than to show how the telegraph could be put into operation. It was three years after this, in 1835, when Professor Morse continued these experiments with the view of devising a practical telegraph. Three years later he had perfected his alphabet of dots and dashes but did not succeed in securing the necessary public support for the telegraph until 1842. Professor Henry's generosity and public spirit is strikingly shown in a letter which he addressed to Professor Morse at this time. The following are the most important passages:

"MY DEAR SIR:

"I am pleased to learn that you have again petitioned Congress in reference to your telegraph; and I most sincerely hope you will succeed in convincing our representatives of the importance of the invention. . . . Science is now fully ripe for this application, and I have not the least doubt, if proper means be afforded, of the perfect success of the invention. The idea of transmitting intelligence to a distance by means of the electrical action has been suggested by various persons, from the time of Franklin to the present but until within the last few years, or since the principal discoveries in electro-magnetism, all attempts to reduce it to practice were necessarily unsuccessful. The mere suggestion however of a scheme of this kind, is a matter for which little credit can be claimed, since it is one which would naturally arise in the mind of almost any person familiar with the phenomena of electricity: but the bringing it forward at the proper moment when the developments of science are able to furnish the means of certain success, and the devising a plan for carrying it into practical operation, are the grounds of a just claim to scientific reputation as well as to public patronage. About the same time with yourself, Professor Wheatstone of London, and Dr. Steinheil of Germany, proposed plans of the electro-magnetic telegraph; but these differ as much from yours as the nature of the common principle would well permit; and unless some essential improvements have lately been made in these European plans, I should prefer the one invented by yourself.

"With my best wishes for your success, I remain with much esteem,

"Yours truly,
"JOSEPH HENRY."

It was two years after the date of this letter in May, 1844, that the first telegraphic message was transmitted from Washington to Baltimore.

In 1831 he made what was probably the first observation of a magnetic storm in this country. This term is applied to very small changes in the direction in which a magnet points, and in the force which the earth produces upon it, that occur from time to time. These disturbances of the magnetic needle are called "storms" because they behave much like a storm of wind in moving the magnet about. On the same evening in which the storm was first noticed a brilliant aurora commenced. It has since been found that unusual displays of the aurora are nearly always accompanied by magnetic storms.

The next discovery of Henry was one in which, although it was quite original, he was anticipated in publication by Faraday. This was the production of magneto electricity. When it was known that electricity could make iron into a magnet in the way I have described, the idea naturally occurred that, conversely, magnets might also produce electricity. Efforts to produce electricity in this way were unavailing until Henry showed that the mere presence of a magnet was not sufficient, but that the magnet must move. Henry's discovery may be explained in the following way. Let us suppose a long piece of wire wound round and round in a coil, like a coil of rope, but without anything inside of it. Then bring the two ends of the wire into contact. Of course this alone would be nothing but a commonplace coil of wire. Now take a powerful magnet and insert it inside the coil. While you are doing this an electric current will pass through the coil, but the moment you get the magnet inside and stop the motion, the current stops also. Now take the magnet out and the current again flows, but in the opposite direction.

Here we have the principles on which the modern dynamo is constructed, by which electric roads are now run. Unfortunately there were very few scientific societies and scientific men in this country; and Henry himself had no idea what an epoch-making discovery this was; so he did not publish it immediately, but went on trying to perfect it before describing it in print. While he was doing this he found that Faraday had made the same discovery in England, and published it to the admiring scientific world. It was a remarkable illustration of Henry's high character that he never complained of not receiving the credit of having been another discoverer, but subsequently spoke of "Faraday's admirable discovery" as if it was something with which he had nothing to do.

Another discovery which Henry was the first to publish, and for which he has entire credit, is that which is known as the self-induction of an electric current. Under certain circumstances when a long current is suddenly broken there is a momentary flash in the opposite direction, and the longer the wire through which the current is passing the stronger is this flash. This is the cause of the bright flashes that are so often seen at night on the trolley of an electric car as it is running along the wire. The trolley makes a slight jump; the current is thus broken, and the self-induced current jumps across the space with the brilliant flash which we all must have so often noticed.

Another of Henry's discoveries and one of a very curious character was that, when a flash of electricity suddenly passes through a wire—when a Leyden jar is discharged, for example—what takes place is not a single passage of electricity, but a vibrating of electricity back and forth through the wire. These vibrations are so rapid that they all take place in a much smaller time than the human faculties could ever appreciate, perhaps the ten thousandth or one hundred thousandth of a second, perhaps I ought to say the fraction of a millionth of a second. The question may arise how is it possible to determine invisible motions back and forth in a millionth of a second.

Henry's method was very simple. He passed the electric discharge through a wire round a needle. This object being of highly tempered steel retained the magnetism communicated to it by the current. Henry found that, when the needle was examined after the current had flashed around it, its north and south poles were not always at the ends which should have been produced by the discharge, but were often in the opposite direction, the north pole being the one that should have been south. He immediately saw what was the cause. The electricity must have flashed first in one direction and then in the opposite one. In perhaps the millionth of a second it not only destroyed the magnetism which had first been produced by the current but induced a magnetism of the opposite kind.

Henry's active and fertile mind was by no means confined to electricity. Everything he could find in the heavens or on the earth to investigate, he was ready to actively take hold of. He delighted in experimenting on the properties of matter, and left behind voluminous notes of his results in this field.

About 1832 Professor Henry was called to the chair of Natural Philosophy in Princeton College. Although the duties of an American college professor seldom allow much time for original investigation, he soon resumed his electrical researches, and the first of a regular series was communicated to the American Philosophical Society in 1835. On February 6 of that year he continued the subject of the self-induction of the electric current with especial reference to the influence of a spiral conductor upon it. The series of experiments on this subject are very elaborate, but cannot be fully described without going into details too minute for the present sketch.

Among the little known works of Professor Henry during this period are his researches upon solar radiation and the heat of the solar spots. In connection with his relative, Professor Stephen Alexander, he may be said to have commenced a branch of modern solar physics which has since grown to large proportions, by comparing the temperature of the solar spots with that of other parts of the sun's disk. The first experiments were made on January 4, 1845. A very large spot was then visible upon the sun, the image of which was thrown by a four-inch telescope upon a screen in a dark room. A thermopile was placed in such a position that the image of the spot and of the neighboring parts of the solar disk could be thrown upon it in quick succession. The result of observations extending through several days was that decidedly less heat was received from the spot than from the brilliant part of the photosphere. It is believed that it was these experiments which started Secchi on the brilliant investigations in solar physics which he carried on in subsequent years.

In one of his numerous communications presented to the Philosophical Society he appears as one of the inventors of the electro-chronograph. On May 30, 1843, he presented and read a communication on a new method of determining the velocity of projectiles. It was in its essential parts identical with that now generally adopted. It consisted, he says, in applying the instantaneous transmission of the electrical action to determine the time of the passage of the ball between two screens placed at a short distance from each other on its path. For this purpose the observer is provided with a revolving cylinder, moved by clockwork at the rate of at least ten turns in a second, and of which the convex surface is divided into a hundred equal parts, each part therefore indicating in the revolution the thousandth part of a second or less. Close to the surface of this cylinder, which revolves horizontally, are placed two galvanometers, one at each extremity of a diameter; the needles of these being furnished at one end with a pen for making a dot with printers' ink on the revolving surface. In the appendix to the paper he proposes to dispense with the galvanometer and produce the marks by direct electromagnetic action, as is now done in the familiar astronomical chronograph.

It is impossible in the course of this short sketch to present any full account of Professor Henry's scientific researches. He was a born experimentalist; one who knew how to cross-examine Nature as an astute lawyer would cross-examine a witness and thus bring

out her inmost secrets.   He was one of those men by whom it
seems as if Nature loves to be cross-examined.   Whether his
questions pertained to the most familiar phenomena of every-day
life or the most complex combinations in the laboratory, they are
all marked by the qualities of the author's mind,—acuteness in
research, a clear appreciation of the logic of science, and an enthusiasm for truth irrespective of its utilitarian results.   During the
period of his residence at Princeton, he was a voluminous contributor to the *Transactions* of the American Philosophical Society, an
association already famous in the history of science by the names
of Franklin and Rittenhouse to which his own name was now to
be added.

On December 3, 1846, Henry was chosen the first Secretary of
the newly organized Smithsonian Institution.   The work of the
remaining years of his long life is so intimately connected with this
institution that the organization must be described to understand
the man.   The inducement is all the stronger to do this because
there is probably no foundation for the promotion of science or
original research which shows so many features interesting by
their mysterious character and by the novelty of the idea.

James Smithson, a private English gentleman of fortune and
scientific tastes, and a chemist of sufficient note to be elected a
Fellow of the Royal Society, led a comparatively retired life, and
died unmarried, in 1829.   He does not seem to have left any near
relatives except a nephew.   On opening his will it was found to
be short and simple.   Except an annuity to his servant, he left
the nephew, for his life, the whole income from his property, and
the property itself to the nephew's children should he leave any.
In case of the death of the nephew without leaving a child or
children, the whole property was bequeathed "*to the United States
of America, to found at Washington, under the name of the Smithsonian Institution, an establishment for the increase and diffusion
of knowledge among men.*"

Probably few men have ever written a clause so well fitted as
this to excite a curiosity which can never be gratified.   The views
and motives of the writer in making this provision are involved

in impenetrable obscurity. The first idea to strike a reader would be that Smithson had some especially kind feeling toward either the United States or its form of government. But no evidence of this has ever been discovered. He is not known to have had the personal acquaintance of an American, and his tastes were supposed to have been aristocratic rather then democratic.

It would also have been supposed that the organization of an institution which was to carry his name down to posterity would have been a subject of long and careful thought, and of conversation with friends, and would have been prescribed in more definite language than that used in the will. Some note, some appended paper would certainly be found communicating his views. But nothing of the sort has ever come to light.

We thus have the curious spectacle of a retired English gentleman, probably unacquainted with a single American citizen, bequeathing the whole of his large fortune to our Government to found an establishment which was described in ten words, without a memorandum of any kind by which his intentions could be divined or the recipient of the gift guided in applying it. The nephew, named Hungerford, died in 1835. An amicable suit in chancery was instituted by our Government, through the Hon. Richard Rush, as its agent, the defendant being the Messrs. Drummond, executors of Smithson. Although there was no contest at any point, the suit occupied three years. On May 9th, 1838, the property was adjudged to the United States, and during the next few months disposed of by Mr. Rush for about £105,000. The money was deposited in the Treasury in the following autumn.

The problem now presented to Congress was to organize the Institution described by Smithson. The writer must confess that he does not share the views of those who maintain that the intent of Smithson was too clear and definite to be mistaken, and that the difficulty which our legislators found in deciding upon a plan shows their lack of intellectual appreciation. It is very much easier to see the right solution of a problem after it is reached than before. It ought to be a subject of gratitude rather than criticism that it took the country eight years to reach a solution. The plan at length adopted was better than any of those previously proposed, and the form into which the Institution grew was still in advance of the plan which at length passed Congress.

After a seven years' discussion of all sorts of combinations, the act under which the Institution was at last organized became a law in August, 1846. It provided that the business of the Institution should be conducted by a Board of Regents, who should choose a suitable person as Secretary of the Institution. It also provided for the erection of a suitable building of plain and durable materials and structure, without unnecessary ornament, for the reception of objects of natural history, a chemical laboratory, a library and gallery of art, and the necessary lecture-rooms. The Secretary had charge of the building and property of the Institution, and was also to discharge the duties of librarian and keeper of the museum, and, with the consent of the Board of Regents, to employ the necessary assistants. All the officers were removable by the Board of Regents whenever in their judgment the interests of the Institution required them to be changed.

The Board of Regents created by the act immediately commenced active operations. In December, 1846, a committee of the Board, consisting of Mr. Robert Dale Owen, Mr. Henry N. Hilliard, Professor A. D. Bache, Mr. Rufus Choate, and Mr. Pennybacker, made a report on the plan of organization. Among the recommendations of this report the qualifications desired in the Secretary are of interest to us. It was pointed out as an almost necessary condition that the Secretary should become the chief executive officer of the Institution. After some general remarks respecting the qualifications of Secretary the report proceeds:

"Your committee think it would be an advantage if a competent Secretary could be found, combining also the qualifications of a professor of the highest standing in some branch of science. If to these be added efficiency as an executive officer and a knowledge of the world we may hope to see filling this distinguished post a man who, when brought into communication with distinguished men and societies in this and other countries, shall be capable, as representative of the Smithsonian Institution, to reflect honour on the office, not requiring to borrow distinction from it.

"Your committee will not withhold their opinion that upon the choice of this single officer, more probably than on any other act of the Board, will depend the future good name and success and usefulness of the Smithsonian Institution."

Previous to the election of Secretary the following resolution, from the same comittee, was adopted by the Board:

"*Resolved*, That it is essential, for the advancement of the proper interests of the trust, that the Secretary of the Smithsonian Institution be a man possessing weight of character, and a high grade of talent; and that it is further desirable that he possess eminent scientific and general acquirements; that he be a man capable of advancing science and promoting letters by original research and effort, well qualified to act as a respected channel of communication between the Institution and scientific and literary societies in this and foreign countries; and, in a word, a man worthy to represent before the world of science and of letters the Institution over which this Board presides."

Although couched in general terms it may be supposed that these expressions had direct reference to the subject of our notice, and were meant to justify the Board in selecting a scientific investigator of so much eminence to take charge of the establishment. Professor Henry was elected on December 3, 1846, and signified his accceptance a few days later. It was a frequent remark of his in after years that he had never sought a position, and had never accepted one without fear and trembling. Of the few positions he ever accepted we might well suppose that this was one on which he entered with most hesitation. Held in the highest esteem by the authorities of the college, his position at Princeton was in every respect most agreeable. His enthusiasm as a teacher could not fail to bring around him an appreciative body of pupils. He was not moved by any merely worldly ambition to seek a larger and more prominent field of activity. He thus enjoyed what is almost the happiest lot of man, that of living in a community suited to his tastes and pursuits, and of being held in consideration by all with whom he came in contact. He was now to take a position around which had raged for eight years a conflict of opinion which might at any time break out anew. That all parties could be satisfied was out of the question, and his aversion to engaging in anything which would lead to controversy was so great that he would hardly have accepted had it not been for the urgent solicitation of Professor Bache. The latter pointed out to him that the proper administration of Smithson's munificent bequest was at stake, and that he, Henry, was the only man available to whom all parties could turn with the assurance that the Institution would be carried through its difficulties. This was an appeal which he could not understand; he therefore determined at least to make the attempt, and entered upon his duties with the assurance from the college authorities that, should he fail, his position at Princeton would always be open to him, and his friends ever ready to welcome him back.

After two or three years the divergent views respecting the proper direction to be given to the activities of the Smithsonian Institution gradually began to aggregate themselves into two groups, and thus to assume a partisan aspect. Many of the projects which, during the eight years of discussion, had found supporters, were entirely given up, such, for instance, as the agricultural college, a great observatory, the instruction of women and the establishment of a school of science. But the act of Congress provided, as already stated, for a library, a museum, a gallery of art, and courses of lectures. Henry, while yielding to the necessity imposed upon the Institution of complying with the law directing the establishment of these accessories, was in the main opposed on principle to their permanent support by the Institution. The position he took was that as Smithson was a scientific investigator, the terms of his endowment should be construed in accordance with the interpretation which he himself would have put upon his words. The increase of knowledge would mean the discovery of new truths of any sort, especially the truths of Nature. The only way in which an extended diffusion of knowledge among men at large could be effected was by publication.

The departments of exploration, research, and publication were therefore those to which Henry was most inclined to devote the energies of the Institution. While he made no factious opposition to the collection of a library, he did not consider it as increasing knowledge or contributing to that wide diffusion of it which Smithson provided for. True, it might indirectly contribute to such diffusion by giving authors the means of preparing books; but this assistance was of too local and indirect a character to justify the appropriation of a large proportion of the Smithson funds to it. Nearly the same objections applied to the museum. The objects therein preserved were the property of the Government, or such as were necessary to supplement the governmental collections.

Perhaps the project on which the Secretary looked with most disfavor was the building. The system of operations which he would have preferred required little more than a modest suite of office-rooms. The expenditure of several hundred thousand dollars on an architectural structure seemed to him an appropriation of the funds to which he could give no active encouragement. In later years one of the warnings he often gave to incipient institutions of learning was not to spend more money in bricks and mortar than was absolutely necessary for the commencement of operations, and it can hardly be doubted that his sentiments in this direction had their origin in his dissatisfaction with the large expenditure upon the Smithsonian building.

We must not be understood as saying that Henry antagonized all these objects, considered them unworthy of any support from the Smithsonian fund, or had any lack of appreciation of their intellectual value. His own culture and mental activities had been of too varied a character to admit of his forming any narrow view of the proper administration of the establishment. The general tenor of his views may be summed up in two practical propositions:

(1) The Institution should undertake nothing which could be done by other agencies. A paper or report which would naturally find its outlet in some other channel was never to be published by the Institution. A research made for a commercial object would find plenty to engage in it without his encouragement. It was the duty of the Government to provide room for its own collections and to make them accessible to investigators, rather than to draw

upon the Smithson fund for this purpose. As a natural corollary of these views the Institution should not engage in competition with other organizations in any enterprise whatever.

(2) Objects of merely local benefit, which no one could avail himself of except by a visit to Washington, were to be regarded as of subsidiary importance, as not well fitted to carry out the views of Smithson to the wide extent he would have desired, and as properly belonging to the local authorities.

Putting both these principles, the library, the museum, the art gallery, the courses of lectures, and the Smithsonian building were looked upon as things only temporarily undertaken by the Institution, to be turned over to other agencies whenever such could be found ready to assume the responsibility of the operations connected with them.

The position taken by Professor Henry resulted in a contest of parties which was for the time being decisive of the policy of the Institution. A considerable party in the Board of Regents as well as several officers of the Institution were opposed to his views. Among these was the librarian, a gentleman of much learning and good standing in the literary world. He naturally wanted all the money he could command to increase the library, a proceeding to which Henry was opposed, holding that as this was only a local benefit, it should be provided by Congress. But the librarian was a man of such influence that it became evident to Henry that the carrying out of his own policy was impossible while he was in office. He, therefore, took the bold course of removing him.

This brought up the whole subject of the power of the Secretary to remove the officers and employees of the Institution. The leader of the minority was the Honorable Rufus Choate of Boston. He was an active supporter of the library scheme and showed his dissatisfaction with the conclusion by resigning his position as regent. This led to the subject being referred to a committee of the Senate, which made a unanimous report in favor of the Secretary and the majority of the Board of Regents. In the House of Representatives, of which Mr. Choate was a member, the matter assumed a more serious aspect. Mr. Choate read a letter criticiz-

ing the Board of Regents which was referred to a select committee
of five, appointed to inquire and report to the House whether the
Smithsonian Institution had been managed and its funds expended in accordance with law, and whether any additional legislation was necessary. After a careful examination, extending
through a period of six weeks, the committee seems to have been
unable to agree upon a report. Two reports were, in fact, made.
One, signed by Mr. Upham, the chairman, took ground against
the power of removal by the Secretary of the Institution, and
against the restriction of the increase of the library as contemplated.
Another very elaborate report, signed by two members, sustained
the Secretary and the majority of the Board. The remaining two
members of the committee signed neither report; nor did either
report propose any action on the part of Congress except the pay-
ment of the clerk of the committee. The contest which had been
going on for a period of seventeen years thus ended in a complete
vindication of Professor Henry and the position he had assumed.
During the remainder of his life he had the great satisfaction of
feeling that he was held in constantly increasing esteem both by
the Regents and the public.

In January, 1865, an event occurred which though an almost
irreparable calamity, tended materially toward the appropriation
of the Smithsonian fund income toward those objects which the
Secretary thought most proper. A considerable portion of the
upper story of the main building, and a part of the lower story
were burned. The incipient art gallery, the chemical laboratory,
and the lecture-room were all involved in the destruction. Happily
the library and the museum remained nearly intact. An opportunity thus offered itself to have some of the trusts imposed upon
the fund undertaken by other agencies. The Library of Congress
was rapidly growing into a great national institution, so that there
was no longer any sound reason for collecting a separate Smithsonian library. An act was, therefore, passed by Congress providing for the deposit of the Smithsonian books in the Library of
Congress, so that all could be consulted together, and the Institution at the same time be relieved from their care. The necessity

for reconstructing the art gallery was obviated by the prospective establishment of the Corcoran Art Gallery in a neighboring part of the city. The erection of Lincoln Hall and the establishment of a course of lectures, sometimes of a high intellectual character, by the Young Men's Christian Association, did away with the necessity of reconstructing the lecture-room. The principal immediate drawback was that the building had to be reconstructed at the expense of the Smithsonian fund, although Professor Henry was not entirely satisfied that so large a building was necessary for the Institution.

The only serious burden which remained upon the Institution was the National Museum; but the expense of its support was now undertaken by the Government, and it therefore ceased to be a charge upon the Smithsonian fund except in this indirect way that the building which housed it had been paid for out of that fund. No advantage would therefore have been gained by removing the museum unless the building was purchased by the Government. The Secretary was, therefore, desirous of effecting such a sale, but his views do not appear to have met with the entire concurrence of the Board of Regents. The latter were not unnaturally averse to seeing the Institution surrender its imposing habitation and the associations which clustered around it. A very natural compromise would have been for the Government to pay the Institution a suitable moderate rent for those portions of the building devoted to the care of government property, but it does not appear that this measure was ever proposed.

The position of the Smithsonian building in the public grounds led Professor Henry to take an active interest in measures for the improvement of the city. Among his latest efforts in the direction were those made with the object of having the old canal which bounded the Mall filled up. Some may still remember a witty argument with which he urged this measure upon the Board of Public Works. "The great inefficiency of the Smithsonian had been said by its opponents to be illustrated by the fact that, although formed to diffuse knowledge over the whole world, it had not diffused knowledge enough among the local authorities of the place where it was situated to make them see the necessity of abating the pestilential nuisance of this obsolete canal." The work of filling up was immediately commenced by the Board to which the argument was addressed.

The administration of the Smithsonian Institution was so heavy a task from a business point of view that it was impossible for Professor Henry to continue his personal scientific researches. His function was now not so much to carry on investigations of his own as to encourage and support investigations by others. One of the most important measures toward this end was the publication of original scientific works, which would both promote knowledge and diffuse it among men. From this point of view, the correctness of which no one will contest, this was the most effective step by which Smithson's purpose could be carried out. A medium of publication was all the more necessary because at that time our scientific societies were so poor that investigators found great difficulty in securing the publication of their works. Naturally such works, especially if printed in proper style, are quite expensive. They frequently require illustrations and these formerly cost a great deal more than they do now. Seeing this urgent want Professor Henry commenced the issue of the *Smithsonian Contributions to Knowledge*, a series of memoirs going on from year to year, now forming an important part of every great scientific library. In order to make it certain that only important publications should be published, every paper before being accepted was referred to a committee, to report upon its originality and scientific value.

In bringing out the spirit of Henry's work, which placed pure knowledge ahead of practical applications, it must not be supposed that he was indifferent to the latter. If he seemed to pay little attention to utility it was because he well knew that there would be a score of men all ready to put discoveries to a useful end for every one person who was qualified to make them. But when this was not the case he was ever ready to promote the practical application of science. One of his enterprises in this direction sowed the seed from which our present weather service grew. One of the first works of the Smithsonian Institution was to arrange a system of meteorological observations at various points in the country. The commencement of work at the institution chanced to be coeval with the extensive application of the electric telegraph. In 1874, Henry called the attention of the Board of Regents to the facilities which lines of telegraph would afford for warning observers to be on the watch for the approach of a storm. As a part of the system of meteorology, the telegraph was to be employed in the investigation of atmospheric phenomena. The advantage to agriculture and commerce to be derived from a knowledge of the approach of a storm was recommended as a subject deserving the attention of the Government. About 1850 a plan of mapping the weather was instituted. A few now living may remember the large maps of the country suspended in the entrance of the Institutution, on which the state of the weather in different regions was indicated by movable signs. This system continued until 1861, when the breaking out of the Civil War prevented its further continuance.

After the close of the war a renewal of the system was proposed and some effort made for the attainment of this object. But with this, as with every other enterprise, Professor Henry would never go on with it after anyone else was found ready to take it up. In 1869 Professor Abbe commenced the issue of regular weather bulletins from the Cincinnati Observatory, showing the state of the weather at a number of telegraphic stations, followed by a brief forecast of the weather which would probably be experienced at Cincinnati during the next twenty-four hours. About the same time provision was made by Congress for a national system under the direction of the Chief Signal Officer of the Army. This received the cordial support of Professor Henry, who gave every facility at the disposal of the Institution to General Myer for the completion of the organization, and, indeed, turned over the whole practical part of the subject to him.

Among the services of Professor Henry outside of the field of pure science and of the administration of the Smithsonian Institution the first place is due to those rendered in connection with the

Lighthouse Board. This Board was organized by act of Congress in 1852 to discharge all administrative duties relating to the lighthouse establishment on the American coasts. The duties assigned to Professor Henry in this connection included experiments of all kinds pertaining to lights and signals. The illuminating power of various oils was made the subject of exact photometric experiments, and large sums were thus saved to the Government by the adoption of those illuminators which gave most light in proportion to cost. The necessity of fog-signals led to what are, for our present purpose, the most important researches in this connection, namely, his investigations into the phenomena of sound. Acoustics had always been one of his favorite subjects. As early as 1856 he published a carefully prepared paper on the acoustics of the public buildings, and he frequently criticized the inattention of architects to this subject. His regular investigations of sound in connection with the Lighthouse Board were commenced in 1865. It had long been known that the audibility of sounds at considerable distances, and especially at sea, varies in a manner which has seemed quite unaccountable. There were numerous instances of a sound not becoming audible until the hearer was immediately in its neighborhood, and others of its being audible at extraordinary distances. Very often a sound was audible at a great distance and was lost as the hearer approached its source. The frequency of fogs on our eastern coasts and the important part played by sound signals in warning vessels of danger rendered it necessary to investigate the whole theory of the subject, and experiment upon it on a large scale.

One of the first conclusions reached related to the influence of reflectors and of intervening obstacles. That a sound in the focus of a parabolic reflector is thrown forward and intensified in the manner of light has long been a well-known fact. The logical consequence of this is that the sound is cut off behind such a reflector, so that at short distances it is many times louder in front of the reflector than behind it. In the case of light, which moves in right lines, it is well known that such an increased volume of light thrown in one direction will go on indefinitely. But in the case of sound the law was found to be altogether different—the farther the observer went away from the source, the less the influence of the reflector, and at the distance of two or three miles the latter was without effect,—the sound being about equally audible in whatever direction the reflector might be turned. Another important discovery, made the following year, was that when a sound was moving against the wind it might be heard at an elevation when it was inaudible near the surface of the water.

The observations resulted in collecting an immense mass of facts, including many curious abnormal phenomena. Henry was always extremely cautious in formulating theories of the subject, and had no ambition of associating his name with a generalization which future researches might disprove. The result of his observations, however, was to show that there were none of these curious phenomena which might not be accounted for by a species of refraction arising from varying atmospheric currents. The possible effects of this cause had been pointed out by Professor Stokes of England in 1857, and the views of the latter seem to have been adopted by Henry. One of the generalizations is very clearly explained on this theory: A current of air is more rapid at a short height above the water than at its immediate surface. If a sound-wave is moving with such a current of air its upper part will be carried forward more rapidly than its lower part; its front will thus be presented downward and it will tend to strike the water. If moving in an opposite direction against the wind, the greater velocity of the latter above the water will cause the upper part of the sound-wave to be retarded. The wave will thus be thrown upward, and the course of the sound will be a curved line convex to the water. Thus an observer at the surface may be in a region of comparative silence, when by ascending a few yards he will reach the region of sound vibration.

It was at the lighthouse station in the month of December, 1877, that Professor Henry noticed the first sympton of the disorder which terminated his life a few months later. After passing a restless and uncomfortable night, he arose in the morning, finding his hand partially paralyzed. A neighboring physician being sent for made a prognosis of a very serious character. Although no prospect of recovery could be held out, it was hoped that the progress of the disease would be so slow that, with his healthy constitution, he might still endure for a considerable period. This hope, however, rapidly faded, and it soon became evident that his work was approaching its end, but his intellect was not for a moment clouded nor his interest in what was going on diminished. Only a day or two before his death he asked whether the transit of Mercury had been successfully observed and the appropriation for observing the total eclipse secured. He was then gradually sinking, and died at noon on May 13, 1878.

We should make a great mistake if we measured Henry's usefulness simply by what he ostensibly did, much as the latter would have redounded to his credit. He was one of those men, now becoming altogether too rare, who felt that his activities should not be bounded by the requirements of official duty, but that one should strive to leave behind him something which would make the world better. He appeared in Washington as a recognized leader of science, whom those connected with the Government could readily consult and by whose advice they could profit. Our present system of government science had then scarcely begun. About the only institution of a scientific character which the Government had established was the Patent Office, to which was attached an officer whose duty it was to collect statistics relating to agriculture. Out of this little beginning grew the present Agricultural Department.

A circumstance not to be lost sight of is that Henry, in obedience to one of the great principles of his life, voluntarily relinquished to others each field of investigation at the very time when he had it so far cultivated that it might yield him fame and profit. It is an unfortunate fact that the world, in awarding its laurels, is prone to overlook the sometimes long list of those whose labors have rendered a result possible, and to remember only the one who gave the finishing stroke, or applied previously known principles to some useful result. There are few investigators to whom the criterion in question would do less justice than to the subject of our notice. In his unselfish devotion to knowledge he sowed that others might reap, on the broad humanitarian ground that a valuable harvest would be sure to find a reaper while the seed might wait in vain for a sower. Had this been done solely in his individual character we should have looked upon his course with admiration; but in bringing the principle into the Smithsonian Institution he avoided a danger and rendered a benefit for which we cannot be too grateful. To this principle is due the fact that the Institution never appeared as a competitor, seeking an advantage for itself, but always as the active coöperator in every enterprise tending to carry out the object prescribed by its founder.

So vast was the field which even with these restrictions Henry had before him that this readiness to abandon portions of it to others might seem very natural did we not know by experience how apt the contrary view is to prevail. Besides his electric researches and his establishment of a meteorological system his field of work took in such subjects as the physical geography of his native state, terrestrial magnetism, capillarity, molecular physics, observations of meteors, phosphoresence, solar physics, protection from lightning, observations of the aurora, the radiation of heat, the strength of building materials, experiments on an alleged spontaneous separation of alcohol and water, aëronautics, the ventilation of buildings, the phenomena of sound, and various other subjects hardly admitting of classification.

One of his interesting traits of character, and one which powerfully tended to make the Smithsonian Institution popular and useful, was a certain intellectual philanthropy which showed itself in ceaseless efforts to make others enjoy the same wide views of nature which he himself did. He was accessible to a fault, and ever ready to persuade any honest propounder of a new theory that he was wrong. The only subject on which the writer ever had to express to him strong dissent from his views was that of the practicability of convincing "universe-makers" of their errors. They always answered with opposing arguments, generally in a tone of arrogance or querulousness which deterred even the modest Henry from replying further; but in spite of oft-repeated failure he still considered it a duty to do what he could toward imbuing the next one of the class who addressed him with correct notions of scientific principles.

It is hardly necessary to say that in Professor Henry's mental composition were included a breadth of intellect, clearness of philosophic insight, and strength of judgment, without which he could never have carried out the difficult task which his official position imposed upon him. His mental fiber was well seen in the stand which he took against the delusions of spiritualism. On no subject was he more decided than on that of the impossibility and absurdity of the pseudo-miracles of the mediums, who seemed to him to claim no less a power than that of overruling the laws of nature. An intellectual person yielding credence to their pretensions seemed to him to be in great danger of insanity. An old and respected friend, who had held a prominent position in the government service, in speaking to him on the subject, once described how he had actually seen a spiritual medium rise in the air and waft himself out of the window. " Judge," answered the Professor, "you never saw that, and if you think you did, you are in a dangerous mental condition. If you do not give this delusion up you will be in the insane asylum before you know it. As a loving friend I beseech you to take warning of what I say, and to reflect that what you think you saw is a mental delusion which requires the most careful treatment."

He once related to the writer a curious circumstance as an illustration of the character of this "spiritual" legerdemain. A noted spiritualist had visited Washington during Mr. Lincoln's administration and held several séances with the President himself. The latter was extremely desirous that Professor Henry should see the medium, and give his opinion as to how he performed his wonderful feats. Although Henry generally avoided all contact with such men, he consented to receive him at the Smithsonian Institution. Among the acts proposed was that of making sounds in various quarters of the room. This was something which the keen senses and ready experimental faculty of the Professor were well qualified to investigate. He turned his head in various positions while the sounds were being emitted. He then turned toward the man with the utmost firmness and said, "I do not know how you make the sounds, but this I perceive very clearly: they do not come from the room but from your person." It was in vain that the operator protested they did not, and that he had no knowledge how they were produced. The keen ear of his examiner could not be deceived.

Some time afterward Henry was traveling in the east, and took a seat in a railway car beside a young man, who finding who his companion was, entered into conversation with him, and informed him that he was a maker of telegraph instruments. His advances were received in so friendly a manner that he went further yet, and confided to the Professor that his ingenuity had been called into requisition by spiritual mediums, to whom he furnished the apparatus necessary for the manifestations. Henry asked him by what mediums he had been thus engaged, and was interested to find that among them was the very man he had met at the Smithsonian Institution. The sounds which the medium had emitted were then described to the young man, who in reply stated that the apparatus had been constructed by himself, and explained its structure and working. It was fastened around the muscular part of the upper arm, and so devised that the sounds would be produced by a simple action of the muscle, unaccompanied by any motion of the joints of the arm, and therefore entirely invisible to a bystander.

On the whole we must class Joseph Henry among those men whose lives afford the most interesting examples for the guidance of youth. He who, at the present day, has to do with public life may well be discouraged by the selfishness of its spirit and the extent to which routine takes the place of reason in all its operations. Under these circumstances the spectacle of a man animated by the most exalted impulses, devoting his energies to the promotion of good works on the highest plane, and leaving after him none but fragrant memories, ought to be a source of encouragement and inspiration to every young man who is able to follow in his footsteps.

LOUIS AGASSIZ

ZOÖLOGIST

1807–1873

By Charles Frederick Holder

"I wish to be a good son, a good citizen, and the first naturalist of my time. I feel within me the strength of a whole generation to work towards this end, and I shall reach it, if the means be not wanting." So wrote young Agassiz to his father on the threshold of his career. He was a good son, he became a good citizen and in the opinion of many of his peers he was the first naturalist of his time, ranking with Darwin, Huxley and Spencer, and if brevity alone was desired the historian might stop here, and let his own outline of principles stand.

It is a pleasure to have known Louis Agassiz, to have seen his genial smile, and to remember his strong personality. The writer lived at Lynn, and with the late Dr. J. B. Holder often walked over to Nahant and visited Agassiz in his artistic home on the rocky peninsula which reaches out into Massachusetts Bay. In Dr. Holder's correspondence covering nearly twenty years' acquaintance with Agassiz many interesting letters occur referring to collecting tours and dredging in Massachusetts Bay, which ended in Dr. Holder going to Tortugas, Florida, to make an elaborate study of the Florida reef, which was carried on for six or seven years. During this period the writer had, for the pleasure it afforded, an active participation in the collective part of the plan of the work; and recalls the remarkable interest of Agassiz in the work, his long and interesting letters, his delight at the many new species found and described. Even when Dr. Holder's deductions regarding the growth of corals were, to some extent antagonistic

147

to his own, the result was not a tragedy, as some of the breaking of fond theories appear to be. Agassiz had placed himself on record as believing that corals and coral reefs grew very slowly. Dr. Holder proved the contrary, and with the writer kept coral heads in partial confinement on the reef, which doubled their diameter in a year. Such a specimen is to be seen in the American Museum of Natural History and is figured in the writer's *Elements of Zoölogy*.

Agassiz impressed me as a strong, virile man of remarkable mold. Had he not been a naturalist, he would have been a leader of men in some other direction. As an organizer he was preëminent; as a scientist profound. He was a theorist and idealist yet his attitude was essentially scientific; he sought the truth and worked along the lines of logical investigation, feeling his way from fact to fact, not jumping at conclusions; and it is this quality of mind that has given him the position in the scientific history of the world as its greatest teacher in the department of zoölogical science.

It is rare that an alien has become so thoroughly identified with the country of his adoption as Agassiz. He was born in Switzerland May 28, 1807, in the little village of Mottier, in the canton of Vaud, and came from a long line of intellectual men and women; and possibly the deep religious feeling which dominated his entire life and to some extent influenced his career, can be traced to heredity, as his father was the sixth clergyman in a direct line from a divine who came down from a Burgundian Huguenot who fled from France to escape the persecutions which characterized the reign of Louis XIV.

While Agassiz had a life struggle to attain the prominence he succeeded to, it can be said that he was a born genius in the fields in which he later became conspicuous. When a youth he developed a remarkable taste for nature study. He was conscientious, indefatigable, studious, earnest, and possessed of a masterly power of overcoming obstacles that would have appeared insurmountable to the average youth. An illustration of this is to be seen in his attempts to become a naturalist. His father was deter-

mined that he should be a business man or a physician; the son
was equally determined to follow the study of his choice and he
won by the very greatness, the loftiness of his appeals, and the
logic of his well-supported arguments.

The very element of semi-poverty would have discouraged the
average boy alone, but to Agassiz it was another reason for success, and in this determination, reinforced by lucid demonstrations, one sees the explanation of his successes in the various epochs
of his career which led to the lofty pinnacle upon which he stood
when he passed on into history.

Agassiz's youth was spent in the open. Until the age of ten he
roamed the fields a devoted student of every branch of nature,
from the song of the birds to the deep snows and glaciers of his
mountains. During this period he studied with his parents. He
displayed not only a remarkable love for animals, but a peculiar
desire to know all about them, their structure, and habits; and at
this time we find him an all around investigator, not only studying
living fishes in a home-made aquarium, but watching the work of
mechanics of various kinds and copying their work. At ten years
of age he entered the University of Bienne, and at twelve had
a remarkable collection of animals and plants, committing the
Latin names to memory and compiling remarkable manuscripts;
in fact, tutoring himself "in the rudiments of many desperate
studies" and methods which, doubtless, had in later years to be
unlearned. Indeed he says, "I am conscious that at successive
periods of my life I have employed very different systems of study."

When very young Agassiz began to buy books relating to the
studies of his choice. In the later years of his life at Bienne, he
announced his strong desire to become a naturalist, but his father
believing it would mean a life of comparative poverty, determined
that he should follow a business career, and while Agassiz was
secretly preparing to become the great *savant*, the father was
laying plans for his entering the firm of his uncle at Neuchatel;
but Agassiz succeeded in holding off the decision, and entered
the College of Lausanne where he met many scientific men who influenced his career. Here he had first access to collections of

scientific value. Here in 1823 he listened to his first lecture in Zoölogy.

Seeing that they could not influence him his family virtually surrendered, or a compromise was effected through Dr. Mathias Mayor, and Agassiz entered the medical school at Zurich which he considered a step in the right direction. Some idea of the charming personality of Agassiz can be formed from the following incident. With a few friends he was on a walking trip through the country where he met *en route*, a gentlemen who invited them to join him at lunch, during which, he was so impressed with the young student that he later expressed a desire to adopt him, and to undertake his complete education, a consummation which would have been accomplished had not family ties between the boy and his parents been so strong. All who met young Agassiz fell under the potent charm of his personality and it was noted that his professors took exceptional interest in him. In this way his acquaintance was increased and he was enabled to meet men of importance, and to borrow books. It is difficult for the reader to-day, when every village has its library, to realize that young Agassiz had the greatest difficulty in obtaining books. They were rare, and he did not possess the money to buy them; and that this can be thoroughly appreciated, it may be said that he spent days and weeks copying books that he had borrowed, which he could not afford to buy, that he might at least own a copy, while pages and chapters of others were committed to memory. It would be difficult to imagine a modern boy copying two volumes of Lamarck's *Animaux sans Vertèbres*, that he might have the material at hand.

The character of Agassiz was influenced greatly by the men he associated with at this time. This is not strange, but it is remarkable that he should have sought the friendship of such men and preferred it; and that he might reap the full value of this association he entered Heidelberg University in 1820. He now met Leuckart, Tiedemann and Braun, who gave him every possible aid. His life now was that of a student actuated by a remarkable prescience. The ordinary frivolities of youth did not enter into his composition; not that he was not full of life, fond of sports, but he seems to have been gifted with that rare faculty in the young, of looking ahead. He planned his career and was working up to it with a sagacity that was almost abnormal. He was confined to his books and lectures, yet he did not neglect outdoor life and exercise. He was a skilled fencer; few could tire him in walks over the country, and to this was due his lusty frame and commanding figure and later in life his power to withstand fatigue.

Perhaps no feature of Agassiz's life has attracted so much attention among laymen as his thoroughly religious feeling and attitude, and this never changed. He possessed it all though life, and in the great intellectual conflicts in which he became engaged in later years, his religious nature was always a dominant factor to be counted with. We find this cropping out in his student life. His home training, the influence of his mother, and the traditions of his family were strong within him, and the "rare comet in the Heidelberg horizon," as Braun describes him at this time, was a student with strong religious proclivities that could not be overcome by even the jokes of his more or less jovial fellows.

In 1827 Agassiz entered the University of Munich, one of the epochs of his career, accomplished not without a struggle, as his family were people of moderate means, and he was sustained at every step of his career only by the greatest effort. He writes at this period:

"I cannot review my Munich life without deep gratitude. The city teemed with resources for the student in arts, letters, philosophy, and science. It was distinguished at that time for activity in public as well as in academic life. The King seemed liberal; he was the friend of poets and artists, and aimed at concentrating all the glories of Germany in his new university. I thus enjoyed for a few years the example of the most brilliant intellects, and that stimulus which is given by competition between men equally eminent in different spheres of human knowledge. Under such circumstances a man either subsides into the position of a follower in the ranks that gather around a master, or he aspires to be a master himself."

Already Agassiz's marked personality was making itself felt upon his compatriots. The "Little Academy" came into being, a meeting of men of congenial tastes and spirit, where papers were discussed and great projects with all the enthusiasm of youth, proposed.

Mr. Dinkel, who was the artist of Agassiz, in describing the "Little Academy" says that the members all had nicknames, as "Molluscus," "Cyprinus," and "Rhubarb." The room was small and so filled with specimens, seat and floor, that visitors not only had to stand up, but sometimes could not move around, while the walls were covered with sketches of all kinds of animals, and their skeletons and grinning skulls, to the possible terror of the landlady.

Here Agassiz outlined the Brazilian trip which came later, suggested by Martius who told of his experiences in this lotus land of the entomologist.

That Agassiz was influenced by the strong personality of Von Martius is evident. The latter was the friend of the King of Bavaria; a man of ripe scholarship, who with Spix, had made for his majesty an important trip through South America. Spix died, and Von Martius, to the astonishment and delight of Agassiz, gave him the fishes of this great expedition to work up, this being in a way a notable step in his career. It was the turning of the roads to Agassiz. His parents hoped that he would graduate and become a practicing physician, but Agassiz did not take them wholly into his confidence and tell them of his association with Von Martius, or the signal honor that had fallen to him, as he knew that it would cause them annoyance; so he began on the great work at night, pursuing his medical studies by day, determining to use the work as a lever to induce his parents to consent to the scientific career.

To his father he wrote, "If during the course of my studies I succeed in making myself known by a work of distinction, will you not then consent that I shall study, at least during one year, the natural sciences alone, and then accept a professorship in Natural History, with the understanding that if in the first place, and in the time agreed upon, I shall take my Doctor's degree?" His father replied, "Let the sciences be the balloon in which you prepare to travel through higher regions, but let medicines and surgery be your parachutes."

The secret could not be kept, and the spectacle of Agassiz at twenty-one years of age making a report on the fishes of Brazil to the Government, was so signal an honor that it silenced all opposition. The work gave him fame, and when completed, the name of Agassiz appeared upon the title-page as a Doctor of Philosophy, which was soon followed by his degree of M. D.

At twenty-three Agassiz was well-known in Europe, an author and naturalist of national reputation, a position not accomplished without great mental and physical effort; the details of which cannot be given in a sketch so limited. It was now that Agassiz met Cuvier and Von Humboldt, who both recognized the inherent genius of the young man and aided him in every way possible. Cuvier placed in his hands his notes on fishes, a signal honor. Agassiz was delighted, but as his father had foreseen, the life of a naturalist was not productive in a pecuniary sense, and in 1832 he possessed an income of but forty dollars a month, out of which he paid his artist twenty-five, leaving him but fifteen dollars to live upon. At this period, working fifteen hours a day, his only regret appears to have been that he was so poor, that he did not have a suitable coat to wear when he presented letters of introduction. The severest privations did not sway or influence him from his object which was to become the greatest teacher of science of the day, and he even refused a salary of two hundred dollars per annum from a journal, that desired him to edit a zoölogical section, on the ground that he would be obliged to give up two hours a day from his studies. Investigators in Psychology to-day will find the following story of Agassiz of more or less interest. He was working on a fish, which ultimately appeared in his *Recherches sur les Poissons Fossiles*. One fish puzzled him; he could not trace its characteristics. One night he dreamed he saw it worked out in the rock; for two nights he had this dream, but in some way, after the fashion of dreams, it evaded him when he awoke; so on the third night he placed paper and pencil at his bedside. Again he had the dream, and seizing the pencil he drew the outline roughly as it appeared. The following day he went to the *Jardin des Plantes*, and there he cut away the stone of a fossil fish, *Cyclopima spinosum* and found the figure of his dream, which is pictured in the above mentioned work, Vol. IV, tab. 1, p. 21.

With the death of Cuvier dark days fell upon Agassiz; he became more and more impoverished, he was forced to relinquish his artist and then, owing to complications which followed, he was absolutely forced to face the possible abandonment of the career he had laid out for himself. He even decided to return to his native town and teach, to leave Paris and all its treasures, which meant so much to the student. But Agassiz was a man of destiny, and in this instance destiny may be translated to mean the logical result of true and conscientious effort in a given direction. When his fortunes were at the lowest ebb, out of a clear sky came a letter from Von Humboldt inclosing a letter of credit for one thousand francs. This was another stepping-stone in his career, and from then on Humboldt became his friend and patron. Through the author of *Cosmos* he secured a professorship at Neuchatel, which while small, eighty louis per annum, was guaranteed for three years. Baron Von Humboldt's letter to the college authorities contains the following: "He (Agassiz) is distinguished by his talents, by the variety and substantial character of his attainments, and by that which has a special value in these troubled times, his natural sweetness of disposition."

Von Humboldt advanced Agassiz's interests as rapidly as possible, and in 1832 we find him a national figure as a professor delivering his first lecture "upon the relations between the different branches of Natural History and the then prevailing tendencies of all the sciences." It was at this period that Leopold Von Buch, the famous geologist, said that he dreaded to knock at the door of Agassiz of Neuchatel. "Why," asked a friend. "I fear that he will take me for a new species," was the witty rejoinder, which spoke volumes for Agassiz at the time. Agassiz, now about twenty-six years of age, married the sister of his friend, Cecile Braun, and honors came thick and fast and recognition from scientists all over

the world.   Agassiz was an international figure and as a teacher of
the sciences, he occupied a distinguished position.   He now took
the Wollaston prize of seven hundred francs, a godsend as he had
expended his last cent in producing a volume of his splendid work,
Researches Among the Fossil Fishes, which was only finished in
1843, occupying ten years for its completion.

Agassiz now visited England and was enthusiastically received,
meeting Lyell, Murchison, Buckland, Egerton, Lord Coll, and
before these leaders of the day he demonstrated his marvelous
insight into the secrets of nature.   At a meeting he was asked to
give his idea of a fish that *might* belong to a certain ancient geological horizon.   He of course had never seen such a fish nor did he
know that one had been found in this ancient stratum, but he
walked to the board and made a sketch of the fish as he thought
it would appear, a rousing cheer greeting his work.   Then to his
amazement some one pulled aside a screen and showed the fossil
specimen.   Agassiz had anticipated and figured it perfectly.

To such an extent said Dr. Stebbins "had this great scientist
advanced in a knowledge of the plan of God in nature."   Agassiz
now became interested in glaciers and in the following years gave
the world his splendid works, opinions based on observation of
these marvelous phenomena of the Alps, and his work aroused
the greatest interest and discussion all over Europe and in scientific centers of America.   His views received criticism in many
quarters, but they prevailed and his masterly handling of the
subject made him still more famous, and in 1838, when thirty
years of age, he received the membership of the Royal Society of
London.

It is impossible to even mention the books and subjects which
Agassiz had in mind, during this and following years, in the limited
space of this paper.   America, where he was destined to rise to the
highest pinnacle of his career as a great teacher of science, first
came seriously into his mind in 1842 when a trip was suggested
by the Prince of Canino.   His books were contributions to science,
and their production was often a continual drain, keeping him
impoverished, but when an offer came from America for a course

of lectures, and the King of Prussia gave him fifteen thousand francs for investigation, he decided to accept it, and in 1846 he arrived in Boston and began his lectures on the "Plan of Creation." Agassiz was now thirty-nine years of age, in his prime, and he made so strong an impression upon the people of the Republic that they determined to keep him. American ideas appealed to him. He was necessarily a lion and in constant demand, but avoided publicity, declining invitations when he could, giving as a reason that he was in the employ of the King of Prussia.

Many could not understand him, and a servant said he was a "queer stick" spending his time at the fish markets, and the market men thought he was "daft" as the fishes he preferred were the ones the men generally threw away. The course of lectures at the Lowell Institute was so successful that he began another on Glaciers. The American idea was slowly but firmly taking possession of his heart and mind. He was captured by the hospitality of the Americans. He says in writing to a friend:

"I am constantly asking myself which is better, our old Europe where the man of exceptional gifts can give himself absolutely to study, opening thus a wide horizon for the human mind, while at his side thousands barely vegetate in degradation or at least in destitution; or this new world where the institutions tend to keep all on one level as part of the general mass,—but a mass, be it said, which has no noxious elements, yes, the mass here is decidedly good. All the world lives well, is decently clad, learns some things, is awake, is interested.

"Instruction does not, as in some parts of Germany for instance, furnish a man with an intellectual book and then deny him the use of it. The strength of America lies in the prodigious number of individuals who think and work at the same time.

"It is a severe test of pretentious mediocrity, but I fear, it may also efface originality."

To Milne Edwards he wrote,

"Naturalist as I am, I cannot but put the people first, the people who opened this part of the American continent to European civilization. What a people!"

If the American people made an impression on Agassiz he certainly made one upon them. At this time he was a splendid type of manhood of noble presence. Enthusiasm beamed in every glance, he had a benignant air, and was a notable figure, fascinating, magnetic, yet simple with all, a great leader along the paths of his choice. Inducements were held out to Agassiz to remain in America and he soon had many pupils and with his determination to remain began a new epoch in American science.

In 1848 the King of Prussia gave him an honorable discharge from his services, and Agassiz was offered the chair of the Amos Lawrence Scientific School at Cambridge. So at the age of forty he became a professor at Harvard University and joined the charmed intellectual circle made up of Longfellow, Peirce, Fulton, Asa Gray, Wyman, Channing, Holmes, Emerson, Whittier, Ticknor, Motley, Lowell and other American immortals.

Agassiz now sent for his family, and soon his home was the center of scientific interest. He impressed American men of science by the thoroughness of his methods, the boldness of his theories, and at once established new methods, new lines of thought and became the greatest science teacher the world has ever seen. His coming was epoch-making not only along the line of original investigation, but for the dissemination of knowledge among the people. He established new methods. He began the Museum of Comparative Zoölogy at Cambridge, and under his influence, science took on new interests, a fresh impetus along many lines. The Government offered him every facility for original investigation, and through the Coast Survey and other sources he began lines of work which were far reaching, not to say revolutionary. He made science popular in America by his lucid methods and the charm of his engaging personality. New works were continually coming from his hand, as years went on, and his bibliography as published in the writer's *Life* or in the records of the Government constitutes a monument of enduring fame, a stupendous record of work, which in the main was a labor of love; the disinterested labor of a lifetime devoted to science. Agassiz married a second time in 1850, Elizabeth Graves Cary, a woman of superlative gifts and many graces of character.

Of her Arnold Guyot in his memoir of Agassiz in the National Academy writes: "Her literary talents, to whom we owe the interesting account of the Florida reefs and perhaps the final appearance of more than one of his later works, are acknowledged by all. Her deep and absolute devotion, her soothing influence secured for him the peace of mind and heart so necessary for an undisturbed mental activity. To her also science owes a debt of gratitude."

Agassiz was the same vigorous collector in America he had been in Europe and had soon visited all sections of the country from the Lake Superior copper regions, which he explored, to southern Florida, and the Pacific coast. While on a trip with the coast survey vessel he visited Charleston and was there offered a professorship in the Medical College, it being a more remunerative position than the one he held at Harvard. This he retained until 1853, ever hampered by the lack of adequate funds to carry on his elaborate publications and explorations. He established with his wife a school for young ladies in Boston in 1855, which became one of the institutions of the region, and was continued for eight years, materially aiding his work in the accumulation and knowledge relating to marine zoölogy and its dissemination.

European nations, particularly France, never quite forgave Agassiz for going to America, and continually offered him inducements to return. The French Emperor tendered him a position that probably no other living scientist, of France at least, would have refused and in 1857 he was invited to take the chair of Paleontology in the French Museum of Natural History, a position which had been held by D'Orbigny, and despite his continued refusals the Emperor conferred upon him the order of the Legion of Honor. His reply was characteristic, he had become imbued with American sentiments. "Were I offered absolute power for the reorganization of the *Jardin des Plantes* with a revenue of fifty thousand francs I should not accept it. I like my independence better."

The idea of a great museum now filled his heart and mind, and after many years' work, needless trials and struggles, the Museum of Comparative Zoölogy as it stands to-day was founded and equipped on land provided by Harvard University and the state, an institution which has grown and been added to by his distinguished son, Alexander Agassiz. The museum was dedicated in 1860, and the present writer for the pleasure of it made large and extensive collections with Dr. J. B. Holder, late curator of Zoölogy of the American Museum of Natural History, New York, on the Florida reef for Agassiz at this time, forwarding them all during the Civil War by every passing vessel, many of which were captured by the various Confederate cruisers, so failed to reach their destination.

Agassiz's energy at this time was boundless, and he began a series of elaborate volumes, ten in number, entitled *Contributions to the Natural History of the United States*, the expenses of which were met by public subscription, and four of those monumental works were completed before his death. The first volume was completed on his fiftieth birthday, which was celebrated by his pupils, who serenaded him, giving at midnight the grand Choral of Bach. The event was also emphasized by the Saturday Club of which he was an honored member, at which Longfellow read a poem entitled "The Fiftieth Birthday of Agassiz." Dr. Holmes says, "I cannot forget the delicate unusual way in which he read his charming verses":

> It was fifty years ago,
>   In the pleasant month of May,
> In the beautiful Pays de Vaud,
>   A child in its cradle lay.
>
> And Nature, the old nurse, took
>   The child upon her knee,
> Saying: "Here is a story-book
>   Thy Father has written for thee."
>
> "Come wander with me," she said,
>   "Into regions yet untrod,
> And read what is still unread
>   In the manuscripts of God."

And he wandered away and away
　　With Nature, the dear old nurse,
Who sang to him night and day
　　The rhymes of the universe.

And wherever the way seemed long,
　　Or his heart began to fail,
She would sing a more wonderful song,
　　Or tell a more marvellous tale.

So she keeps him still a child,
　　And will not let him go,
Though at times his heart beats wild
　　For the beautiful Pays de Vaud;

Though at times he hears in his dreams
　　The Ranz des Vaches of old,
And the rush of mountain streams,
　　From glaciers clear and cold.

And the mother at home says, "Hark!
　　For his voice I listen and yearn;
It is growing late and dark,
　　And my boy does not return."

May 28, 1857.

The Saturday Club had a warm place in the affections of
Agassiz—here he met the friends of his choice.

Dr. Wendell Holmes in referring to it said:

"At one end of the table sat Longfellow, placid, quiet, benignant, soft-voiced, a most agreeable rather than a brilliant talker,
but a man upon whom it was always pleasant to look, whose
silence was better than many another man's conversation.　At
the other end sat Agassiz, robust, sanguine, animated, full of talk,
boy-like in his laughter.　The stranger who should have asked
who were the men arranged along the sides of the table would
have heard in answer the names of Hawthorne, Motley, Dana,
Lowell, Whipple, Peirce, the distinguished mathematician, Judge
Hoar, eminent at the bar and in the cabinet, Dwight the lead-

ing musical critic of Boston for a whole generation, Sumner the
academic champion of freedom, Andrew, ' the great war governor '
of Massachusetts, Dr. Howe, the philanthropist, William Hunt,
the painter, with others not unworthy of such company."

Among the many experiences of Agassiz was being taken for a
harmless lunatic by some country men when on a trip through
New Hampshire. With some friends he collected insects and
pinned them to his hat and coat. Some one asked the driver of
the coach who the men were who acted so strangely, and he replied, "Their keeper says they are naturals, and I should say
they was." The trip of Agassiz to Brazil was one of his great
explorations, which lack of space will not permit reviewing. He
followed this in 1869 with a cruise on the *Hassler* to the coast of
Cuba, and during all these years his days, hours and moments
were filled with labors of the most exhaustive kind. In 1871, he
made a trip around the Horn to San Francisco in the *Bibb*, and in
1872 we find him again working upon the plan for a great marine
laboratory and school which finally took shape, due to the gift of
John Anderson of New York, who gave the island of Penikese for
the purpose and the sum of fifty thousand dollars for equipment.
Many of the leading naturalists of to-day were students of Agassiz
here, and to Dr. David Starr Jordan, President of Stanford
University, the writer is indebted to the following memories of
days with the greatest teacher of science the world has ever produced:
"Penikese is a little island containing about sixty acres of very
rocky ground, a pile of stones, with intervals of soil. It is the last
and least of the Elizabeth Islands, lying to the south of Buzzards
Bay, on the south coast of Massachusetts. The whole cluster was
once a great terminal moraine of rocks and rubbish of all sorts,
brought down from the mainland by some ancient glacier, and
by it dropped off into the ocean off the heel of Cape Cod. The
sea has broken up the moraine into eight little islands by wearing
tide channels between hill and hill. The names of these islands
are recorded in the jingle which the children of that region learn
before they go to school:

Naushon, Nonamesset,
Uncatena, and Wepecket,
Nashawena, Pesquinese,
Cuttyhunk, and Penikese.

" And Penikese, least and smallest of them, lies, a little forgotten speck, out in the ocean, eighteen miles south of New Bedford. It contains two hills, joined together by a narrow isthmus, a little harbor, a farm-house, a flagstaff, a barn, a willow tree, and a flock of sheep. And here Agassiz founded his school. This was in the month of June in the year 1873.

" From the many hundred applicants who sent in their names as soon as the school was made public Agassiz chose fifty, thirty men and twenty women, teachers, students, and naturalists of various grades from all parts of the country. This practical recognition of co-education was criticized by many of Agassiz's friends, trained in the monastic schools of New England, but the results soon justified the decision. These fifty teachers should be trained as far as he could train them in right methods of work. They should carry into his schools his views of scientific teaching. Then each of these schools would become in its time a center of help to others, until the influence toward real work in science should spread throughout our educational system.

" None of us will ever forget his first sight of Agassiz. We had come down from New Bedford, in a little tugboat in the early morning and Agassiz met us at the landing-place on the island. He was standing almost alone on the little wharf, and his great face beamed with pleasure. For this summer school, the thought of his old age, might be the crowning work of his lifetime. Who could forsee what might come from the efforts of fifty men and women, teachers of science, each striving to do his work in the best possible way? His thoughts and hopes rose to expectations higher than any of us then understood. His tall, robust figure, broad shoulders bending a little under the weight of years, his large round face lit up by kindly dark-brown eyes, his cheery smile, the enthusiastic tones of his voice, all these entered into our first as well as our last impressions of Agassiz. He greeted us with great warmth as we landed. He looked into our faces to justify himself in making choice of us among the many whom he might have chosen. Among the students in the school at Penikese, who come to my mind as I write, are Dr. Charles O. Whitman, now of the University of Chicago; Dr. William K. Brooks, of Johns Hopkins; Dr. Frank H. Snow, afterwards Chancellor of the University of Kansas; Dr. W. O. Crosby, of the Boston Society of Natural History, then a boy from Colorado interested in rocks and minerals; Samuel Garman, Walter Faxon, Walter Fewkes, and Charles Sedgwick Minot, all of them still connected with the work at Cambridge; Ernest Ingersoll, then just beginning his literary work; Professor J. G. Scott, of· the Normal School at Westfield; Professor Stowell, of the school at Cortland; Professor Apgar, of Trenton, N. J.; Professor Fernald, of Maine; Miss Susan Hallowell, of Wellesley College; Miss Mary Beaman (Mrs. Joralemon); Mr. E. A. Gastman, of Illinois; and other well-known instructors. With these was the veteran teacher of botany at Mount Holyoke Seminary, Miss Lydia W. Shattuck, with her pupil and associate, Miss Susan Bowen. Professor H. H. Straight and his bride, both then teachers in the State Normal School at Oswego, were also with us. These four, whom all of us loved and respected, were the first of our number to be claimed by death.

" Among our teachers, besides Agassiz, were Burt G. Wilder, Edward S. Morse, Alfred Mayor, Frederick Guyot and Count Pourtales, early associates of Agassiz, already in the fullness of years. Mrs. Agassiz was present at every lecture, note-book in hand, and her genial personality did much to bind the company together.

" The old barn on the island had been hastily converted into a dining-hall and lecture-room. A new floor had been put in, but the doors and walls remained unchanged, and the swallows' nests were undisturbed under the eaves. The sheep had been turned out, the horse stalls were changed to a kitchen, and on the floor of the barn instead of the hay-wagon, were placed three long tables. At the head of one of these sat Agassiz. At his right hand always stood a movable blackboard, for he seldom spoke without a piece of chalk in his hand. He would often give us a lecture while he sat at the table, frequently about some fish or other creature, the remains of which still lay beside our plates.

" Our second day upon the island was memorable above all the others. Its striking incident has passed into literature in the poem of Whittier, 'The Prayer of Agassiz.'

" When the morning meal was over, Agassiz arose in his place and spoke, as only he could speak, of his purpose of calling us together. The swallows flew in and out of the building in the soft June air, for they did not know that it was no longer a barn but a temple. Some of them almost grazed his shoulder as he spoke to us of the needs of the people for better education. He told us how these needs could be met, and of the results which might come to America from the training and consecration of fifty teachers.

" This was to him no ordinary school, still less an idle summer's outing, but a mission work of the greatest importance. He spoke with intense earnestness, and all his words were filled with that deep religious feeling so characteristic of all his thoughts. For to Agassiz each natural object was a thought of God, and trifling with God's truth as expressed in Nature was the basest of sacrilege.

" What Agassiz said that morning can never be said again. No reporter took his language, and no one could call back the charm of his manner or the impressiveness of his zeal and faith.

" At the end he said, 'I would not have any man to pray for me now,' and that he and each of us would utter his own prayer in silence. What he meant by this was that no one could pray in his stead. No public prayer could take the place of the prayer which each of us would frame for himself. Whittier says:

> On the isle of Penikese,
> Ringed about by sapphire seas,
> Fanned by breezes salt and cool,
> Stood the Master with his school.
>
> *   *   *   *   *   *   *
>
> Said the Master to the youth:
> "We have come in search of truth,

Trying with uncertain key
Door by door of mystery;
We are reaching, through His laws,
To the garment-hem of Cause
Him, the endless, unbegun,
The Unnamable, the One
Light of all our light the Source,
Life of life, and Force of force.
As with fingers of the blind,
We are groping here to find
What the hieroglyphics mean
Of the Unseen in the seen,
What the thought which underlies
Nature's masking and disguise,
What it is that hides beneath
Blight and bloom and birth and death.
By past efforts unavailing,
Doubt and error, loss and failing,
Of our weakness made aware,
On the threshold of our task
Let us light and guidance ask,
Let us pause in silent prayer!"

*　*　*　*　*　*　*

Even the careless heart was moved,
And the doubting gave assent
With a gesture reverent,
To the Master well beloved.
As thin mists are glorified
By the light they cannot hide,
All who gazed upon him saw,
Through its vail of tender awe,
How his face was still uplit
By the old sweet look of it,
Hopeful, trustful, full of cheer,
And the love that casts out fear.

*　*　*　*　*　*　*

"And the summer went on with its succession of joyous mornings, beautiful days, and calm nights, with every charm of sea and sky, the master with us all day long, ever ready to speak words of help and encouragement, ever ready to give us from his own stock of learning.   The boundless enthusiasm which surrounded him like an atmosphere, and which sometimes gave the appearance of great achievement to the commonest things, was never lacking.

" Essentially Latin in his nature, he was always picturesque in his words and his work.   He delighted in the love and approbation of his students and his friends, and the influence of his personality sometimes gave his opinions weight beyond the value of the investigations on which they were based.   With no other investigator have the work and the man been so identified as with Agassiz.   No other of the great workers has been equally great as a teacher. His greatest work in science was his influence on other men.

" In an old note-book of those days " continues Doctor Jordan, " I find fragments of some of his talks to teachers at Penikese. From this note-book I take some paragraphs, just as I find them written there:

" ' Never try to teach what you do not know yourself and know well.   If your school board insist on your teaching anything and everything, decline firmly to do it.   It is an imposition alike on pupils and teacher to teach that which he does not know.   Those teachers who are strong enough should squarely refuse to do such work.   This much needed reform is already beginning in our colleges, and I hope it will continue.   It is a relic of mediaeval times, this idea of professing everything.   When teachers begin to decline work which they cannot do well, improvements begin to come in.   If one will be a successful teacher, he must firmly refuse work which he cannot do successfully.'

" ' It is a false idea to suppose that everybody is competent to learn or to teach everything.   Would our great artists have succeeded equally well in Greek or Calculus?   A smattering of everything is worth little.   It is a fallacy to suppose that an encyclopædic knowledge is desirable.   The mind is made strong not through much learning, but by the thorough possession of something.'

" ' Lay aside all conceit.   Learn to read the book of nature for yourself.   Those who have succeeded best have followed for years some slim thread which has once in a while broadened out and disclosed some treasure worth a life-long search.'

" ' A man cannot be Professor of Zoölogy on one day and of

chemistry on the next, and do good work in both. As in a concert all are musicians one plays one instrument, and one another, but none all in perfection.'

" 'You cannot do without one specialty. You must have some base line to measure the work, and attainments of others. For a general view of the subject, study the history of the sciences. Broad knowledge of all Nature has been the possession of no naturalist except Humboldt, and general relations constituted his specialty.'

" 'Select such subjects that your pupils cannot walk without seeing them. Train your pupils to be observers, and have them provided with the specimens about which you speak. If you can find nothing better, take a house fly or cricket, and let each one hold a specimen and examine it as you talk.'

" 'In 1847 I gave an address at Newton, Mass., before a Teachers' Institute conducted by Horace Mann. My subject was grasshoppers. I passed around a large jar of these insects, and made every teacher take one and hold it while I was speaking. If any one dropped the insect, I stopped until he picked it up. This was at that time a great innovation, and excited much laughter and derision. There can be no true progress in the teaching of natural science until such methods become general.'

" 'There is no part of the country where in the summer you cannot get a sufficient supply of the best specimens. Teach your children to bring them in themselves. Take your text from the brooks, not from the booksellers. It is better to have a few forms well known, than to teach a little about many hundred species. Better a dozen specimens thoroughly studied as the result of the first year's work, than to have two thousand dollars worth of shells and corals bought from a curiosity shop. The dozen animals would be your own.'

" 'You [1] will find the same elements of instruction all about you wherever you may be teaching. You can take your classes out and give them the same lessons, and lead them up to the same subjects you are yourselves studying here. And this method of teaching children is so natural, so suggestive, so true. That is the charm of teaching from Nature herself. No one can warp her to suit his own views. She brings us back to absolute truth as often as we wander.'

" 'The study of Nature is an intercourse with the highest mind.

---

[1] In this paragraph, quoted by Mrs. Agassiz (*Life and Letters of Agassiz*, p. 775) I have adopted the wording as given by her.

You should never trifle with Nature. At the lowest her works are the works of the highest powers, the highest something in whatever way we may look at it.'

" 'A laboratory of Natural History is a sanctuary where nothing profane should be tolerated. I feel less agony at improprieties in churches than in a scientific laboratory.'

" 'In Europe I have been accused of taking my scientific ideas from the church. In America I have been called a heretic because I will not let my church-going friends pat me on the head.'

" Of all these lectures the most valuable and the most charming were those on the glaciers. In these the master spoke, and every rock on our island was a mute witness to the truth of his words.

" He often talked to us of the Darwinian theory, to which in all its forms he was most earnestly opposed. Agassiz was essentially an idealist. All of his investigations were to him not studies of animals or plants as such, but of the divine plans of which their structures are the expression. 'That earthly form was the cover of spirit was to him a truth at once fundamental and self-evident.' The work of the student was to search out the thoughts of God, and as well as may be to think them over again. To Agassiz these divine thoughts were especially embodied in the relations of animals to each other. The species was the thought-mind at the moment of the creation of the first one of the series which represents the species. The marvel of the affinity of structure, of unity of plan in creatures widely diverse in habits and outward appearances, was to him a result of the association of ideas in the divine mind, an illustration of divine many-sidedness. To Darwin these same relations would illustrate the force of heredity acting under diverse conditions of environment.

" Agassiz had no sympathy with the prejudices worked upon by weak and foolish men in opposition to Darwinism. He believed in the absolute freedom of science; that no power on earth can give answers beforehand to the questions which men of science endeavor to solve. Of this I can give no better evidence than the fact that every one of the men specially trained by him has joined the ranks of the evolutionists. He would teach them to think for themselves, not to think as he did."

No one can contemplate the character of Agassiz, without realizing its nobility, its strength, its sweetness and his joyous nature. He was notably a Christian in all the term implies. He held to the belief in an all wise Creator. He was the great theistic philosopher of his day and time. Nature was to him so much evidence of an enduring mind, a divine intelligence.

In his essay on classification he says: "All the facts proclaim aloud the one God whom we know, adore, and love, and Natural History must in good time become the analysis of the thoughts of the creator of the Universe as manifested in the animal and vegetable kingdoms."

Holding such views it is not surprising that Agassiz opposed Darwin and it may be said that he led the anti-Darwin forces; a controversy which was waged all over the civilized world, at one time. Agassiz held out to the last, but it is interesting to note that his pupils, I believe with few, if any exception, went over to the forces of evolution, as understood at the time. The views of Agassiz did not mitigate against him as a scientist. The question of a divinity or no divinity, is beyond the pale of science, is not a scientific question, is not susceptible to argument from the standpoint of science, and the influence of Agassiz, as a great teacher, as a dominant educational force and factor stood, stands to-day unimpaired. His appearance in America was the beginning of a new era, was a scientific *renaissance* and his beneficent influence radiated around the world like the ripples from a pebble dropped upon the serene and glass-like surface of a pool. In 1873, Agassiz, the colossus of workers, Agassiz who had been warned years before by Von Humboldt that the intense work he was doing "kills," began to break down.

"I want rest," he said, "I am ready to go; I am tired; but I will work while I live, while I have strength I will labor," and here was the secret of his success, of all success, in life. And so he passed on; a good and faithful servant who found eternal rest on December 14, 1873. No man has a greater or more enduring monument than he. His influence, his works rise, a pillar of Hercules that will stand potent; virile so long as time lasts.

Jeffries Wyman

JEFFRIES WYMAN

ANATOMIST

1814–1874

By Burt G. Wilder

AMONG those in whose honor this series has been prepared probably no one is less generally known than Jeffries Wyman. He never published a book, rarely a magazine article or newpaper communication. He seldom spoke in public or upon other than strictly scientific topics. He never claimed credit or took part in a controversy. Yet for nearly half a century he was devoted to the increase and diffusion of knowledge. His discoveries were numerous and important, some almost startling. He aided the determination of momentous issues. His writings were models of clearness and conciseness. His teaching was admirable and highly appreciated. His museum was unique. In his special branches his authority was recognized the world over. Confidence in him was absolute; and rarely has any man gained from friends and pupils an affection so deep, sincere and enduring. At his death the governing body of the institution with which, as pupil or officer, he had been connected for three-fourths of his life, voiced the sentiments of all who knew him in terms appropriately simple and direct:

"The President and Fellows of Harvard University recall with affectionate respect and admiration the sagacity, patience and rectitude which characterized all his scientific work; his clearness, accuracy and conciseness as a writer and teacher; and the industry and zeal with which he labored upon the two admirable collections which remain as monuments of his rare knowledge, method and skill. They commend to the young men of the University this signal example of a character modest, tranquil, dignified and independent, and of a life simple, contented and honored."

The father of Jeffries Wyman was Dr. Rufus Wyman, born in Woburn, Mass., and graduated at Harvard in 1799; he studied medicine under Dr. John Jeffries of Boston, and during the latter part of his life was physician to the McLean Asylum for the Insane; in this, the earliest institution of the kind in New England, Dr. Wyman had the wisdom, the courage and the power to introduce radical improvements in the care and treatment of mental defectives. His wife was Ann, daughter of James Morrill, a Boston merchant; this family name was continued in the baptismal name of the second son, Dr. Morrill Wyman, of Cambridge, who was held in the highest honor and affection until his death, January 30th, 1903.[1]

[1] For the family history, for the earlier life of Professor Wyman, for various information, and for a revision of the completed manuscript I am indebted to Professor Wyman's daughters, Miss Susan and Miss Mary Morrill Wyman; to the only son, who inherited his father's name and has transmitted it to his son; and to Dr. Henry P. Walcott, a connection of Professor Wyman by marriage. Aid has been received also from Mr. Glover Morrill Allen, a relative of Professor Wyman; from President Charles W. Eliot; from Professors Thomas Dwight and James C. White of the Harvard Medical School; from Dr. Francis H. Brown and other pupils of Professor Wyman; and from Mr. Allen Danforth, Comptroller of Harvard University. A friend and former teacher discovered in the Boston papers of the period announcements and notices of Wyman's Lowell Institute lectures and abstracts of some communications to the Natural History Society, presumably sent by its secretary. There have been consulted the memoirs or articles by Asa Gray (Address at the Memorial Meeting of the Boston Society of Natural History, October 7th, 1874, reprinted from the *Proceedings*, vol. 17, pp. 96–124; also his Remarks, as Curator, *pro tempore*, of the Peabody Museum of American Archæology and Ethnology, in the Eighth Annual Report, presented April 8th, 1875 (*Reports*, vol. 1, pp. 7–11, with portrait); by Oliver Wendell Holmes (*Boston Daily Advertiser*, September 12th, 1874, and, at greater length, under the title, "A Memorial Outline," the *Atlantic Monthly*, November, 1874, pp. 611–623); by S. Weir Mitchell (under the title, "The Scientific Life," *Lippincott's Magazine*, March, 1875, pp. 352–356); by Alpheus S. Packard (reprinted from *Biographical Memoirs of the National Academy of Sciences*, vol. 2, 1886, pp. 77–126); it was read April 18th, 1878, and contains a Bibliography

Jeffries was the third son and was named for his father's medical preceptor. He was born at Chelmsford, near Lowell, Mass., August 11, 1814. His early education was received at a school in Charlestown, kept by Horatio Gates. Of this period, while he was between seven and ten years old, there is preserved a record consisting of weekly entries in a little book dated from October 20th, 1821, to March 27th, 1824. The first entry is "Studies very well"; the last, "Is a good boy." Between are "A fine little fellow"; "at the head of his class," etc. Later he attended the Academy at Chelmsford and prepared for college under Dr. Benjamin Abbott. He entered Harvard in 1829, the first year of the presidency of Josiah Quincy, and was graduated in due course; of the fifty-three members of the class of 1833 six, including Wyman, became professors in their *alma mater*.

In the spring of his senior year, Wyman had a dangerous attack of pneumonia which, says Dr. Holmes, "seems to have laid the foundation of the pulmonary affection that kept him an invalid and ended by causing his death." To recover from the effects of this attack he passed the following winter in Georgia and South Carolina. This flight southward at the approach of winter was the precursor of many others by which his life was undoubtedly prolonged.

His interest in natural objects was early manifested. When less than ten years old he spent his holidays largely along the banks

of Wyman's writings which, although marred by errors and omissions, was reproduced in the volume, *Animal Mechanics*, (articles by Sir Charles Bell and Jeffries Wyman, edited, with portrait, by Morrill Wyman in 1902); by Frederick W. Putnam (Report of the Council [on Deceased Members] in *Proceedings of the American Academy of Arts and Sciences*, n. s., vol. 10, 1875, pp. 496–505, including a Bibliography). Wyman's relations with the Lowell Institute, as Curator and Lecturer, are stated, with a portrait, in the *History of the Lowell Institute*, by Miss Harriette Knight Smith, 1898, p. 18. From September, 1859, to July, 1862, I was a pupil of Professor Wyman, and acted as his unofficial assistant during the latter half of the period; my recollections are very distinct; of the third year I have a Diary, and I have preserved all his letters, more than thirty in number. My previous tributes were published in *Old and New*, November, 1874, pp. 533–544, and in the *Popular Science Monthly*, January, 1875, pp. 355–360, with a portrait.

of rivers and creeks, and nearly always returned with some specimen, living or dead. In college the same preference continued, and he made many dissections, especially one of a mammoth bullfrog, once an inhabitant of Fresh Pond, which was an object of great interest to his classmates.[1]

Early, too, were displayed the taste and talent for drawing that proved so helpful in later years. With little instruction, he copied Hogarth's picture of the politician who was so absorbed in his paper that his hat caught fire from the candle.   When ten or twelve years old he executed upon a panel, with house-paints, a portrait of himself; the likeness was recognizable, but the tints were imperfect, the hair being colored green!

While at the Phillips Exeter Academy the impression made by young Wyman upon his fellow-pupils is recorded in a letter to Dr. Holmes from his classmate, Professor Bowen:

"He was pure-minded, frank, playful, happy, careless, not studious, at least in his school-books, but not mischievous. He *would* take long rambles in the woods and go a-fishing, and draw funny outline sketches in his school-books, and whittle out gimcracks with his pen-knife, and pitch stones or a ball farther and higher than any boy in the academy, when he ought to have been studying his lessons. Only a few years ago, when we were chatting together about our early life at Exeter and in college, he said, in his frank and simple way, with a laugh and half a sigh, 'Bowen, I made a great mistake in so neglecting distasteful duties, though you may think I made up for it by following the bent of my inclinations for catching and dissecting bullfrogs. I have been obliged, even of late years, to study hard on some subjects distinct from and yet collateral with my especial pursuits which I ought to have mastered in my boyhood." [2]

[1] This may be the "Skeleton of a frog, North America," numbered 1335 in his manuscript catalogue of the specimens now at the Boston Society of Natural History.

[2] According to the college records, in his senior year Wyman stood No. 50 in a class of fifty-three; let no budding anatomist, however, expect to achieve scientific eminence by contenting himself with a corresponding rank; some of the earlier pupils of Agassiz were none the wiser for their imitation of his excessive smoking at a certain period.

It does not appear that young Wyman had any special preference for the practice of medicine; he was emphatically a born naturalist. But at that period naturalists, as a class, hardly existed; the very word, as in the well-known anecdote of Agassiz and his colleagues in the White Mountains, was in danger of interpretation as equivalent to "naturals." The lecture-room and the illustrated magazine had not then become familiar mediums for scientific instruction and personal income. With few exceptions the naturalists of the time were practitioners; their vocation was medicine; science was merely an avocation. At all events Wyman could see no means of gratifying his natural history tastes other than by joining his father's profession. Soon after his graduation, in 1833, he entered the Harvard Medical School, and pursued his studies, partly with his father and partly with Dr. John C. Dalton, father of the distinguished physiologist of the same name.

In the spring of 1837, he received the degree of M. D., presenting a graduation thesis, entitled "De oculo," with drawings. This was never printed; but soon afterward (September, 1837) he published in *The Boston Medical and Surgical Journal* his first paper, "On the Indistinctness of Images Formed by Oblique Rays of Light," a physiologic essay for which his anatomic thesis constituted a natural foundation.

Soon after graduation he opened an office in Boston on Howard Street (not Harvard or Washington, as sometimes stated). What practice he had is not known; we may be assured that he prepared for it diligently, awaited it patiently, and attended to it faithfully. He was soon appointed demonstrator of anatomy at the medical college under Dr. John C. Warren. It is the duty of the demonstrator to aid the lecturer by making in advance the dissections and preparations needed to illustrate the exposition of the structure of an organ or region; for this office Wyman was particularly well equipped, and he held it for two years. In July, 1838, he also received a temporary appointment as assistant physician at the Massachusetts General Hospital.[1]

[1] To replace Dr. J. B. S. Jackson who was himself performing the duties in

The compensation as demonstrator was slight and Wyman felt that his father had already done enough in educating his sons. He lived within his means, but there is no reason to think that his health, strength or efficiency was impaired by undue frugality. As was the custom in those days of a volunteer fire-department, he accepted from Samuel A. Eliot, Mayor, an appointment dated September 1, 1838, and was assigned to Engine No. 18. The rule was that the first comer to the engine-house should bear the lantern and be absolved from other work; Wyman lived near by and his promptitude generally saved him from all severe labor than that of enlightening his company.

During this period there was offered a really extraordinary opportunity for usefulness and self-support. In 1839, by the bequest of John Lowell, Jr., there had been founded in Boston the Lowell Institute. This provided for the delivery, each winter, of several courses upon various subjects by lecturers invited from all parts of the civilized world. It has thus not only instructed the public but also proved an incentive and an aid to the advancement of knowledge. The first trustee, John Amory Lowell, appointed Wyman as curator at $500 per annum. He held the office for three years, and during the second (1840–41), gave a course upon Comparative Anatomy which proved so attractive that its repetition was demanded.[1] For the lectures the compensation was liberal (and has since been increased); with the funds thus earned by his first essay in teaching others he went abroad to seek further instruction for himself.

He reached Paris in May, 1841. Although Cuvier had then

the absence of Dr. Henry I. Bowditch. There is no evidence that Jeffries Wyman served as house-physician during his medical course.

[1] The *Boston Evening Transcript* of December 3, 1840, and January 12, 1841, has somewhat extended notices of the opening and closing lectures of this course. While regarding his manner and delivery as perhaps too quiet they recognize that "he was a perfect master of the subject and indefatigable in his efforts to disseminate among his hearers that ardent love of science which is so manifest in himself. The drawings (the work of the lecturer himself) were spirited and conspicuous, very well executed, and precisely of the kind wanted for illustration to a popular audience."

been dead nearly twelve years that city was still the center of biologic science. Wyman attended the lectures of Flourens, Longet and Majendie on Physiology, and those of de Blainville, Dumeril, Milne-Edwards, St. Hilaire and Valenciennes on Zoölogy and Comparative Anatomy. In the summer of 1842, after the lectures were over, he made pedestrian tours along the Loire and the Rhine, returned through Belgium and then went to London. There, while studying the Hunterian collections at the Royal College of Surgeons, he learned that his father was alarmingly ill; he departed as soon as practicable but, to his intense grief, arrived too late to see his beloved parent alive.

After his return to Boston he wrote for *Silliman's Journal* (*American Journal of Science and Arts*) reviews of three widely different publications, viz., DeKay's *Zoölogy of New York*, Vogt's *Embryologie des Salmones*, and Agassiz's *Monographies d'Echinoderms, vivans et fossiles*.[1] These, and the two that appeared in the same journal twenty years later of Weir-Mitchell and Morehouse's *Respiration of Turtles* and Owen's *Monograph of the Aye-Aye*, are apparently his only reviews; it may be inferred that he did not prefer the attitude of critical commentator.

Congenial occupation was offered in 1843 by his appointment as professor of anatomy and physiology in the medical department of the Hampton-Sidney College at Richmond, Virginia; this involved his absence from Boston only in the winter and spring, when the milder climate was advantageous.

In 1847, upon the death of Dr. J. C. Warren, the instruction in anatomy and physiology at the Harvard Medical School in Boston was intrusted to Dr. Oliver Wendell Holmes (who was an accomplished anatomist as well as poet and writer); his was the Parkman professorship, named in honor of Dr. George Parkman. At the same time, Wyman, then thirty-three years old, was

[1] The monographs of his future colleague were characterized as follows: "They constitute one of the most important additions which have been made to modern zoölogy, no less in consequence of the completeness of the plan upon which they have been conceived than the fidelity with which they have been executed."

appointed Hersey Professor of Anatomy in the Lawrence Scientific School, a part of Harvard College in Cambridge.[1] Wyman made the single word, *anatomy*, cover Embryology and Comparative Physiology, both with reference to Vertebrates rather than Invertebrates. They thus became complementary to the courses of Agassiz (appointed at about the same time) on Geology and Paleontology, and on Zoölogy with more special reference to the Invertebrates. In this connection it may be added that while the title of the likewise newly established chair of Asa Gray was the comprehensive one of Natural History, his instruction was practically confined to Botany.

Upon the subjects above named Wyman gave two courses of lectures. His enforced migration southward in midwinter threw the courses into the fall and spring. During my pupilage, 1859–62, Wyman's lectures constituted a senior elective. The limited time allowed, and the lack of preparation of his hearers, did not permit him to offer a complete exposition of any one topic. But every word told. He spoke from notes, which were yearly revised and rewritten so as to embody the latest information.[2]

The writer heard both courses three times, and *feels that he profited more by the last than by the first*. Wyman had many and accurate diagrams, made by himself; and they were always carefully arranged before each lecture. His use of specimens for illustration was really profuse, notwithstanding the fact, which he greatly lamented, that the museum was on the floor above the lecture-room, involving a laborious and perilous transfer by the stairs or by a sort of dumb-waiter. At that period

[1] The fund for this chair represented the consolidation of bequests made successively between 1772 and 1812 by Ezekiel Hersey, Sarah Derby, John Cumming, Abner Hersey, and Esther Sprague. During Wyman's incumbency the income varied from $827.39 to $1,375.85, but in the earlier years it was not all paid to him.

[2] Among the interesting documents preserved by his family is a set of his "Notes." The sheets measure 19 cm. by 16.5 (7.5 by 5.5 in.); the paper cover bears at the left margin, "1849, *Comp. Physiology;*" the complete title is: "Harvard University. Lectures on Comparative Physiology in the Scientific School (April 11 to June 18), 2d term, 1849. J. Wyman, Hersey Prof."

experimental physiology had made little progress in this country, but Wyman devised some most ingenious and effective pieces of apparatus, which he too modestly called "dodges"; among these was one for the demonstration of ciliary movement.[1] In a letter criticizing a recently issued text-book of physiology for the lack of experimental detail, he adds, "Everything that can be reinforced by experiment should be." Yet I never knew him inflict needless pain upon any creature.

He used the blackboard perhaps less readily and picturesquely than Agassiz, but with more care and accuracy and with great effect. He did not look constantly at his audience, and he never spoke for applause. His hearers respected his wish that the only expression of approval should be perfect silence and attention; but occasionally a quiet smile would usher in some quaint illustration of his subject, and embolden the audience to a subdued demonstration. At the close, he always remained for an hour, explaining specimens, and discussing questions with interested students.

With the Boston Society of Natural History he was identified during almost his whole scientific life. Joining in October, 1837, he early served as secretary and as curator of several departments.

At the annual meeting, May 17, 1843, at the age of twenty-nine, he delivered an address which is thus mentioned in the *Proceedings*, vol. 1, p. 116:

"Then followed the Annual Address, from Dr. J. Wyman, a learned and interesting discourse on the progress of science in the various branches of Natural History during the past year. At the close of the address it was voted 'That the thanks of the Society be presented to Dr. Jeffries Wyman, for his interesting and instructive address, and that a copy be requested for publication.'" [2]

Elected President in 1856, he at first declined, holding that he

[1] In a letter of November 25th, 1869, feeling that it would be useful in my own instruction, he devotes to it two pages and a diagram; it was not published until 1871.

[2] There is no evidence that the address was ever published; the manuscript is in possession of his daughter. It will be noted that this was not the presidential address; to that office he was chosen thirteen years later.

could be more useful as merely a member. Prevailed upon to accept, he was retained in the office, in spite of repeated resignations, until his connection with the Peabody Museum of Archæology and his temporary absence in Europe forced the society to relieve him in 1870. He almost invariably attended the meetings, and almost as invariably had something interesting to communicate; but he always waited until others had spoken.

Under his administration, the society prospered in every way. The membership increased; the collections were enlarged and displayed; a new building was erected with funds partly given by a friend of his;[1] public lectures were delivered; and the value of the society to the community and to science was brought to the highest point. Some idea of the extent of his activity may be gained from the fact, that, during the ten years from 1860 to 1870, the titles of his communications are about fifty in number, some of them being elaborate and extended papers. Among the rest is a loving memorial of his friend Dr. A. A. Gould, many passages of which might now be applied to himself.

Wyman was a member of the American Academy of Arts and Sciences[2] (in Boston), but attended its meetings less constantly than those of the Natural History Society. Of the National Academy of Sciences he was named one of the original members in 1863. He does not appear to have attended the meetings as his name is absent from the rolls in 1865–70, but in 1871 it is included among the Honorary Members; in the following year it was "transferred to the list of Active Members."

Wyman was one of the administrative "Faculty" of the Museum of Comparative Zoölogy from the date of its formation; and his relations with its founder were always of the most cordial nature, however they might differ upon some questions.[3] He recognized

---

[1] Dr. William J. Walker.

[2] The *Memoirs* of this Academy, vol. 9, 1867, contain one of Wyman's most important papers, "On the Development of Raia batis" (a ray or skate), and his "Notes on the Cells of the Bee" was printed in the *Proceedings*, vol. 7, 1868.

[3] As to Evolution, see the extracts on p. 193.

JEFFRIES WYMAN   181

and admired the powers of his zoölogic colleague; and Agassiz,
for his part, never tired of praising Wyman, and of advising his
students to attend his lectures; his good opinion of the teacher
was tranferred to the pupils of the latter; and indeed, in all anatomical and medical circles Wyman's name was a passport to
favor and opportunity.[1]

From personal participation in the Civil War Wyman was
excluded by his age and health; but his lively interest in it was
practically shown in various ways and is evinced by the following
extracts from letters dated, respectively, August 20, 1862, December 21, 1862, May 8, 1863, May 26, 1864, and January 15, 1865:

"Knowing how many there are connected with the hospitals
who shirk their duties . . . I do not know when you and Adams
(see p. 201, note) will have a better chance to do good than that
now at your disposal." "The weather here is severely cold, and
if such prevails on the Potomac the sufferings of the soldiers must
be fearful." "I presume you will have enough to do for the
present to take care of the wounded from the Fredericksburg dis-
aster, the consequences of downright folly on the part of the managers of the war." "I could not help feeling indignant when I
read the account of the attack at Honey Hill, to find that our
troops were again marched, as they have been so often, in the
face of a battery where it was equally disastrous to advance or
retreat; it does seem to me that there was a disgraceful blunder
on the part of some one. . . . At Thanksgiving time I visited
the Army of the Potomac. I went to the picket-lines and took a
deliberate look with my glass into a rebel battery; they did not
pay me the compliment to offer a single bullet; of course I don't
complain."

On the 8th of October, 1866, Mr. George Peabody gave one
hundred and fifty thousand dollars "in trust for the foundation and

[1] The writer is sure that to Wyman's name more than to his own merits
were due the invitation from Dr. Francis H. Brown, also a pupil, to serve
under him as medical cadet at the Judiciary Square Army Hospital in Washington in July, 1862; the request to perform the necropsies there; the proposition to give the course in anatomy at a medical college; the detail to assist
Dr. John H. Brinton on "The Surgical History of the War"; and the special
opportunities for taking examinations for higher grades in the service.

maintenance of a museum and professorship of American archæology and ethnology in connection with Harvard University."
Wyman was named one of the original seven trustees and became
curator.

Into this work Wyman entered with all the zeal and enthusiasm
of youth. As was his wont, he did all himself: every specimen
passed through his hands. Under date of January 2, 1869, his
ideas and methods were clearly set forth:

"I once thought my collection of thigh-bones and other long
bones uselessly large; but having just received more or less complete skeletons of over fifty!![the exclamation-points are his own]
moundbuilders from Kentucky, I find that, for the purposes of
comparison there is no such thing as too many, since everything
turns on averages. I see six months work ahead, and wish you
were here to help me. Just think of measuring fifty skulls, each
by twenty-five different measurements."

His seventh and last report contains an account of *Cannibalism among the American Aborigines* based upon evidence that
he had been accumulating since 1861. This portion of the Report
is reproduced entire in the *American Naturalist* for July, 1874,
and there are quoted here only the characteristically judicial summary of the evidence and the grimly humorous comments upon
the motives for the origin and maintenance of cannibalism:

"It would perhaps be going too far to say that the presence of
human bones, under the circumstances above described, amounted
to absolute proof of cannibalism. The testimony of eye-witnesses
would be the only sure evidence of it. There is, however, nothing
with regard to them which is inconsistent with this practice, nor
does any other explanation occur to us which accounts for their
presence so well. [Surely no professed logician could state that
better.]
"The idea of eating human flesh as ordinary food, may, perhaps, have had its origin in eating it as a necessity. Once tasted
and found to be good, as all cannibals aver that it is, under the
influence of savage instincts and passions, the conversion of an
enemy's flesh into meat to eat would be very natural. . . . The
New Zealander loves human flesh as a choice food, and also eats
it under the superstitious belief that he thus not only incorporates

the body of his enemy with his own, but absorbs also his enemy's soul, so that ever after the two are one. To the victor this had an especial significance, for believing in a future §tate and the presence of his enemy there, if he eats him in this life he makes sure of it that there will be no trouble with him hereafter, for he possesses him body and soul already [p. 411]."

One of the pleasantest incidents in Professor Wyman's life, and one known to comparatively few besides those directly concerned, was the presentation to him, upon the eve of a visit to Europe, of a testimonial in the double form of a sum of money and a letter expressing the "warm feelings of gratitude and respect" entertained toward him by those who had worked in his laboratory between the years of 1850 and 1870.[1] Wyman's acknowledgment was characteristically simple and modest, and is here reproduced:

"CAMBRIDGE, Jan. 19, 1870.
"GENTLEMEN:—I received, yesterday, the letter bringing your good wishes and expressions of regard. They are most gratifying to me, and recall, too, the great pleasure I have always enjoyed from personal intercourse with you. Such testimonials are among the greatest rewards a teacher can receive.

"Besides these, there is the unexpected and most generous gift you send. I thankfully accept it; and, following one of your suggestions, shall gladly devote it to the acquisition of some instruments which I very much need; and so through your kindness, shall not only be able to do my work as a teacher better, but shall have the most pleasant associations connected with the means you give me.

"Offering to each of you my heartiest thanks for this your re-

---

[1] According to the Circular as to this Testimonial, issued October 20, 1869, after he had ceased to receive students preparing to study medicine, the total number communicated with was seventy-two. Of these the large majority had became practitioners; at least three, the two Worcesters and Mills, entered the ministry; the following, and probably others, became teachers or private investigators: LeConte, '50; Dean, Wilder and Moore, '59; Warriner and Lombard, '60; Rothrock, '61; Amory and James, '63; Derby and Fitz, '64; Bowditch, '65; and Farlow, '66; thirteen in all. The years under which the names are grouped indicate the dates of beginning study with Wyman; comparatively few remained long enough to obtain a degree with him before graduating in medicine.

membrance of me, I am, gentlemen, with the kindest regards and best wishes,

"Always sincerely yours,
"[Signed]   J. WYMAN.
"Drs. J. T. G. Nichols, Francis H. Brown, H. P. Walcott, Norton Folsom, H. E. Townsend."

His forethought and personal attention to details were nowhere more clearly shown than in his preparations for expeditions, or for the annual flight to Florida or South America. In no other way can we account for the extent of the collections and information gathered during these absences from Cambridge. In fact, his vacations were only alternations of work; and his European tours in 1853 and 1870 were less occasions of rest to himself than of gain to the institutions with which he was connected.

Wyman was chosen to the Phi Beta Kappa, and attended the annual meetings; he was not a Mason or a member of any other secret organization. He did not smoke, and used wine with moderation upon occasion.

Professor Wyman was twice married; in December, 1850, to Adeline Wheelwright, who died in 1855, leaving two daughters; in August, 1861, to Annie Williams Whitney, who died in February, 1864, shortly after the birth of an only son; there survive the son and the younger daughter; see note to p. 172.

The following statements are derived from the memoir of Asa Gray (see note to p. 172).

"Although Wyman's salary, derived from the Hersey endowment (see p. 178) was slender indeed, he adapted his wants to his means, foregoing neither his independence nor his scientific work. In 1856 came unexpected and honorable aid from two old friends of his father who appreciated the son and wished him to go on with his scientific work without distraction. Dr. William J. Walker sent him ten thousand dollars outright. Thomas Lee, who had also helped in his early education, supplemented the endowment of the Hersey professorship with an equal sum, stipulating that the income should go to Wyman during life, whether he held the chair or not. Seldom, if ever, has a moderate sum produced a greater benefit.

"Winter after winter, as he exchanged our bleak climate for that of Florida, we could only hope that he would return. Spring after spring he came back to us invigorated, thanks to the bland air and the open life in boat and tent, which acted like a charm;— thanks, too, to the watchful care of his attached friend, Mr. Peabody,[1] his constant companion in Florida life. In 1874 it was late in August when he left Cambridge for his usual visit to the White Mountain region, by which he avoided the autumnal catarrh; and there, at Bethlehem, New Hampshire, on the fourth of September, a severe hemorrhage from the lungs suddenly closed his valuable life."

Half a century ago science was far less extensive and specialism was less imperative. It was possible for one individual to be a naturalist in a very broad sense. Wyman was not only an educated physician and for a time an actual practitioner; his two courses of lectures embraced embryology, anatomy and physiology, mainly of vertebrates, yet of invertebrates in no small degree. Most of his publications deal with the comparative anatomy of vertebrates, but there are papers upon the structure, habits and development of insects, shell-fish and worms; upon infusoria; upon fossil remains and prehistoric human bones and implements; upon plants and the marks made by ripples and raindrops; the remarkable discussion of the irregular forms of the cells of the bee involved mathematic computations.

At a moderate estimate, Wyman's published communications, nearly two hundred in number, would cover about one thousand octavo pages, with many figures of his own making. A part, at least, of his unpublished drawings and notes could be incorporated with what he had already given to the world. Brought together and properly edited, his works would be at once a benefit to science, a memorial of their author, and an earnest of that which he was so often urged to undertake, but which his successors should now aim to accomplish; namely, a comparative anatomy of vertebrates based upon American forms.

The year of Wyman's inauguration as professor at Harvard was signalized by his recognition of the gorilla as a new species

[1] George Augustus Peabody, Esq., Burleigh Farm, Danvers, Mass.

of ape. In order to appreciate the significance of the event itself
and the nature of Wyman's part in it some preliminary statements
are needed.

At that time, in addition to the many kinds of monkeys—with
tails of greater or less length and lacking the vermiform appendix
of the intestinal cecum—there were known several anthropoids
or man-like apes, with no trace of a tail but having an appendix
substantially like that of man.   These apes comprised several
species of gibbons from Asia and Asiatic islands; the reddish-
brown orang of Borneo and Sumatra; and the black chimpanzee
of West Central Africa. The gibbons were not discussed by Wyman and need not be considered here; the chimpanzee was sometimes spoken of as the "Black orang." [1] Wyman had already
published an important paper on the structure of the chimpanzee
in conjunction with Dr. Thomas S. Savage, a corresponding member of the Boston Society of Natural History; while serving as a
missionary on the West Coast of Africa, Dr. Savage obtained the
specimens that were examined by Wyman, and himself contributed
Observations on the External Characters and Habits.

The first scientific account of the gorilla was given by Wyman
in the summer of 1847, after the reception of specimens sent him
by Dr. Savage from New York on the 16th of July. The communication was made to the Boston Society of Natural History on the
18th of August; [2] see the *Proceedings*, vol. 2, pp. 246–247.

The paper was printed in full, with four plates, in the *Boston*

[1] "The term *Orang*, more commonly but incorrectly written *Ourang*, is
strictly applicable to the eastern species only. *Orang* is a Malay word which
means a reasonable being, and is also given to man and the elephant. *Outan*
means *wild* or *of the woods; Orang-outan*, wild man, *Cambang-outan*, wild
goat. *Outang*, the word generally used as the adjective, signifies a robber.
See Cuvier, *Animal Kingdom*, McMurtrie's Translation, vol. I, p. 57, note."
Footnote to Wyman's first paper on the Gorilla, p. 417.

[2] At the meeting of the association of American Geologists and Naturalists
in Boston, beginning September 20th, the specimens were also shown and
commented upon by Wyman, who that year was the Secretary. That association was the precursor of the American Association for the Advancement of
Science which was organized at Philadelphia the following year.

Journal of Natural History, vol. 5, part 4, pp. 417–443.[1] The *Journal* was in octavo form, and the large plates had to be folded. Evidently Wyman realized the importance of the subject since he took the unusual trouble to have the article reprinted in quarto form with the plates on heavier paper and the text repaged and very slightly rearranged but not otherwise altered, excepting as to the title-page, which reads as follows:

A DESCRIPTION OF THE CHARACTERS AND HABITS OF TROGLODYTES GORILLA. BY THOMAS S. SAVAGE, M. D. CORRESPONDING MEMBER OF THE BOSTON SOCIETY OF NATURAL HISTORY. AND OF THE OSTEOLOGY OF THE SAME, BY JEFFRIES WYMAN, M. D. HERSEY PROF. ANAT. IN HARVARD UNIVERSITY.
(From the *Boston Journal of Natural History*.)
BOSTON: PRINTED BY FREEMAN AND BOLLES. 1847.

How many copies of this quarto edition were printed I have not been able to learn. In the possession of Wyman's family is his private copy, handsomely bound up with 26 leaves of ruled paper; upon these, in Wyman's unmistakable handwriting, are copies of letters relating to the gorilla, prefaced by an account of the early stages of the discovery.

This account is signed, and dated Cambridge, June 18, 1866. Although referred to in the memoirs by Gray and Packard, it has never been printed so far as I am aware, and it is reproduced here because in several respects it is a unique document. Not only is the topic of unusual zoölogic and anthropologic interest; it embodies a really extraordinary evidence of self-abnegation upon the part of both the men most directly concerned; and it constitutes, so far as I know, the sole instance of Wyman's claim for priority; yet, it will be noted, even this was merely written for

---

[1] This paper and the part of the *Journal* containing it seem to be very rare; the writer will be grateful for information as to the location of copies.

the sake of his family with no hint of a wish that it be published, even after his death.

To the writer its presentation here appears as almost a sacred duty, a duty to the man, to his family, to his university and to the nation.[1]

TROGLODYTES GORILLA, SAVAGE

HISTORY OF THE DISCOVERY

The existence in Africa of a large ape, which without doubt was the gorilla, was mentioned by Battell,[2] and by Bowdich in his *Mission to Ashantee*,[3] but it does not appear that either of them saw the animal. In April, 1847, the Rev. J. L. Wilson brought to the notice of Dr. Thomas S. Savage, while the latter was on a visit to Gaboon, the skull of a large ape. Dr. Savage became convinced that it was not known to naturalists, and was able to obtain through the aid of Mr. Wilson other crania and various portions of the skeleton, including the pelvis and some of the long bones. He also sent drawings of a male and female skull to Professor Owen, who satisfied himself from them, that the ape in question was not the pongo of Borneo, but expressed (in a letter) the belief that the crania might prove to be those of an old, adult male and female chimpanzee. He, however, threw out the suggestion that as there were two species of apes in Borneo, Africa might also possess two species.

The collections of crania and bones belonging to Mr. Wilson and Dr. Savage were placed by the latter in my hands for description, Dr. Savage reserving for himself an account of the

[1] Were a dozen persons, ordinarily intelligent and well-informed, to assign offhand the credit for introducing to science "the most portentous and diabolic caricature of humanity that an atrabilious poet ever conceived," probably at least one-half would name Huxley; three, Darwin; two might name Owen, or perhaps one of these would recall the traveler, Du Chaillu; certainly not more than one, if any, would mention either Savage or Wyman. Even in the American edition of an ostensibly reliable work, Hartmann's *Anthropoid Apes* (International Scientific Series, 1886), the index omits Wyman's name; in the text (p. 5) it is misspelled; and his prior contribution is recorded after that of Owen.

[2] Purchas, *His Pilgrimes*, London, 1625, Part II, p. 984.

[3] London, 4to, 1819, p. 440.

outward characters and of the habits. A joint memoir was presented by us to the Boston Society of Natural History, August 18th, 1847.

In the meantime Mr. Samuel Stutchbury, Curator of the Bristol Museum in England, having learned of Dr. Savage his discovery, obtained through Captain Wagstaff, three crania which he immediately placed in the hands of Professor Owen for description. An account of them was presented to the Zoölogical Society of London, February 22, 1848, six months after our memoir had been read in Boston.

Professor Owen in a letter to Dr. Savage acknowledges that our description established the specific characters of the gorilla and that priority belonged to us. Through a vote of the Council of the Zoölogical Society the osteological characters, as set forth by me, were printed as an appendix to Professor Owen's memoir, It does not appear, however, either in the *Proceedings* or the *Transactions* of the Society *at what time our memoir was published nor that we had anticipated him in our description.*[1]

The credit of the discovery clearly belongs to Drs. Wilson and Savage, chiefly to the latter, who first became convinced of the fact that the species was new and who first brought it to the notice of naturalists. The species therefore stands recorded *Troglodytes gorilla*, Savage.

In the following account the notice of the external characters and habits was prepared by Dr. Savage. The introductory portion and the description of the crania and bones, and also the determination of the differential characters on which the establishment of the species rests, was prepared by me. In view of this last fact Dr. Savage thought, as will be seen in letter, that the species should stand in my name; *but this I declined.*[2]

In a conversation I had with Dr. A. A. Gould with regard to a suitable name, when I informed him that Hanno stated that the natives called the wild men of Africa *Gorillæ*, he at once suggested the specific name *gorilla*, which was adopted.

[1] The italics are mine. I am unable to ascertain or even to conjecture the date of Owen's reception of the first information as to the paper of Wyman and Savage. His letter to Wyman, dated July 24, 1848 (copied in the latter's private copy of the gorilla memoir already described), begins: "I duly received," etc., but *duly* is a very indefinite word. Upon this matter no light is thrown in the *Life* of Owen by his son.

[2] The italics are the present writer's.

In October, 1489, Dr. G. A. Perkins brought to me two additional crania which formed the subject of a second memoir.

In 1859, Mr. P. B. Du Chaillu arrived in New York with a large collection of the skins and skeletons of the gorilla. These he kindly placed at my disposal. My notes on his collection were printed in his book of travels. The account of the dissection of a young gorilla preserved in alcohol and which he presented to me was printed in the *Proceedings of the Boston Society of Natural History*, vol. 7, 1860, p. 211, and in vol. 9, p. 203.

[SIGNED] JEFFRIES WYMAN, CAMBRIDGE, June 18, 1866.

His studies of the two African apes naturally led Wyman to compare them with one another and with man. His second paper on the gorilla (*American Journal Science and Arts*, n. s., vol. 9, 1850, pp. 34–45) contains unusually positive expressions:

"Owen regards the gorilla as the most anthropoid of all known brutes. After a careful examination of his memoir I am forced to the conclusion that the preponderance of evidence is unequivocally opposed to the opinion there recorded. . . . There seems to be no alternative but to regard the Chimpanzee as holding the highest place in the brute creation [p. 41]. No reasonable ground for doubt remains, that the Engé-ena [gorilla] occupies a lower position and consequently recedes further from man than the Chimpanzee [p. 42]." [1]

The same paper contains a really extraordinary—indeed, for Wyman, almost anomalous—feature, viz., the formulation of a generalization without intimating the actual or probable occurrence of exceptions. On p. 41, in describing the cranium of a gorilla, he says:

"In man, the intermaxillary bones form a projecting ridge on the median line both in and below the nasal orifice and at the

[1] It will be noted that two questions are involved, *viz.*, (a) of the two African apes, gorilla and chimpanzee, which resembles man the more nearly? and (b) is either of them the highest animal? Both Wyman and Owen appear to assume that it is merely a choice between the two. Waiving for the present the interesting question as to whether even man is the highest from a purely structural standpoint, there are certain features of the brain of the Bornean ape, the orang, that are more anthropoid than those of the two African forms.

middle of the border of this opening form the projec.ing 'nasal spine,' which is not met with in any of the lower animals, and is therefore *an anatomical character peculiar to man.*"

The italics are his, a rare instance of emphasis of his own views.[1]

Intimately associated with the subjects of the papers just named is his elaborate exposition of *The Cancellated Structure of those Bones which have a Definite Relation to the Erect Position which is Naturally assumed by Man alone.* Communicated to the Natural History Society in 1849, it was not published until 1857; fortunately, as stated in the note to p. 173, it was reprinted in 1902 by Wyman's elder brother as part of a volume on *Animal Mechanics.* There are described and figured, from sections of human bones, arrangements of the lamellæ and intervening spaces, mechanically adapted to sustaining the weight of man in the erect attitude; he adds: "The only animals in which I have detected any approach to the structure of the neck of the thigh [bone] in man are the chimpanzee and the gorilla. . . . In these slight traces of the trusswork exist."

Wyman's judicial temperament was never more needed or more conspicuous than in his treatment of the ever-vexing problems of the differences and relative rank of the several human races; then, as now, in this country, those problems constituted a "Negro Question."

As early as 1847, in his first gorilla paper, his views were thus stated: "It cannot be denied that the Negro and the Orang[2] do afford the points where man and the brute, when the totality of their organization is considered, most nearly approach each other."

Granting any racial differences, and assuming the descent (or ascent) of the human species from one or more ape-like forms now extinct, the validity of the view that from those ancestral stocks

---

[1] In certain apes and even monkeys has been detected a trace (beginning or *proton*) of the nasal spine; and there have been recorded several cases of its more or less nearly complete absence in man; practically, however, as stated by Wyman, it constitutes a constant and peculiar human character.

[2] Here, as explained on p. 186, he uses the one word for all the anthropoid or tailless apes.

the white race, *as a whole,* has advanced further than the black, will be no more denied by thoughtful negroes than by the average man of to-day would be denied the superior physical perfection of, *e. g.,* the type of the Apollo Belvedere.

But, in the first place, upon several occasions, Wyman took pains to specify that, in respect to the location of the foramen magnum (the orifice at the base of the skull through which the brain is continuous with the spinal cord), the North American Indians are more ape-like than the Africans.[1]

In the second place, the same paragraph quoted above from his gorilla paper contains the following emphatic declarations: "Any anatomist who will take the trouble to compare the skeletons of the Negro and the Orang, cannot fail to be struck at sight with the wide gap which separates them. The difference between the cranium, the pelvis, and the conformation of the upper extremities in the Negro and the Caucasian, sinks into comparative insignificance when compared with the vast difference which exists between the conformation of the same parts in the Negro and the Orang." A similar remark is made in his later paper on the Hottentot, *B. S. N. H., Proceedings,* December 16th, 1863.

We may imagine the scorn with which Wyman would have repudiated the implication of a novelist that an intelligent person could not distinguish between the skull of a gorilla and that of a negro.[2]

Wyman's trusted janitor, Clary, was a dark mulatto. During the Civil War, the action of the United States paymaster in offering, at first, the Massachusetts regiments of colored troops the wages of laborers instead of the pay of soldiers, as had been promised,[3] was vigorously condemned by Wyman in a letter dated

---

[1] *Observations on Crania,* Boston Society of Natural History Proceedings, vol. II, April 15th, 1858; reprint, p. 14; also November 20, 1867, pp. 322–323.

[2] For the later qualification of this implication and for some comparisons between African and Caucasian brains see the writer's address, "The Brain of the American Negro." *Proceedings of The Annual Conference of The National Negro Committee for 1909.*

[3] This incident was related by me in an address, "Two Examples of the Negro's Courage, Physical and Moral," at the Garrison Centenary in Boston,

May 26, 1864: "All you say about the pay of the soldiers puts
the government in a very shabby light; its members are disgracing
themselves in the eyes of the world."

Evolution was a real and serious issue during the last fifteen
years of Wyman's life. The first edition of Darwin's *The Origin
of Species* appeared in the fall of 1859.[1] Like Asa Gray, William B. Rogers and some others Wyman felt no antagonism toward
the new theory and was even somewhat prepossessed in its favor.
But the formulation and publication of his views were delayed and
modified by his natural deliberation and dislike of controversy;
possibly, also, by the pronounced opposition of his nearest colleague, Agassiz. His first distinct public expression of opinion
seems to have been in the following paragraph from his review
of Owen's "Monograph of the Aye-Aye," in the *American Journal
of Science*, 2d series, vol. 36, 1863, pp. 294–299:

"We conclude with expressing the belief, that there is no just
ground for taking, and that we arrive at no reasonable theory
which takes, a position intermediate between the two extremes.
We must either assume, on the one hand, that living organisms
commenced their existence fully formed, and by processes not in
accordance with the usual order of nature as it is revealed to human minds, or, on the other hand, that each species became such
by progressive development or transmutation; that, as in the individual, so in the aggregate of races, the simple forms were not
only the precursors, but the progenitors of the complex ones, and
that thus the order of nature, as commonly manifest in her works,
was maintained."

For Wyman the foregoing was quite emphatic. How keenly
he realized the situation appears in the following extract from a
letter written in 1871 (undated, but received by me on May 30):

December 10th, 1905, printed in *Alexander's Magazine* for January, 1906.
See also the address referred to in the previous note.

[1] At that time the present writer had just entered Wyman's laboratory and
begun to attend the meetings of the Boston Society of Natural History. He
recalls with awe the earnest discussions among the intellectual giants of the
day.

"At present I am giving a few lectures on Embryology and its bearing on Evolution in general. It is a curious fact that the opponents of evolution have as yet started no theory except the preposterous one of immediate creation of each species. They simply deny. After many trials I have never been able to get Agassiz to commit himself to even the most general statement of a conception. He was just the man who ought to have taken up the evolution theory and worked it into a good shape, which his knowledge of embryology and palaeontology would have enabled him to do. He has lost a golden opportunity, but there is no use in talking of that." [1]

That this divergence upon a vital question did not estrange them personally is greatly to the credit of both these great men.

In the posthumous paper on the shell-heaps of Florida,[2] which Packard believes to have been written in 1873 or early in 1874, he reiterates his general view and in a way applies it to the early stages of the human species:

"The steady progress of discovery justifies the inference that man, in the earliest periods of his existence of which we have knowledge, was at the best a savage, enjoying the advantage of a few rude inventions. According to the theory of evolution, which has the merit of being based upon and not being inconsistent with observed analogies and processes of nature, he must have gone through a period when he was passing out of the animal into the human state, when he was not yet provided with tools of any sort, and when he lived simply the life of a brute."

The question of Abiogenesis ("spontaneous generation") was considered by Wyman with his habitual caution. He performed two extensive series of experiments with flasks [3] containing boiled solutions of organic matter. The earlier (1862) seemed to indi-

---

[1] In his memoir (referred to on p. 172, note) Asa Gray relates a conversation in which Wyman expressed the same regret and recalled a conversation of his own with Agassiz, when the latter said that Humboldt had told him that Cuvier missed a great opportunity in taking sides against St. Hilaire.

[2] Fresh-water Shell-mounds of the St. Johns River, Florida. Fourth memoir. Peabody Academy of Science, Salem, Mass., 1875.

[3] One of these historic flasks has been appropriately placed in the charge of Theobald Smith, M. D., Professor of Comparative Pathology in Harvard University.

cate the possibility of the reappearance of life after treatment and under conditions that were supposed to be fatal. But in the later series (1867), when the solutions were boiled for five consecutive hours, living organisms did not afterward appear therein. Two years later, under date of November 25th, 1869, he wrote: "After five hours boiling all flasks fail to sustain life. Nevertheless, while I do not believe spontaneous generation proved, I by no means consider it disproved." What a perfect illustration of the aphorism of his friend and colleague, Asa Gray (I quote from memory): "Upon many subjects a truly wise man remains long in a state of neither belief nor unbelief; but your intellectually short-sighted person is apt to be preternaturally clear-sighted, and to find his way very promptly to one side or the other of every mooted question."

Wyman was early interested in the study of monsters, not so much as curiosities as because he felt the truth of Goethe's axiom, "It is in her mistakes that Nature reveals her secrets;" his account of a double fetus[1] concludes with a discussion of the proximate causes of organic arrangement:

"The force, whatever it be, which regulates the distribution of matter in a normal or abnormal embryo always acts symmetrically; and, if we look for any thing among known forces analogous to it, it is to be found, if anywhere, in those known as polar forces. The essential features of polarity, as in symmetry, are antagonism either of qualities or forms. Studying the subject in the most general manner, there are striking resemblances between the distribution of matter capable of assuming a polar condition, and free to move around a magnet, and the distribution of matter around the nervous axis of an embryo."

Closely associated with these considerations is the problem of the relationship between the arms and legs, to which he had long given much thought, and upon which he published a very remarkable paper.[2] The opening words are as follows:

[1] *Boston Medical and Surgical Journal*, March 29, 1866.
[2] *On Symmetry and Homology in Limbs*. Proc. Boston Soc. Nat. Hist., June 5, 1867, p. 32.

"Anatomists who have compared the fore and hind limbs of men and animals have mostly described them as if they were parallel repetitions of each other, just as are any two ribs on the same side of the body. By a few they have been studied as symmetrical parts, repeating each other in a reversed manner from before backwards, as right and left parts do from side to side. We have adopted this last mode of viewing them, because, though open to grave objections, as will be seen further on, the difficulties met with are, on the whole, fewer than in the other, and because, too, it is supported by the indications of fore-and-hind symmetry in other parts of the body." [1]

Those who have adopted his view, and who hope, in time, to show that fore-and-hind symmetry is a fundamental law of vertebrate organization, are encouraged by the reflection that their leader seldom gave even a qualified assent to any doctrine which did not prove in the main correct.

For some reason Wyman devoted comparatively little attention to neurology. Under date of July 25, 1864, he wrote:

"I shall try to work in a direction in which I have hitherto done but little, viz., the nervous system."

The papers on the brains of the frog (1852) and opossum (1869), while admirable and suggestive so far as they go, fall short of what might have been expected. The former, indeed, contains what is, so far as I know, the sole instance, in all his writings, of a serious misapprehension, viz., as to the developmental and morphologic significance of the fusion of the right and left olfactory bulbs in the frog.

It fell to Wyman to report upon the brains of two notable men, Daniel Webster (1853), and Louis Agassiz (1873). To them he refers in the last letter received from him, dated June 17, 1874, less than three months before his own death. He says:

"Agassiz' brain weighed 1,495 grams, Webster's 1,500 and a trifle more. Practically the two were alike as far as absolute weight

[1] The writer has a sheet of paper upon which, on Christmas Day, 1861, Wyman made five hasty but most graphic and suggestive sketches of the ideal vertebrate, with its viscera and limbs symmetrically arranged with reference to a central neutral point.

goes. Neither was in a healthy condition; Webster's was somewhat atrophied and did not fill the skull, and Agassiz' had no doubt diminished from its healthy weight." [1]

About two years after Wyman's Harvard appointment there devolved upon him the painful duty of aiding the conviction of a colleague of the crime of murder. On the 23d of November, 1849, Dr. George Parkman (in whose honor was founded the chair of anatomy held by Dr. Holmes) was killed in the college building by John W. Webster, professor of chemistry. The latter tried to dispose of the corpse by various means, including fire, and the fragments of bone were identified by Wyman with characteristic skill and caution; his evidence related also to the manner of dismembering the body and to the determination of blood-stains.[2]

So predisposed was Wyman, by temperament and habit, to recognize imperfections in brilliant and apparently perfect generalizations, that, had he written a Latin grammar, he probably would have set the rules in small type; the exceptions thereto in type of medium size; and the exceptions to the exceptions in the most conspicuous. In 1865, the commonly accepted assertion of Lord Brougham that in the cell of the bee there is perfect agreement between theory and observation, was tested by measurements and by pictures ingeniously produced by the cells themselves. He concluded that "it may reasonably be doubted whether a type cell is ever made."

In 1833 the sensational newpaper report as to a "shower of flesh and blood" was disposed of by Wyman's recognizing fragments as similar to what he had seen disgorged by turkey-buzzards during his sojourn at Richmond. In 1845 were exhibited, under the name, *Hydrarchos*, what were claimed to be the bones of an

[1] According to the above figures, reckoning the avoirdupois ounce as equivalent to 28.35 grams, each of the brains weighed about 52.7 ounces. This is not the place for an attempt to reconcile the figures with slightly higher ones published elsewhere.

[2] The execution took place August 30, 1850. The descriptions in the newspapers so impressed the present writer, then nine years old, that he hanged himself in order to see how it felt; his first scientific experiment nearly proved his last.

enormous extinct reptile. Wyman demonstrated that 'they were cetacean or whale-like, and did not belong even to one and the same individual; in short that they were a factitious agglomeration.

Among Wyman's numerous other contributions to the knowledge and the interpretation of Nature, the following possess perhaps the more general interest: The recognition of a new species of manatee (sea-cow) from West Africa, 1849; an account of the brain, organ of hearing and rudimentary eyes of blind-fish from the Mammoth Cave, 1843, 1853–56; the jet from the blowhole of whales, shown to consist chiefly of the condensed moisture of the breath, 1848–51; the gestation of the Surinam toad, the male of which "plants" the eggs upon the back of the female, where they are carried until hatched, 1854–56; the mode of formation of the rattle of the rattlesnake, 1861; on the alleged "sea-serpent," 1863; the occurrence, in Florida, of a true crocodile, a genus distinct from the alligator and previously supposed to be restricted in this hemisphere to the southern half, 1870; the change in habit of cows, found grazing under water in Florida, 1874. The same state, his winter refuge and work-place for so many years, yielded a really astonishing discovery, communicated to the Natural History Society on the 7th of October, 1868, under the title, "On a Threadworm Infesting the Brain of the Snake-bird," printed in the *Proceedings*, vol. 12, pp. 100–104, and partly reproduced in the *Monthly Microscopical Journal*, vol. 2, 1869, pp. 215–216. The snake-bird, *Plotus anhinga* (now *Anhinga anhinga*), is commonly called " water-turkey," but is more nearly related to the Divers and Cormorants, differing from them in the form of the bill and in the length of the snake-like neck. In *seventeen out of the nineteen individuals examined*, Wyman found, coiled up on the brain a mass of "threadworms," measuring each from three to six centimeters (about one and one-fourth to two and one-half inches) in length; the number varied from two to eight; they were always upon the cerebellum, just behind the cerebral hemispheres, and in some cases produced a distinct depression. "They are viviparous and immensely prolific. Their presence constitutes what may be called the normal condition of the bird. Their earlier stages are unknown, as likewise the manner in which the transfer of the embryos is effected outwardly to some other animal, or the water, and then back to another Anhinga." Surely almost any other man than Wyman would have found in this surprising combination a medium of greater scientific reputation, if not, indeed, newspaper notoriety. But that was not his way, and all exploitation of his achievements has yet to be accomplished.

Wyman described very few species, and never permitted one to be named after him. Less and less, too, year by year, did he seek to draw conclusions as to relationship from his studies of animal forms. His interpretations were either teleologic or purely morphologic; that is, they either illustrated function, or the relations of single parts, without reference to the entire organism.

This feature rendered Wyman's anatomic work absolutely free from zoölogic bias, and his statements were always received as gospel by both parties to a controversy. He might not tell the whole truth, for he might not see it at the time; but what he did tell was "nothing but the truth," so far as it went. He is one of the very few naturalists who "never told a lie," simply because he never allowed his imagination to outstrip his observation. The hottest partisan felt that a figure or description of Wyman's was, so far as it went, as reliable as Nature herself.

The peculiar value of Wyman's writings and of his collections depends not so much upon their extent as upon their *absolute trustworthiness*. He worked and thought and wrote by and for himself. His facts and ideas were his own; and the smallest specimens bear the impress of his personal manipulation. All were carefully labeled by himself, and in the descriptive catalogue are rich treasures of fact and thought as yet unrevealed.[1]

It was not strange that he carefully guarded the fruit of his life; and the writer can never forget the solemn sense of responsibility with which he first received the keys and the "freedom" of the collection.[2] And although the demands upon Wyman's time and

[1] The collection and its catalogue are now in charge of the Boston Society of Natural History.

[2] My diary of November 28, 1861, chronicles the permission (without

strength made by the Archæological Museum debarred him from anything like his former care, yet he never forgot his first love; and, during the last summer of his life, the writer found him, as of old, coat off and brush in hand, dusting and rearranging the precious things,—the very children of his own industry; every one of them reminding him of some special time in the bygone years.[1] With almost a sigh he looked about him, and said, "No one man should try to establish a great museum alone; for it absorbs all his time and attention, and sooner or later ruins him, or falls itself into decay."

Nor was this a temporary feeling, born of the day's weariness, or the recent death of his colleague, Agassiz. Seven years earlier, he had embodied the same conviction in the advice *not to aim at a multiplicity of specimens, but to select typical and representative forms and parts.* And, nearly as we may think that his own museum approaches his ideal, it can hardly be doubted, that, under Providence, had it been one-half so large, Wyman's work would have been lighter, his writings fuller, his life longer, and his fame greater. But the past cannot be recalled. The man is gone. His monument remains, its intrinsic value doubled by our recollections of its builder.

To the ardent naturalist the sharpest temptation is that forbidden by the tenth commandment. A rare specimen, a new fact, a brilliant idea, these are the things which he covets, and can hardly refrain from appropriating, upon an unconscious conviction that he is best capable of using them for the world's benefit, and that the end justifies the means. How far Wyman was thus tempted, he alone could tell; but that he never yielded in word or deed would be unhesitatingly declared by all who knew him. In this, as in other respects, his was an almost "impossible morality."

This freedom from the failings of ordinary men extended to language and demeanor under all circumstances. The writer

precedent, I understood) to take out of town his finest gorilla cranium and humerus.

[1] See Asa Gray's reference to the same period in the memoir named in the note to p. 172.

never knew him to lose his temper. The nearest approach to profanity was the result of the catastrophe now to be described.

As has been stated already, Wyman's courses constituted a senior elective. Those who attended them were not commonly admitted to the laboratory. During the second year (I think) of my pupilage, he determined to occupy a lecture-hour with the exhibition of objects through microscopes. It was a great innovation; never, so far as I know, had such an exhibition been held before and the result did not encourage its repetition. In the forenoon of the previous day the tables in our laboratory were arranged, the instruments were adjusted, and each of us had his station assigned as expositor of one or more specimens. That afternoon Wyman did not come to the building at all; would that I also had absented myself. In the corner near the sink, and near the door of entrance, was the "macerating closet" communicating with a ventilating flue through which bad odors could escape. The floor of the closet was at about the height of a table. Near the front stood a large glass jar containing a cat's carcass at an advanced stage of maceration; that is, after the removal of the skin and viscera and most of the flesh, the bones had been put into a jar of water and allowed to stand until the remaining flesh had decomposed and come off, leaving the bones free. I had occasion to get something at the back of the closet. In descending from it the tail of my dissecting-gown caught upon the top of the jar and pulled it over after me; it broke and the contents spread over the floor and entered the cracks. The intensity of the odor may be inferred from the fact that my bespattered clothing had to be destroyed. The janitor was summoned in haste and we all coöperated toward purification, but with slight success. It was decided—rather pusillanimously, as it now appears to me—not to notify the professor. The windows were left open and we hoped it would not be so bad after all.

Next morning Wyman arrived before me. What happened was witnessed by a fellow-student.[1] The professor opened the door, stopped short upon the threshold, threw up his hands, and ejacu-

[1] J. F. Alleyne Adams, now a distinguished physician of Pittsfield, Mass.

lated "By George, what a confounded smell!" Under the circumstances, from most men this would have seemed a very mild exclamation; from Wyman's lips it fell upon his listeners like lightning from a clear sky.

To conclude the episode; as the seniors arrived each sniffed and asked whether the laboratory always smelt like that. The exhibition was never repeated. Yet Wyman did not reproach me nor did he ever again refer to the incident.

In those days listeners to anatomical lectures in some colleges and medical schools were too often shocked by words or innuendoes alike unworthy of the speaker and insulting to his hearers. Wyman never uttered a word that might not have been published abroad.

By some, this purity of life, reaching as it did into things great and small, will be regarded as of no avail, unless a satisfactory account is given of his religious convictions. This is out of the writer's power, and even further from his purpose. I do not recall a remark of Wyman's upon any theological topic whatever. His daughters, however, inform me that "in term time he regularly attended the college services, in vacations the Unitarian church, and joined in the Communion. He was a lover of hymns, was fond of reading the Bible and was distinctly a religious man." To me he seemed almost above the need of spiritual information or correction. His life was blameless. The heaviest of all human afflictions was endured by him with a resignation to which no set forms of piety could have contributed aught of value. He worked on for science and for his fellow-men, thinking always of others rather than of himself, and always doing better than he could hope to be done by. And is not this the essence of true religion?

Still we may gain some idea of his convictions respecting the Creator, the relation of mind to matter, and the other life, from passages in the notice of Dr. Burnett, already referred to:

" He seems to have had a pervading perception of God in his works, and often in eloquent words gave expression to his feelings when some new manifestation of divine wisdom was uncovered to his inquiring mind. . . . He had religious faith and religious hope. . . . There is a moment when, if ever on earth, the heart, if it opens itself, does so without disguise; it is that dread moment when death approaches so near, that there is no alternative but to look upon this earthly life as finished, its account made up, and when all that remains for the mind to dwell upon is the dissolution of the body, and the realization of another life."

Admired and trusted by his associates, by the younger naturalists Wyman was absolutely adored. Ever ready with information, with counsel and encouragement, so far from assuming toward them the attitude of a superior, he on several occasions permitted his original observations to be more or less merged within their productions. His generous desire to accord all possible opportunity and credit to others was early exemplified in his relations with Dr. Savage in respect to the gorilla, as described on p. 189. Dr. S. Weir Mitchell has records and recollections of like manifestations toward himself. In the following instances the persons concerned were former pupils and much younger than Wyman. His account of the brain of the opossum was published as an appendix to the Osteology and Myology of the same animal by Eliot Coues. Edward S. Morse has a letter urging him to publish his own elucidation of a morphologic point to which Wyman had already given considerable attention; indeed, in a letter to me, dated January 15, 1872, he gives a diagram and alludes to a certain fact as a "bombshell." Referring to the thesis of Norton Folsom, which included an exposition of Wyman's own views upon "fore-and-hind symmetry," he wrote me, May 26, 1864: "I do not know exactly what ideas he brought forward, but I suppose they were not unlike those we have all talked over [wholly his own]. I am *very glad that they are beginning to find their way into the minds of young men, for the older ones will never listen to them.*" (The italics are mine.) On the 27th of February, 1863, while my own thesis was under revision for belated publication, he wrote: "I do not know that I have anything to add with regard to 'fore-and-hind symmetry,' but if you find it convenient to make use of the talks we have had about it, of course I should be glad to have them turned to account."

The universal regard in which he was held is, in the writer's case, intensified by the sense of peculiar obligations which might cloud the estimate of any ordinary individual.[1] But to no man more fitly than to Wyman could be addressed the lines:

> "None knew thee but to love thee,
> Nor named thee but to praise."

Nor were any strictures ever made upon him, from any quarter, other than as to his extraordinary lack of personal ambition, and his aversion to public notice or display. If there exist already no such words as *inegotism* and *inegotistic* they really need to be coined in order to designate a characteristic of Jeffries Wyman so pronounced that it almost ceased to be a virtue.

His attitude toward criticism and critics is well exemplified in the following extracts from letters of March 1, 1863, and October 23, 1872, respectively:

"I do not think it worth the while to trouble yourself about what Professor ——— or anyone else chooses to say by way of criticism of my experiments [on 'spontaneous generation']. One thing is certain; if they are good, they will stand, and in the long run fight their own way. The verbal criticism of anyone cannot affect them.

"Have you seen the notice by ——— of your paper, and mine too [how characteristic the order]? It is quite comic to see how he charges us with ignoring, etc. At first I thought of correcting some of his mistakes, but all such things pass out of mind so soon that it seemed useless, and so I am satisfied that the best way is to say nothing."

Wyman rarely referred to what he had already done, and still more rarely to what he intended to do. The only prognostication

---

[1] In most cases the reprints of Wyman's papers were repaged, without even adding the original page numbers in brackets. Probably this was due to the preference of the printer and was simply overlooked by the author. The defect is specified partly because it is still tolerated by some writers, but mainly for the sake of showing that my affection and admiration for my friend and teacher have not rendered me absolutely incapable of criticism.

of this sort known to me occurs in his early and very suggestive paper, "Analogies Which Exist Between the Structure of the Teeth of the Lepidostei (Gars or Gar-pikes), and those of the Labyrintho-donts (extinct Amphibia)." *Bost. Soc. Nat. Hist.*, *Proceedings*, 1843, vol. 1, pp. 131–132; the report (for which, indeed, he may not have been responsible, says: "Other analogies were found in the osteology, but of these he proposes to speak in a future com-munication." No such appears to have been made.

Wyman's language, in both speech and writing, was always sim-ple and unaffected. The single instance of what might be termed, in the usual sense, "fine writing," occurs in his notice of the life and writings of Waldo I. Burnett, while speaking of the cell:

"The nucleated cell!—that minute organic structure which the unaided eye cannot discern, yet constituting the first stage of every living being, the seat of so many of the complex phenomena of animal and organic life, and the agent by which even the mind itself retains its grasp, and exerts its influence upon the living structures with which it is associated."

Wyman certainly never aimed at epigram, yet some of his say-ings deserve at least to be called aphorisms. Of the following the first two have been quoted already: "For the purposes of comparison there is no such thing as too many, since everything turns on averages." "Everything that can be reinforced by experi-ment should be." "The isolated study of anything in Natural History is a fruitful source of error." "No single experiment in physiology is worth anything." "Here [as to the form of the bee's cell], as is so often the case elsewhere in nature, the type-form is an ideal one, and with this, real forms seldom or never coincide." "The cat's anatomy should be done first because it would also serve as an introduction to human anatomy and thus become an important aid to medical education." "In organizing your department aim to fulfil these four conditions, viz. (1) Let the museum, laboratory and lecture-room be on one floor. (2) Light the museum from above. (3) Select representative forms; for what you want pay liberally if necessary; decline other things even as gifts. (4) Give not more than two lectures a week, so as to secure time for preparation, for research, and for the instruction of advanced pupils."

As may be inferred from his character and from what has been said on p. 205, Wyman preferred simple and vernacular terms. During the years 1871–72 several of his letters contain frank animadversions upon certain of my terminologic novelties. A discussion of the subject would be out of place here. The following representative extracts from a letter of October 23, 1872, should be regarded in the light of two facts: First, his own studies of the brain had been practically restricted to forms (frog and opossum) where that organ is comparatively simple; secondly, it had not been then proposed that the antagonistic preferences of the "classicists" and the "vernacularists" might compromise in the employment of paronyms, *i. e.*, national slight modifications of the common Latin antecedent; *e. g.*, *hippocampus*, which becomes *hippocampo* in Italian, *hippocampe* in French, *hippocamp* in English, and *Hippokamp* in German.

"I really do not think the time has come to establish a general nomenclature, that is, one covering the whole ground, for the reason that the subject is still in its infancy and not ready for it. The muddle growing out of human anatomy will naturally disappear in the course of time, as the horizontal method of viewing animals must prevail. The term, *Intermembral*, strikes me as good, although at first I relucted at it." [1]

Notwithstanding Wyman's exceptionally mild disposition his regard for verity was almost fierce, and upon occasion he could rejoice in the tragedy implied in the phrase (from Huxley, I think), "The slaying of a beautiful hypothesis by an ugly fact." At Wyman's hands, however, the sacrifice would be accomplished

[1] In this connection it is interesting and instructive to note that, in his *Memoir on the Development of the Ray*, 1867, p. 35, Wyman consistently employs, if, indeed, he did not coin, the singularly appropriate term of Greek derivation, *protocercal*, for the "primary, embryonic condition" of the tail; this alone would warrant the use of the international *proton* rather than "*Anlage*," the international and (to French anatomists, particularly) objectionable heteronym.

(like the killing of mortally wounded soldiers by old Ambrose Paré), "doucement et sans cholère."

This rare combination of judicial severity with gentle toleration in Wyman's character is admirably portrayed by Dr. Holmes:

"If he had been one of the twelve around the Master, whom they had seen hanging on the cross, no doubt, like Thomas, he would have asked to see the print of the nails, and know for himself if those palms were pierced, and if that side had received the soldier's spear thrust. But if he had something of the questioning follower in how many ways he reminded us of the beloved disciple! His characteristic excellencies recall many of the apostle's descriptions of the virtue which never faileth. He suffered long and was kind; he envied not; he vaunted not himself; he was not puffed up; he sought not his own; was not easily provoked; thought no evil; and rejoiced in the truth. If he differed from Charity in not believing all things, he followed the apostolic precept of trying all things, and holding fast that which stood the trial."

Without brilliancy, Wyman combined qualities rarely found in the same individual. No man of our time has surpassed him in the love of nature for its own sake, free from the hope of position, power, or profit, in keenness of vision both physical and mental, in absolute integrity with the least as well as the greatest things, in industry and perseverance, and in method, whether for the arrangement of collections, or the presentation of an idea. And if to these had been adjoined a tithe of the ambition displayed by lesser men, and had his health and strength been at all equal to his mental powers, no one can doubt that his attainments, his productions, and his reputation with the world at large would have been surpassed by those of none of his contemporaries.

However much we may, for our own sakes, regret that such was not the case, we know that into his mind never entered the shadow of bitterness. His recognition of others' labors was full and generous: his mind was upon the facts and principles of nature, and regarded not the medium through which they were obtained; and, if he ever prayed for health and strength, it was surely not for his own advancement, but because he felt within himself the desire and the ability to learn and to teach the truth.

His reputation was less widespread than that of some others, but it was more deeply rooted. And as the years roll on, and as the final estimate is made of the value of what has been done in this country, we may be sure that the name of Jeffries Wyman will stand high among those who have joined rare ability and unwearied industry with a pure and noble life. To use his own words upon a like occasion, "Let us cherish his memory, and profit by his example."

This account of Jeffries Wyman may close fitly with tributes from two who were not only friends and colleagues but masters of the art of expression, Oliver Wendell Holmes and James Russell Lowell:

"A more beautiful and truly admirable character would be hard to find among the recorded lives of men of science. The basis of all was in his personal qualities, his absolute truthfulness, his great modesty, his quiet enthusiasm, his inexhaustible patience. He never boasted, he never sneered, he never tired, he put forward no pretensions to infallibility, though he was never caught making mistakes; he was always exact and positive as to what he had seen, but willing to suspend his opinion, however tempting a generalization might offer itself, if it was only probable and not proved. He was prompt to recognize the merits of those whom he considered in any way his superiors, generous in his estimate of his equals, and a willing helper of those who looked to him for any kind of knowledge he could impart. In a word, he was always the same honest-minded, sagacious, unprejudiced, sweet-souled, and gentle-mannered creature of God, whom it was a joy to meet, a privilege to listen to, a regret to part from, whom it is a sorrow to lose, and whom it will always be a precious inheritance to remember."

"The wisest man could ask no more of Fate
Than to be simple, modest, manly, true,
Safe from the Many, honored by the Few;
Nothing to count in World or Church, or State,
But inwardly in secret to be great;
To feel mysterious Nature ever new,
To touch, if not to grasp, her endless clue,
And learn by each discovery how to wait.

He widened knowledge and escaped the praise;
He wisely taught, because more wise to learn;
He toiled for Science, not to draw men's gaze,
But for her lore of self-denial stern.
That such a man could spring from our decays
Fans the soul's nobler faith until it burn."

Reproduced by permission from the engraving on wood by Gustav Kruell.   Copyright, 1890.

ASA GRAY

BOTANIST

1810–1888

BY JOHN M. COULTER

ASA GRAY became the foremost botanist of America, with a place in the esteem and affection of American botanists so unique that it is not likely to be duplicated. His reputation as a scientific man was perhaps greater in Europe, for at that time his most important work could be appreciated better there; but his hold upon his American colleagues was more that of a genial and helpful teacher than that of an impersonal investigator.

His boyhood gave little promise of this great future, for there was nothing in his surroundings that suggested a life devoted to science. It would be interesting to account for his unusual career by discovering something in his ancestry or in his own early experiences that brought it to pass. Unfortunately such records are too scanty to be used in such a way, and Dr. Gray was too busy with his work to supply more than the barest outline of his early life. His father was a tanner in Sauquoit, Oneida County, New York, where Gray was born, November 18, 1810. While he was very young the family moved to a small settlement about a smelting furnace—Paris Furnace—where the father established a tannery. The child was set the monotonous task of feeding the bark-mill and driving the old horse that furnished its motive power. Those who have seen these old mills can appreciate that a keen, active boy, restless in mind and body, would find such an occupation depressing; but it may have been good training.

Mrs. Gray has recorded her impressions of the father and mother as follows:

"The father was quick, decided, and an immense worker; from him the son took his lively movements and his quick eagerness of character, perhaps also his ready appreciation of fun.

"The mother was a woman of singularly quiet and gentle character, with great strength and decision, and possessed a wonderful power of accomplishing and turning off work; a woman of thoughtful, earnest ways, conscientious and self-forgetting."

There are some records of young Gray's precocity; for his schooling is said to have begun when he was three years old; and we are told that at six or seven he was a champion speller at the numerous "spelling matches" that once furnished the chief excitement of country neighborhoods. This was not bad training in accuracy of observation and tenacity of memory, and both qualities were later shown in high degree by the great botanist.

Professor Gray was not "college-trained," and his formal education would be regarded now as vague and irregular and not very effective; and yet, even in purity and felicity of literary expression, which is often supposed to belong peculiarly to university culture, he was not surpassed. If the best that formal education can do is to make self-education possible, Gray needed no more of it than he received. He was one of many strong men, full of initiative, who develop in spite of lack of opportunities and contrary to the most approved principles of pedagogy.

For a time he studied at a "select school" taught by the pastor's son, and at twelve he was sent to the Clinton Grammar School. There he studied for two years, spending his summer vacations in the harvest-field. After another year of study at the academy in Fairfield, his general education was brought to a close, at a point that one might roughly estimate as about half through a good high school of to-day.

His practical father thought the time had come to turn education into useful channels, and persuaded him to begin at once the study of medicine. This advice to a partly trained boy of fifteen was a testimony not only to his reputation as a student, but also to the current notion as to the amount of general education necessary for a physician. In 1826, therefore, Gray entered the "Medi-

cal College of the Western District," at Fairfield. His medical
training was a patchwork of lectures at the college and study in
the offices of practicing physicians, chiefly that of Dr. John F.
Trowbridge of Bridgewater; but it continued for five years, when
in 1831 he received the degree of M. D., a few months before he
was of age. His medical studies, however, served chiefly to introduce him to botany, which became a growing desire throughout
his preparation for a medical career.

Fortunately we have Gray's own record of his distinct "call"
to botany. He says that during the winter of 1827–28 he chanced
to read the article "Botany" in Brewster's *Edinburgh Encyclopædia*, and this aroused so greatly his interest in the subject that
he bought Eaton's *Manual*, read it eagerly, and longed for spring.
When the first flowers appeared, he tried his *Manual*, and he tells
us that "spring beauty" (*Claytonia*) was the first plant he named.
This seems to have been like putting a brand to a mass of dry fuel,
for his interest became a consuming one, and the fire was never
extinguished. The call came, therefore, not through the personal
inspiration of a teacher, but directly from Nature; and to most
great naturalists the call has come in this way.

In the botany of that day there was a peculiar charm to the real
naturalists, for it meant the forest and the field, the "search for
hid treasure," the triumphant discovery, the gradual accumulation
of material, the ever-widening horizon of "exchanges" and
friendships. To-day botany has made very great advances, and
there are many botanists who have never had these inspiring
experiences; but those who have had them recall the old thrill as
a beautiful memory. When Asa Gray became interested in botany, the classification of plants—chiefly of flowering plants—
was the whole of botany; and it remained so in America well
through his long life. In a certain sense, North America was then
virgin territory, and its rich flora was awaiting discovery and
description. Naturally this was the first duty of American botanists, and it was a task that bred enthusiasm, just as the discovery of a new country is more exciting than its cultivation.

With the collection and naming of plants there came naturally for Gray the beginnings of an herbarium, the best record of his discoveries. In those days the naming of ordinary plants was by no means so simple a thing as Gray afterwards made it for the botanical fraternity through his admirable *Manual*. Descriptions were often meager and indefinite and scattered; and the frequent uncertainties of determination would have discouraged any but the most ardent. Hence in Gray's herbarium there began to accumulate his perplexities—plants that he could not identify.

Up to this time botany for him seems to have been only a fascinating recreation, his serious purpose still being the medical profession; but his undetermined plants brought him into his vital botanical connection, and so determined his career. In 1830, a year before he received his medical degree, he went to New York City to buy medical books for his instructor, Dr. Trowbridge. A package of undetermined plants was taken along, for he hoped to get the assistance of Dr. John Torrey, at that time the best known American botanist. He failed to find him, but left the plants. Presently there came a letter from Torrey, inclosing the names of his plants, and doubtless also containing kindly expressions of encouragement. In any event, this letter began their life-long acquaintance and intimate association, until Dr. Torrey's death in 1873.

Then came the struggle for a botanical opportunity, a struggle that continued for seven or eight years. There was abundant opportunity for botanical work, but in those days there were no botanical positions. Botany was cultivated chiefly by practicing physicians, clergymen, or those who had an income sufficient to permit it. It was distinctly not recognized as a means of livelihood. Gray did not want to practice medicine; he did want to devote himself to botany; and he had no income. For six years he seems to have lived "from hand to mouth," teaching during the winters, chiefly in Utica, and using the money thus earned in making collecting tours during the summers. One summer he spent in Western New York; and another in the "pine-barrens" of New Jersey, where he was sent by Dr. Torrey. Those who knew him later, when his great reputation had become established, can well imagine that his bright, cheery spirit carried him through these uncertain years in the hope that some opportunity would present itself. It was in the midst of this period, December, 1834, that he read his first paper before the New York Lyceum of Natural History; and it showed that the young botanist did not flinch before the most difficult groups of plants, for it was a monograph of North American Rhynchosporeæ, a group of sedges.

Dr. Torrey became so much impressed with his ability that in 1835 he invited him to become his assistant; but the offer was withdrawn later on account of the poor outlook for paying his salary, which doubtless was to have been meager enough. To young Gray this must have been a keen disappointment, for it seemed to shut the door of a great opportunity. It would have seemed to most men that botany should be abandoned as a means of living and serious attention given to establishment in some recognized profession. But Gray returned to his father's house and spent the year in preparing his *Elements of Botany*, which was published in May, 1836, and was the first of that remarkable series of text-books which for many years dominated botanical instruction in the United States, and which are marvels of clear, masterful presentation.

In 1836, through the influence of Dr. Torrey, Gray was appointed curator of the collections of the New York Lyceum of Natural History, and in its new building he made his home. It may be said that his career as a professional botanist began with this appointment. Although it was to be regarded as only a temporary makeshift, his whole time could now be devoted to his chosen pursuit. About this time an opportunity presented itself to the young botanist that seemed to promise great things. A government exploring expedition in the South Pacific was being organized, and Gray secured appointment as botanist. But there were vexatious delays and changes in organization, and it was not until 1838 that the expedition finally sailed, under command of Captain Wilkes. It is useless to imagine what would have been the result of Gray's personal study of the regions visited by this expedition; but from his subsequent contributions it is safe to assume it would have included much more than the description of new plants. The unknown field of large geographical distribution thrust itself upon him even at a distance; and it is certain that a personal survey of vegetation in the mass would have made the subject far more real and urgent. In the meantime, however, another opportunity had presented itself, and a choice had to be made. Gray decided to resign his appointment to the expedition; but later its collections came to him for study and he obtained a glimpse of what he had missed. He made the most of this glimpse, for it gave him that large contact with plants outside of North America which always entered into his perspective.

What he regarded as the larger opportunity was the invitation to become the junior author with Dr. Torrey of the contemplated *Flora of North America*. While waiting for the Wilkes' Expedition to sail, Gray "tried his hand," as he says, upon some of the families for the first part of the *Flora*, with the result that he was asked to become joint author. It is hard for botanists now to imagine the chaotic condition at that time of descriptions of the North American flora. Even for the best known region publication was in confusion; while the vaster western area was practically unknown. To bring together in some definite organization the plants already described, and to describe those brought back by various exploring parties in the great west, was the task undertaken by the two authors. With characteristic energy Gray threw himself into the work, and the first two parts—about half of the first volume—appeared in July and October, 1838.

At last a definite and congenial position was open to him, for in 1838 he was elected Professor of Natural History in the newly organized University of Michigan. In his work on the *Flora*, he had become impressed with the necessity of studying the North American plants stored in the great herbaria of Europe. Among them were many of the types, that is, the actual plants upon which the original descriptions had been based. Nearly all of the earlier collections of North American plants were sent to Europe for description; and the subsequent determinations of American botanists were based upon descriptions often imperfect and ambiguous, with no opportunity of comparison with the types. It is easy to understand how incorrect determinations would be made, how these would be perpetuated, and how descriptions would finally be changed to suit the wrongly named plants. In Gray's first work on the *Flora* he discovered that many American plants were masquerading under false names; but to discover the real plant to which a name belonged could only be done by examining the type specimen. He felt that no more of the *Flora* should be published until these types had been examined. Hence, although accepting the Michigan appointment, he asked for and obtained leave of absence to visit Europe, agreeing to serve the university at the same time by buying books for the library.

In November, 1838, he sailed, and entered upon those personal relations with the most distinguished European botanists that continued with increasing intimacy until his death. His letters show that he met almost every distinguished worker in systematic botany, and their strong personal liking and admiration for him is still freely expressed in the great herbaria he visited. In addition to the herbaria of England and Scotland, he visited those of Paris, Lyons, Geneva, Munich, Berlin, Halle, Hamburg, and Vienna. In all he made six more or less prolonged visits to Europe and put the identity of the older described American plants upon a sure basis.

Upon Gray's return from his first trip to Europe, in 1839, his leave of absence was extended by the University of Michigan. In fact he never entered upon his duties there, the furlough merging into his appointment at Harvard College. In the spring of 1842, he visited Mr. B. D. Greene in Boston, and while there met President Quincy of Harvard. Soon afterwards he was elected to the Fisher Professorship of Natural History, and continued in this position for the rest of his life. The large opportunity had come at last, and it was at Harvard that Gray made his great reputation, entering upon his duties there as teacher, author, and investigator with an enthusiasm and an ability that soon made Cambridge the center of botanical instruction and investigation in America. He was a most prolific writer, but a complete list of his publications would give no adequate impression of Asa Gray as an inspiring teacher, a keen and kindly critic, and a bright and genial companion. Such impressions come only from personal contact, but they go to make up the appeal to affection; and in the case of Professor Gray they accounted in no small way for his hold upon American botanists.

Reference has been made to the fact that Gray's scientific reputation during his life was perhaps greater in Europe than in America, for his real scientific colleagues were chiefly in Europe. Now that American botany has developed a larger perspective, some unprejudiced estimate of Gray's place in the science may be made by an American botanist. During the period of Gray's botanical activity, the science of botany in the United States consisted almost exclusively of the determination of its flora. The Atlantic states had been explored in a general way, and enough was known to justify the publication of a few manuals. Isolation from Europe, however, where the types were stored, had filled these manuals with incorrectly determined plants. But the flora of the much greater west remained practically unknown. Public and private enterprise had organized exploring expeditions that touched this flora slightly, and scattered reports contained descriptions of many plants. In short the flora of North America was partly in confusion and more largely unknown when Gray began his work. His mission was to organize this chaotic material into some orderly form, clearing away confusion, bringing together scattered and often ill-considered publications, and establishing American systematic botany upon a secure foundation. His was the first serious and successful attempt to grasp the flora of the whole continent and relate it properly to all previous publications. It may be said that American systematic botany as a definite organized science, rather than a mass of isolated, sporadic efforts, dated from the work of Asa Gray. To appreciate this fact, one has only to compare the condition of systematic botany in America before and after Gray. In his chosen subject, therefore, Gray stands for its permanent transformation in America.

Work on the *Flora of North America* was pushed forward

rapidly after Gray's first return from Europe; but at this time there began the memorable series of great transcontinental surveys, each returning with notable collections of the plants of the regions traversed. Naturally most of this material came to Torrey and Gray for determination, and these botanists began to get some glimpses of the riches of the American flora. Report after report was published, and they are now well-known classics in American systematic botany. So rapidly did the new material appear and so endless did it seem that the *Flora of North America* was hopelessly out-of-date before half of it had appeared. Any attempt to include the whole flora of North America in a single publication was clearly out of the question at that time, and so its completion was postponed indefinitely. Many years later, after the successive waves of new material had subsided a little, Dr. Gray renewed the attempt in what he called the *Synoptical Flora of North America*. It began where the old *Flora* of Torrey and Gray stopped; then it began to traverse again the ground of the older publication; and it is still in process of publication. It was hoped that it could be completed by Dr. Gray; for although he could delegate his work, he could not delegate his great grasp and vast experience. But he did leave a reorganized science, and a better conception of what such work demands in the way of research and equipment.

No one was more competent to estimate Gray's place in systematic botany than his life-long friend Sir Joseph Hooker, the great English botanist, who wrote in *Nature*, upon the occasion of Gray's death:

"When the history of the progress of botany during the nineteenth century shall be written, two names will hold high positions; those of Professor Augustin Pyrame DeCandolle (Geneva) and Professor Asa Gray. One sank to his rest in the Old World as the other rose to eminence in the New. Both were great teachers, prolific writers, and authors of the best elementary works on botany of their day."

The preparation of the large *Floras* referred to was but the bringing together in organized form of the great mass of monographs and "contributions" of new species that was constantly issuing from Cambridge; and the present student of the American flora can hardly find a region of his subject that is not underlaid by a substratum of Gray's work. The amount of such work, when Gray's numerous other publications are considered, is surprising. In addition to his tireless industry, he had a remarkable quickness for discerning characters, seeing at once what many would have to obtain by the drudgery of analysis and patient comparison. At one time the writer was preparing a monograph of a small family of plants under the direct supervision of Dr. Gray. In the course of the work a snarl of confusing forms presented themselves, and the most laborious examination brought no satisfactory results. The material seemed too abundant to classify, for intermediate forms persisted in contradicting every suggestion as to grouping. Into the midst of this situation Dr. Gray came, and spreading out the troublesome forms upon a series of tables so that his eye could run over them all at once, with surprising quickness he pointed out characters that proved to be exactly the trail that was needed. To see Gray run through a bundle of newly arrived plants was a revelation to the cautious plodder. Every character he had ever met seemed vivid in his memory and ready to be applied instantly; and the bundle was "sorted" with a speed that defied imitation. It seemed like intuition, but it was vast experience backed by a wonderful memory; perhaps it could be called genius. Besides this facility for work, Gray's descriptions were marvels of aptness and lucidity. As his long-time friend W. M. Canby has written, he had "a rare faculty of conveying his own knowledge to others by felicitous and accurate description." When one compares Gray's brief but complete descriptions, containing no unnecessary or inappropriate word or phrase, with the long, labored, repetitious and ineffective descriptions of many systematists, this characterization will be appreciated.

Turning from Gray's work as the great organizer of systematic botany in North America, to his work as a teacher, his personal contact with students, his large correspondence, and his text-books are all to be considered. Perhaps no more intimate description of Professor Gray in the class-room has been given than that by Dr. Farlow, first his pupil and afterwards his colleague at Harvard University. His first impressions are recorded as follows:

"I expected to find an elderly and rather austere man; but I found a young-looking man, with strikingly bright and expressive eyes, quick in all his motions, and so thoroughly in earnest and absorbed in his subject that he assumed that all his hearers must be equally interested. There was an air of simplicity and straightforwardness, without a trace of conscious superiority or pedantic manner. He was always young in spirit and his enthusiasm was contagious."

He was a great teacher, not in the sense of exacting a rigid discipline, but in the far better sense of transforming interest into enthusiasm. Nor did he coddle interest, but trained it, often severely. The writer very distinctly remembers submitting to him a piece of work that must have been callow in the extreme, but which seemed to its author fairly creditable. Glancing through it with characteristic quickness, Gray sat down and took a half hour out of an extremely busy day in performing a most searching and relentless piece of dissection. As the flimsy fabric was torn to tatters, the victim felt all the sinking of heart and discouragement that must come to a man convinced that he is a complete failure. Afterwards he discovered that the operation was not to destroy but to train, and the lesson was never forgotten. It brought a perspective that no amount of coddling could have done. Another phase of Gray's teaching, and one far too much neglected by scientific men, is well brought out by an incident in the experience of Dr. J. T. Rothrock, who says:

"It was not sufficient that the conclusions should be correct, but they must be stated in exactly the right way. An artistic turn of a sentence, making it graceful as well as logical, was in his eyes of the utmost importance. 'There now, that is neatly stated,' is an expression which yet rings in my ears. It was uttered by Dr. Gray, when at last I had succeeded in 'putting a point' as he thought it should be. I had written my first scientific paper at least six times, and each time thought it was as well done as could be; certainly as well done as I was capable of doing it. But my

critic was merciless. I mentally resolved each time that I would
not re-write it; but I did re-write it; and was obliged to continue
doing so until he thought it might be allowed to pass. It was the
most helpful lesson I ever received in the art of stating things."

Gray insisted upon developing initiative in the student. Perhaps
work in systematic botany lends itself more kindly to a slavish
following than almost any other. It is so much easier to copy
descriptions than to make them afresh, especially when they seem
clear and appropriate. This slavish following Dr. Gray could not
endure, and when the writer submitted him some pages of a contemplated manual, he was informed that he was to act as an investigator rather than a recording machine. To see the plant vividly,
to seize the essential features, and then to describe them aptly
was to him as much a matter of individual style as the production
of a literary composition.

Gray's work as a teacher through his *Manual* touched his
greatest audience. The first edition appeared in 1848, and seven
editions were published. Probably no manual of botany was ever
so widely used for so long a time, and it well deserved its success.
It was a model of clear arrangement and masterly description.
It was simple enough for use by the beginner; its keys were easily
understood; and its descriptions were marvels of brevity and completeness. Long drawn out descriptions are confusing and to the
beginner they are baffling and often misleading; but the *Manual*
selects the essential features of each species and makes it stand out
sharply. It easily supplanted all preceding manuals, and for half
a century it has been the constant companion of every botanist
within its range. This made Gray's name a household word
wherever botany was either studied or only cultivated as a pas-
time, and helped in no small way to establish his singularly preëminent reputation in this country.

Not only through his more technical scientific work, but more
largely through his *Manual*, he developed an enormous correspondence. Collectors everywhere sent him plants for determination or confirmation, and he never turned them aside. It was
always a mystery how he found time to write so fully to so many

botanists of all grades, from the beginner to the intimate associate. With considerable trepidation the writer, then a very amateurish collector, sent some plants to Dr. Gray, which he thought might be of interest. It seemed presumptuous to intrude upon the time of one so occupied with larger matters, and with plants which were probably common enough to him. The surprise came in the form of a letter so full of kindly suggestion and encouragement that it stimulated the ambition and aroused the affection of the recipient so effectively that it determined his career and secured his unbroken devotion. This case was far from being a solitary one, for just such letters went daily from the study at Cambridge, prompted by the kind heart of the great botanist; and it is little wonder that he held all the younger botanists of the country in the hollow of his hand, and became to them the court of final appeal. It was the combination of his opportunities and his genial helpfulness that secured for him so unique a position. In fact, so complete was his domination that to those outside it might seem to have the appearance of autocratic control; but those inside knew that it was only the natural control that belongs to a strong and helpful man in a peculiarly favorable position to be of service.

Systematic botany lends itself peculiarly to this kind of friendly contact, for it involves much correspondence and exchange of material; so that its devotees cannot work isolated from their fellows, but must form a great fraternity. This accounts for the strong personal hold Gray had upon many whom he never met. Such a hold is not possible now, aside from any peculiar power that may have belonged to Gray; because several important centers of systematic work have been established, botanists have become more independent, and botany has become a many-sided science.

Associated with the *Manual* were the various text-books of all grades, from *How Plants Grow* to the *Structural Botany*. To say that they are marvels of clear, flowing style is only to repeat the common opinion concerning them. They are models of style for elementary texts in general, as well as masterly presentations of the subject as it was understood at that time. The first of the series was the *Elements of Botany*, which appeared in 1836; and the last and most important one, written from the university standpoint, was the *Structural Botany*, published in 1879. Very few great and hence much-occupied investigators are willing to take the trouble to prepare text-books of their subject, much less elementary text-books. But Gray was also a great educator, and his ambition was to develop the science of botany by training the greatest possible number, from the elementary schools to the university. Never did he lose interest in this part of his work, and for nearly half a century he taught not only the teachers but also the children. From the text-books, often said to be "the finest set of text-books ever issued in the English language," Gray's greatest popular reputation came; for the great majority of Americans knew of him as the author of their text-book in botany rather than as a great investigator.

Gray's work did not end with the organization of systematic botany in America and with teaching his science to Americans, but he was also conspicuous as a great critic. His reviews of current work were continuous through his long life, and it seemed impossible that he could read so much. These reviews included not only American work, but also all European work that was important. In fact for years he was the principal channel through which foreign publications reached the majority of American botanists, publications dealing not only with systematic botany, but with all phases of the science. Apparently he wrote with no effort; and his graceful, flowing style, with now and then some fine humor, was very characteristic. He recognized the responsibility of his position as critic, feeling that the science and those who depended upon his opinion must be served. Hence his reviews were not of the kind that either speak well of everything or speak well of nothing; but they were sharply discriminating. He was often severe, but never ill-natured or personal; and always contrived to find something for commendation. A chronological collection of this great series of reviews would form a most instructive commentary on the history of botany for half a century. An incident related by Mr. Thomas Meehan illustrates Gray's feeling in reference to his duty as a critic, and explains how a man with such evident kindly feeling and consideration for all could sometimes seem so harsh in criticism.

"Once a very zealous collector, to whom science was under many obligations, described and published a large number of plants from imperfect material, with undue haste, and without competent knowledge. Dr. Gray had to show that really there were very few new species among them, and in so doing his criticism was unusually severe. In writing to Dr. Gray I ventured to remonstrate with him upon the severity he had used. The reply was, 'In my heart I would have been more tender than you, but I cannot afford to be. I am, from my present position before the world, a critic, and I cannot shrink from the duty which such a position imposes upon me. If you were in the position that I am, with a short life and a long task before you, and just as you thought the way was clear for progress some one should dump cart-loads of rubbish in your path, and you had to take off your coat, roll up your sleeves, and spend weeks in digging that rubbish away before you could proceed, I should not suppose you would be a model of amiability.'"

This critical care of his science appeared not only in his published reviews, but also in the more numerous private letters to authors. After any publication, it was the common thing for the author to receive from Dr. Gray some characteristic comment, very friendly but faithfully keen; and it always helped the next performance. When the *Botanical Gazette* was established in 1875, the enterprise was encouraged and the name suggested by Dr. Gray. But he followed up this responsibility faithfully, and for some time after each issue the editor would receive a letter full of commendations or caustic comments. It was quite characteristic of the man that when the criticism had been unusually savage and the editor was feeling that perhaps the journal had better be abandoned, Dr. Gray would send a paper of his own for publication.

Gray's interest extended beyond the somewhat narrow limits of his special work in systematic botany, and included the general philosophical aspects of biology. One of his most brilliant papers was a discussion of the *Relation of the Japanese Flora to That of*

North America. The conclusions as to a former arctic connection were all the more remarkable since at that time the testimony from the boreal fossil flora was not in.

It was this larger biological interest that compelled Gray to become the foremost expounder in this country of Darwin's theory of natural selection. It was at the opening of the Civil War that the notable discussion began, and perhaps it would have attracted even larger public attention than it did if men's thoughts had not been so engrossed by the terrible experiences through which the country was passing. Gray was almost alone at first in meeting the skepticism and opposition aroused by what was soon called Darwinism; and his task was all the more difficult because of the opposition of his very influential colleague Agassiz. What he contended for was not so much belief in the theory of natural selection, for he himself did not accept it in all its fulness, as for an attitude of mind that could recognize its bearings without prejudice and could see that it was consistent with theistic belief. Hence he was its expounder rather than its defender. He debated with skeptical scientists and unbelieving theologians; and especially with the latter antagonists were his breadth and keenness shown. All of his scattered writings upon this subject were later brought together in a volume bearing the appropriate title *Darwiniana.* It is an admirable commentary on the theory of natural selection, in which the author now explains it with wonderful lucidity, as a great teacher; now defends it against unjust attack, as a great champion; now pierces the statements of theologians with most brilliant logic, as a great debater; by one means and another routing enemies and winning friends. In the midst of the general storm aroused by the *Origin of Species*, Darwin himself learned to rely upon the judgment and support of Gray, as shown by their correspondence. In Darwin's letters to Gray will be found the following statements:

"You never touch the subject without making it clearer;" "I look at it as even more extraordinary that you never say a word or use an epithet which does not fully express my meaning;" "Others who perfectly understand my book, sometimes use expressions to which I demur;" "I hope and almost believe that the time will come when you will go further in believing a much larger amount of modification of species than you did at first or do now."

The contest involved a great principle, and Asa Gray should be regarded as the great and successful champion in this country of the freedom of scientific investigation from theological domination.

In 1873, Gray retired from instruction, to give his undivided attention to the preparation of the *Synoptical Flora* and the monographic studies connected with it. His priceless herbarium and library had been given to Harvard University on condition that they be housed in a fire-proof building. This building, in the Botanic Garden at Cambridge, connected with Dr. Gray's house, his own study being the connecting link between the two, is full of associations for American botanists. Those who consulted the herbarium, and all who published were compelled to do this sooner or later, will never forget the rapid steps that now and then issued from the study and hastened into the adjoining library; the occasional words of friendly greeting; the still more prized invitation to the study; and the genial hospitality of the home that was open to all who loved plants.

After Cambridge became a receiving center for nearly all important collections of North American plants, it might be supposed that Gray would be compelled to become exclusively a herbarium botanist. The pressure of important work thrust upon him would certainly seem to have justified it. But he began botany in the "open," and he always returned to it at every opportunity. His visits to the most interesting regions of the North American flora, from the "pine barrens" of New Jersey and the mountains of the South Atlantic states to the Rocky Mountains, were not only the greatest delight to him, but memorable occasions to those who were fortunate enough to accompany him. Like a boy at home during a short vacation, he bubbled over with enthusiasm and activity. The interesting plants were hailed with as keen a pleasure as though they were new; perhaps with even greater pleasure because they were old and prized friends. His light and wiry body kept pace with his enthusiasm, and to be with him for a day's tramp tried the endurance of the most experienced walkers. One could not be with him long in the field without catching the contagion and finding himself running about as eagerly as a boy after butterflies.

He was preëminently a companionable man, delighting in his friends, very vivacious, and always looking at his experiences with the eyes of fresh youthfulness, as though his whole business was to have a good time. From the hard strain of work he always rebounded joyfully, never retaining the air of abstraction or weariness. This secured for him the warm friendship of Cambridge associates and of those whom he met in his travels; and his presence always brought good cheer.

In 1848 Dr. Gray was married to Jane L. Loring, the daughter of Charles Greely Loring, a lawyer in Boston. In all of his travels Mrs. Gray was his constant companion, and established that familiarity with his work and his associates that made her a constant help and delight. Their home life was charming, and although childless, Dr. Gray was passionately fond of children, always greeting them cordially, stopping to talk with them, and at times romping with them in boyish abandon.

Gray's reading was always omnivorous, and this, after all, he says, was the larger part of his education. In his early boyhood there was no great choice, and so everything was read that could be obtained. He says, "History I rather took to, but especially voyages and travels were my delight." At first very few novels were available, but an introduction to the Waverley novels made Scott his life-long favorite. Mrs. Gray, in her *Letters of Asa Gray*, writes:

"In later life the novels were always saved for long journeys. The novel of the day was picked out, and one pleasure of a long day's ride in the train was to sit by his side and enjoy his pleasure at the good things. The glee and delight with which he read Hawthorne, especially the *Wonder-Book* and *Tanglewood Tales*, make days to remember. So he read George Eliot, and *Adam Bede* carried him happily through a fit of the toothache. Scott always remained the prime favorite, and his last day of reading, when the final illness was stealing so unexpectedly and insidiously

on, was spent over *The Monastery*, which he had been planning
to read on his homeward voyage in 1887."

Gray was of Irish ancestry, his great-great-grandfather having
emigrated from Ireland to Massachusetts as a member of a Scotch-
Irish colony composed of rigid Presbyterians, who desired to
leave Ireland to escape various persecutions. This religious inheritance had not faded out when it reached Gray, and although to
some at the time he seemed far from orthodox in his champion-
ship of Darwin, he was always a theistic evolutionist. In the
preface to *Darwiniana* he makes the following distinct statement
of his religious views:

"As to the natural theological questions which are here throughout brought into what most naturalists, and some other readers,
may deem undue prominence, there are many who may be interested to know how these increasingly prevalent views and their
tendencies are regarded by one who is scientifically, and in his
own fashion, a Darwinian, philosophically a convinced theist, and
religiously an acceptor of the ' creed commonly called the Nicene,'
as the exponent of the Christian faith."

A glimpse of the man and the estimate of him by his colleagues
may be obtained from an extract taken from a letter written by
his friend Dean Church to Mrs. Gray.

"There is a special *cachet* in all Dr. Gray's papers, great and
small, which is his own, and which seems to me to distinguish
him from even his more famous contemporaries. There is the
scientific spirit in it, but firm, imaginative, fearless, cautious, with
large horizons, and very attentive and careful to objections and
qualifications; and there is besides, what is so often wanting in
scientific writing, the human spirit, always remembering that,
besides facts and laws, there are souls and characters over against
them, of as great account as they, in whose mirrors they are reflected, whom they excite and delight, and without whose interest
they would be blanks. The combination comes out in his great
generalizations, in the bold and yet considerate way in which he
deals with Darwin's ideas, and in the notices of so many of his
scientific friends, whom we feel that he was interested in as men,
and not only as scientific inquirers. The sweetness and charity,
which we remember so well in living converse, is always on the

lookout for some pleasant feature in the people of whom he writes, and to give kindliness and equity to his judgment.

"And what a life of labors it was! I am perfectly aghast at the amount of grinding work of which these papers are the indirect evidence. . . .

"For they [his religious views] were a most characteristic part of the man, and the seriousness and earnest conviction with which he let them be known had, I am convinced, a most wholesome effect on the development of the great scientific theory in which he was so much interested. It took off a great deal of the theological edge, which was its danger, both to those who upheld and those who opposed it. I am sure things would have gone more crossly and unreasonably, if his combination of fearless religion and clearness of mind, and wise love of truth, had not told on the controversy."

On November 18, 1885, Professor Gray's seventy-fifth birthday, there was an outpouring of expressions of admiration and affection from American botanists that was remarkable. At the suggestion of the editors of the *Botanical Gazette*, the expression took the form of a silver memorial vase and personal letters of congratulation. The responses were so prompt and generous that the whole movement was really spontaneous, waiting only for the opportunity. The legend upon the vase read

"1810 November eighteenth 1885
Asa Gray
in token of the universal esteem of American botanists"

Beautifully wrought upon the vase were appropriate representatives of the North American flora; and it was a keen pleasure to see with what almost boyish delight the venerable but ever youthful botanist recognized and named them. There were also greetings from 180 American botanists; in fact from all who could be notified of the anniversary; and James Russell Lowell contributed the following sentiment:

"Just Fate, prolong his life well-spent
Whose indefatigable hours
Have been as gaily innocent
And fragrant as his flowers."

Professor Gray's published reply to this overwhelming tribute was so characteristic in sentiment and in style that it must be repeated. Addressing the American botanists he said:

"As I am quite unable to convey to you in words any adequate idea of the gratification I received, on the morning of the 18th. inst., from the wealth of congratulations and expressions of esteem and affection which welcomed my 75th birthday, I can do no more than to render to each and all my heartiest thanks. Among fellow-botanists, more pleasantly connected than in any other pursuit by mutual giving and receiving, some recognition of a rather uncommon anniversary might naturally be expected. But this full flood of benediction, from the whole length and breadth of the land, whose flora is a common study and a common delight, was as unexpected as it is touching and memorable. Equally so is the exquisite vase which accompanied the messages of congratulation and is to commemorate them, and upon which not a few of the flowers associated with my name or with my special studies are so deftly wrought by art that one may almost say 'the art itself is nature.' . . ."

A little more than two years after this notable anniversary, on January 30, 1888, Asa Gray died, stricken with paralysis; and it was the common voice of American botanists that they had lost their leader and friend.

James D. Dana

JAMES DWIGHT DANA

GEOLOGIST

1813–1895

BY WILLIAM NORTH RICE

JAMES DWIGHT DANA [1] was born in Utica, New York, February 12, 1813. He was a descendant of Richard Dana, who is believed to have emigrated from England to Massachusetts about 1640. Among the numerous posterity of Richard Dana are included a remarkably large number of men of eminent achievement in science, literature, and politics, in the ministry and the law.[2] The history of the family prior to the emigration of Richard Dana is uncertain. It appears probable that the family name is of Italian origin, and that some ancestor of Richard emigrated from Italy

---

[1] In the preparation of this sketch, the principal sources (aside from personal memories of a revered teacher and friend, and from Professor Dana's own works) have been the biography by President Gilman (*The Life of James Dwight Dana, Scientific Explorer, Mineralogist, Geologist, Zoölogist.* New York and London, 1899), and the appreciative articles by Professors E. S. Dana (*American Journal of Science*, series 3, vol. 49, pp. 329–356), Le-Conte (*Bulletin of the Geological Society of America*, vol. 7, pp. 461–479), Williams (*Journal of Geology*, vol. 3, pp. 601–621), Farrington (*Journal of Geology*, vol. 3, pp. 335–340), and Beecher (*American Geologist*, vol. 17, pp. 1–16).

[2] Among the most eminent descendants of Richard Dana may be mentioned Francis Dana, member of the Continental Congress, Chief Justice of Massachusetts; Richard Henry Dana, poet; Richard Henry Dana, Jr., jurist; Samuel Whittlesey Dana, United States Senator from Connecticut; John Winchester Dana, Governor of Maine; James Freeman Dana, chemist and mineralogist; Samuel Luther Dana, chemist; Charles Anderson Dana, editor, Assistant Secretary of War.

to England. A number of Italians bearing the name of Dana have had honorable careers in various intellectual professions. The intense vivacity of mind and body which always characterized Professor Dana may have been due in some degree to his inheritance from the sunny land of Italy.

The parents of James Dwight Dana were intelligent, energetic, and earnestly religious people, and the atmosphere of the home was thoroughly wholesome. "Honesty, virtue and industry seem almost to be our natural inheritance," said Professor Dana in after years, in grateful memory of the influences under which he and his nine brothers and sisters had been reared. There is, however, no evidence that the associations of his childhood home tended to inspire or cultivate an interest in scientific investigation. One of his aunts, who was a member of the household in which his boyhood was passed, describes him as "a merry boy, always ready for a game of romps." She informs us that he began collecting specimens at an early age, and that "he had quite a cabinet before he was ten years old." How much significance belongs to these early efforts, it is impossible to estimate.

The earliest influence tending to awaken into activity his scientific taste and talent was found in an academy which had been established in Utica by Charles Bartlett. The science teacher in that school, Fay Edgerton, was a graduate of Rensselaer Polytechnic Institute, and was far in advance of his time in his methods of scientific instruction. His students were taught in large degree by laboratory methods. Especially instructive and inspiring were his short field excursions in term time, and his longer tours with his students in the summer vacations, in which they collected minerals, fossils, plants, etc., and acquired the mental habitudes which come from first-hand contact with nature. Mr. Edgerton was succeeded in his position by Asa Gray, the illustrious botanist. It does not appear, however, that Dana was ever a pupil of Gray,[1]

[1] According to M. M. Bagg (quoted by Gilman, p. 16), Gray commenced teaching in Utica in 1829; but a letter of Gray to Torrey (*Letters of Asa Gray*, p. 37) shows that Gray's work in Utica did not begin till 1832. This was after Dana had entered college.

though their friendship and helpful mutual influence certainly commenced early in life.

In 1830, Dana entered the Sophomore Class of Yale College, and he was duly graduated from that institution in 1833. His standing in general scholarship was creditable though not brilliant. Those were the days of the fixed curriculum in which the staples were classics and mathematics. Dana's preparation in the classics had been defective, and in college he did not distinguish himself in that department. He attained, however, a high grade in mathematics; and it is needless to say that he made the most of the rather scanty opportunities which an American college then afforded for the study of the sciences of nature. Undoubtedly the strongest influence in his college life towards the shaping of his future career was that of the elder Benjamin Silliman, whose pioneer work in chemistry and geology was already giving renown to Yale College.

In the spring of 1833, Dana received an appointment as schoolmaster in the navy. He was ordered to report June 15, at Norfolk, Virginia, for service on the U. S. ship *Delaware*, in a cruise in the Mediterranean. The school for the instruction of midshipmen on the ship was presided over by the chaplain. Dana's work was that of instructor in mathematics. The routine duties of his position left him much leisure, and he devoted a large portion of his time to the study of crystallography. He had opportunities for observation of the geology of various localities on the Mediterranean shores. The earliest of his long series of scientific publications was a letter to Professor Silliman, describing Vesuvius as it appeared in July, 1834, which was published in the *American Journal of Science* in the following year. He returned to this country near the end of the year 1834, and retired from the naval service.

The return from the Mediterranean cruise was the beginning of a period of perplexity. Already young Dana clearly heard the inward call to a distinctively scientific career, but in those days the opportunities to secure a livelihood in such a career were far less abundant than at present. A great encouragement to the aspirations of the young scientist was his appointment as assistant to Professor Silliman in 1836. The routine duties of the position occupied but little time. He had the benefit of stimulating association with other scientific men, and the use of the library and the already respectable mineralogical collection of the college.

His studies at this period were chiefly in mineralogy; and in 1837 appeared the first of his great scientific works, the *System of Mineralogy*. It is certainly remarkable that a book representing so large an amount of research should have been produced by a man only twenty-four years old, and only four years out of college. Successive editions of the work were published in 1844, 1850, 1854, and 1868. In the fifth edition Professor Dana had the assistance of Professor George J. Brush. That edition included only descriptive mineralogy, but was more voluminous than the previous editions which had included crystallography also. A sixth edition, completely rewritten by Professor Edward S. Dana, the son of James D. Dana, was published in 1892.

The four years from the summer of 1838 to that of 1842 stand strongly in contrast with the remainder of Professor Dana's career. In those years he had an experience of the adventures, the hardships, and perils, and no less of the joys, of the explorer of unknown lands and seas. The remainder of his life was in the main the quiet and uneventful life of the student. To him, as to his great contemporary, Charles Darwin, a period of world-wide travel, coming early in his career, with its opportunities of seeing most varied aspects of nature and life, was doubtless of immense value in storing his memory with material for scientific thought, and in leading him to broad views of cosmic processes. Most of all to a geologist is wide and varied travel an experience of inestimable importance.

The United States Exploring Expedition, under the command of Lieutenant (afterwards Admiral) Charles Wilkes, sailed from Norfolk, Virginia, August 18, 1838. The expedition consisted of six vessels—the *Vincennes*, the *Peacock*, the *Porpoise*, the *Relief*, the *Sea-gull*, and the *Flying-fish*. Of these, the first two were sloops-of-war, and were the principal vessels of the little squadron.

The last two were pilot boats. Asa Gray had been appointed Botanist of the expedition, and it was largely through his influence that Dana was induced to join the scientific staff as Mineralogist and Geologist. The lifelong friendship of these two great men, which was so full of inspiration to both in their long scientific careers, had already begun. Various causes, however, led Gray to resign his position before the departure of the expedition. The limits of this article will not allow any consideration of Wilkes' memorable voyage along the coast of the Antarctic continent, of the important work done by the naval officers of the expedition in charting seas and islands previously unknown, or even of the work of the other naturalists. Only an outline can be given of the journeys, explorations, and experiences in which Dana himself had a share. At the start, Dana was assigned to the *Peacock*, and he shared the fortunes of that vessel most of the time until the shipwreck which ended her career.

The expedition crossed the Atlantic to Madeira, where Dana had an opportunity for some study of the geology of the island. Then a short visit was paid to the Cape Verde Islands, after which the squadron sailed to Rio Janeiro, where it remained about six weeks. The long stay at Rio was for the purpose of making repairs and taking additional supplies. After leaving Rio, the voyagers doubled Cape Horn, and the ships assembled in Orange Harbor on the west side of Nassau Bay. From this point some of the ships sailed southward for exploration in the Antarctic regions, while the *Relief*, to which Dana had been transferred, was ordered to a cruise in the Strait of Magellan. Unfavorable and violent winds baffled for many days the attempt to enter the strait. The troubles of this part of the expedition culminated in a terrific storm of three days' duration, in which the ship lost all but one of her anchors and very narrowly escaped shipwreck. The *Relief* then sailed to Valparaiso, and in the course of a few weeks the *Vincennes* and the *Peacock* arrived at the same port. Dana and the other naturalists improved the opportunity to make some excursions into the Chilian Andes. From Valparaiso the squadron proceeded northward to Callao, and then sailed westward across the Pacific in the summer of 1839. The main work of the expedition—the exploration and charting of the Polynesian archipelagoes—was now to begin. They reached first the Paumotu or Low Archipelago, where Dana had his first introduction to the problems of the coral islands. Next, Tahiti was visited, where Dana and others ascended Mount Aorai, and made important geological observations. After a visit to the Samoan Islands, the expedition proceeded to Sydney, Australia, where they arrived about the first of December. From this point Wilkes sailed southward with the *Vincennes*, the *Peacock*, and the *Porpoise*, and on January 16, 1840, discovered the Antarctic Continent—the most important geographical result achieved by the expedition. When the navigators started on the Antarctic cruise, the naturalists were left at Sydney. After some weeks spent in the study of the geology and natural history of Australia, they proceeded to New Zealand, where the expedition reassembled in the spring of 1840. The Tonga and Fiji groups of islands were then explored. The murder of two of the officers of the expedition by the then savage Fijians was one of the tragedies of the voyage. In the early autumn of that year the explorers reached the Hawaiian Islands, where already the labors of American missionaries had been crowned by the development of a Christian civilization. The magnificent volcanoes of these islands afforded Dana the material for most important and fruitful study. In December, the *Peacock*, to which Dana was again attached, left Oahu on a long cruise in the Pacific, in which numerous groups of islands were visited. The ship narrowly escaped wreck by grounding on a reef among the Kingsmill Islands, whose cannibal inhabitants would have been far from hospitable to shipwrecked mariners. The cruise actually ended in the wreck and total destruction of the ship on the bar of the Columbia River, July 18, 1841. The lives of all on board were saved, but an important part of the scientific collections of the expedition was lost. A party of which Dana was a member then proceeded up the Willamette River and down the Sacramento to San Francisco, then a village of a few shanties. In October of that year the surviving vessels of the expedition assembled at San Francisco;

and a brig, the *Oregon*, was purchased to take the place of the *Peacock*. The squadron returned to the Hawaiian Islands for supplies. After some study of the Kuroshiwo, or Japanese Current, the expedition made a short visit to the Philippine Islands, then proceeded to Singapore, and returned home by way of the Cape of Good Hope, visiting on the way Cape Town and Saint Helena. The arrival at New York was in June, 1842.

In the next few years Dana's task was the preparation of reports of the scientific work of the expedition. He had undertaken, in the first organization of the scientific staff, the mineralogy and geology; but, in consequence of the retirement of one of the party at the beginning, and of another during the course of the expedition, he was led to undertake also two parts of the zoölogy, viz., the study of the crustacea and that of the corals. The report on Zoöphytes appeared in 1846, that on Geology in 1849, the first part of the report on Crustacea in 1852, and the remainder in 1854. The reports were issued in magnificent style, that on Crustacea forming two great quarto volumes, the others each one volume, and each report being accompanied by a folio atlas. It is, however, only in a very accommodated sense of the word that the scientific reports of the expedition can be said to have been published. The number of copies authorized by Congress to be printed was so small that they have been from the beginning inaccessible to most of the students who would have profited by their use, only a very few of the largest libraries possessing complete or nearly complete sets. This absurd policy contrasts strongly with the enlightened liberality with which the more recent scientific publications of the United States government have been distributed. For about two years after the return of the expedition, Dana worked in Washington, but in 1844 he returned to New Haven, where he resided until his death.

He married, June 5, 1844, Henrietta Silliman, a daughter of his teacher and friend, Benjamin Silliman. The home life of more than half a century which thus began was most happy. Mrs. Dana and four children survived him. The oldest son, Professor Edward Salisbury Dana, of Yale University, is a distinguished mineralogist, and was the editor—perhaps it should rather be said, the author—of the last edition of the *System of Mineralogy*.

In 1846, Professor Dana became associated with his former teacher, Professor Silliman, as one of the editors of the *American Journal of Science*. The history of that periodical is indeed a remarkable one. Founded by the elder Silliman in 1818, it has continued ever since under the editorial charge of a single family, though a considerable number of the most eminent scientific men of the country have been for longer or shorter periods associate editors. Professor J. D. Dana was the chief editor from 1871 until his death. His son, Professor E. S. Dana, succeeded him. In the earlier years the journal was entitled *American Journal of Science and Arts*. Gradually its scope came to be restricted to pure science, and in 1880 the words, "and arts," were dropped from the title. The successive volumes of the Journal form a history of American scientific work for more than three-quarters of a century. The intelligence and liberality and the thoroughly non-partisan spirit with which it has been conducted, have made it a most potent and a most salutary influence in American science.

In 1850 Dana was elected Silliman Professor of Natural History in Yale College, and he remained a member of the faculty of that institution until his death. He did not, however, enter upon the work of teaching until the college year 1855–56, being occupied in the meantime in the preparation of the reports of the Exploring Expedition. In 1864, his title was changed from Professor of Natural History to Professor of Geology and Mineralogy. He was actively engaged in the work of teaching (with short interruptions due to ill health) until 1890. In 1894 he was formally recognized as *Professor emeritus*. During his term of service the little college of the middle of the century grew into the great university of the close of the century. He was influential in the organization of the Sheffield Scientific School, though his own teaching was always chiefly, and most of the time exclusively, in the college proper.

Professor Dana's clearness of exposition, his enthusiasm for his subject, and his genial spirit made him an inspiring teacher.

His field excursions with his classes are gratefully remembered by multitudes of students whose interest in geology was merely incidental. The small number of advanced students who were destined to be themselves geologists, came to know more intimately the mind and heart of their master, and cherish his memory with reverent love.

A certain amount of teaching is undoubtedly a help to the investigator. The work of exposition is an aid to clear thinking. The human interest of imparting knowledge and awakening the intellectual life of others gives a new fervor to one's own intellectual life and a new zest to the work of acquiring knowledge. It is, however, the misfortune of many teachers to be so overloaded with routine duties as to have no time for the work of investigation, of which they might otherwise be capable. It was the good fortune of Professor Dana to have enough of teaching and not too much. His teaching made him greater as an investigator, and left him time for investigation.

The career of Professor Dana reminds us in various ways of that of Darwin. In the great duration of productive activity, in the number and variety of the subjects which engaged their attention, in the adventurous world-wide exploration at the beginning of the career of each, and the half-century of peaceful home life that followed, the two careers were much alike. The experience of the two great scientists was alike also in the fact of impaired health, and of pathetic struggle to husband a scanty capital of physical vigor and endurance so as to make it yield the largest possible income of intellectual achievement. When about forty-five years of age, Dana found his health showing signs of breakdown from the effects of overwork. In 1859–60 he was compelled to take a year of rest, which was spent in travel in Europe. The months of travel brought only partial restoration of health, and he was not able to resume his college duties till 1862. In December of that year he wrote to Darwin: "I have worked to great disadvantage, from one to three hours a day, and often not at all. An hour's intercourse with the students in the lecture-room is a day's work for me." The two illustrious sufferers could well sympathize with each other. Professor Dana was compelled to drop his college work, for longer or shorter periods, in 1869, 1874, and 1880, and in 1890 he finally relinquished the work of teaching. All through the last four decades of his life he worked under the oppressive limitations of nervous exhaustion. He conscientiously avoided all social excitements, very rarely attending even the meetings of scientific associations. By thorough self-control, by careful regimen as regards sleep and exercise, by the conscientious economizing of the short working periods which his weary head could bear, and by the watchful care of his wife, he was enabled to keep up his intellectual activity and productiveness beyond the age of four-score.

In 1862 was published the book which has probably had, on the whole, a larger influence on the general intellectual life of the world than any other of Dana's writings—the *Manual of Geology*. Later editions of this work were published in 1871, 1880, and 1895. The fourth edition was the last important labor of his life, appearing only a few weeks before his death. In 1864, Dana published a smaller book entitled, *Text-book of Geology*, of which several later editions have been published, and which has been very widely used in the colleges and high schools of this country.

In 1872 was published *Corals and Coral Islands*—an elegantly illustrated book, in which were presented in semi-popular form some of the results of Dana's work in the Exploring Expedition. A second edition of this work was published in 1890

In the summer of 1887, Dana visited again the Hawaiian volcanoes, which he had first studied almost a half-century before. Great changes in means of communication and in the condition of the Hawaiian Islands had taken place since 1840, and the journey was a far easier one than at the earlier date. It was nevertheless somewhat of an adventure for a man seventy-four years of age.

In 1890 was published *Characteristics of Volcanoes*. In this work the Hawaiian volcanoes are very fully described, and the general theory of vulcanism is discussed. In addition to the studies of the Hawaiian Islands in 1840 and in 1887, Dana had seen in his circumnavigation of the globe and in his European tours a great variety of volcanic phenomena. The book was the fruit of manifold observation and mature thought.

His intellectual activity and clearness of thought continued to the very end of his life. In the last months he corrected the proofs of the fourth edition of the *Manual of Geology*—the noblest of all his works. He had commenced a revision of the *Text-book of Geology*, but the completion of that work was reserved for the hand of a friend and pupil. The *Journal of Science* for March, 1895, contained a brief article on *Daimonelix* signed with the initials, J. D. D. On Friday, April 12, he wrote a letter to Mr. Frank Leverett, containing a clear discussion of the conditions of eolian work and the limits of its effects. Two days later, on the evening of Easter Sunday, he passed into the eternal rest.

The appreciation of the work of Dana by other scientific men was testified by the honors which came to him in abundance. Amherst, Harvard, and Edinburgh gave him the degree of Doctor of Laws, Munich that of Doctor of Philosophy. He was President of the American Association for the Advancement of Science and of the Geological Society of America, and Vice-President of the National Academy of Sciences. He was elected to membership in the Royal Societies of London, Edinburgh, and Dublin, and the Academies of Paris, Saint Petersburg, Vienna, Berlin, Güttingen, Munich, Stockholm, and Buda-Pesth. He received the Copley Medal of the Royal Society of London, the Wollaston Medal of the Royal Geological Society of London, the Clarke Memorial Medal of the Royal Society of New South Wales, and the Walker Prize of the Boston Society of Natural History.

The science to which the early years of Professor Dana's productive activity were chiefly devoted was mineralogy. The *System of Mineralogy*, published in 1837, took rank at once as a standard treatise—rather, one might be justified in saying, *the* standard treatise of the science.

In the first two editions, Dana followed the so-called " natural classification " of Mohs, in which the groups depended chiefly on conspicuous physical characters, such as hardness, luster, and specific gravity; and he proposed an original Latin nomenclature similar to that used in botany and zoölogy. In the third edition (1850), the "natural classification" was abandoned, with the frank statement that it was "false to nature in its most essential points;" and Dana's own Latin nomenclature was not even mentioned in the synonymy. It had become obvious that the primary basis of mineralogical classification must be found in chemistry, while, within the groups established on chemical grounds, subdivisions must be based largely on crystalline form. It was further recognized that the more comprehensive groups must be founded not on the metallic, or electropositive, constituents, but rather on the non-metallic, or electronegative, constituents, and very largely on the type of the chemical formula. For instance, the iron-holding minerals, or the copper-holding minerals, would form an utterly heterogeneous group; but the sulphides, or the carbonates, or the silicates, would form a relatively homogeneous and consistent group. Among the sulphides, again, the monosulphides and the disulphides would form rational subdivisions. A system of classification based primarily on chemical principles as now understood, with subdivisions characterized by identity or similarity of crystalline form, recognizes all the true relations which were expressed in the so-called " natural system," and which the earlier forms of chemical classification conspicuously failed to recognize. In Part VI of his third edition, Dana outlined the "chemico-crystallographic classification"—a classification whose general plan has been almost universally adopted, though the progress of mineral chemistry has made possible great improvement in the details.[1] This classification was proposed tentatively in the third edition, a merely provisional classification being used in the arrangement of the descriptive part of the book. The new classification was definitively adopted in the fourth edition (1858).

The fourth edition introduced a remarkably elegant system of symbols for crystalline forms. The treatment of crystallography, in this, as in the previous editions, followed in general the method

[1] A classification essentially similar to Dana's was proposed two years later by Gustav Rose, in his *Krystallo-chemisches Mineral-system.*

of Naumann. In the sixth edition (edited by E. S. Dana), the system of Miller is followed, though the symbols of J. D. Dana adapted to the system of Naumann are also given.

The fact is worthy of incidental mention that J. D. Dana constructed a series of glass models of crystals as early as 1835— probably the first models of this kind.

The fifth edition of the *System of Mineralogy* is a monumental work in the thoroughness with which the literature of the science was ransacked to give completeness and accuracy to the synonymy. The changes made in the successive editions have kept pace with the progress of science; and the book still stands, as it stood more than seventy years ago, at the head of the encyclopedic treatises on descriptive mineralogy.

Dana's reputation as a zoölogist rests chiefly upon the Reports on the Zoöphytes, and on the Crustacea, of the United States Exploring Expedition. Each of these great works is illustrated with a magnificent folio atlas, many of the figures being colored. All the figures of Crustacea and most of those of Zoöphytes are from Dana's own drawings. More than two hundred new species of coral animals, and more than five hundred new species of Crustacea, are described. Besides the vast amount of detail work represented by the description of so many new species, these reports contributed to the progress of science by the advanced views on classification which they presented.

The Report on Zoöphytes especially was an epoch-making work in that department of science. The number of known species of coral animals was almost doubled by Dana's collections. Moreover, most of the species previously described had been based on the skeleton (coral) alone, few naturalists having had any opportunity to see the creatures alive or to study their soft parts. Naturally, therefore, the relations of the known species were but imperfectly understood. Dana's report, accordingly, did not confine itself to the species collected in the expedition, but included all species then known. It was thus a monograph of the entire group. The number of species of the coral animals recognized was 483, of which 229 were new. The Zoöphytes were divided into the two orders, Actinoidea and Hydroidea; and the former of these orders was divided into the two suborders, Actinaria and Alcyonaria. The order Actinoidea, as defined by Dana, is equivalent to the class Anthozoa, or Actinozoa, as generally recognized by zoölogists to-day; and his two suborders of Actinoidea exactly represent the two orders into which most naturalists would divide the class to-day. In Dana's work, then, was published for the first time a classification involving both a correct delimitation of the group of Anthozoa (sea-anemones and coral animals), and a true discrimination of its two main divisions. The advance of knowledge in the last half-century has made important changes in the details of the classification, but in its broad outlines Dana's classification has stood the test of time.

The study of the Crustacea was in a more advanced state than that of the corals before Dana's work. There was no occasion, therefore, for a revision of the whole group in his Report on the Crustacea. It is, however, a striking proof of the diligence with which the work of collecting was prosecuted under manifold difficulties that he catalogues six hundred and eighty species collected in the Expedition, of which over five hundred were new.

The study of this group of animals suggested to Dana a striking generalization, which was first enunciated in the Report on Crustacea, but which was later discussed more fully in a number of papers, most of which were published in the *Journal of Science* (1863–66)—the principle of *cephalization*.

In the Crustacea, as in the Arthropoda in general, each segment of the many-jointed body bears typically a pair of jointed appendages, which are serially homologous, though appropriated to different functions. In the highest Crustacea, as the crabs and lobsters (Decapoda), the eight anterior segments bear appendages cephalic (*i. e.*, sensory or oral) in function; namely, two pairs of antennæ, one pair of mandibles, two pairs of maxillæ, and three pairs of accessary mouth-organs (maxillipeds); while the next five segments bear the principal locomotive appendages. In a lower group represented by the sow-bugs and sand-fleas (Arthrostraca), the second and third pairs of maxillipeds are represented by legs, so that these creatures have only six cephalic (sensory and oral) segments, and seven, instead of five, locomotive segments. In still lower Crustacea (Entomostraca), the number of functionally cephalic appendages is still less, even the antennæ becoming sometimes organs of locomotion or adhesion. Moreover, in the crabs (Brachyura), which form the highest division of the Decapoda, the posterior part of the body is greatly reduced in size, and most of its segments are destitute of appendages. The whole body seems almost, so to speak, absorbed into the head. The larger number of appendages appropriated to cephalic functions in the higher Crustacea is naturally correlated with a greater development of the cephalic ganglion. It was natural that the contemplation of facts like these should suggest to a mind so fond of generalization as was that of Dana the broad principle that, as "anteroposterior polarity" characterizes animals in distinction from plants, so the grade of different animal forms in comparison with each other is shown by the "degree of structural subordination to the head and of concentration headward in body structure."

The principle is an important and valuable one. Certainly, as we pass from the lower, and in general the earlier, types of animal life, to the higher, and in general the later, types, there is a tremendous advance in cephalization. From a protozoan, destitute even of a mouth (the earliest cephalic feature to be developed), or from a sea-anemone, whose symmetry is radial rather than bilateral, and in which therefore there is but faint indication of an anteroposterior axis, to man, with his immense brain, there is a tremendous advance in "degree of structural subordination to the head." In Dana's application of the principle of cephalization to zoölogical classification, there was much of ingenuity. But it cannot be denied that he sometimes gave undue weight to mere analogies. A notable example of this is his argument for the ordinal distinctness of man from other mammals, on the ground that his anterior limbs, instead of being locomotive in function, are used for prehension and manipulation. They are, according to his conception, cephalic organs—organs appropriated to the immediate service of the brain. Now, among the Crustacea, the Decapoda, as we have seen, have eight pairs of cephalic organs and five pairs of locomotive organs, while the Arthrostraca have six pairs of cephalic organs and seven pairs of locomotive organs, the second and third pairs of maxillipeds in the former group being homologous with the first two pairs of legs in the latter. In like manner, the last pair of oral (cephalic) appendages in Insects—the labium—is believed to be homologous with the first pair of legs in the Arachnoids. Dana's argument was, accordingly, that the distinction in regard to the use of the anterior limbs in man and other mammals was analogous to the cases cited among the Arthropoda, and that man must therefore be made at least a distinct order in the classification. There is of course no homology between vertebrate limbs and arthropodan appendages; and Dana's argument, based on a mere analogy, and not a very close analogy, has no force as viewed from the standpoint of zoölogy to-day. Viewing Dana's discussion of cephalization from the modern evolutionary standpoint, one might make the general criticism that the distinction of high and low, which he emphasized, is of vastly less significance than that of generalized and specialized. Low forms may be primitive, or they may be degenerate. A vertebrate destitute of limbs would naturally be regarded as a low, or degraded type. But the lamprey is destitute of fins because it is a survival of a primitive type antedating the evolution of limbs, while the snake has lost the legs which its lizard ancestors possessed. Writing before he had adopted the theory of evolution, Dana of course failed to appreciate this distinction.

Dana was not an early convert to the theory of evolution. It is interesting to compare, with reference to their attitude toward the theory of evolution, the three men who were the leading naturalists of this country in the middle of the nineteenth century—Gray, Agassiz, and Dana. Gray was ready to welcome the Darwinian theory when first promulgated. In a letter to Dana in 1857, he wrote the prophetic words, "You may be sure that before long there must be one or more resurrections of the development theory in a new form." One year later the prophecy was fulfilled by Darwin and Wallace. Agassiz remained till his death a strenuous and bitter antagonist of the evolution theory. Dana at first opposed the theory, but later, with characteristic candor, gave it a somewhat qualified assent.

About the middle of the nineteenth century, the majority of naturalists regarded the theory of evolution in any form as dead beyond hope of resurrection. The general conception of transmutation of species was supposed to have been buried in the same grave with the crudities of Lamarck and of the "Vestiges of Creation." Weismann says, "We who were then the younger men, studying in the fifties, had no idea that a theory of evolution had ever been put forward, for no one spoke of it to us, and it was never mentioned in a lecture." Dana himself, in his *Thoughts on Species*,[1] had formulated the somewhat metaphysical doctrine that "a species corresponds to a specific amount or condition of concentered force defined in the act or law of creation." This formula was supposed to apply alike to chemical elements and compounds —the species of the inorganic world—and to the species of plants and animals. The permanence of species seemed to follow *a priori* from this conception. Dana was also disinclined to the theory of evolution on theological grounds, since he was under the influence of a phase of natural theology then prevalent, which found the most convincing evidence of a personal God in the supposed breaks in the continuity of nature. Another cause of the lateness of Dana's accession to the evolution theory was the fact that the date of publication of the *Origin of Species*, approximately coincided with the date of the breakdown of Dana's health. On this account he did not read Darwin's book for several years after its publication, and naturally failed to appreciate how greatly the status of the evolution theory was changed. We know from the correspondence between Dana and Darwin that Dana did not read the *Origin* till some time after February, 1863.

In the second edition of the *Manual of Geology* (1871), Dana still maintained the permanence of species. "Geology," he declared, "has brought to light no facts sustaining a theory that

[1] *American Journal of Science*, series 2, vol. 24, pp. 305–316.

derives species from others." But in the second edition of the *Text-book of Geology*, published in 1874, he took a somewhat qualified evolutionary position, in the following statements: "The evolution of the system of life went forward through the derivation of species from species, according to natural methods not yet clearly understood, and with few occasions for supernatural intervention. The method of evolution admitted of abrupt transitions between species. For the development of man there was required, as Wallace has urged, the special act of a Being above nature." In the two remaining decades of Professor Dana's life, his faith in evolution became somewhat more decided. In the last edition of the *Manual of Geology*, he gave much fuller recognition than before to Darwin's principle of natural selection, though holding more nearly a neo-Lamarckian than a strictly Darwinian view of the method of evolution. He still maintained that "the intervention of a Power above nature was at the basis of man's development." In the same paragraph he declared that "nature exists through the will and ever-acting power of the Divine Being," and that "the whole universe is not merely dependent on, but actually is, the will of one Supreme Intelligence." One is tempted to ask why, if all nature is thus divine, we need to assume for man a supernatural origin. A truer evolutionary theistic philosophy recognizes so fully an immanent God in the continuity of nature that it seeks no apparent breaks of continuity wherein to find him.

Though Professor Dana's faith in the doctrine of evolution was, even to the end, a little hesitant, it must be recognized as a remarkable proof of his open-mindedness and candor that, at an age when most men's opinions are already petrified, he was able to make so radical a change, and frankly to adopt the views he had so long and so ably opposed. In 1863, Darwin wrote to Dana as follows: "Pray do not suppose that I think for one instant that, with your strong and slowly acquired convictions and immense knowledge, you could have been converted. The utmost that I could have hoped would have been that you might have been here or there staggered." But the unexpected happened; and in the course of the next decade Darwin could rejoice over his friend's conversion. The accession to the ranks of the evolutionists of one whose learning was so vast and varied, whose thinking was so conservative, and whose spirit was so devout, was a very potent factor in promoting the acceptance of the doctrine among thinkers outside the ranks of scientific specialists.

Valuable as were the investigations of Professor Dana in mineralogy and in zoölogy, his great work was in geology. The last three decades of his life were devoted almost entirely to that science. After the publication of the fifth edition of the *System of Mineralogy*, in 1868, he scarcely published anything outside of the field of geology. No other science was so well adapted to the tastes and capabilities of a mind so strongly disposed to broad views of comprehensive relations. As Dana himself remarked, "Geology is all the sciences combined into one." In such a science such a mind might well find its chosen field.

The *Manual of Geology*, has been since its first publication the one indispensable book of reference for any American geologist. Apart from its unique character as a manual of American geology, it is unquestionably one of the best manuals of geology in general. But it must not be forgotten that Dana's contributions to geology include more than one hundred and fifty books and papers of greater or less length and importance besides the encyclopedic *Manual*.

Perhaps the most characteristic contribution of Dana to geology was in rendering more clear and definite the conception of the scope and significance of the science. There is a little exaggeration in Le Conte's statement that "geology became one of the great departments of abstract science, with its own characteristic idea and its own distinctive method under Dana." [1] Yet the statement contains an important truth. More or less clearly all geological investigators must have felt that the distinctive idea of geology is that the structures shown in the rocks of the earth's crust, whether on the large scale or on the small scale, whether seen in the panoramic view of the landscape or discerned by the micro-

[1] *Bulletin of the Geological Society of America*, vol. 7, p. 463.

scope, have their supreme significance as monumental inscriptions, the deciphering of which may reveal to us the history of the earth. Yet surely this conception had never been so clearly formulated, and the whole treatment of the subject never so consistently adjusted thereto, as in the writings of Dana. The portion of previous manuals dealing with the distribution of the series of strata had generally borne some such title as "Stratigraphical Geology"; and very commonly the series had been traced backward, commencing with the most recent strata.[1] The phrase, "Historical Geology," which forms the title of that part of Dana's *Manual*, involves a distinct clarification of the general view of the science. Starting with this conception, of course he deals with the earliest formations first. In treating of each era, he endeavors to reconstruct, from the evidence afforded by the kinds and distribution of the rocks, the physical geography of the time. In accordance with this general principle, the sections of the Historical Geology in the *Manual* were not characterized as series, systems, and groups of strata, but as eras, periods, and epochs of time. The common use in recent geological writings of such phrases as "Silurian era," rather than "Silurian system," etc., is a testimony to the influence of Dana's mode of treatment.[2] The key-note of Dana's conception of geology as history is clearly sounded in his presidential address before the American Association for the Advancement of Science in 1855. The title of the address is significant—*On American Geological History*. In that address occurs the following passage: "Geology is not simply the science of rocks, for rocks are but incidents in the earth's history, and may or may not have been the same in distant places. It has its more exalted end,—even the study of the progress of life from its earliest dawn to the appearance of man; and instead of saying that fossils are of use to determine rocks, we should rather say that the rocks are of use for the display of the succession of fossils."

To Dana we owe the formulation of a doctrine now almost universally adopted by geologists—the doctrine of the permanence

[1] As in the manuals by Lyell and De la Bèche.
[2] Williams, in *Journal of Geology*, vol. 3, p. 606.

of continents and oceans. It is of course a fact familiar to all students of geology that nearly if not quite the whole surface of our existing continents has been covered at some time by the waters of the sea. This naturally suggested the belief which was held by Lyell, the great master of geology in the middle of the nineteenth century, as it had been held in general by his predecessors, that continent and ocean have repeatedly changed places. Moreover, the strictly uniformitarian doctrine of Lyell was adverse to any notion of progressive change in any definite direction. Lyell, accordingly, conceived of a perfectly indefinite, kaleidoscopic interchange of continent and ocean in the course of geological time. The Lyellian doctrine finds beautiful expression in the familiar lines of *In Memoriam:*—

> "There rolls the deep where grew the tree.
> O earth, what changes thou hast seen!
> There, where the long street roars, hath been
> The stillness of the central sea."

Dana, on the contrary, believed that our present continents and oceans were outlined as areas of relative elevation and depression, respectively, in the crust of the globe, in the very beginning of geological time. The progress of geographical evolution has been, in the broadest view, a subsidence of the ocean bottoms, a withdrawal of the waters more and more into the deepening basins, and consequently a progressive emergence of continental lands. The substantial truth of this view, enunciated by Dana in 1846,[1] hardly admits of doubt; though there has been an amount of oscillation, in connection with the progressive deepening of the oceans and emergence of the lands, which Dana seems not to have adequately appreciated. The greater density of the sub-oceanic masses in comparison with the subcontinental masses, as shown by pendulum observations, indicates that the distinction between continent and ocean depends on the heterogeneity of the material in the interior of the earth; and the determining conditions must therefore have had their origin in the initial aggregation of

[1] *American Journal of Science*, series 2, vol. 2, p. 353.

the part of the primitive meteoric swarm which formed the earth; or, perhaps, as suggested by Chamberlin and Salisbury, in the changes attendant upon the beginning of the formation of the ocean. The study of the sedimentary formations which cover our existing continents shows that almost all of them were deposited in shallow waters, many of the strata, indeed, in waters so shallow that the layers of mud and sand were from time to time exposed by the receding tide or subsiding freshet, to dry and crack in the sun or to be pitted by raindrops. Scarcely any of the strata bear evidences of deposition in water of very considerable depth. Even the chalk of England and of Texas was probably not deposited in waters of oceanic depth.

Another general topic in dynamical geology for whose elucidation we are greatly indebted to the writings of Dana is the process of mountain-making.[1]   That the main cause of mountain elevation is the tangential pressure in the earth's crust resulting from internal contraction, is now somewhat generally acknowledged; though there may be doubt whether the main cause of contraction is the cooling of the earth from an incandescent condition, as assumed in the commonly accepted form of the nebular theory, or the gravitational adjustment of an incoherent aggregation of planetesimals, as assumed in the more recent hypothesis of Chamberlin and Moulton. Whatever the cause or causes of internal contraction, its effect in causing crustal wrinkles would be the same. As, in Dana's homely illustration, the smooth skin of the plump, fresh apple becomes wrinkled when the apple dries and shrivels, so the earth's skin must wrinkle if the interior decreases in volume. The idea of the contractional origin of mountains was not original with Dana. A glimmer of the idea appears in the writings of Leibnitz. Constant Prévost appears

---

[1] The views of Le Conte on this subject are in most points similar to those of Dana; but, while Le Conte's discussions have been of great value, the priority in the general development of the theory belongs to Dana. See the noble and generous tribute of Le Conte, in his obituary of Dana, read before the Geological Society of America, and published in vol. 7 of the *Bulletin* of the Society.

to have been the first to develop the idea into a definite scientific theory. But the elaboration of the theory into its present form is largely the work of Dana. His earliest discussion of the subject appeared in the *Journal of Science* in 1847. In later years he returned to the subject again and again; and the theory, as shaped by his maturest thought, appears in the last edition of the *Manual*. In his earlier writings, his views of the origin of continents and mountains are developed on the assumption of a liquid globe. In later years he abandoned that view, and adjusted his theories to the more probable doctrine of a globe substantially solid.

Dana's conception of the origin of mountains may be formulated somewhat as follows: In the contraction of the earth's interior, the suboceanic crust is the chief seat of subsidence. As the suboceanic crust, in its subsidence, necessarily flattens, so that its profile continually approaches the chord of the arc, it exerts a tangential thrust towards the continental areas. The rather abrupt change in the radius of curvature, in passing from the oceanic to the continental areas, determines lines of weakness along the continental borders, which mark in general the location of the great mountain wrinkles. The crustal wrinkles will involve upward and downward folds—*geanticlines* and *geosynclines* (in distinction from simple anticlines and synclines, which are foldings of strata on a much smaller scale both in breadth and depth). A gradually subsiding geosynclinal trough along the border of a continent may naturally be kept full of sediment deposited *pari passu* with the subsidence. Thus strata may accumulate in narrow tracts to immense thickness, as in the case of the Appalachians, taken by Dana as a type of mountain structure, where the strata are more than six miles in thickness. The progressive subsidence carries the lower strata of the mass to a depth where they are affected by the internal heat of the earth, since the isogeotherms are nearly parallel with the surface. These water-loaded sediments are softened in much greater degree by the high temperatures which they encounter than the nearly anhydrous crystalline rocks which they have displaced. The geosynclinal trough at last becomes so weak that the ever persistent tangential pressure crushes it together. The strata are thrown into alternating anticlines and synclines, or one part forced over another in great thrust faults, while slaty cleavage and more decided forms of metamorphism may be produced. A mountain range thus produced Dana calls a *synclinorium*. In such a process, the final crushing of the geosyncline is a movement relatively rapid in comparison with the age-long accumulation of sediment in the subsiding trough. Hence, in the history of any region, there are long ages of comparative tranquillity alternating with brief epochs of rapid geographical change—"revolutions," as Dana has somewhat poetically called them. These revolutions are the time boundaries of geological history, delimiting the eons and eras into which geological time is divided. Thus an evolutionary geology recognizes the truths in the two systems of catastrophism and uniformitarianism which it has displaced.

While in most mountain regions the thick masses of strongly folded, thrust, and metamorphosed strata bear witness to the crushing of a geosyncline, Dana also recognized that a geanticline may result in a permanent elevation. Such a mountain range he proposed to call an *anticlinorium*. There is reason to believe that the actual history of most mountain ranges is complex. Thus, the Appalachian range was formed by the crushing of a geosyncline at the close of Paleozoic time, degraded nearly to base-level by atmospheric and aqueous action in Mesozoic time, and again elevated by a broad geanticlinal movement early in Cenozoic time. In these two phases of elevation it may serve to illustrate Dana's two types of mountain range—the synclinorium and the anticlinorium. Its present topography of ridge and valley is due to erosion subsequent to the Cenozoic elevation.

There are unquestionably weak points in the theory of mountain-making as thus developed; and, in our ignorance of the conditions in the interior of the earth and of the forces there in action, it ill becomes us to be dogmatic. But the theory is certainly a beautiful one, and is worthy of a provisional acceptance as the most plausible explanation of orogenic processes yet suggested.

Dana has illustrated his conception of geographical evolution by the concrete example of the development of the continent of North America.[1] The continent is pictured at the beginning of Paleozoic time, showing a V-shaped area of land composed of Archæan rocks, with the apex of the V in the region of Lake Superior, and its arms extending northeastward to Labrador and northwestward to the Arctic Ocean, while other linear areas of Archæan rock (*protaxes*) mark the positions of the Appalachian chain on the east and the Cordillera on the west. Between the Appalachian and the Cordilleran protaxis lies a vast Mediterranean sea of shallow water (the Mississippian Sea, as it has been appropriately named), in which sedimentary deposits are gradually accumulating, while its northern shore-line along the Archæan V moves gradually southward, as the progressive oceanic subsidence allows strip after strip of dry land to emerge and to be annexed to the primitive nucleus of the continent. So the Paleozoic strata crop out in parallel bands through New York and westward. The tranquil progress is interrupted by the Taconic revolution (post-Ordovician), uplifting a mountain range in western New England and eastern New York, and probably other ranges now in ruins farther south; and later by the Appalachian revolution (post-Carboniferous), uplifting the Appalachian range from the Catskills to the mountains of Alabama. The eastern half of the continent becomes permanent dry land at the close of the Paleozoic, while the evolution of the western half—a newer territory geologically as well as politically—goes on through later time. The Sierra revolution (post-Jurassic) and the Laramide revolution (post-Cretaceous), uplifting respectively the Sierra Nevada and the main ranges of the Rocky Mountains, serve as time boundaries for the later ages of geological time, as the Taconic and the Appalachian revolutions for earlier ages.

The picture is a noble one, and in its main outlines true, though the actual history was less simple than the student would naturally

[1] Notably in his presidential address before the American Association for the Advancement of Science, in 1855; most fully, of course, in the *Manual of Geology.*

infer even from the last edition of the *Manual*. Dana recognizes indeed the occurrence of oscillations in the progressive emergence of the continent, but he seems not to appreciate adequately their magnitude and importance. In earliest Cambrian time, for instance, the area of dry land was far greater than in later Cambrian or Ordovician time. In the earliest Cambrian (Georgian period), the Mississippian Sea was only a sound or strait, the greater part of the area of the Mississippian Sea of later Cambrian and Ordovician time being then dry land. While the progressive deepening of the oceans and emergence of the continents is unquestionably a great truth, the oscillations were so considerable that an alternation of marine and terrestrial conditions over vast areas must be equally recognized. But we do not refuse the honor due to Copernicus, though he made the planetary orbits circular, instead of elliptical; and to Dana belongs no less the credit of the great conception of continental evolution, though he made the curve too simple.

Dana's first introduction to the problem of coral islands was at the Paumotu Islands in 1839. The coral animals, whose skeletons, broken or comminuted by the waves, furnish materials for the reefs, live only in shallow water, seldom ranging much below a depth of one hundred feet. It is accordingly readily intelligible that the debris of these skeletons may accumulate to form fringing reefs, closely bordering the shore of a continent or island. But a more difficult problem is presented by the barrier reefs and atolls. The barrier reefs may be separated from the shore by a channel ten or fifty miles in breadth or even more, and hundreds of feet in depth. Still more startling are the atolls—rings of coral reef, which may be crowned with scattered islets or with a more or less complete crest of dry land, inclosing a comparatively shallow lagoon, and surrounded by water deepening rapidly to thousands of feet, and far from any other land. The supposition that the reef has actually been built up from a depth of a thousand feet or more, is obviously inconsistent with the fact that the animals live only in shallow water. When Dana arrived at Sydney in the latter part of the year 1839, his mind was full of the problem, which he had not yet solved to his own satisfaction. Darwin had been at work at the problem three years earlier, and at Sydney Dana learned of Darwin's theory. It seemed to him then to explain the phenomena he had studied in the regions of barrier reefs and atolls which he had already visited; and the larger acquaintance with coral formations which he gained in the course of the next two years seemed to him only to bring ampler evidence of its truth. Although the original conception was Darwin's, Dana had the opportunity to study a vastly greater number and variety of coral formations than Darwin had ever seen, so that he was able to support the theory with a greater wealth of evidence than Darwin himself. Darwin welcomed most cordially so powerful an ally. Writing to Lyell, after receiving a copy of the Report on the Geology of the Exploring Expedition, he refers to the substantial agreement of Dana's views with his own, and adds, "Considering how infinitely more he saw of coral reefs than I did, this is wonderfully satisfactory to me. He treats me most courteously."

The theory of Darwin and Dana may be summed up in a single word—*subsidence*. If there occurs, along a coast of continent or island bordered by a fringing reef, a subsidence not more rapid than the upward growth of the reef, the coral growth and consequent reef formation will be most rapid on the outer margin of the reef, where the water is purest, and the supply of oxygen and of floating life available for food is greatest; and the channel between the reef and the shore will consequently become wider and deeper. Thus the fringing reef becomes a barrier reef. If an island is girt with a coral reef, the ultimate effect of a progressive subsidence will be to carry the original island entirely under water, leaving an atoll as a monument to mark its place of burial. The most important difference between Darwin's own conception of the theory and that of Dana was that Darwin, in the spirit of the Lyellian geology, thought of the Pacific area of coral islands as very likely marking the site of a drowned continent; while Dana, in accordance with his own doctrine of the essential permanence of continent and ocean, conceived the drowned lands to be only volcanic peaks, such as may be formed by submarine volcanic action in regions remote from continental land.

The history of the Darwinian theory has been a singular one. When first announced, it produced on most scientific minds the same impression of complete satisfaction that it produced upon the mind of Dana. The subsidence of large areas of the ocean bottom which it postulates, is sufficiently probable *a priori;* and the theory possesses that same charm of simplicity which characterizes Newton's conception of gravitation and Darwin's own theory of natural selection. Very naturally, therefore, for three or four decades, it was generally accepted as the one complete theory of barriers and atolls. Later researches, however, have shown conclusively that both barrier reefs and atolls may be formed without subsidence. At the southern extremity of Florida, three successive barrier reefs have been formed, all of which now have their crests almost at the same level, showing that there has been no crustal movement of any consequence. Chamisso long ago showed that an atoll might be formed on a submarine volcano, or on a shoal of any other origin, simply by the more luxuriant growth of corals on the margin than in the middle. Of course it was impossible to believe that several hundred submarine volcanoes had been raised to within about a hundred feet of the same level; but Murray showed that no such assumption of coincidence was necessary. A submarine volcano that did not rise into the zone of coral growth, could be built up by the accumulation of skeletons of other kinds of marine life until it reached that zone; while a volcano that rose a little above the sea-level might be degraded to a shoal by wave-action.

But, while it is certain that both barrier reefs and atolls can be formed without subsidence, it still seems probable that there has been a very extensive subsidence in the central part of the Pacific Ocean, and that this subsidence has been an important factor in the origin of the numerous atolls and barrier reefs of that region. In going northeastward from the zone of fringing reefs of the New Hebrides and Solomon Islands, one would traverse successively zones of barrier reefs, large atolls, small atolls, and blank ocean—

an arrangement which is strongly suggestive of a subsidence progressively increasing towards the middle of the ocean. The association of fringing reefs with active volcanoes and of barrier reefs with extinct volcanoes, as pointed out by Darwin, indicates that in some way the different kinds of coral formations are correlated with hypogene actions; and it is probable that the explanation of that relation lies in the theory that crustal elevation in any region diminishes the pressure on the rock masses in a condition of potential liquidity a few miles below the surface, thus lowering the melting-point, so that actual liquefaction takes place, and the molten materials find their way to the surface. The active volcanoes should therefore be in regions where the crust has been recently undergoing elevation, while in subsiding areas the volcanoes should be extinct. The lagoons in the larger atolls often show a depth much greater than the limiting depth of coral growth. This is probably evidence of subsidence, since there are very strong objections to Murray's notion that the lagoons are extensively widened and deepened by the solvent action of the sea-water. The core brought up from a bore eleven hundred feet deep, recently made on the island Funafuti in the Ellice group, is said to show no important change of character through its entire length. It appears, therefore, probable that a true coral reef rock extends down to the bottom of the bore and we know not how much farther. Such a thickness of reef could of course be formed only by subsidence. For these and other reasons it seems probable that Darwin and Dana were right in believing that the multitudinous barriers and atolls of the Pacific are evidence of subsidence of a vast area. It is hardly necessary to say that Dana's conception of the drowning of a multitude of oceanic volcanoes is more probable than Darwin's conception of the drowning of a continent.

Next to the study of the coral formations, the most important geological work done in the Exploring Expedition was in the study of volcanoes. Especially important was the detailed investigation of the Hawaiian volcanoes, though numerous extinct volcanoes were also studied in the course of the expedition. Dana's work contributed, with that of Scrope and Lyell, to the demolition of von Buch's theory of craters of elevation and the establishment of a true theory of the origin of volcanic cones. A volcanic cone is not a sort of blister on the earth's crust, formed by the uplifting of the strata by intumescent lavas beneath, but is simply a pile of erupted material.

In the years from 1871 to 1888, Dana was engaged in the investigation of the so-called "Taconic Question." A great series of schists, quartzites, and crystalline limestones, extending from Canada through western Vermont, Massachusetts, and Connecticut, and southeastern New York, had been described by Ebenezer Emmons, in 1842,[1] as the Taconic system, and by him and his followers was claimed to be older than the Champlain group of the New York geologists (now classified as Cambrian and Ordovician). Dana devoted much time to the investigation of the subject in the field. He also fortunately got hold of the notes of Rev. Augustus Wing, and thus rescued from undeserved oblivion the discoveries of a patient and conscientious investigator who had been too modest to publish his work. The result of the labors of Dana, Wing, Walcott, and others was the conclusive proof that the so-called Taconic system is not pre-Cambrian but metamorphosed Cambrian and Ordovician.

The Taconic question was not merely, though it was primarily, a question of local stratigraphy. The settlement of the age of the Taconic rocks fixed the date of the first important epoch of orogenic disturbance in the post-Archæan history of North America. The Taconic revolution stands as a time boundary between Ordovician and Silurian time. The settlement of the Taconic question was important, also, as establishing a perfectly clear case of somewhat highly crystalline rocks of Paleozoic age. It was thus a refutation of the belief of a school of geologists now extinct or nearly so, that all the crystalline schists and associated rocks are Archæan, and that a crystal is as good as a fossil to determine the age of a rock.

When the first edition of the *Manual of Geology* was published, opinions were still divided in regard to the origin of the hetero-

[1] *Geology of New York*, Part 2, pp. 135–164.

geneous mantle of clay, gravel, and boulders, covering much of the area of Canada and the northeastern United States, as well as northwestern Europe, and commonly called "drift." In opposition to the older diluvial theories, Agassiz had advocated the doctrine that the drift was due to the action of a glacier of continental extent. Dana clearly indicated his sympathy with the views of Agassiz in his presidential address before the American Association for the Advancement of Science in 1855, and in the *Manual* in 1862 the glacier theory of the drift was unqualifiedly adopted. Thenceforward the great influence of the *Manual of Geology* was unquestionably an important factor in the rapid progress of the glacier theory to substantially unanimous acceptance.

Dana gave much attention to a study of the terraces and other phenomena connected with the melting of the ice sheet, as shown in the vicinity of New Haven and in the Connecticut valley. The results of these studies were given in a number of papers published in the years from 1870 to 1883. While these papers show much of conscientious observation, their conclusions must be considerably modified in the light of more recent studies of the Glacial period.

The results of another study of Dana's own locality are given in an elegant little volume entitled *The Four Rocks of the New Haven Region*, published in 1891. In the careful study of East Rock, West Rock, Pine Rock, and Mill Rock, he showed unmistakably that the trap-rock of these picturesque hills formed intrusions in the Triassic sandstones. He was, however, in error in extending the same conclusion to the long series of ranges of trap hills from Saltonstall Ridge to Mount Holyoke. Though these hills are topographically similar to the New Haven "Rocks," and consist of similar material, it has been conclusively shown by Davis, Emerson, and others that the trap in them has the relation not of intrusions but of lava sheets outpoured upon the surface.

With Professor Dana's profound faith in Christianity, he could not be indifferent to the relations of science and religion. Believing that the opening chapters of Genesis contain the record of a divine revelation of the fact of creation, and, in some degree, of the order and method of creation, he could not be satisfied without asking and answering the question whether his scientific beliefs were in harmony with that revelation.   He published in 1856 a scheme of reconciliation of Genesis and geology,[1] for whose main outlines he acknowledged indebtedness to Professor Arnold Guyot. He further expounded the scheme with much learning and ingenuity in several later publications, and seems to have retained his faith in it to the end of his life.   It was one of the schemes of reconciliation in which the "days" of the first chapter of Genesis are regarded as symbolic of indefinite periods.   We need not in this connection take time for its discussion.   All these schemes of reconciliation belong to an obsolescent stage of religious thought. Intelligent and progressive theologians to-day generally believe that the reconciliation of scientific theories and Hebrew traditions is as unnecessary as it is impossible, and that Christian faith is in no wise dependent upon the scientific accuracy of Genesis or the inerrancy of Scripture in general.

So long as science is progressive, the study of the works even of the greatest scientists must be largely a study of errors.   Already we have outgrown some of the geological views which Professor Dana held to the end of his life, and which find expression even in the latest edition of the *Manual;* as, for instance, on the origin of many of the gneissoid rocks, the extent of climatic oscillations in the Glacial period, the conditions of the rivers during the formation of post-Glacial terraces, the relations of the igneous to the sedimentary rocks in the Trias of Connecticut and New Jersey. But, when we consider the number and importance of the fruitful ideas in geological science of which we owe to Dana the origination or the elaboration, and the breadth of view and the judicial temper and the just sense of perspective which gave to the *System of Mineralogy* and the *Manual of Geology* a character so authoritative, we shall feel like assenting to the words of Professor John W. Judd, in a letter to Professor E. S. Dana on the occasion of his father's death: "Geologists and mineralogists all over the world will feel that the greatest of all the masters of our science has now passed away."

[1] *Bibliotheca Sacra*, vol. 13, pp. 110–129.

The consideration of the life and the scientific work of James Dwight Dana has already made us acquainted with some of his most marked traits of character. Yet it may be worth while to conclude this sketch with an attempt at a picture of the man.

The characteristic that most impressed all who came to know him, whether through the reading of his works or through personal intercourse, was his profound sense of the sacredness of truth. With absolute sincerity he sought to know the truth and to communicate to others the truth as it had revealed itself to him. No pride in what is wrongly called consistency wrought in him unwillingness to accept new light. Even to extreme old age he remained hospitable to new truth and ready to change opinions. It was said of a very learned man that his forte was science and his foible was omniscience. Dana had no such foible. He seemed to take pleasure in confessing ignorance or error. In the third edition of his *System of Mineralogy*, when he cast aside the classification and the Latin binomial nomenclature of the former editions, he wrote in the preface: "To change is always seeming fickleness. But not to change with the advance of science is worse; it is persistence in error." He said to me, in speaking of the changes introduced in the third edition of the *Manual of Geology*, "When a man is too old to learn, he is ready to die; or at least he is not fit to live." The frankness with which he changed his opinions and his teachings on the subject of evolution, when past threescore years of age, is a striking illustration of his loyalty to truth, and of the perennial intellectual youth which is the reward that truth gives to her loyal worshipers. The same exquisitely delicate sense of truth which made him so ready to change opinions, made it easy for him to hold opinion in abeyance. He knew that he did not know some things, and he would not assert plausible conjectures as truths. Professor Farrington has preserved some of the aphorisms which he uttered from time to time, and which might well be adopted as maxims by all students of science.[1] "I think it better to doubt until you know. Too many people assert and then let others doubt." "I have found it best

[1] *Journal of Geology*, vol. 3, p. 335.

to be always afloat in regard to opinions on geology." "I always like to change when I can make a change for the better."

His liberality in the treatment of difference of opinion was another phase of his devotion to truth. Sensible of the liability to error attending the beliefs of all men, he recognized that only by the criticism of opposing views could truth be reached. The pages of the *Journal of Science* were always freely open for the presentation of views most widely divergent from those of the editor. "More," he said, "could be learned by studying unconformities than conformities," and this he believed to be as true of unconformable opinions as of unconformable strata.[1]

His loyalty to truth was in part an intellectual and in part a moral trait. Intellectually it was related to the clearness of his conceptions. It is the man who never knows exactly what he thinks that falls most easily into the vice of saying something different from what he thinks. But Dana's character was intensely ethical. And with him ethics was always sanctified and glorified by religious faith. His view, alike of nature and of human life, was profoundly theistic. Disloyalty to truth was infidelity to God. In his scientific investigation he always felt, like Kepler, that he was thinking God's thoughts after him.

Dana was not only a theist but a Christian. Religion was a dominant principle in his life. The influences of his childhood home were strongly religious, and in his early manhood he made public profession of Christian faith. While residing in New Haven as assistant to Professor Silliman, he became a member of the First Congregational Church in that city. His letters written amid the perils of shipwreck and cannibals in the Exploring Expedition reveal the sincerity of his faith in the providential care of a Heavenly Father. His patience under the restraints imposed upon him by the impairment of his health, and the serene light which brightened the long evening of his life, were in part doubtless the effect of a naturally cheerful spirit, but surely in large part the effect of religious faith. A few months before his death he wrote to Professor J. P. Lesley: "I, too, feel age encroaching on old

[1] Farrington, *loc. cit.*

privileges. I used to have a spring in my walk, and get delight out of it. But for a little over a month, owing to a weakening of some strings, my heart has compelled me to take what I should before have called a creeping gait. Such encroachments are reminders that the end is coming. But it will be peace, rest, and, I believe, joy unending. Life were worth living if it were only for the end." One is reminded of Browning's noble lines—

> "Grow old along with me!
> The best is yet to be,
> The last of life, for which the first was made."

As a thinker, Dana was eminently characterized by breadth of view. Though facts might be, as Agassiz so nobly said, "the words of God," they were meaningless unless they could be arranged in sentences. Dana was eminently a generalizer and a systematizer. The *Manual of Geology* is for every American geologist the most indispensable book of reference for its encyclopedic array of facts. But the general conception of the meaning of geological fact with which the whole book is luminous is the greater glory. If Dana sometimes mistook analogy for identity, and sometimes grouped facts in a pseudo-system, he only showed "the defects of his qualities." The only man who has made no unsound generalizations is the man who has never generalized at all.

There is a certain intellectual kinship between the philosopher and the poet. The loftiest generalizations of science involve a flight of imagination approaching the poetic. The minds most gifted with the power to see the scientific meaning of natural phenomena are often most keenly sensitive to the inspiration of nature's beauty. Some of the descriptive passages in the *Corals and Coral Islands*, and gem-like sentences which flash here and there from the pages of the *Manual of Geology*, show a poet's sense of nature's manifold and resistless charm.

Dana was fond of music, and played the flute and the guitar. In his early manhood he made some attempts at musical composition. Among these efforts was the music for an ode to the ship

Peacock, written during the Exploring Expedition by Dr. J. C. Palmer, the surgeon of the ship. In later years, however, the exacting demands of his scientific work left little time for the cultivation of an art which for him could be only a recreation.

His personal appearance was at once attractive and impressive. The inspiring flash of his deep blue eyes and the exquisite sweetness of his smile will ever haunt the memory of all who had the privilege of his society. His hair, which had been light brown in earlier years, turned white as he advanced in age, but ceased not to be abundant. His latest portrait is the most impressive. The thin, eager, vivacious, kindly face, encircled with its halo of silver hair, was inspiring in its dignity and sweetness. For him the hoary head was a crown of glory. He was of medium height or rather less, and light and slender. The quickness of all his movements was remarkable. Even in old age he walked uphill and down at a pace which the students who went on his geological excursions found it easier to admire than to emulate. The quickness of his physical movements was an expression of the same sensitiveness of nervous organization which made possible the marvelous vivacity of his mental working.

The restraints imposed by the failure of his health isolated him from society in general. Yet he was delightfully companionable to those who had the privilege of entering the precincts of his quiet and secluded life. His conversation was enlivened with a delicate humor, and in controversy he could be sarcastic. The courtesy which endeared him to all who knew him was the expression of real kindness of heart. His helpful interest in the work of young scientific men has left rich store of grateful memories. As son, brother, husband, father, friend, his life, in all the relations of most intimate affection, was pure and gentle.

His was a genius to be admired, a character to be reverenced, a personality to be loved.

Spencer F Baird

SPENCER FULLERTON BAIRD

ZOÖLOGIST

1823–1887

By Charles Frederick Holder

In the introduction to Professor G. Brown Goode's *Bibliography of Professor Baird*, published under direction of the Smithsonian Institution, I find the following lines referring to his portrait, which is slipped into, but not bound in the volume: "Professor Baird having refused to allow it to be inserted in this work, it will be distributed separately to as many recipients of the *Bibliography* as is practical to reach. Those who received it are requested to attach it permanently to copies of the book."

Professor Goode doubtless did not intend it, but he could not have written a more speaking panegyric on the character of Professor Baird had he tried, nor can I do better than to quote it, to illustrate what always impressed me as one of the most charming qualities of the great naturalist and organizer,—his modesty.

This virtue does not always indicate greatness, but in this instance it did, and in an acquaintance with Professor Baird, which extended over many years, it always seemed to me to be a dominant factor in all the acts of his career.

In the correspondence of my father, dating back to 1846, I find voluminous letters from Spencer F. Baird, asking for Dr. Holder's lists of the birds, mammals and plants of Essex County, Massachusetts, and offering his own lists of the same near Reading, Pennsylvania, in return, and out of this correspondence grew a friendship which held through life between the two men. My first impression of Professor Baird came in the fall of 1859 when we were on the way to the Florida reef. Professors Baird and

Agassiz having induced Dr. Holder [1] to throw up a lucrative practice as a physician in Lynn, Massachusetts, and go to what in all probability was the most desolate spot within the confines of the government—Garden Key, or Tortugas, to study the fauna in the interests of science. We visited Professor Baird en route, and I well remember his strong, robust personality, his kindly responsive nature, the evident nobility of his character, his intense interest in nature, and a certain sweetness of character, difficult to associate with a man of heroic mold which found its expression in his innate modesty and purity of life. If I should be called upon to paint a word-picture, to conjure up from the imagination a figure which should fully represent the typical American as he is, as he should be, to meet the ideals of a great and patriotic people, the form and features, the character, the virtues, and intelligence of Spencer F. Baird, would insensibly present themselves. He was a typical American of a heroic type, a man of many parts, virtues and intellectual graces, and of all the zoölogists science has given the world, it can doubtless be said, he was most prolific in works of practical value to man and to humanity.

Professor Baird belonged to the time of Agassiz, Huxley, Spencer and Darwin, being but sixteen years younger than Agassiz, and came upon the field in a period notable for its activity in science along many lines. Reading, Pennsylvania, claims him as an honored son, where he was born February 3, 1823, and after several years of public schools he entered Dickinson College, from which he graduated at the age of seventeen. Like Agassiz and Darwin, he was a born genius, with predilection for scientific pursuits and all his energies from early youth were expended along these lines of thought and practice.

Like Agassiz, he studied medicine, but never completed his studies although he was given the degree of M.D. *honoris causa* from the Philadelphia Medical College.

During his early college days he attracted wide-spread attention for his studies and observations in Nature, and when the true his-

[1] The late Joseph Bassett Holder, Curator of Zoölogy of the Museum of Natural History, N. Y., from its founding to 1888.

tory of the Smithsonian and National Museum comes to be written it can be said that the foundation of the splendid museums of these institutions was largely laid by young Baird in this period. He was a powerful, robust specimen of young manhood, an assiduous collector with a strong intuition for the work, and with abnormal perceptions for one of his age; hence he accomplished much in his tremendous walks of from twenty to fifty miles a day across country, not only laying the foundation for an exalted scientific career, but for a constitution which served him well in later years, when he was obliged to renounce field-work and assume the head of the great lines of special scientific research which his active mind conceived, and brought into being. Professor Baird at this period not only made remarkable collections in a variety of fields, but he began an extraordinary system of exchanges with naturalists all over the country, which later on formed the basis for the fine and far-reaching system of exchanges which became a policy of the Smithsonian and National Museums. When he was twenty-two years of age, he was tendered the chair of Natural History at Dickinson College, and later his duties also included the chair of Chemistry and up to 1850 he was the recipient of many honors; in that year, when but twenty-seven years of age, being offered the assistant secretaryship of the Smithsonian Institution, which he accepted.

The motto of James Smithson, the one which he gave to the Institution which bears his name, was "the increase and diffusion of useful knowledge among men," and that Professor Baird adopted this and followed it closely is evident to any one who will seriously study the quality of his life-work, as it differs from that of almost any scientist of the century. His original researches were brilliant and far-reaching, but his greatest work, his best energies were exerted along those lines that produce results of practical benefit to the human race. To illustrate my meaning, the works of Agassiz, his discoveries among fossil fishes, his elaborate books on glaciers and their causes were of inestimable value to science, but Professor Baird's work in the United States Fish Commission alone was of far more practical and immediate value to humanity now and in the future.

His studies among food-fishes, his efforts to protect them, to regulate their catch, to discover new grounds in the interest of trade and commerce, carried on side by side with studies of a more scientific character, were in a direct line with the sentiment of Smithson: "the diffusion of useful knowledge among men." Professor Baird was, like Agassiz and Darwin, a strenuous type, an indefatigable worker, and the amount of work he produced was monumental. In twelve years, the period between 1858 and 1870, he produced works which would have been the normal output of a well rounded lifetime of an ordinary man. During this period he wrote the catalogue of *North American Serpents; The Birds of North America; The Mammals of North America; The Review of North American Birds; The History of North American Birds* in collaboration with Brewer and Ridgeway, besides innumerable reports and papers on a variety of subjects. For many years he was the editor of Harper's scientific department, and during this time he wrote the yearly encyclopedia called *The Annual Record of Science and Industry.* These titles tell at once the story of his wide range of thought, of his versatility, and stamp him as a naturalist of the widest range. It is not unusual to-day to meet men of the most distinguished attainments in certain branches of zoölogy, men who are masters of the cephalopods, we may say, to whom the fishes are a closed book. In a word, naturalists have taken Agassiz's advice literally and become specialists, but Baird belonged to the school that believed that a naturalist in the broadest sense should have a good, even thorough knowledge of all the animal kingdom first, as a base upon which to stand, this accomplished, he should then take up some speciality and follow it to a logical and exhaustive finish.

I have often accompanied Professor Baird in a round of the Smithsonian or the Collection of the American Museum of Natural History and have been impressed by the remarkable range of his knowledge. One afternoon in New York, we were discussing taxidermy with John Bell, the friend and companion of Audubon;

Bell was telling his experiences with the great naturalist and how he almost had a serious break with him. Bell was traveling with Audubon, and every day new species were found; one day Bell said that he made up a bird with the head of a snipe, the body of something else, the wings and legs of another. Audubon had been away for a week, and when he returned Bell displayed the bird, saying that he had mounted it at once as it was in bad condition. Audubon was completely mystified and proportionately delighted. He described the new bird and sent the account to Europe, and it was weeks before Bell, then a young man, had the temerity to confess. When he did Audubon fell into a rage, but finally laughed, and acknowledged the cleverness of his assistant. I noticed that Professor Baird was fully conversant with Bell's work, and doubtless had views of his own regarding taxidermy which were adopted in the National Museum. One could not easily exaggerate the versatility of Professor Baird, and the diversity of his interests is well shown by even a casual glance at his journal while studying medicine in New York. This was in 1848. One day we find him closeted with Audubon studying his drawings, then dissecting a fox for him. The next day he is with Le Conte, visits De Kay, and studies his report of the zoölogical survey of New York. The following day we find him studying drawing under Audubon, then he obtains bird skins from Peale and sends him snails, fossils and coins in return.

In the morning he is studying the fine collection of Siberian fossils of T. A. Conrads and in the evening we find him taking tea with Isaac Lea that he may go over this gentleman's large collection of shells; straws which indicate the wide range of interest taken by the young naturalist; and when it is remembered that he was noted for the profundity of his investigations and the thoroughness of his work even to the minutest detail, the character of his life-work and its extent can be realized.

In 1871, General Grant appointed Professor Baird a commissioner of United States Fish and Fisheries, an honorary position which added greatly to his work. This move was epoch-making and marked the recognition by the government of Professor

Baird's views on the economic value of animals, and the necessity of having laws to conserve animal life in the interest of humanity of to-day and to-morrow. The appointment of Baird to this unremunerative position marked an epoch in the development of economic science in America, and the growth and evolution of the United States Fish Commission alone shows better than anything else the comprehensive views of its chief and his remarkable grasp upon questions requiring the highest powers of a systematist. His work showed that he was an organizer and administrator of the highest rank. For twelve years he devoted his energies to the arduous labors of the United States Fish Commission. He constructed the entire framework of the new department, and organized it under the following general plan: "To prosecute investigations on the subject of the diminution of valuable fishes with the view of ascertaining whether any and what diminution in the number of food-fishes of the coast and lakes of the United States has taken place, and, if so, to what cause the same is due and also whether any and what productive, prohibitory or precautionary measures should be adopted in the premises and to report the same to Congress. It is impossible to more than hint at the work of Professor Baird in this direction in this limited paper, but it was of far-reaching importance, and comprised a comprehensive plan to prevent the depletion of fishes, either in sea or river.

Experts were sent all over the country, hatching stations were established, and available fish were carried from one part of the country to another, and the interests of humanity conserved in many ways. As an illustration, the striped bass, which has been gradually disappearing on the Atlantic coast or at least assuming lesser proportions, were introduced into the Sacramento River and to-day it is the highest priced fish and the best in quality on the Pacific coast, being caught in large quantities and an economic factor of great value to the people of the coast. The bass have wandered five hundred miles to the south, having been caught at Redondo, and Terminal, opposite the island of Santa Catalina in Southern California. The famous rainbow trout of California was transplanted east and trout and other fish hatcheries established all over the country to ensure an adequate supply of food-fishes of all kinds. At the same time vessels searched the sea for new fishing-grounds contiguous to the coast that would be of value to fishermen, and the new bureau made of vital importance and value to the public.

Professor Baird had the faculty of adapting himself with unusual tact to subordinate positions, and when in command he gave evidence of executive ability equally remarkable. His desire to build up a national museum which should give the United States a standing second to none resulted in the establishment and exploitation of a number of expeditions, and by using the government, its consuls and various good offices, he succeeded in sending agents, collectors and expeditions to the four quarters of the globe, which soon resulted in an enormous inflow of matter in every branch of science; no guilty man escaped. Even the author of *Home Sweet Home* was aided to a consulate, on the suggestion that he would also scour the country to which he was accredited for "bugs" and other things, and when he departed for his station he was taken for a naturalist with cans of alcohol, fishing-nets and various devices. For thirty-three years, from 1850 to 1883, Professor Baird gave his strength and ability to the upbuilding of the Smithsonian Institution, and what it is to-day, is mainly due to his genius for work. For twenty-eight years he was the principal executive officer of the Smithsonian. In training, tastes, line of thought, he differed very materially from his chief, Professor Henry, who in turn had little or no fondness for zoölogy, being a physicist. The two men represented the antipodes of thought and scientific habit, and it is to the credit of Professor Baird that his work with his chief was harmonious. In 1878 upon the death of Henry, he succeeded him as secretary of the Smithsonian. Owing to the diversity of tastes of the two men, many of Professor Baird's ideas had been held in abeyance, but now, having full rein, his marvelous executive and administrative ability became more clearly apparent, and it was never better illustrated than when he was attempting to obtain appropriations for the institutions under his charge.

The salary was always inadequate to the responsibilities of the situation, and it devolved on the head to present the claims and induce Congress to make liberal appropriations, a most difficult and disagreeable work for a man of his training, requiring tact and diplomacy of no ordinary character; but in this work he was remarkably successful, and his addresses to the committees of appropriations of the House and Senate were invariably received with attention, and his claims allowed. He had a remarkable faculty of inspiring confidence, while his innate modesty gained him friends among those who believed they knew a strong honest man, when they saw one.

Baird never demanded more than was reasonable, and his policy was to educate the people in advance to the necessities of the situation, so that congressmen as a rule gave his demands attention and their hearty support. Professor Baird never lost sight of the fact that while the head of the Smithsonian Institution he was the custodian of a public trust, and a public servant. He was conscientious in all his methods, and always drove a good bargain for the government and people. This was well known in Congress, and an influential senator is quoted as saying: "I am willing to vote the money asked for by Professor Baird, for he will get two dollars worth for every dollar we give him, one-half by direct purchase and one-half by gift." This statement while true does not do full justice to the remarkable administrative skill of the incumbent. He literally turned every branch of the government into a clearing-house for the National Museum and the Smithsonian Institution; the consulates, the agents of the government, surgeons, army officers, ministers, soldiers, lighthouse keepers, revenue service, officers of the army and marine corps, the engineer department, no branch of the service was overlooked by this indefatigable collector who had the power to interest everyone in his work and to induce them to send in animals, plants, minerals, fossils, fruits and flowers, or Indian implements from the localities in which they were stationed, while consuls and ministers were induced to arrange for exchange with foreign nations. In this way he had an enormous corps of enthusiastic helpers and aids which, if they had been paid, would have cost the government enormous and impossible sums.

There is a feature of the life of Professor Baird which commends itself to many naturalists; this was his influence over young men and the cordial aid he always stood ready to give them. He was a remarkable organizer, and as such possessed a keen insight and discernment of a remarkable quality. He recognized the fact that the great museum he was building up was not for to-day, but for all time, and that new men would be required in the future and should be trained to fill the positions in the various departments; hence he was always on the lookout for young men of promise and marked ability, and scores of the leading naturalists in the United States to-day owe their prominence to his good judgment; and the methods of study which he advocated. Dr. John Billings in his life of Agassiz, cites an illustration which bears on this point. The Institution had received some interesting Semitic inscriptions, and a young man named Mason who had been making studies along these lines called to see them. Professor Baird gave him a hearty welcome and listened quietly to his explanations. When Mason completed his work and was about to leave, Baird said to him, "I want you to give up your Semitic work and devote yourself to American ethnology. We have two continents awaiting some one, you are the one, you must stay with us." In this way America gained one of its greatest ethnologists, and Dr. Otis T. Mason is still connected with the government Institution—a living example of the good judgment of the late secretary.

The sagacity, the positive genius of his discernment is shown in the selection of his assistant, the late Professor G. Brown Goode, who was appointed to share the administrative work, as his assistant, in 1887. Dr. Goode was already connected with the Fish Commission and he was given the charge of the National Museum. The two men were alike in their modesty and their many virtues, and their only serious difference during many years of arduous work is related by Miss Baird. Baird and Goode had been working along some identical line in the museum in which both were interested. Baird in making a report upon it gave Goode the credit. Goode resented the implication and retorted with a minority report insisting that the credit belonged to his chief. This perhaps is the only instance where Goode was even suspected of insubordination, or where the distinguished master of science was known to be unjust, in trying to shirk credit that doubtless belonged to himself, or at least in part. A more speaking commentary on the fine sense of honor possessed by these two American gentlemen could not be imagined, for which I am indebted to T. D. A. Cockerell's life of Baird, in *The Popular Science Monthly*. In Washington Professor Baird's home was the rendevous of men of science throughout the city and country and the Sunday nights there were looked forward to by many with the greatest pleasure. The splendid building of the National Museum is a result of Professor Baird's business methods. Dr. Hall tells the story. An attempt had been made to induce Congress to appropriate money to build it without result, but finally the government consented to make an appropriation for the Centennial at Philadelphia. It was not believed possible in Congress for Philadelphia to return this money, it was not believed that so vast an exhibit could be made a financial success, hence Congress in reply to the importunities of Professor Baird said, that if Philadelphia returned the loan, he could have half of it for the much desired and needed building. This was enough for the energetic secretary, and he called a meeting of his subordinates and explained the situation. They must lend all their efforts to make the exhibition one that would redound to their credit, please the people and Congress. This was carried out. Philadelphia repaid the loan, and Congress in 1879 voted the appropriation and the new building was occupied in 1882; hence it is very evident that Professor Baird was the father of the National Museum.

Professor Baird was a notable figure among the men of science of his time, and the world did not fail to recognize his signal ability, and the fact that he stood at the head of American naturalists.

As early as 1850, he was honored by Dickinson College with a Degree of Doctor of Physics, and in 1875, that of Doctor of Laws from Columbia University. In 1878, he received the silver medal of the Acclimatization Society of Melbourne. In 1879, the gold medal of the Society of Acclimatization of France, and in 1880, the *erster Ehrenpriez* of the International Fischerei Ausstellung at Berlin, given him by his majesty the Emperor of Germany. From the King of Norway and Sweden he received in 1875 the decoration of Knight of the Royal Norwegian Order of St. Olaf.

Professor Baird was one of the early members of the National Academy of Sciences, and a member of its council, and but for his extreme modesty many more honors would have been conferred upon him. He was one of the early secretaries of the Society of the American Association for the Advancement of Science. He was a trustee in numerous institutions, among them the Corcoran Art Gallery, and Columbia University. He was also President of the Cosmos Society and many scientific societies in this country.

Foreign societies vied with those of this country in doing him honor. He was a member of the Linnæan Society of London, the Zoölogical Society, Honorary Member of the Linnæan Society of New South Wales, and a member of all the leading French, German and Italian scientific bodies. While this short paper can only be considered a glance at the fine picture presented by this well-rounded life, and of necessity devoted to his public works and utilities, I cannot pass by the social and home life of the great naturalist. Those who knew him will remember the genial hospitality, the firm grasp of his hand, the strong ring of his friendship, the fine sense of honor, and the full measure of the personal graces with which nature had invested him.

To me he was that ideal, the type of the American gentleman of the old school which should be perpetuated. He was a type to be held up as an example of what an American boy can accomplish, what an American citizen can attain. His home life was an inspiration, and its charm was realized by a large contingent of friends and acquaintances from many lands, who shared in it, and the graceful hospitality dispensed by his gifted wife and daughter.

Professor Baird represented a sturdy American type. He came
of a sterling people who came to this country in the seventeenth
century. During the war of the Revolution his grandfather, the
Rev. Elihu Spencer of Trenton, was so potent'a factor for independence that the British put a price on his head, and both branches
of the family were conspicuous for their services to the people,
the state and their country.

Professor Baird married Mary Helen Churchill in 1846, the
only daughter of Sylvester Churchill, Inspector General, U. S. A.
Mrs. Baird was a woman of high culture and marked intelligence,
who had a strong influence upon her husband's life and work,
while his daughter, Miss Baird, was in close sympathy and com-
panionship with her distinguished father and was a constant and
indispensable aid to him, in all of his many and diverse interests.

The seaside laboratory at Woods Hole, the summer head-
quarters of the United States Fish Commission, was of peculiar
interest to Professor Baird, as one of the results of his comprehensive grasp upon the great plan of zoölogical work in connection
with the government, and it was here that he passed the last period
of his active life. For some time he had been failing, and his
physicians ordered a complete rest; Professor Langley assumed
charge of the Smithsonian, and Dr. Goode of the National Museum,
and the great organizer, the man who had reared the great institution for the people, stepped aside into the shadow of a coming
change. It was hoped that he would rally, that the wasted energies would be restored, but this was not realized and in the summer
of 1887, with intellect still clear and unimpaired, amid the scenes
of his greatest triumphs at what his friend Major Powell fitly
termed the greatest "biological laboratory of the world," reared
by his hands, planned by him, he passed into history revered,
mourned, honored as few men have been in this or any land.

I shall not attempt to sum up the value of his work or its relation
to the present or to posterity. I have sounded his virtues in passing
as they have occurred to me in this brief review of his life, but it
seems fitting to add the words of his well-beloved friend and
colleague, Professor G. Brown Goode: "Future historians of

American science will be better able than are we to estimate justly
the value of the contributions to scientific literature which are
enumerated in the biography; but no one not living in the present,
can form an accurate idea of the personal influence of a leader
upon his associates, and upon the progress of thought in his special
department, nor can such an influence as this well be set down in
words. This influence is apparently due not only to extraordinary
skill in organization, to great power of application and concentration of thought constantly applied, and to a philosophical and
comprehensive mind, but to an entire and self-sacrificing devotion
to the interests of his own work and that of others."

O. C. Marsh.

OTHNIEL CHARLES MARSH

PALEONTOLOGIST

1831–1899

BY GEORGE BIRD GRINNELL

IN the scientific world, the name of Marsh stands forth as that of a man of strong personality, of keen powers of observation, and of high attainments. He brought to the service of science great enthusiasm and zeal, and his learning placed him in the front rank of American anatomists and paleontologists. Like Baird, he was an explorer and collector, taking immense pleasure in his expeditions, in the vast collections of vertebrate fossils thus acquired, and in the elaboration of this rich material. His early success came through perseverance, concentration of effort, and hard and continuous labor. While others may reap greater fame in his chosen field, he was one of the illustrious trio who blazed the path to the broader domain, and it is in large measure due to his work as an enthusiastic pioneer that vertebrate paleontology has assumed its present importance in America. When Marsh died, science lost a devoted ally, American paleontology an eminent leader, and Yale University a distinguished son.

From 1636 to 1881, that branch of the Marsh family living within the bounds of old Salem, Massachusetts, had occupied but four places of residence, all in that part of the town afterwards called Danvers, now Peabody, and in the house last built Caleb Marsh, whose son furnishes the subject of this sketch, was born November 8, 1800. In 1827, he married Mary Gaines Peabody, also a native of Danvers, and a descendant of Lieut. Francis Peabody, who established himself in Ipswich in 1635. After his

283

marriage, Mr. Marsh took up his residence in Lockport, New York, and here on Chestnut Ridge his eldest son, Othniel Charles Marsh, was born October 29, 1831, in the eighth generation from John Marsh of Salem, the founder of the family in this country.

In his third year, the boy had the misfortune to lose his mother, an admirable woman whose influence in her family was strong, and who bequeathed to her son qualities that brought him his highest success. After his mother's death, with an elder sister he was taken by his father to Danvers and placed in the care of an aunt, remaining two years in the home built by his ancestors in 1766 but destroyed by fire in 1881. In 1836, Mr. Caleb Marsh returned to Lockport, and soon after married Miss Mary Latten, daughter of Judge Latten of that place. Six children were born of this second marriage. The family subsequently lived at Bradford, Massachusetts, but a few years later returned to Lockport, where the father died in 1865.

Mr. Caleb Marsh was an industrious farmer, energetic and enterprising, with a keen interest in current events and marked ability in the acquisition of knowledge. Being endowed with a remarkable memory, his attainments, it is said, were such as to cause him to be regarded as a sort of village oracle. He was, however, both stern and impulsive, and not being always in sympathy with the tastes of his strong-willed son, he occasionally inflicted severe punishment on the boy. Brought up in the country, healthy in body and alert in mind, the sturdy lad was chiefly interested in out-of-door affairs, and early showed individuality and resolute character. Obliged, like most country boys, to make himself useful when quite young, he still found time to indulge his predilection for hunting and fishing. The robust health and vigorous constitution enjoyed until within a year or two of his death were doubtless due to the open-air life of these early years, while to habits of observation thus acquired he owed much of his scientific success.

When Marsh was twelve years of age, his father purchased a farm in the western part of Lockport, close to the Erie Canal. At that time the enlargement of the canal was in progress, and great quantities of rocks were blasted out by the workmen. These limestones contained various minerals and fossils which so engaged the attention of the boy, that under the guidance of Colonel Jewett, a collector in that region, he soon became ardently interested in these specimens. So determined and absorbed was he in this undertaking that he absolutely refused to work on his father's farm, often spending whole days in adding to his store of minerals, and further provoking parental discipline. Indeed, from this time on he seems to have had no taste for farming.

At the outset Marsh met with difficulty in gaining an education, for it was during the winter only that his father permitted him to attend school; yet inheriting an aptitude for learning and a retentive memory, it was necessary for him to read his lessons over but once in order to learn them, and he generally stood at the head of his class. He must have made good use of his time, for at the age of nineteen he taught during the winter in a district school, receiving sixteen dollars a month for his services. With this money, he left Lockport for South Danvers, and spent the rest of the year 1851 at the old Marsh homestead. A diary kept during the months succeeding his arrival begins:

"Danvers, June 1st, '51.
"Believing that a diary, with regular additions, will be highly advantageous in improving my style of writing, and penmanship, and also a valuable assistant to my memory, I shall now commence to note down the most important events of each day, in as plain and concise a manner as possible.
"O. C. Marsh."

This diary shows that during the formative period of his life, Marsh displayed the same energy, industry, and enthusiasm characteristic of his more mature years. Up to this time, however, there is no hint of pursuing further study; yet later, through the influence of a maternal aunt, who had enlisted the generosity of her brother (Mr. George Peabody of London) in his behalf, Marsh was induced to enter Phillips Academy, Andover, and, late in the autumn of 1851, he became a student in the English Department of that institution. At first he showed little ambition to excel in his studies, although he devoted some of the time to subjects relating to natural history, spending his leisure in exploring the surrounding country. The next winter, however, he took hold in real earnest, confessing that during the previous year he "was playing backgammon with the boys half the time. I changed my mind," he stated, "during an afternoon spent on Dracut Heights [Lowell]. I resolved that I would return to Andover, take hold, and really study." This resolve he carried out with characteristic energy, and while most of the boys took but three studies, Marsh took four. When asked why he worked so hard, he replied: "To make up for lost time; I have spent enough time shooting ducks to fit myself for college."

Previous to 1852, he apparently came to no decision regarding an academic career. The encouragement of his father and aunt coupled with the liberality of his uncle, Mr. Peabody, turned the scales in favor of a higher education, and Marsh finally declared his intention of going to Yale College. Accordingly, in the spring of 1853, he began his preparation by entering the Classical Department of Phillips Academy as third junior, at the same time continuing his studies in natural science. Three years later he was graduated from that institution as valedictorian of his class. In describing this period in Marsh's career, an intimate friend has written:

"In Phillips Academy there were then two paths of glory; one was high standing in the class, the other was the Philomathean Society, a boys' debating club.

"After Marsh really began to study, he stood first in class every term without exception. He studied intensely, but tried to make the impression that he achieved his success without any work at all. In the debating club, he also took hold strongly, although he was at this time a slow and halting speaker, and never in his life was anything of a rhetorician. His superiority in managing practical affairs soon impressed all, and he became manager of the society and held the whole thing in his hands. But he was older than the rest of us, and was an experienced man of the world moving among a set of crude boys.

"I remember an instance of his foresight and shrewd management—shrewd with a touch of cunning in it. The President of the society for the third term had been taken from the senior class for years, but one year the candidate was unpopular, a revolution started, and the middlers resolved to run a candidate of their own. Marsh, then a junior, threw himself into the movement with might and main. He said to me: 'We can elect the middler and next year I will be candidate; the precedent for the election of a middler will be established.' He worked with much energy and skill and caused the election of the middler, now Dr. Alexander McKenzie of Cambridge. The next year this President left school, and his place was supplied by the Vice-President, now Dr. Franklin Carter, ex-President of Williams College. Carter was the best candidate the seniors had for the third term presidency, and would have been a hard man for Marsh to beat. But Marsh, with some assistance from myself, persuaded the Vice-President to remain in his place and perform the President's duties during the remainder of the term. Then all the school politicians said that Carter had practically been the President for a term, and of course could not run again. This took him out of the way; the time for nomination approached; the seniors put up a weak fellow, but fought for him like tigers, not wanting their class to be defeated. Marsh organized the middlers with great skill, held the class firmly together, picked up the loose votes lying around the school, and defeated the senior candidate by a majority of one. The excitement in the school was tremendous, and Marsh became a great hero. The foresight shown in pushing in a middle-class candidate a year before, and getting McKenzie and Carter on the shelf by previous elections so as to provide a weak opponent for himself was quite exceptional in one so young.

"Marsh entered his senior year having gained all the honors of the Philomathean, politics no longer pressed his mind, and he gave his entire time to study. He secured the valedictory and gave the address at the school exhibition, but his oration was quite ordinary. He had made a clean sweep of all the honors of Phillips Academy; there was no desirable honor which he did not get while there."

During his school-days at Andover and throughout his college course he was a devoted student of mineralogy, and in the summer of 1852 displayed his unabated interest in the subject by arranging the collection of the Essex Institute at Salem, his vacation being given up to this work and to explorations in Massachusetts and New York State. It was during these years that various trips to

Nova Scotia were made for the purpose of investigating the geology of that peninsula and of adding to his specimens. In 1855, with his intimate friend and classmate Park, he explored the famous Coal-Measure section at South Joggins, where he found the remains of a unique extinct animal, *Eosaurus*, the description of which was not published until seven years later. This important discovery eventually changed the course of his scientific career, these two vertebræ serving as the basis of his future work in vertebrate paleontology.

The summer preceding his entrance to college was employed in field work in New Hampshire, Vermont, and New York, most of the time in company with his lifelong friend Van Name; the autumn of 1856 saw him a freshman at Yale. After his brilliant career at the academy, where he had been the acknowledged leader in all society matters and class affairs, it was to be expected that he would meet with disappointment in his new surroundings. Some of his college instructors were apparently less able men than those under whom he had been studying, and failed to arouse the enthusiasm and earnestness inspired by his Andover professors. He was also exhausted by the intense work of the three preceding years and suffered a natural reaction; his scholarship therefore fell below the remarkably high standard previously maintained. Socially, too, he soon discovered a marked difference between the position of leading senior at Andover and that of freshman at Yale. He suffered some humiliations, but the experiences were doubtless beneficial, for his extraordinary success at Andover had perhaps given him too exalted an opinion of himself.

In July, 1857, his uncle and benefactor, Mr. George Peabody of London, visited him for the first time at New Haven, and exhibited a keen interest in his scientific pursuits. This first visit doubtless laid the foundation for Mr. Peabody's subsequent liberality to Yale in bestowing the fund which finally resulted in the present Peabody Museum.

While in college, Marsh gave much of his leisure to the study of the natural history of various parts of Connecticut, and his vacations were often spent in examining the geology and paleontology of Nova Scotia and New Brunswick, a third scientific excursion to these provinces having been made in 1857, in company with three classmates (Abernethy, Clay, and Post).

In 1858, he again devoted the summer to collecting, this time in New York State; and in the following long vacation, when a junior, made his fourth trip to Nova Scotia, Post again accompanying him. A fifth expedition to this peninsula took place in 1860, after graduation, and like those preceding it resulted in valuable additions to his scientific wealth.

At the end of his collegiate course he ranked eighth in a class of one hundred and nine members, the largest and one of the ablest classes that had ever been graduated at Yale. He was given a high oration appointment and his attainments in classics were such as to entitle him to the Berkeley Scholarship, other honors coming in the guise of the Latin prize and an election to Phi Beta Kappa.

In accordance with the terms on which the income of the Berkeley Scholarship is granted, Marsh remained two years longer at Yale as scholar of the house, studying mineralogy, geology, and chemistry at the Sheffield Scientific School. This graduate work led to the degree of M.A., conferred by Yale in 1862. When the Civil War broke out, Marsh was offered a major's commission in a Connecticut regiment, but defective eyesight obliged him to decline this military honor. During the following summer occurred his final trip to Nova Scotia, where he explored the gold fields, then newly discovered. His observations were apparently the earliest published on the subject and were embodied in his initial scientific paper: " The Gold of Nova Scotia " (*Amer. Jour. Sci.*, Nov., 1861). Two additional contributions to mineralogy were subsequently published, but after 1867 his active interest in minerals ceased.

The year 1862 witnessed the publication of an elaborate and detailed description of the enaliosaurian vertebræ found in Nova Scotia in 1855, the only specimens of the kind ever discovered. Previous to the appearance of this article, the fossil had been brought to the attention of the elder Agassiz, who at once recognized its value and importance, as shown by his letter to Professor

Silliman, which appeared in the *American Journal of Science* for March, 1862.

In the succeeding summer, Marsh refused the professorship offered him by his Alma Mater, and in November, 1862, started on his first European trip, visiting the International Exhibition in London and spending some time in the various museums of England. Later he entered Berlin University as a student of mineralogy and chemistry, under G. and H. Rose, respectively, and of microgeology under Ehrenberg.

In the spring of 1863, his studies were continued at Heidelberg University, under the direction of Bunsen, Blum, and Kirschoff, and it was during this semester that he became a fellow of the Geological Society of London, his name having been proposed by Sir Charles Lyell. The following summer was devoted to an extended trip through Switzerland, during which a special study of glaciers was made. Returning to Berlin, he began researches in paleontology, a professorship in that branch of science having been instituted for him at Yale College. This subject was diligently pursued throughout the academic year, and further preparations for his prospective work were made in extensive collections of books and specimens. He again studied at Berlin in 1864 under the eminent scholars Beyrich, Peters, and Ehrenberg, and made various excursions to the Hartz Mountains and other parts of northern Germany. Several short papers giving the results of his investigations on invertebrates were presented to the Geological Society of Germany, of which he had then recently been elected a member. The results thus obtained, however, were never fully published, and two brief notes on annelids, another on *Ceratites*, a description of the fossil sponge *Brachiospongia*, and a short paper on the color markings of *Orthoceras* and *Endoceras* constitute his principal articles dealing with invertebrate fossils, the series closing in July, 1869, with a paper on a new species of *Protichnites* from New York. This paper virtually ended his miscellaneous contributions to science, and henceforth the study of vertebrate paleontology became his sole aim.

In the summer of 1864, Marsh made extensive geological explo-

rations in Switzerland and the Tyrol, which resulted in some discoveries of interest. Entering Breslau University later, he spent
the winter studying under Roemer, Grube, and Goeppert. He
was again at Berlin, in the spring of 1865, but soon after went to
Paris, making frequent stops *en route* in order to visit various
museums and important geological localities. A little later, while
working in the British Museum, Marsh became acquainted with
Dr. Henry Woodward, Keeper of Geology, the warm friendship
that ensued lasting throughout life.

After joining Mr. Peabody in Ireland for the purpose of salmon
fishing, Marsh sailed from Queenstown for Boston in August,
1865, and soon after his arrival in this country began a systematic
study of American geology as then known, devoting the autumn
to the investigation of characteristic localities in New York,
Ohio, and Kentucky.

That a fair idea may be gained of Marsh's early environment
and subsequent training, prominence has here been given the
events of his life leading up to the time of entering on the career
in which he was to achieve signal success in many lines, and by
means of which he earned a place among renowned scholars in
the world of science. He was already a skilled explorer, an enthusiastic collector, and a promising scientific writer when he accepted
the Chair of Paleontology at Yale College, to which he was appointed at Commencement, 1866. Equipped with the best preparation afforded by the institutions of this country and of Germany,
and endowed with ability, energy, and perseverance, he assumed
the duties of a professorship apparently the first established in
that branch of science. In the absence of Professor Dana, he
began his college work by giving instruction in geology to the senior
class, continuing this with succeeding classes for several years.
But he did not wish to make his professorship a teaching one,
and preferred to serve Yale without salary in order that his time
might be devoted to research and exploration. During the last
years of his life, however, he delivered a few lectures on vertebrate
paleontology, and also directed the work of several graduate
students.

A just appreciation of the value and importance of vertebrate fossils had been acquired by Marsh during his studies and observations abroad, and the supposed poverty of this country in such resources being generally admitted, his genius for collecting was called out anew to meet the deficiency. The years succeeding his return from Europe had been devoted to the careful study of the Cretaceous and Tertiary faunas of New Jersey, from which he had obtained some fossils of interest. He had also made scientific excursions into Canada and had investigated the geology of the Connecticut Valley and of New York. But it became apparent to him while on his first short trip to the Rocky Mountains in 1868, that paleontological fields far wider than any in the East existed in the West, and he had the genius to comprehend their great possibilities and to realize what personal exploration of the West might yield. The initial journey over the then newly opened Union Pacific Railroad produced results of no small scientific interest, though not strictly pertaining to vertebrate paleontology. From an alkaline lake in Wyoming, he obtained living specimens of larval Siredons, or "fish with legs," as they were called, the remarkable development of which, observed by him after his return to the East, called forth the notable paper: *On the Metamorphosis of Siredon into Amblystoma.*

On this trip he secured various interesting Tertiary fossils that had been thrown out during the excavation of a well in an ancient lake bed at Antelope Station, Nebraska. Among these specimens were the first of the equine mammals that were destined to play so important a rôle in the list of Marsh's brilliant discoveries. The paper describing his new and diminutive fossil horse (*Equus parvulus*) appeared in November, 1868.

This preliminary investigation, confirming the work of Leidy on the vertebrate material collected by the Hayden Survey, convinced Marsh of the wonderful fertility of the western country in geological and paleontological resources, and he immediately began preparations for its systematic exploration. Owing to an Indian war in 1869, in the region he wished to explore, his plans were not fully matured until the following year.

Foremost among the successes of these early days was the series of private expeditions originating in 1870, with which Marsh's name is so closely identified. In the spring he made an extensive trip through the southern states, with special investigation of the phosphate beds of South Carolina and the Cretaceous deposits of Alabama, and on his return to New Haven organized the first Yale expedition, the party consisting of twelve students or recent graduates under the leadership of Marsh. This party started in June, and after an absence of five months returned to New Haven ladened with fossil treasures. Military escorts from various posts along the route insured their safety, and explorations in numerous Tertiary and Cretaceous deposits in Nebraska, Colorado, Wyoming, Utah, California, and western Kansas resulted in the discovery of over a hundred species of extinct vertebrates new to science—fossil horses, peculiar ungulates, carnivores, turtles, serpents, fishes, aquatic reptiles, toothed birds, and a single flying dragon, or pterodactyl.

During the four years that ensued, Marsh annually led other expeditions scarcely less successful than the first, the later parties being made up chiefly of competent assistants, specially fitted for original research. Localities proving most fertile in vertebrate remains were repeatedly visited, and the fossils thus collected soon came to be estimated by tons rather than by hundreds or thousands of specimens. The difficulties under which Marsh labored and the zeal shown in the pursuit of his aim may be inferred from the fact that the regions traversed were wild and sometimes dangerous from hostile Indians. Sometimes there was suffering from lack of food and water—the usual difficulties of early western travel. There was then but one transcontinental railroad in the United States, and away from that, travel through a region practically unknown was slow and difficult and involved a great expenditure of time and means. After 1874 no expeditions were undertaken on the previous grand scale. Although under the escort and protection of United States troops, accompanied by Indian and local guides, the heavy expense of these the first private scientific expeditions to the Great West was borne chiefly by Marsh, who during his life contributed more than a quarter of a million dollars to the sole object of completing his paleontological collections, in the acquisition of which he crossed the Rocky Mountains twenty-seven times.

It was on his perilous expedition to the Bad Lands near the Black Hills in 1874 that Marsh was twice driven back by the Sioux Indians, who supposed him to be searching for gold rather than for bones. In endeavoring to appease the savages, he held various councils with Red Cloud and other chiefs, and at last gained permission to proceed with his party only by promising Red Cloud to take his complaints, with samples of his rations to the Great Father at Washington. The fulfilment of this promise together with an exposure of the frauds that Marsh had seen practised upon the Indians led to his conflict with Secretary Delano and the Indian Ring, in which fight this department of the Government was thoroughly defeated, subsequent events substantiating all the charges made by Marsh. Later, Red Cloud presented his benefactor with an elegant pipe and tobacco pouch as tokens of his gratitude, sending with them the complimentary message that the "Bone-hunting Chief" was the only white man he had seen who kept his promises. A full account of Marsh's contest with the Indian Ring is embodied in *A Statement of Affairs at the Red Cloud Agency* and *Report of the Special Commission appointed to investigate the Affairs of the Red Cloud Indian Agency*, 1875.

The large series of equine mammals collected by Marsh previous to Huxley's memorable visit to this country in 1876, not only rendered the pedigree of the Equidæ more complete, but was the means of convincing the British anatomist that the specimens in the Peabody Museum "demonstrated the evolution of the horse beyond question, and for the first time indicated the direct line of descent of an existing animal." In the life and letters of his father, Huxley's son tells of the visit to Yale and of the western wonders stored in its natural history museum.

After examining these collections and weighing the evidence offered by the fossil remains, Huxley recast much of his New York lecture which treated of the genealogy of the horse based on

European specimens, and announced the fact that "through the Tertiary deposits of Western America Marsh tracked the successive forms by which the ancient stock of the horse has passed into its present form."

It was during his visit to New Haven in 1876 that Huxley made the jocular drawing which accompanies this sketch. He had been going over the horse material in the museum and at the end

of a session sat down at a laboratory table with Marsh to discuss the fossils he had seen. As he talked, he began to sketch with his pencil on a sheet of brown paper, and presently said, "That is my idea of *Eohippus*." Then suddenly he added, "But he needs a rider" and with a few strokes of his pencil he completed the sketch as it stands to-day. There was some laughter over it, and then Marsh said, "But the rider must have a name. What shall we call him?" "Call him *Eohomo*," said Huxley, and Marsh wrote under the sketch the legend as it appears.

The layman must understand that all this was pure fun; that the name *Eohomo* does not exist; that in the geological horizon from which *Eohippus* comes no tailless apes have yet been found. The whole thing was fun, and is not to be taken seriously.

On the 16th of August Huxley left to join the "Alexander Agassiz" at Newport whence he wrote the following letter:

"NEWPORT, Aug. 19, 1876.

"To Mr. Clarence King,

"MY DEAR SIR: In accordance with your wish, I very willingly put into writing the substance of the opinion as to the importance of Professor Marsh's collection of fossils which I expressed to you yesterday. As you are aware, I devoted four or five days to the examination of this collection, and was enabled by Prof. Marsh's kindness to obtain a fair conception of the whole.

"I am disposed to think that whether we regard the abundance of material, the number of complete skeletons of the various species, or the extent of geological time covered by the collection, which I had the good fortune to see at New Haven, there is no collection of fossil vertebrates in existence which can be compared with it. I say this without forgetting Montmartre, Siwalik, or Pikermi—and I think that I am quite safe in adding that no collection which has been hitherto formed approaches that made by Professor Marsh, in the completeness of the chain of evidence by which certain existing mammals are connected with their older tertiary ancestry.

"It is of the highest importance to the progress of Biological Science that the publication of this evidence, accompanied by illustrations of such fulness as to enable paleontologists to form their own judgment as to its value, should take place without delay.

"I am yours very faithfully,
"THOMAS H. HUXLEY."

During the years succeeding 1874, the rapid development of the West and the accessibility of many fossil fields to the railroads made it possible for small, less expensive parties to carry on the work of exploring for extinct vertebrates. After 1876, therefore, trained local collectors and others were annually sent into the field

by Marsh, and these men working under his instructions packed
the accumulated specimens on the ground and shipped them to
New Haven. Not until 1879 did Marsh again personally visit the
West, but his success in ferreting out new material was undi-
minished.

Marsh was appointed Vertebrate Paleontologist on the United
States Geological Survey, July 1, 1882. The experience gained in
the preceding fourteen years of investigation of the geology and
paleontology of the Rocky Mountain region and other parts of
the West peculiarly fitted him for this position, which also relieved
him from the personal expense attendant upon keeping parties
in the field, although during his connection with the Survey he
devoted all the salary annually received from that source to the
advancement of the work in hand.

In making collections for the Survey he had two objects in view:

"(1) To determine the geological horizon of each locality where
a large series of vertebrate fossils was found, and
"(2) To secure from these localities large collections of the
more important forms sufficiently extensive to reveal, if possible,
the life history of each."

In the first of these objects he demonstrated his belief "that
vertebrate fossils are the key to the geology of the western regions
for all formations above the Paleozoic, and that most stratigraphical questions can be solved by them alone"—a belief not shared
by all paleontologists and geologists. The second object resulted
in the vast collections he procured through various western parties
exploring under his direction, for during the ten years' connection
with the Survey he personally visited the West only four times.
From the Jurassic, Cretaceous, and Tertiary formations he obtained series of fossils of the greatest scientific value, the following
being especially noteworthy:

"(1) An extensive series of gigantic Dinosaurs from Colorado
and Wyoming, the largest land animals known, and found only
in a single horizon of the Jurassic.
"(2) A series of small primitive mammals from the same localities, the discovery of which was of great importance.

"(3) A large collection of the gigantic horned Dinosaurs of the Laramie, one of the most unexpected discoveries made in paleontology.

"(4) From the same horizon, a large series of Cretaceous mammals, a discovery of still greater importance, as such fossils had long been sought in vain in various parts of the world.

"(5) The discovery and full investigation of the remains of a new order of gigantic Eocene mammals, the *Dinocerata*, known only in this country, and from a limited area.

"(6) From the Miocene formation, a large series of the remains of another group of gigantic mammals, the *Brontotheridæ*, also unknown except in this country; and the investigation of all the important forms of this family."

When Marsh was forced to relinquish field-work for the Survey in 1892, he stated that during the preceding ten years the number of large bones shipped from the West alone was over one thousand, averaging more than one hundred a year. Several hundred small boxes and parcels containing vertebrate fossils, many of them of great value, were also sent as part of the same collections made in the West by his division. The scientific value of this entire collection Marsh believed to be far greater than that of any other collection of fossils made by any geological survey in any part of the world.

It has been stated elsewhere that "the methods of collecting and preparing these fossils for study and exhibition which he . . . introduced in the course of his long experience form the basis very largely of all similar work in almost every paleontological laboratory of the world, and it is a matter of common remark that nearly all the noted collectors and preparateurs have acquired their training under his influence."

Marsh surely deserved all the praise accorded him at home and abroad for his skill in accumulating the vast amount of material going to make up the Government collections, as well as those belonging to him personally. A firm believer in the theory of evolution, he was naturally gratified over the light thrown on geological history by his western discoveries, for among the specimens acquired were many forms which filled gaps in the paleontological series. In addition to the collection of fossil vertebrates, he made important contributions to the geology and natural resources of the regions explored.

It was the understanding with Survey officials that the material collected by Marsh should remain in his custody until thoroughly investigated and the results published. After his death, therefore, all specimens belonging to the Government were promptly transferred from New Haven to Washington. He suffered some adverse criticism in his work of collecting for the Geological Survey, but the aspersions cast on his methods had no foundation in truth and were happily silenced by the correspondence which appeared in *Science,* January 5, 1900.

Marsh's contributions to scientific literature were chiefly the fruit of three lines of investigation—mammals, birds, and reptiles— and modern text-books of geology and paleontology show how much he added to the prominence now accorded American forms. Though not an easy writer, he took great pains to express himself clearly and in correct English, and his papers exhibit none of the carelessness of expression that often mars the literary work of scientific men. The careful and methodical distribution of his writings to scientific centers throughout the world gave him eminence in practically every country.

His work on the Tertiary formations, both East and West, was productive of numerous papers on fishes, serpents, birds, crocodiles, lizards, amphibians, ungulates, rodents, carnivores, insectivores, and primates. Most of the species of fossil horses discovered by him were described before 1876, yet the two editions of *Polydactyle Horses* were published in 1879 and 1892, respectively, and include the illustrations made for Huxley in 1876, to show the progressive adaptation in the teeth and limbs of extinct equine mammals. Recent examples of what Marsh considered atavism, however, cited in these papers, are not so regarded by some noted vertebrate paleontologists, who look upon them merely as deformities or duplications, like the sixth finger in the human hand.

The unearthing of various Miocene ungulates which he called *Brontotheridæ* formed the basis of many descriptions of genera and species, and enabled him to publish a restoration of the principal type, but the projected volume on this peculiar group was never completed. With a group of horned animals nearly equalling the elephant in size—the gigantic mammals from a restricted area in the Eocene—he was more successful, and the series of papers descriptive of these forms culminated in 1886 in his second monograph, that on the *Dinocerata*. These huge beasts existed in great numbers in central Wyoming, where many of them were entombed and preserved, and more than two hundred individuals now have representation in the Yale collection.

Rivaling these investigations in the Tertiary deposits were those made in the Mesozoic of the West, which furnished material for numerous contributions to science from 1871 on. Previous to this he had described a few remains of birds from the Cretaceous of New Jersey and from various Tertiary deposits in this country, but all pertained to comparatively small species and apparently belonged to families still existing. In a letter to Professor Dana, under date of November 29, 1871, Marsh announced the discovery of his Kansas Cretaceous birds, although the fact of their possessing teeth was not learned until 1873. This announcement was soon followed by a preliminary description of *Hesperornis regalis*. Subsequent discoveries in the same region in Kansas, accompanied by the investigation of accumulating material and by the publication of results, finally led to the appearance, in 1880, of Marsh's first great monograph: *Odontornithes*, or *The Extinct Toothed Birds of North America*, a work which included complete restorations of two distinct types, *Hesperornis* and *Ichthyornis*, the one possessing teeth in grooves and the other teeth in sockets. It was published as one of the volumes of the U. S. Geological Exploration of the 40th Parallel, of which Clarence King was the chief. This work subsequently called forth the following letter from Darwin:

"MY DEAR PROFESSOR MARSH: I received some time ago your very kind note of July 28th, and yesterday the magnificent volume. I have looked with renewed admiration at the plates, and will soon read the text. Your work on these old birds, and on the many fossil animals of North America, has afforded the best support to the theory of Evolution, which has appeared within the last twenty years. The general appearance of the copy which you have sent me is worthy of its contents, and I can say nothing stronger than this.

"With cordial thanks, believe me,
"Yours very sincerely,
"CHARLES DARWIN."

In 1881, Huxley also paid a tribute to Marsh's discovery of these ancestral birds:

"The discovery of the toothed birds of the cretaceous formation of N. America, by Prof. Marsh, completed the series of transitional forms between birds and reptiles, and removed Mr. Darwin's proposition that, 'many animal forms of life have been utterly lost, through which the early progenitors of birds were formerly connected with the early progenitors of the other vertebrate classes,' from the region of hypothesis to that of demonstrable fact."

This notable volume on toothed birds taken in connection with papers preceding and following it made Marsh easily the first authority on the extinct avian class in America, and to-day most of the knowledge of fossil birds in this country, from the Jurassic to the Post-Pliocene, will be found in his writings.

Western Kansas which in 1870 also furnished the first pterodactyls found on this continent, on reëxamination yielded a large series of specimens pertaining to forms of unusual size, which were described by Marsh in various papers from 1871 to 1884. Not until 1876, however, was it found that, unlike European forms, one of the distinctive features of American types of Pterosauria was the absence of teeth, indicating a new group to which Marsh gave the name *Pteranodontia*.

Investigations on American forms of this group have recently been continued at the Yale University Museum, and a forthcoming memoir on *Pteranodon* furnishes interesting proof of Marsh's keen insight and rare skill in interpreting the evidence afforded by incomplete specimens. In a discussion of the skull of this flying dragon, it is stated in regard to the crest: "In figuring this strange outgrowth . . . Professor Marsh gave an example of his exceptional shrewdness in working from fragmentary material. As seen in [the] Plate, there remains only the basal portion of the great crest once borne by the type skull. From the evidence offered by this he was able to anticipate later discovery by figuring and describing an enormous crest that formed about one-third the entire length of the skull." It was during recent researches on these pterodactyls that the "enormous crest" mentioned in the quotation was disclosed in the matrix. The previous conjectural restoration of this part of the skull by Marsh is of interest in connection with a remark often made by him to one of his graduate students: "Young man," he would say, "remember that we don't any of us know much about this business."

The Cretaceous chalks of western Kansas further yielded remains of numerous sea-serpents, described by Marsh in a series of papers also beginning in 1871. Mosasaurs, though comparatively rare in other parts of the world, were remarkably developed in eastern and western sections of the United States. Marsh cleared up many obscure points in the structure of these marine reptiles, and was the first to determine some of the essential characters of the skeleton. New genera and species of other types of swimming reptiles were established by him, among which were a few forms allied to *Ichthyosaurus*.

Although Marsh's toothed birds and toothless pterodactyls, together with his fossil horses, may seem to constitute the more brilliant of his discoveries, yet probably the vertebrates that have added most to his fame are those comprised in the reptilian group called *Dinosauria*. Beginning in 1877, the notable discoveries of these monsters of antiquity in both Jurassic and Cretaceous deposits of the West, and later in the Triassic of the Connecticut Valley; the description and illustration of various suborders, families, genera, and species and the portrayal of their many peculiar characters were brought out in numerous papers contributed to the *American Journal of Science*, fourteen of which were reprinted in the *Geological Magazine* of London. In the *Dinosaurs of North America*, his third notable volume, which appeared in

1895, his long researches were compiled into a synoptic whole, yet the affinities and detailed treatment of these enormous lizards were reserved for the final monographs Marsh purposed to write. The volume under discussion, however, serves as the only monument of this class of his writings extant. The work accomplished on other volumes is mainly represented by numerous costly plates, including restorations of principal forms. The Dinosaurs found in the Triassic of the Connecticut Valley offered Marsh the needed evidence that some of the so-called bird tracks, of which Yale possesses a fine series, were made by carnivorous forms of these terrestrial reptiles, the larger species of which were bipedal. Unfortunately, much of the knowledge of this difficult group of extinct reptiles was held in Marsh's remarkable memory; his notes generally are not sufficiently amplified to make them available to others.

It will thus be seen that while Marsh wrote a great number of what he considered preliminary papers and published three large volumes, he left a vast amount of unfinished work. Although he published various general articles late in his career, after 1895 he seemed to lose sight of the fact that time was passing, and that his indebtedness to the Government in the way of volumes on which large sums of money had been expended for illustrations was still uncanceled. Habits of procrastination grew on him, and this fact combined with a lack of facility in readily formulating his thoughts will account for most of his literary failures. Some provision for the continuation of his uncompleted work was made in the eighth article of his will, which reads:

"The sum of Thirty thousand dollars which by the Terms of the First Family Trust of Mr. George Peabody, founded in 1867, I am authorized to dispose of by will, I hereby give and bequeath to said Corporation of Yale University in New Haven to be expended by the Trustees of said Peabody Museum in preparing for publication and publishing the results of my explorations in the West."

After 1892 no large collections were added to the Yale series until 1898, when active field-work was resumed under the direction of Marsh. A few fossil cycads had been previously received at New Haven, but the bulk of this collection was made during the summer and autumn of the latter year. More than seven hundred of these fossil trunks came from the Black Hills alone, and these taken in connection with the specimens since added constitute the most important series of the kind in the world. A few vertebrates were also obtained at about this time, notably the unique dinosaurian type *Barosaurus* and various remains pertaining to the largest turtles yet discovered.

But Marsh did not confine his efforts entirely to the making of vast collections; he devoted much of his energy to the proper housing of them. During a visit to his uncle at Homburg in 1863, he broached the subject of establishing a museum of natural history at Yale, and before the visit was over Mr. Peabody had given him assurance that the building, with proper endowment, should become a reality.

When in England, he had been strongly urged by Sir Charles Lyell to make a special study of the antiquity of man in America. With this in view, he commenced researches in the sepulchral mounds of Ohio. While thus engaged the idea of a museum of archæology and ethnology at Cambridge presented itself to his mind, and his plans for establishing scientific museums at both Harvard and Yale were fulfilled in 1867, when he assisted Mr. Peabody in organizing gifts to these universities and to the Peabody Academy of Science at Salem. In connection with the first of these Marsh was offered a professorship at Cambridge, a second offer coming in 1874, both of which were declined. He was appointed a trustee of the other two foundations and became Curator of the Yale Geological Collections, a position retained throughout life. The right wing of the Yale museum was completed in 1875, and much to his regret remained the only portion of the building to be finished during his régime, although he used every effort to overcome this adverse condition.

Early in 1898 by deed of gift Marsh presented all his scientific collections, including vertebrate and invertebrate fossils, fossil footprints, recent osteology, American archæology, minerals, and fossil cycads, to Yale University. The acceptance of this splendid gift was recorded in the following resolutions offered by the Corporation of the University:

"YALE UNIVERSITY,
"January 13, 1898.
"The President and Fellows, having received a deed of gift from Professor Othniel C. Marsh, presenting to the University his very valuable collections now in the Peabody Museum, which represent the labor of many years on his part and also the expenditure of a large amount from his personal fortune, desire, as they accept the gift, to communicate to him, and to place on record, an expression of their grateful acknowledgment of his generosity.

"In this grateful acknowledgment they are confident that all the graduates and friends of Yale will unite, when they learn of this most recent manifestation of his long-continued interest in the University, even as they already appreciate the unselfish devotion of his time, his talents, and his energies, for more than thirty years, to the scientific researches which have given him such personal distinction and have brought such renown to the institution.

"TIMOTHY DWIGHT, President."

Although the collection of vertebrate fossils combined with that of recent osteology constitutes by far the most important of these gifts to Yale, yet science is also indebted to Marsh for his zeal in gathering together a large amount of material pertaining to archæology and ethnology. On his return from Europe in 1866, he saw the importance of beginning a collection of American antiquities, and both before and during his western expeditions large numbers of ancient implements found their way to New Haven. Purchases were also made from collectors in various states, and through the liberality of friends of Yale many specimens have at various times been added. No provision was originally made for installing specimens of this kind in the museum, and a room on the fourth floor was devoted to this purpose, but its size combined with other disadvantages precludes the possibility of making an adequate display of the large number of objects acquired, which have been greatly augmented since Marsh's death. Notable in this collection are the thousands of specimens from the Province of Chiriqui,

Republic of Panama. These antiquities came mainly from prehistoric graves and represent the culture of Indians who in this respect ranked next to the Aztecs and the Peruvians under the Incas. The collection, said to be by far the most valuable and complete of the kind owned by any institution, has never been placed on exhibition, although received at the museum years ago. Another noteworthy series in the archæological collection is made up of a large number of Egyptian scarabs, which an eminent authority has recently declared the most comprehensive in America.

In recognition of his genius and of his zeal for science, Marsh won distinction both in this country and abroad. The appreciation of his ability as a collector has steadily grown, until he holds a foremost place among makers of vast scientific collections. What has not been so fully recognized is his great ability as an anatomist and the unerring certainty with which he seized on the characteristic features of a specimen and its relation to other forms.

Marsh was either a correspondent or an honorary member of many learned societies, the last honors of this kind coming to him in 1898, when he was elected correspondent of the Institute of France (Ácademy of Sciences) and foreign member of the Geological Society of London. Harvard University conferred upon him the degree of LL.D. in 1886, and he received an honorary Ph.D. from Heidelberg University the same year. At the time of his death he still held the position of Honorary Curator of Vertebrate Paleontology in the United States National Museum and of Vertebrate Paleontologist on the Geological Survey.

He became a member of the American Association for the Advancement of Science in the summer of 1866, while attending the Buffalo meeting, reading his first paper before that body at Burlington the following year. Two years later he was elected Secretary of the Association, and in 1876 its Vice-President, succeeding the next year to the position of presiding officer. His celebrated Nashville address on the *Introduction and Succession of Vertebrate Life in America* was delivered at the time of his retirement as Vice-President, and on leaving the office of President he made a second address: *History and Method of Paleontological Discovery*. In the first of these he showed his great knowledge of vertebrates by tracing in a masterly way the introduction and succession of the various types then known from this country, beginning with the lowest Devonian fishes and culminating in the highest primate—Man; while in the second he gave a comprehensive account of the progress of the science of paleontology from earliest times.

In 1877, Marsh was awarded the first Bigsby medal by the Council of the Geological Society of London. In transmitting this medal to Marsh, the President of the Geological Society said in part:

"The Medal is given in recognition of the great services which Prof. Marsh has rendered to the palæontology of the Vertebrata. He has distinguished himself by studying the fossil remains of nearly every great group of the Vertebrata from the Palæozoic, Cretaceous, and Cainozoic strata of the New World. The field of his research has been immense, but it has been very correct; and his descriptive and classificatory palæontological work indicates his effective grasp of anatomical details, and his great power as a comparative osteologist."

Marsh's first paper before the National Academy of Sciences was read by invitation at Northampton in 1869, and treated of his new western fossils. He was not elected to membership in the Academy, however, until 1874. Four years later he became Vice-President, and in May, 1878, on the death of the first President, Professor Henry, he served as Acting President. While substituting in the later capacity, the first instance occurred in which the advice of the Academy was asked by direct act of Congress. This action related to a consideration on the part of the Academy of "the methods and expenses of conducting all surveys of a scientific character under the War or Interior Department, and the surveys of the Land Office," with a request to report to Congress "a plan for surveying and mapping the Territories of the United States on such general system as will, in their judgment, secure the best results at the least possible cost." By virtue of his office, Marsh held the chairmanship of the committee appointed to carry out the wishes of Congress, and that portion of the report concerning geological surveys and the appointment of a commission on public lands became a law in 1879. Thus originated the present Geological Survey, with the designation by the Chief Executive of Clarence King as first Director.

In 1883, Marsh succeeded Professor W. B. Rogers as presiding officer of the National Academy of Sciences, and for twelve years he led the deliberations of that body with dignity and ability. He took pride in the fact that from the time of his election as Vice-President in 1878, he never absented himself from a meeting of the Academy—a record that probably few members can boast. His resignation took effect in April, 1895.

One of the most distinguished honors received by Marsh was the Cuvier Prize, awarded him by the Institute of France (Academy of Sciences) in 1898—a prize given every three years for the most remarkable work either on the animal kingdom or on geology. In submitting the report setting forth Marsh's claim to this distinction, Professor Gaudry, after rapidly reviewing the researches of the principal American savants in paleobotany and in invertebrate and vertebrate paleontology, announced that it was proposed to award the prize in 1898 to one of the paleontologists of the United States, Professor Marsh, who "stands unquestionably the chief of the constellation of distinguished men who are giving their attention to fossil vertebrates." [1]   The various phases of Marsh's work were dwelt upon in some detail, the report closing as follows:

"It is impossible to enumerate here all the creatures which the hammer of Mr. Marsh has drawn from the rocks and which his genius has restored. The discoveries which are now being made in the United States and in Patagonia open immense horizons before paleontologists. We believe that we are honoring the memory of Cuvier in awarding the prize which bears his name to

[1] " reste le seule chef incontesté de la pléiade d'hommes distingués qui s'occupe des vertébrés fossiles."

Prof. Marsh, one of the most skilful of those who are carrying forward the science whose foundations he laid." [1]

Marsh was a frequent visitor to England, and attended many meetings of the British Association for the Advancement of Science, where he read numerous papers on his western researches. He paid a last visit in 1898, having been appointed a delegate from this country to the International Congress of Zoölogists at Cambridge, subsequently attending the Association meeting at Bristol. He traveled extensively on the continent, and attended various congresses, both geological and zoölogical, in 1897 going as far as Russia as one of the delegates to represent the United States Geological Survey at the International Geological Congress at St. Petersburg.

The conditions of Marsh's early life tended to the formation and growth of certain peculiarities which at times laid him open to criticism. When he entered college he was years older than his classmates—a man when they were boys. He had not, at the formative period of his life, been thrown with other boys of his own age, and subjected to that process of attrition by which angles are worn off. Absorbed in his work, he never married, and thus missed that further smoothing off of roughness which family life is likely to bring.

His indomitable will brought him success and in later life, like many successful men, he was sometimes impatient, intolerant, and even autocratic. He took the ground that a region first investigated by him became his by right of preëmption—a notion that caused him numberless difficulties and brought little sympathy. He was a man of strong convictions—when attacked he would fight—and there were years in his scientific life when he permitted

[1] "Il est impossible de rappeler ici toutes les créatures que le marteau de M. Marsh a tirées des rochers et que son génie a restaurées. Les découvertes qui se font en ce moment, soit aux États-Unis, soit en Patagonie, ouvrent devant les paléontologistes des horizons immenses. Nous croyons honorer la mémoire de Cuvier en attribuant le prix qui porte son nom au professeur Marsh, un des plus habiles continuateurs de la Science dont il a jeté les fondements."

controversy and the struggle for priority to mar his happiness
and hinder his work. His fossils were priceless in his eyes, and he
guarded them with extremest care. A man of less enthusiasm or
of more liberal mind might have turned over certain subjects to
able assistants; Marsh's failure in this respect caused in several
cases a rupture of friendly relations. If his nature had been more
conciliatory—if he had really cared more for peace—these troubles
might have been avoided. He had one or two unfortunate experiences with visitors; hence was somewhat suspicious and disposed
to think that strangers were trying to overreach him. On the other
hand, he was a man of kindly nature, extremely jolly, and very
fond of a joke even though it were directed against himself. He
was generous, also, in the sense that if anyone made a special effort
in his behalf he would in turn go out of his way to assist the one
who had aided him. Marsh's peculiarities were many, some of
them being so marked as to give his enemies an opportunity to
speak ill of him, which sometimes resulted in grave injustice.

His foibles and failings, however, sink into insignificance when
compared with the many rare qualities that made his life successful. To a notable degree, he possessed the faculty of making
even minor things seem worth while; he lent to his surroundings
a strength and dignity that were almost unique. Since his death,
the grievances of most of those who worked under him have been
forgotten in admiration for his achievements. He had but few
close friends in America, yet his relations with men of science in
England were of the friendliest sort; however, Huxley's recorded
estimate of him, that he was "a wonderfully good fellow, full of
fun and stories of his western adventures," will find hearty indorse-
ment in many minds, at home as well as abroad. Marsh was a
keen judge of men, could instantly select the one that he felt would
be of most use to him, and was seldom at fault in his estimate of
character. He was efficient and shrewd, and an aggressive leader.
The quiet humor displayed in parts of the diary to which reference has been made constituted one of his most prominent characteristics.

The last years of his life were shadowed by adversity, yet to the world he showed only his cheerful and optimistic spirit. The financial stress of the early nineties reduced his private income and unfavorable legislation at Washington cut off his salary from the Geological Survey, even his allotment from this source being finally discontinued. So straitened did he become for means with which to carry on his researches that he finally mortgaged his property, and in 1896, although he had served Yale for thirty years without compensation, he was at his own request placed on the list of salaried officers of the University. The vote passed by the President and Fellows at this time shows the estimation in which Marsh's services were held:

"The Corporation of Yale University desires to congratulate Professor Othniel Charles Marsh upon arriving at the thirtieth anniversary of his professorship in health and strength, and to wish him a continuance of the same for many years.

"And they further desire to express to him their appreciation of and their profound sense of obligation for all that he has accomplished in the advancement of science, as well as for the reputation of the University, by creating and building up under its auspices the department of Paleontology and by generally carrying on the elaborate and expensive system of original research, exploration and discovery, by which he has enlarged the boundaries of scientific knowledge and has brought honor to the country, to the University, and to himself."

An English friend, in describing Marsh in 1882, pictured him as "of middle height, with a robust well-knit frame and massive head. Ruddy and of a fair countenance, he has blue eyes which often twinkle humorously." Coming of a hardy race, he possessed a vigorous physique and his consciousness of health was always vivid. Long after middle life he could endure an amount of physical strain that would have tired a younger man, and it was only within a year or two of his death that faith in his own length of days deserted him. While in Russia in 1897, trouble in the leg developed, virtually depriving him of the daily walks so necessary to his health. Lack of exercise, therefore, combined with the disturbance in the arterial system from which he suffered, rendered him unfit to cope with the disease that caused his death. He was seized with a chill on the eleventh of March, 1899, while working at the museum; pneumonia rapidly developed, and in a week, almost before those closest to him knew of his serious illness, he was dead. The tribute of a colleague in the University fittingly closes the story of his useful life:

"The details of his work were so little known by his fellow townsmen and his personality was so unusual that an inadequate impression might easily exist as to the value of his intellectual attainments and the importance of what he accomplished. From the time when . . . he collected minerals on the shores of the Bay of Fundy to the closing weeks of his life, he was ever the same eager, earnest student of science, amassing collections in many different lines with an indomitable energy characteristic of himself.

.   .   .   .

"Deprived of family ties which to most men bring the chief happiness of life and with but few close personal friends, he was ever bright and cheerful and devoted himself to science with a single heart. It is certainly not strange that, situated as he was, his intense personal ambition should have been often self-centered. His standard of scientific accuracy was high and he demanded the same of others; he was none too tolerant of those who opposed his views and who encroached upon a field which he felt he had preoccupied. But whatever may have been his personal peculiarities, Professor Marsh was a great man; great in the thoroughness of his intellectual attainments, great in his grasp of the broad principles of evolution, great in the tireless energy of his spirit.

"Death came to him suddenly before he had completed all the labors he had undertaken. . . . Notwithstanding it is given to few men to erect such a monument as he has done."

E. D. Cope.

EDWARD DRINKER COPE

PALEONTOLOGIST

1840–1897

BY MARCUS BENJAMIN

IN the history of American science there will be found the names
of many who have devoted their lives to the study of natural history. Indeed, according to Goode, Henry Harriot who accompanied Sir Walter Raleigh on his voyage to Virginia in 1584 and
thereafter compiled a *Brief and True Report of the New Found
Land of Virginia*, which is full of interest to the naturalist, was
"the first English man of science who crossed the Atlantic." He
is described as "a man of wide culture . . . a botanist, zoölogist, and anthropologist." From his time to the present there
have been many who have followed in his footsteps and among
them the names of Say, Leidy, Dana, Agassiz, Baird, and Newberry stand out conspicuously in the front rank, like planets among
the stars.

As knowledge grew, men more and more devoted themselves
to specialities, and from naturalists there were differentiated those
who studied living forms and those who occupied themselves with
fossil life, and then zoölogists and paleontologists were recognized,
and now with the everlasting growth of knowledge there are
ornithologists, ichthyologists, conchologists, lepidopterists, coleop-
terists, carcinologists, and many others who devote themselves
exclusively to some one of the almost infinite gradations into which
natural science has resolved itself.

The student of history who recalls the era when the great transcontinental surveys were made to locate a favorable possible
railway route that should extend from the Atlantic to the Pacific

313

will remember that each of these surveys was accompanied by a scientist whose duties were the collection of objects in natural history. These railway surveys were succeeded by the four great scientific surveys which flourished in the seventies of the nineteenth century and were consolidated into the United States Geological Survey in 1879, and the practice of employing trained scientists in connection with their work continued. Among those who have gained high reputation in consequence of this development no one occupies a higher place than Edward Drinker Cope of whom also more than of his contemporaries, it may be said that he "possessed those brilliant mental qualities which are the natural endowment of genius." It is the pleasant mission of the following pages to present his contributions to science.

The Cope family is a distinguished one in the annals of Philadelphia, and in the charming romances that Dr. Weir Mitchell has written so delightfully about the early days in the Quaker City, the name Cope frequently occurs. He tells pleasantly in one of his books how during an epidemic of yellow fever in 1793, Mr. Cope heroically remained in Philadelphia when flight was considered the best policy and devoted his attention to the victims of the plague. It was Mr. Cope also who four years later when the smallpox raged accepted the task of ministering to the wants of the destitute and carried food to the homes of the sufferers.

According to the records of the family Oliver Cope came from Wiltshire, England, about 1687, and settled at Naaman's Creek in the extreme north of what is now the state of Delaware. The original grant of land is dated September 8, 1681, and recites that William Penn of Worminghurst in the county of Sussex, Esquire, in consideration of five shillings, etc., conveys to Oliver Cope of Awbry in the county Wilts tailor, two hundred and fifty acres of land within the province of Pennsylvania.

Oliver's grandson was Caleb Cope, who, in 1761, removed to Lancaster and later settled in Philadelphia. While serving as burgess of Lancaster in 1776, the unfortunate Major André, who had been captured at St. Johns, Upper Canada, by General Montgomery and sent with other British prisoners to Lancaster, arrived in the little town. In spite of the popular excitement against these prisoners of war Caleb Cope offered them an asylum in his home and protected them against the vengeance of a mob which attacked his residence. He is said to have been a member of the Society of Friends and an opponent of the war against England. His son, Thomas Pim Cope, began a commerical career in Philadelphia in 1786, and four years later he established himself in the business of importing. His success was very great and soon warranted him in purchasing his own vessels. This venture likewise proved successful, and in 1821 he inaugurated the first line of packets that ran between Philadelphia and Liverpool, which then continued until about the beginning of the Civil War. His sons, Henry and Alfred, succeeded to the business, and in time the firm assumed the name of Cope Brothers.

Edward Drinker Cope was the eldest son of Alfred Cope and his wife, Hannah Edge. He was born in Philadelphia on July 28, 1840, while his father was yet active in business, but as the child grew to boyhood the family removed to Germantown and there the father, who was a man of cultivated literary taste, freed from the active interests of his commercial pursuits, lived in ease and devoted himself largely to the bringing up of his son.

At a very early age the boy manifested an active and intelligent interest in nature; when only about seven years old during a sea voyage to Boston with his father he is said to have kept a journal which he filled with drawings of "jelly fish, grampuses and other natural objects seen by the way." When eight and a half years old he made his first visit to the Museum of the Academy of Natural Sciences of his native city; this visit was "on the 21st of the 10th mo. 1848" as entered in his journal. He brought away careful drawings, measurements and descriptions of several larger birds, as well as of the skeleton of an ichthyosaurus. His drawing of the fossil reptile bears the explanatory legend in Quaker style: "two of the sclerotic plates: look at the eye, thee will see these in it." At the age of ten he was taken upon a voyage to the West Indies.

His contemporary and lifelong friend, Dr. Theodore Gill, in

a memorial address delivered before the American Philosophical Society said:

"While a school boy he relieved his studies of the classics and the regular course in which boys of his age were drilled by excursions into the fields and woods. Reptile life especially interested him, and he sought salamanders, snakes and tortoises under rocks, stones, fallen trees and layers of leaves, as well as in the ponds and streams of his vicinage. The trophies of his excursions were identified from descriptions in the works in which they were treated, as well as by comparison with identified specimens in the museum of The Academy [of Natural Sciences in Philadelphia]."

Professor Henry F. Osborn, his intimate friend and literary executor, writes, "the principal impression he gave in boyhood was of incessant activity in mind and body, reaching in every direction for knowledge, and of great independence in character and action."

His academic education was received in the Westtown Academy, a Quaker institution, where he came under the influence of Dr. Joseph Thomas and from whom he obtained a passing knowledge of Latin and Greek. In a letter written at this time he says:

"I caught a large water snake or water wampum as they are called here—one of the Colubers in Brandywine, and brought it home. It was about as long as my leg, but very thick for its length, being somewhat more than two inches in diameter in one place. I afterwards found that it had eaten a large bull frog which somewhat increased its natural thickness. The people told me it would bite me, for everybody almost about here thinks water wampums are poisonous, and, indeed the way it struck at me scared me a little, but I soon convinced myself it was not, by examining its mouth which wanted fangs, and as all non-venomous have, it had four rows of small teeth in its upper, and two in its lower jaw, and two rows of scales under the tail."

He does not appear to have had any instruction in any biological science and had no regular collegiate training, although for a year he studied anatomy in the laboratories of the University of Pennsylvania under the illustrious Leidy, but after all, according to Osborn, "it is evident that he owed far more to paternal guidance in the direct study of nature and to his own impulses as a young investigator than to the five or six years of formal education which he received at school."

Thus the boy grew to manhood, and of his appearance at that time Doctor Gill describes him as:

"A young man, nineteen years old, about 5 feet 9 or 10 inches high, with head carried somewhat backwards and of rather robust frame, stood before me; he had an alert, energetic manner, a pronounced, positive voice, and appeared to be well able to take his part in any trouble. His knowledge was by no means confined to herpetology, but covered a wide range of science, and his preliminary education had been good."

In 1859, he visited Washington and joined the group of young naturalists who were associated together in the Smithsonian Institution under Professor Baird. Their names are best recalled by the following stanza, improvised by one of their number, after a hotly contested argument on some disputed point in natural history:

"Into this well of learning dip with spoon of Wood or Horn,
For students Meek and holy silver spoons should treat with scorn.

"If Gabb should have the gift of Gill
As Gill has gift of Gabb,
'Twould show a want of judgment still
To try to Cope with Meek."

In Washington he found not only congenial associates but also a place of abode, and he tells in a letter of how he "located on the sixpenny side of Pennsylvania Avenue near Sixth St." at $25 a month.

Later, on February 1, 1861, he writes:

"I have come to the conclusion that Washington is decidedly a second-rate place. Though there are two professors and a doctor in the boarding house, they are all unsatisfactory trifling people."

Of his associates he says:

"Two fairer men than Profs. Henry and Baird are, however,

hard to find. Theodore Gill, a native of New York, with whom I have been acquainted for a considerable length of time, is an honorable and sincere young man, so far as I know him, though by education different enough from myself."

His first scientific publication was in 1859, when he contributed a paper "On the Primary Divisions of the Salamandridæ, with descriptions of Two New Species" to the *Proceedings* of the Academy of Natural Sciences in Philadelphia. In this paper he presented important modifications of the systems previously adopted in this country. He continued his study of the serpents and made a catalogue of the specimens contained in the museum of the Academy in which he employed an improved system of his own.

During the five years that followed he published frequent papers, describing new species and giving synopses or brief monographs of various genera of lizards and anurous amphibians. In these early papers he manifested the independence and critical spirit which were so characteristic of him later. On this point, Gill says:

"Bold as was the criticism of such herpetologists as Duméril, Bibron, and Günther, it was justified by the facts, and the young author's conclusions have received the endorsement of the best succeeding herpetologists, including even the latest author criticised."

His only deviation from this special subject of reptiles was in 1861, when he made a verbal communication on some cyprinoid fishes, and again in 1862 when he described a new shrew caught by himself in New Hampshire. Again I quote from Gill, who writes:

"He never lost his interest in herpetology and continued to the end of his life to devote much attention to that department. His studies extended to every branch of the subject, covering not only specific details and general taxonomy, but also the consideration of anatomical details, the modifications of different organs, geographical distribution, chronological sequence, genetic relations, and physiological consequences."

The time at the Smithsonian passed quickly and was well spent in hard work—work that was to tell so splendidly in the years yet to come. Partly as a rest from overwork and partly for study, he went to Europe in 1863, and for a year he visited the great museums of England, France, Holland, Austria, and Prussia, systematically examining the collections of reptiles in the chief centers of science.

The broadening influence of foreign travel soon manifested itself, and although herpetology was his first love and continued to be the favorite branch of science to his life's end, he began to develop wider interests and to extend his studies to various other subjects.

The Civil War was in progress during his visit to Europe, and of special interest, therefore, in this connection is the following quotation from one of his letters.

"I hear nothing but bad news from the United States. It is plain that we cannot carry on those works, or achieve the results which require the united systematic efforts of a whole people without a strong government which shall absolutely rule; but it is plain also that such arrangements, as far as I can see here, are the moral ruin and intellectual degradation of a great many people; hence the conclusion that the results to be obtained are not worth the loss incurred in obtaining them; hence the request of the Jews for a king instead of a judge, was a mistake. But as things are, I suppose we shall have a strong government; what my duty would be in case I were drafted, I am as much in the dark about as ever. It seems wrong to withdraw myself from any participation in government at all—yet if one begins it is hard to stop short of armies."

Soon after his return to the United States he was called to the professorship of Natural Science in Haverford College and for three years, from 1864 to 1867, he lectured in that institution. It was while holding that chair that in 1865 he married Anne Pim, daughter of Richard Pim of Chester County, a distant cousin.

Meanwhile his papers, which were increasing in number and which for the most part were published in the *Proceedings* of the Academy of Natural Sciences, more and more, according to Osborn, "showed the impulse of philosophical spirit, complete familiarity

with the history of opinion and marked power of generalization."
For the most part they dealt with recent herpetology and ichthyology and were demonstrative of the main evolution principles in
these groups.

In 1865 he first began to extend his studies among the mammalia, especially of the Cetacea, both recent and extinct, of the Coast
Tertiary. It was also in this year that he described a fossil vertebrate for the first time—the *Amphibamus grandiceps* from the
Coal Measures. Thereafter for many years he devoted his chief
attention to exploration and research. During a portion of this
time he made his home in Haddonfield, New Jersey, a place six
miles southeast of Camden, and there he began the accumulation
of those great collections of specimens, the descriptions of which
form perhaps his greatest contributions to science. In 1866 he
began his studies of the fossil vertebrates found in the Cretaceous
marls of New Jersey, where he procured the remains of dinosaurs,
"describing especially the carnivorous *Lælaps* and grouping these
reptiles into three great suborders, Orthopoda (*Hadrosaurus* and
Iguadon), Goniopoda and Symphopoda (*Megalosaurus*, *Lælaps*,
Compsognathus)." This was essentially his introduction into the
field of vertebrate paleontology, "in which, until his death, he was
considered by many as foremost in America, if not in the world."

In 1867 he examined the Eocene and Miocene beds in the southern part of Maryland between the Potomac and Patuxent rivers,
and there made a collection of fossil vertebrates and mollusks.
There he found a dolphin with a long cylindrical muzzle which
he describes as "one of the most singular known . . . as it is
new, species, genus and family." A year later he traveled through
the marl country with Prof. O. C. Marsh and he writes:

"Prof. Marsh has studied and traveled in Europe for three
years, and is very familiar with their invertebrate fossils. We
have procured three new species of Saurians, apparently of known
genera; one a Mosasaurus, one a Gavial, and one of large size is
very near the Cetacea."

He visited the mountain region of North Carolina in 1869 and
of this trip he writes from Raleigh, on December 11:

"I spent four weeks east of this city investigating the marl region, and collecting its fossils. This region is mostly Miocene, and the formation is more largely developed here than in any part of the United States, excepting perhaps Nebraska."

Adding also:

"I had pretty good success in my fossil collecting, and with more knowledge of the country could have done much better. I will however be able to make some valuable additions to paleontology, and will have all the vertebrate fossils obtained by the state survey, to determine. The majority of mammalia are cetaceans, I have at least 15 species of these."

Between the years 1868 and 1870, the plesiosaurs of the Cretaceous of Kansas began to occupy his attention, and in 1871 he visited these chalk beds and began his own explorations there. His work soon extended further westward. In 1872 for a time he was in Wyoming, and in 1873 he was in Colorado.

From Fort Bridger, Wyoming, under date of October 12, 1872, he writes:

"I found in my sixty-five days' exploration the remains of species of animals according to the following figures: species, quadrupeds, 32; birds, 2; crocodiles, 6; lizards, 4; snakes, 1; turtles, 17; total 62; and 13–14 kinds of fishes."

From the foregoing quotations some idea of his great activity may be had and yet it by no manner of means represents all, for his nights were spent in preparing papers describing new species, many of which were illustrated by drawings from his own pen, which were promptly sent to Philadelphia for publication.

While not neglecting other interests, for a time, at least, his work in paleontology continued to be paramount, and led in 1872 to his appointment as vertebrate paleontologist to the United States Geological and Geographical Survey of the Territories under Dr. F. V. Hayden, and during his connection with this survey he explored and collected in every state and territory west of the Missouri.

It would be difficult, indeed, to follow his career in detail as he journeyed through the west, but it resulted in the discovery of many new types of fishes, mosasaurs, chelonians, and other reptiles which were described in short preliminary papers and then more fully in his larger *Vertebrata of the Cretaceous Formations of the West* (1875), which forms the second volume of the quarto series of the reports issued under the auspices of the Hayden Survey.

Even larger than this is his famous "Book 1" often facetiously called "Cope's Bible" which, however, properly bears the title *The Vertebrata of the Tertiary Formations of the West* and is the third volume of the quarto series of the Hayden reports. It contains over a thousand pages and more than one hundred plates, and was published in Washington in 1883. According to Cope himself it included descriptions of "the vertebrata of the Eocene and of the Lower Miocene, less the Ungulata." He says: "There are described three hundred and forty-nine species, of which I have been the discoverer of all except thirty-two. They are referred to one hundred and twenty-five genera." In further detail he says:

"The most important results which have accrued to paleontology through the researches here set forth, are the following: 1. The discovery of the Laramie genus *Champsosaurus* in Tertiary beds. 2. The discovery of Plagiaulacidæ in Tertiary beds. 3. The discovery of the characters of five families and many genera and species of the Creodonta. 4. The discovery of the characters of the *Periptychidæ* and its included genera. 5. Of the *Meniscotheriidæ*. 6. Of the *Phenacodontidæ* and its genera. 7. The discovery of the characters of the suborder of Condylarthra and of the phylognetic results of the same. 8. The discovery of the characters of the *Pantolambididæ;* and 9. Of the suborder *Taligrada* and its implications in phylogeny. 10. The discovery of the *Anaptomorphidæ* of the Prosimiæ. 11. The reconstruction of Hyracotherium; and 12. Of *Hyrachyus*. 13. The discovery of numerous *Marsupialia* in the Lower Miocene. 14. The discovery of the phylogenetic series of the Canidæ; and 15. The same of the ancestors of the Felidæ."

In his letter of transmittal Hayden well describes this volume "as one of the most important contributions to the rich field of vertebrate paleontology of the Western Territories ever made in this country." As originally contemplated his work was intended to consist of four parts, namely: 1. Puerco, Wasatch, and Bridger faunæ (Eocene); 2. White River and John Day faunæ (Lower and Middle Miocene); 3. Ticholeptus and Loup Fork faunæ (Upper Miocene); and 4. Pliocene. Book 1 covered Part 1 and Part 2, including the marsupials, bats, insectivores, rodents, and carnivora of the Miocene only. The remaining parts were never published.

In March, 1874, he wrote to his father:

"I recently went over the reptiles and fishes of Wheeler's survey with interesting results. I found one new group of fishes pertaining exclusively to the waters of the Western Colorado—the only one peculiar; all the rest are usual forms of the east."

In July of the same year there will be found among his letters one, also written to his father, in which he says:

"I have just returned from Washington, where I have concluded a contract with G. M. Wheeler, of the topographical engineers and director of the Geological survey of the territories west of the 100th meridian. By this I engage to work on the geology and paleontology of the region he surveys until the work is concluded (about a year) at the rate of $2,500 per annum, and $30 per month additional for provisions when in the field, and all expenses of expedition paid."

He at once took the field and spent the time from July to October in New Mexico. I glean the following pertinent paragraphs from his letters.

On September 15, from the " Eocene Lake Formation " he writes:

"We began to find fossil bones. The first thing was a turtle, and then Bathmodon (Cope) teeth! and then everything else rare and strange till by near sun down I had twenty species of vertebrates! all of the lowest Eocene, lower than the lowest at Fort Bridger. The most important find in geology I ever made, and the paleontology promises grandly."

Twelve days later on September 27, writing from Camp Galli-
nas he says:

"I have over 75 species of Vertebrate fossils, many new. . . .
The most remarkable are toxodonts of four species and two new
genera, which I call *Calamodon* and *Ectoganus*, varying from the
size of a sheep to that of a cow. The order has never been found
out of South America before, and is in structure between rats and
hoofed animals, especially elephants."

While on October 11, from "Camp N. W. from Nacimiento,
New Mexico," he writes:

"I have now some 90 species of vertebrates from this bed, six
of them toxodonts. I have also discovered the deposits of another
fresh water lake of much greater age, say lower Cretaceous, not
many miles from here, which contains remains of saurians,—one
like Lælaps; I have a tooth and a vertebra."

The results of his summer's work in New Mexico were published
in several preliminary bulletins and then finally collected to form
a part of the volume on Paleontology which was published in 1877
as the fourth in the quarto series of the reports of the U. S. Geographical Surveys west of the One Hundredth Meridian, under
Lieutenant George M. Wheeler. It bears the subtitle of *The
Extinct Vertebrata Obtained in New Mexico by Parties of the
Expedition of* 1874.

Cope describes his work as follows:

"Of stratigraphical results, I may mention three: first, the
elucidation of the structure of the western slope of the Rocky
Mountains and the plateau to the westward of them, in north
western New Mexico; secondly, the determination of the fresh
water character of the Triassic beds in that region; thirdly, the
discovery of extensive deposits of the Lower Eocene, equivalent
to the Suessonien of western Europe."

The paleontological results were more numerous, and Cope
refers to them in his letter of transmission as follows:

"They are included in the determination of the faunæ of four
periods in basins which had not previously been explored, viz.,

in the Trias, the Eocene, the Loup Fork epoch, and Post-pliocene of the Sandia Mountains. The first vertebrate fossils ever determined from the Trias of the Rocky Mountains are included in the report. The first discovered were obtained by Professor Newberry while attached to Captain Macomb's expedition and one now described for the first time. The determination of the ages of the respective horizons necessarily follows the first determination of the fossils."

He continues:

"An especial advantage enjoyed in the preparation of this report consists in the fact that the author obtained the fossils himself and is thus familiar with their local relations. This is a point of much importance since the fragmentary condition in which the skeletons of extinct vertebrata are usually found, furnishes opportunities for error or doubt which greatly curtailed the value of the work. In the present instance the author has admitted no correlation of fragments without the clearest evidence, and where any uncertainty exists, has stated it."

The number of specimens of extinct vertebrata obtained during the season of 1874 was as follows: Triassic, 4; Cretaceous, 13; Eocene, 87; Upper Miocene (Loup Fork), 30; and Post-pliocene, 2, making a total of 136 specimens which now form part of the collections contained in the U. S. National Museum.

His specimens increased to such an extent that subsequent to 1874 he was obliged to devote more and more attention to working up the material that he had accumulated and consequently less time to field-work; although in 1876 he led an expedition to the Bad Lands of the Upper Cretaceous and returned again in 1877 to further investigate the chalk deposits of Kansas. On both of these trips he was accompanied by Charles H. Sternberg, who has recently pleasantly described his experiences.[1]

For a time he maintained parties in the field, paying their expenses from his private purse. One of these expeditions was sent as far away as South America and returned with a valuable lot of material; however, for the most part they were confined to

[1] See *Life of a Fossil Hunter*, by Charles H. Sternberg, New York, 1909.

the western territories and were under the direction of well-known fossil hunters such as Jacob L. Wortman and Charles H. Sternberg.

Early in 1877 he gave up his residence in Haddonfield and thereafter his home on Pine Street in Philadelphia was used to store his ever-increasing collections; for notwithstanding financial difficulties that came to him owing to unfortunate investments made from the ample fortune bequeathed to him by his father, he persisted in retaining his collections, refusing even to sell portions for which he was offered liberal sums, and at the cost of personal discomfort, held on to them and made his home, for much of the time, in the midst of them, having sold his residential home but keeping his museum. Gill says: "He filled a large house from cellar to topmost story with his collections and resided in an adjoining one."

Of this period, Sternberg tells how he had a standing invitation to eat dinner every Sunday with the Professor and his wife and daughter, a lovely child of twelve summers. He says:

"I shall never forget those Sunday dinners. The food was plain, but daintily cooked, and the Professor's conversation was a feast in itself. He had a wonderful power of putting professional matters from his mind when he left his study, and coming out ready to enter into any kind of merrymaking. He used to sit with sparkling eyes telling story after story, while we laughed at his sallies until we could laugh no more."

I may add that his work in connection with the exploration of the western territories resulted in the discovery of more than one thousand new species of extinct and as many recent vertebrata. It has been said that this work described in more than four hundred separate papers forms "a systematic record of paleontology in the United States." [1]

[1] Professor Oliver P. Hay is authority for the following statement: "According to my examinations of the fossil vertebrates I find that there are something more than 3,200 species described from North America, and of these Cope has given name to 1,115. That is he has named that many species which, with our present knowledge, must be accepted as good. They are distributed as follows: Fishes, 227; Batrachians, 73; Reptiles, 320; Birds, 8; Mammals, 487; Total, 1,115."

According to Osborn "as early as 1868 it may be said that he had laid the foundations for five great lines of research, which he pursued concurrently to the end of his life." Four of these pertaining to natural history, are fishes, amphibians, reptiles, and mammals.

Very briefly I shall present opinions concerning his contributions in these branches of zoölogy.

Of his knowledge of fishes, Osborn, his ever-faithful friend, says: "Cope's work in ichthyology would alone have given him high rank among zoölogists." According to Gill, than whom no more competent authority is possible, "as early as 1864, Cope became interested in the fresh water fishes of the United States and from then on published descriptions and enumerations of many species." Some of the most interesting genera of North America were originally made known by him. He was the first to describe the richness of the cyprinoid and especially the catastomoid fauna of North Carolina. But his greatest work was on classification. Almost from the first he set aside the superficial characters which had been employed in the arrangement of fishes, sympathizing keenly with the morphological study which his colleague, Theodore Gill, was then actively developing. While in Vienna, in 1863, he purchased a large collection of fish-skeletons from all parts of the world which was most useful to him in his comparative study of the various forms. In 1870, he published a paper in which he maintained that the primary divisions of the Telostomi are indicated by their fin structure. He established the fundamental division of the living fishes into five groups, just as they stand at the present day, upon cranial and fin structure. In 1884 he proposed an Elasmobranch subclass, Ichthyotomi, based on the Permian Diplodus, which is firmly established, and in 1889 he proposed the suborder Ostracodermi which is also now accepted. His views with but slight modifications have received the approval of A. Smith Woodward of the British Museum who is accepted as the best informed living student of extinct forms of fishes. Cope continued his studies on fishes until the close of his life and his final opinions and additions to the taxonomy and phylogeny of fishes are contained in the syllabus of his university lectures in 1897.

Passing to the amphibians it may be said that his studies in this branch of natural history are included in more than forty papers. These began with one on the Salamandridæ written in 1859. The classification of the Anura received his attention in 1865 and 1866 when he outlined the larger Ecaudate or Anurous divisions, namely, the Aglossa; the Bufoniformia; the Arcifera; and the Raniformia. It was also in 1865 that he described the fossil *amphibamus grandiceps* from the Carboniferous of Ohio. This was his first extinct amphibian. Soon after, turning to the classification of the amphibians, he proposed the order of Stegocephali to include the labyrinthodonts and smiliar great monsters of the past. This order has been universally adopted. From the Coal Measures of Ohio and the Permian deposits of Texas he obtained many new forms of fossil amphibians which he described and classified, and in 1884 he published the "Batrachia of the Permian Period of North America," in which he summed up his previous contributions. He must also be credited with the "Check List of North American Batrachia and Reptilia" (1875) and with "The Batrachia of North America" (1899) which he contributed to the series of *Bulletins* published by the U. S. National Museum. The former includes a systematic list of the higher groups and also an essay on geographical distribution. The latter forms a volume of over 500 pages with 120 text figures and 86 full page plates. In it "107 species are recognized and these are distributed under 31 genera." According to Dr. George Baur of the University of Chicago: "There never has been a naturalist who has published so many papers upon the taxonomy, morphology and paleontology of the Amphibia and Reptilia as Professor Cope."

His studies of the reptiles developed largely in connection with his western explorations, and according to Osborn may be grouped as: "First, his treatment of the reptiles of the Bridger and other fresh-water Tertiary lakes in connection with the mammalian fauna; second, the continuation of his systematic description of the Kansas Cretaceous fauna; third, the brief papers upon the herbivorous Dinosaurs of the Dakota (1877 and 1878) and the horned Dinosaurs (Monoclonius) of the Laramie formations; fourth, the numerous papers based upon the Reptilia of the Triassic, especially the Permian. The latter must be considered the most important and unique in their influence upon paleontology." They have also been described as his "most epoch-making contributions." Many of his papers on the reptiles were contributed to the *Proceedings* of the American Philosophical Society. Mention was made in the preceding paragraph of his two important works on batrachia and reptilia in the publications of the U. S. National Museum. To them may properly be added his "Catalogue of Batrachia and Reptilia of Central America and Mexico" (1887) also published by the National Museum. In it 197 genera are represented. These include 705 species which are divided between 135 Batrachia and 570 Reptilia. His last large work, completed a few months before his death, was on "The Crocodilians, Lizards, and Snakes of North America." It formed a monograph of 1095 pages with 36 plates and 347 text figures, and was issued as an appendix to the *Report of the U. S. National Museum* for the year 1898. According to Cope this work, together "with my book on the Batrachia published in 1889, and Doctor's Baur's on the Testudinata (in preparation),[1] the access to North American herpetology becomes equal to that which the science of ornithology has long enjoyed." This work gives descriptions in full of all the species and their including categories. The classification which he had already elaborated in various memoirs is adopted, and as in the "Batrachia," the genera and their including groups of the entire world are diagnosed in analytical tables, but full descriptions are given only of the North American types.

Professor Cope's most numerous and voluminous papers were devoted to mammals and more especially to fossil mammals. His conspicuous contributions in this domain are by common consent conceded to be those which have led to the development and establishment of certain fundamental principles which he

[1] The untimely death of Doctor Baur unfortunately prevented the publication of his work.

derived from his experience. The proposition that "the ancestors of the hoofed animals possessed bunodont or hillock-like teeth" was originally advanced by him and then was verified by the opportune discovery of *Phenacodus*. It led to a reclassification by him of the *Ungulates* by foot structure. To Cope is due the chief credit in establishing the principle "that the primitive feet of hoofed animals were plantigrade, like those of the bear with serial unbroken joints," which according to Osborn constituted "the first distinct advance in mammalian classification since Owen demolished Cuvier's 'pachydermata.'" The same authority may be quoted as describing Cope's conclusions as ranking "with Huxley's best work among similar problems, and they afford a basis for the phylogenetic arrangements of the hoofed orders which has been adopted by all American and foreign paleontologists." From his studies of the collections from the Basal Eocene he derived his "Law of Trituberculy," that is, "that all types of molar teeth in mammals originate in modifications of the tritubercular form." This generalization is of the utmost value, for upon it may depend the whole modern morphology of the teeth of the mammalia and the establishment of a series of homologies in the teeth of the most diverse types, applying even to the teeth of man. That "the hoofed orders converge towards the clawed types of Creodonta and Insectivora" is a law which he also laid down and demonstrated by a fortunate discovery in the field. He defined the primitive suborder of Carnivora, now universally adopted under his name of Creodonta; and he added much to our knowledge of the whole order, especially of the true cats. The mechanical origin of the hard parts of the bodies of mammals, especially the teeth, vertebræ, and limbs received his consideration and he published many papers on this subject, which culminated in his memoir on the "Origin of the Hard Parts of the Mammalia" (1889).

Fitting indeed, as a closing paragraph to these brief summaries of his specialties are the following words written by his friend and admirer, A. Smith Woodward of the British Museum:

"One great feature of this systematic work, everywhere conspicuous, is the attempt to define every term, whether specific, generic, of family or higher rank, in a concise diagnosis. Before Cope's time, this method had rarely been applied to extinct animals; even at the present day it does not prevail so widely as it ought to do. Cope, however, made all his definitions as precise as the variously imperfect materials would allow; and he naturally waxed wroth in his reviews of some contemporary literature which contained new names with nothing but an artist's drawing to justify their introduction into scientific terminology."

The consideration of Professor Cope's philosophical writings naturally belongs here. He was never satisfied with the study of morphological details or simple taxonomy. As Gill says: "He aspired to know how animals came into existence; why they varied as they did, and what laws determined their being. His was an eminently philosophical mind, but at the same time with a decided tendency to metaphysical speculation."

And so in 1869, at the very outset of his career he published a remarkable essay of 80 pages, *On the Origin of Genera,* in which he contended that while a large proportion of specific characters are adaptive, few generic characters are so, and the latter evolve separately by the force of "acceleration or retardation" of one of several plans or types of development preordained by the Creator. He did not agree with Darwin that natural selection was a sufficient factor for differentiation but returned to the Lamarckian principle of the effect of the use and disuse to explain variations; but he went further than Lamarck in that he denied that animals are passive subjects. With Hyatt, Ryder, and Packard he became one of the pioneers in the Neo-Lamarckian school of thought.

In 1874, in a letter to his father, Cope wrote :

"There are three forms of evolution doctrines: (1) That non-vital force evolves life; (2) that internal consciousness is the source of non-vital force and life; (3) that external or supernatural force, applied from without, maintains development. My studies have led me to the second position. The third is Professor McCosh's; the first that of the materialists."

His progressive thoughts on evolution and other metaphysical problems may be found in such papers as "On the Hypothesis of Evolution," contributed to *Lippincott's Magazine* in 1871; "Evolution and its Consequences" (1872); "Consciousness in Evolution" (1875) and "The Origin of the Will" (1877) which appeared in the *Penn Monthly* in the years named. Of similar character were his studies "On Archæsthetism" (1882); "The Relations of Mind to Matter" (1887); and "The Theology of Evolution (1887), originally published in the *American Naturalists*, as well as "What is the Object of Life?" (1887) which appeared in *The Forum*.

Many of these are included in the series of twenty-one essays on evolution which he published in 1886 with the title of *The Origin of the Fittest*. In this volume of 467 pages he presents "the doctrine of evolution from a more modern standpoint than that of Darwin and which is at the same time more ancient, namely that of Lamarck." He shows essentially that organic structure or species are the result of movements long continued and inherited and that the character of these movements was originally determined by consciousness or sensibility. Effort or use exerted by the living being on its own body is the reason, he contended, why variations occur for natural selection to play on.

The London *Athenæum* said of this volume:

"As many of the opponents of evolution are, consciously or unconsciously, swayed by the fear that the principle threatens the future of revealed religion, it is proper to add that Professor Cope's method of dealing with metaphysical evolution is hardly one to which any of the various synonyms of 'unorthodox' could be applied."

Among his later essays worthy of special mention are the following: "Evolution and Idealism" (1888); "The Relation of Will to the Conservation of Energy" (1888); "The Theism of Evolution" (1888); "On Inheritance in Evolution" (1889); "The Evolution of Mind" (1890); "Phylogeny of Man" (1891); "The Energy of Evolution" (1894); and "Psychic Evolution" (1897), all of which appeared in the *American Naturalist*. His papers on the relations of individuals during this period were for the most part contributed to the *Monist* and *The Open Court*, both of which are published in Chicago. They include the following: "The Marriage Problem" (1888), "Ethical Evolution" (1889), "On the Material Relation of Sex" (1890), "Foundations of Theism" (1893), "The Effeminization of Man" (1893), "The Present Problems of Organic Evolution" (1895), and "Primary Factors of Organic Evolution" (1896). These essays in time formed the basis of chapters or even constituted chapters themselves in the works that he subsequently published. Many of those that appeared in Chicago were collected and woven into the volume entitled *The Primary Factors of Organic Evolution*, which was published in 1896. This work he describes as "an attempt to select from the mass of facts accumulated by biologists, those which, in the author's opinion, throw a clear light on the problem of organic evolution, and especially that of the animal kingdom."

The evidence presented is chiefly paleontological. He says:

"In the search for the factors of evolution, we must have first a knowledge of the course of evolution. This can only be obtained in a final and positive form by investigation of the succession of life. The record of this succession is contained in the sedimentary deposits of the earth's crust, and is necessarily imperfect. Advance in knowledge in this direction has, however, been very great of recent years, so that some parts of the genealogical tree are tolerably or quite complete. We hope reasonably for continued progress in this direction, and if the future is to be judged of by the past, the number of gaps in our knowledge will be greatly lessened. In the absence of the paleontological record, we necessarily rely on the embryologic, which contains a recapitulation of it. The imperfections of the embryonic records are, however, great, and this record differs from the paleontologic in that no future discovery in embryology can correct its irregularities. On the contrary every paleontologic discovery is an addition to positive genealogy."

Mention is appropriate at this place of his contribution of a paper on "Evolution in Science and Art" to the *Evolution Series* of the Brooklyn Ethical Association in 1891. He also prepared one of the lectures in the series published over the title of *Half Hours with Modern Scientists*, and he was the author of the article on "Comparative Anatomy" contained in the *Universal Cyclopedia*.

His last book, published in 1897, was on *The Primary Factors of Organic Evolution*. In it with his accustomed skill he gives the latest evidence for inheritance of acquired characters.

Gill says of this work:

"He evoked 'evidence from embryology,' 'evidence from paleontology,' 'evidence from breeding'; he considered the 'characters due to nutrition,' 'characters due to exercise of function,' 'characters due to disease,' 'characters due to mutilation and injuries,' and 'characters due to regional influence'; he enquired into the conditions of inheritance,' and he fought against the 'objections to the doctrine of inheritance of acquired characters.' "

This volume is of interest also as containing his views on many sociological and theological problems.

A. Smith Woodward of the British Museum in a most admirable sketch of Cope that appeared in *Natural Science* for June, 1897, sums up his view on philosophy so satisfactorily that even if the statements are of the nature of repetition, I believe them worthy of presentation.

"Cope believed that all organisms, impelled by some inherent growth-force, which he termed 'Bathmism,' varied in certain definite directions, and that all modifications ultimately depended on the mechanical conditions of the environment. Paleontology, according to him proved beyond all doubt that characters thus acquired were inherited. Still further, he promulgated the doctrine, that this development of new characters takes place by an acceleration or retardation in the growth of the parts changed; that, in fact, the adult of an ancestral organism is the exact parallel of an immature stage in its descendant, which only advances or becomes degraded in certain characters during the latest phase of its growth. He was also the first to point out, as the result of these premises, that the genera of systematists, as commonly understood, are often polyphyletic. According to him, it is the species that are permanent, while genera are but our expression of various grades of organisation through which many species pass. The environment moulds species into genera, and genera into families; and a genus or a family by no means contains forms that are of necessity descended from a common ancestor.

"Finally, and not unnaturally, Cope wandered into the domain of mental phenomena, and applied his principles to these. He believed that consciousness preceded the form in which we are accustomed to witness its manifestation, namely organic tissue. His latest definition of life was: 'Energy directed by sensibility, or by a mechanism which has originated under the direction of sensibility.'"

In the year 1878, Cope purchased the rights of the owners of the *American Naturalist*, a scientific periodical founded in 1866 by Messrs. Hyatt, Morse, Packard, and Putnam, then in the splendid strength of their early manhood and fresh from the laboratories of Cambridge where they had been students under the elder Agassiz. This journal was published in Salem, Massachusetts, but Cope transferred its place of publication at once to Philadelphia where it was regularly issued by him at first in association with Professor Packard, and then alone, aided, however, by a staff of eminent specialists. Subsequent to 1887, he was its editor-in-chief and sole proprietor. This medium afforded him an outlet for his continuous stream of shorter articles and for the free expression of his very independent opinions upon current scientific movements and topics. His last words appeared in the numbers issued after his death and the leading article on those remarkable mammals of South America, known as Toxodontia, in the June number for 1897, was from his pen. Twenty octavo volumes (12–31) form the record of his industry in this direction.

With his retirement from Haverford College in 1867 Cope's professorial work was entirely discontinued for more than twenty years, although he gave lectures in his own home to special students and from time to time he delivered public lectures, showing the wonders of his western exploration to enthusiastic audiences.

In 1873 he wrote:

"Some one has just endowed a chair of natural history at Princeton College to be called the Henry chair, and Professor H. recommended me to Professor McCosh to fill it. The latter objected to my evolution sentiments, for those views are much condemned at Princeton. I have not much intention of fixing myself there, as the hours and work generally will probably require too much time, but I may find the University of Pennsylvania better, especially as it is nearer home.   One or the other I will probably undertake."

At the close of the Centennial Exhibition in Philadelphia in October, 1876, the success that had crowned the splendid efforts of the public-spirited citizens of that city led to further efforts on their part to organize a memorial that should be a permanent exhibition, a special feature of which was to be the Educational Department.   Cope was made chief of the division of organic material and did much in the preliminary work of organization of what is now the Pennsylvania Museum in Fairmount Park.

The loss of the greater part of his private fortune led Cope to consider the desirability of increasing his income, by some appointment worthy of his ability.   It was doubtless on that account that in a letter written to Dr. Persifor Frazer he says:

"Some of my friends are exerting themselves to secure for me the place to be shortly vacated by Langley in the Smithsonian. He will in all probability become secretary of the Smithsonian Institution and the place of Assistant Secretary will be vacant.   G. Brown Goode will become director of the National Museum and Chief of the U. S. Fish Commission, but some one will be necessary to fill the other vacancy.   The person must also be a naturalist, since Langley the secretary, is a physicist."

In 1889, he was called to the chair of geology and mineralogy in the University of Pennsylvania, and in the actual charge of this professorship he continued until his death although in 1895, the exact title of the chair was changed to that of "zoölogy and comparative anatomy."

Gill says of him in that capacity:

"Such a man naturally awakened the interest of apt pupils, and he was a facile and entertaining lecturer.   From the stores of a rich memory he could improvise a discourse on almost any topic within the range of his varied studies.   His views were so much in advance of those in any text-book that for his own convenience, no less than for the benefit of his pupils, he felt compelled to prepare a 'syllabus of lectures on geology and paleontology,' but only 'Part III, Paleontology of the Vertebrata' was published.

It appeared in 1891 and is still a valuable epitome of the classification of the vertebrates, recent as well as fossil, giving in dichotomous tables the essential characters of all the groups above families and also the names of all the families."

The honors that came to him were many and well earned. Haverford College gave him the degree of Master of Arts in 1870, and the University of Heidelberg on the occasion of the celebration of the five hundredth anniversary of its foundation conferred on him the degree of Doctor of Philosophy. The Bigsby gold medal of the Geological Society of London was bestowed on him in 1879, and in 1891 the Academy of Natural Sciences of Philadelphia gave him its Hayden Memorial medal. He became a member of the Academy of Natural Sciences in Philadelphia in 1861, and was a curator of that Academy in 1865–73, corresponding secretary in 1868–76, and a member of the Council in 1879–80. In 1866 he was chosen to membership in the American Philosophical Society, and in 1872 was elected to the National Academy of Sciences. His connection with the American Association for the Advancement of Science began with his election in 1868, and in 1875 he was advanced to the grade of fellow. The Section on Biology made him its presiding officer in 1884, and in the following year he delivered a retiring address on "Catagenesis." His name had been frequently urged upon the Association for its highest honor, but it was not until the Springfield meeting in 1895 that this well-merited appreciation came to him. In 1864 he was elected a corresponding member of the Zoölogical Society of London, and in 1881 he was chosen a foreign correspondent of the Geological Society of London. While attending the International Geological Congress held in 1878 in Paris, he was nominated for membership in the Geological Society of France, to which he refers in a letter to his wife as "quite an honor." The Royal academies of Bavaria and Denmark, as well as other learned societies in Europe, testified to their appreciation of his attainments by enrolling his name among their foreign correspondents.

A personal description of the man taken from a sketch by Miss Helen Dean King follows. Doctor King was his assistant for a time and knew Professor Cope well. Her appreciation does full justice to the man:

"Professor Cope was a man of quick decision, boundless energy, and great independence in thought and expression. He had keen and accurate powers of observation and a marvelous memory embracing the most minute details. Strong in his convictions, he was fearless in his criticism of men and institutions when he was convinced that he was upholding the right; yet he was ever ready to admit a mistake or correct an error when it had been proven that he was in the wrong.   He possessed tireless perseverance— an attribute always essential to good scientific work—and when absorbed in his investigations he was completely forgetful of his own personal comfort, going for long periods without food or rest."

Of more than passing interest is the following letter written by him on February 3, 1873. It describes the complimentary dinner given in New York city to Prof. John Tyndall, on the eve of his departure for England, after a successful lecture tour in the principal cities of the United States:

"It was a good assembly of five hundred, mostly naturalists, and though the dinner was good, there was more reason and soul and no conviviality in the usual sense; Evarts, the lawyer presided, and Tyndall, Draper, Barnard, etc., spoke for science, and Beecher and Doctor Bellows for theology. The whole subject was well-handled and I was particularly pleased with Beecher, whose acquaintance I afterwards made. Bellows was not afraid of his audience and told them plain gospel. He told Tyndall that on his departure he should have as many of his prayers as he would believe in, and alluded generally to prayer in a very effective and graceful manner. Tyndall in his remarks spoke largely of a sense of duty, which he considered important."

Of his own beliefs, I venture to quote an extract from a letter written by him in 1886:

"I learned several things in the time I have lived. Nothing affords so much satisfaction to the mind as the consciousness of having done right, not but that the best people must have regrets for having also done wrong on some occasions. Then we can take comfort in the knowledge that God knows our incapacities and our defects, and pities and helps us; the latter especially if we try to help ourselves. But there are many triflers in the world, people who avoid doing anything of any value or importance. It is very desirable not to be compelled to live with such people. Any one who feels the seriousness of life and the certainty of its termination, will not waste it."

The last letter that he ever wrote contains so much that is pertinent to this subject that I cannot forbear from including a large portion of it. He wrote, using the familiar style of the Quakers,— the style of his ancestors and of the faith in which he was born:

"Dear Aunt Jane: I understand that to-morrow is thy birthday and I wish to send my greetings.

. . . .

"I do not expect to leave the world yet awhile, but I shall do so when the time comes with the full belief that it will be a change greatly for the better.

"The relation of the Supreme to men is that of father to children, and if we keep the relation true, He (?) will not fail. To be sick is good for us sometimes. It corrects our perspective of human life, and sets things in a proportion which we must sometimes see. In active life we have our special pre-occupation of mind, and see chiefly those things.

"So we do our work; and must do it; but to take a pause sometime is good. This applies to me, for I have many enterprises going on that need close attention, and other things cannot receive much attention.

"May physical comfort attend thy coming years; mental peace thee knows how to have, and may it remain."

In February of 1897, Cope's health became seriously affected by a nephritic disorder which it is said "might possibly have been remedied by a surgical operation," but this he would not submit to. He soon grew worse and, in March, he wrote to his wife, saying:

"I went to my lecture Tuesday and was the worse for it. I am well cared for by the Doctor and Miss Brown; and between my spells of pain, I can do some work that enables me to pass the time as pleasantly as may be under the circumstances. My pursuits are fortunately such that they are not suspended by imprisonment in the house. This is fortunate for me, as I find inaction very unpleasant, until I am actually disabled and then it comes natural.

"Apparently healthier men than I die about us. . . . My trouble will probably finish me in the course of time, if it goes on, but it can be eradicated by a surgical operation, and that I will probably have to undergo sooner or later. —— gives me a remarkable case of a permanent cure of a worse case than mine by some surgery."

And then a week later he again wrote to his wife pathetically: "The sky looks beautiful out of the window, and I dare say that in a few days the country will be charming. I am anxious to get out, but cannot yet awhile."

Steadily he grew worse and worse, and then on March 31, he wrote with cheerful optimism in that last letter sent to his aunt:

" I have been confined to my room, barring a few walks out, for five weeks to-day; some of the days confined to bed.

"I have suffered great pain and am now recovering slowly from the depression caused by powerful drugs taken for relief. My dangerous symptoms have passed away, but the morphia-bella-donna combination makes the strongest constitution stagger. The mental depression is dreadful so that nothing in life is in any degree enjoyable, except an occasional draught of ice water. So I pity everybody I hear of that is sick, and am glad to see so many people well. To be well seems to me now to be something extraordinarily fortunate."

He continued on until April 12, and then in the room which he had so long used as a study, surrounded by the objects of his life-long attentions, the end came and he passed into the future.

Once he wrote:

"I dare not deny a future life, and as we all probably wish it, in case it should be happy, we may seek for phenomena which indicate the existence of such a state of happiness in the human mind in this world. . . . If we believe in a development into a future life, we must believe that as many have gone before us, that future state must be well populated. If this be true I see no difficulty in supporting that communication, and hence prayer, is a reasonable thing."

The peace that passeth all understanding and the knowledge of the future are now his.

J. Willard Gibbs

WILLARD GIBBS

PHYSICIST

1839–1903

By Edwin E. Slosson

Bacon says there are two kinds of men of science, the ants and the spiders. The ants are the men of experiment who collect facts and use them. The spiders are the men of theory who spin cobwebs from their own minds. He condemns both extremes, and, thanks in part to his exposition of the need of combining theory and practice, the two species are becoming less distinct. The practical man is more and more recognizing the importance of theory, and the theorist is paying better heed to experimentation. Nevertheless, the two mental types persist, and it is usually possible to tell to which any scientist, however great, inclines. The practical man uses a general law as a vaulting-pole to assist him in jumping from one fact to another. The theoretical man uses facts as stepping-stones to reach a general law. The practical man receives his inspiration from mixing with men and perceiving their needs. He produces immediate results and he gets an immediate reward in popularity, praise and wealth. The nature of his work is apparent to everybody, and his achievements are appreciated, indeed often overestimated, by his contemporaries. The theorist, on the contrary, is heard of more often after his death than during his life, for he is apt to be something of a recluse, following his own thread of thought without allowing his attention to be distracted by the shouts of the crowd who cannot understand his work or his temperament, and are always calling him in directions that to them seem more profitable.

Of American scientists Count Rumford and Prof. Willard Gibbs, are the best examples of these two tendencies, and since each was able to make his life the expression of his personality in a very unusual degree, they form as remarkable a contrast in life as in temperament. The former was a man of the court, the latter of the college. The one was a rover, an adventurer, whose changes of fortune would form a theme for a romance; the other lived a cloistered life, absolutely devoid of dramatic incident, the intellectual life in its purest form. Rumford took great delight in the honors, decorations and titles heaped upon him as he journeyed from country to country, and the applause of street crowds was sweet to his ears; the influence of women was a potent factor in his life. Gibbs was shy and modest, a celibate, and was little known personally except to some of his colleagues of the faculty. Anyone of ordinary culture can read understandingly all of Rumford's papers. Gibbs' work is a sealed book to all but a few of mathematical mind and training.

Rumford's work had always a practical purpose, even when he was evolving a general law, and he hastened personally to apply the scientific principles he discovered to the conveniences of daily life. Gibbs paid no attention to the invention of useful articles, or to the promotion of manufactures. Rumford used general principles as guides to his further experimentation; Gibbs left entirely to others the experimental verification of the laws he logically deduced. Rumford carried on researches of the most varied character; Gibbs confined his life-work to a few closely allied studies. Rumford's discoveries were the result of his alert observation and shrewd wit; Gibbs made his deductions by slow and sure process of rigid mathematical analysis.

It would be useless to discuss which type of scientist is the more useful, and it would be unjust as well as futile to blame the one for not being the other. We do not find fault with a great general because he is not also a great poet, and there is need for as wide a diversity of gifts in the advancement of science. The theorist and the utilitarian often fail to understand and to appreciate one another; such narrowness cannot be ascribed to the two men here contrasted, for in their case it was a concentration of personal powers, not a narrowness of mind that made their work so diverse. Gibbs did not despise applied science, nor did Rumford neglect theory. Each did most what he could do best, the work he was fitted by nature to do, and what, in the state of science at the time, was most needed. In the days of Rumford, when physical science was in its infancy, one who devoted himself to its prosecution had to justify such research by constantly showing its value to mankind. Experiments had to be crude because facilities were lacking. But in the time of Gibbs, a hundred years later, the technique of experimentation had reached great perfection, the usefulness of scientific research had been demonstrated, and there were plenty of workers in well-equipped laboratories, but deep abstract thinkers were rare. Ants were numerous and busy, but spiders were hard to find.

Chemistry is in a peculiar state. It started as a practical science and its advance has been so rapid that the theoretical has never caught up with it. By a century of very successful experimental work there have been accumulated a larger number of verified facts than was ever before at the disposal of a science, but there is an almost complete lack of guiding theories and correlating hypotheses. Hundreds of thousands of chemical compounds have been made and studied; their melting-points, boiling-points and solubilities have been determined; their properties and reactions are known; but why they look and behave as they do no one can tell. The chemist who mixes together two compounds can guess only by means of vague and uncertain analogies how they will act. Whether a given salt will be more or less soluble in hot water than in cold, whether two solutions of salts when mixed will precipitate a solid, evolve a gas or remain unchanged he has no way of determining for sure except to try and see.

A successful chemist needs the memory of a politician; he has to exert himself continually to enlarge his circle of acquaintances, and to remember as much as possible about their behavior under all circumstances. He envies his brother physicist, who needs only carry in his head a neat little collection of formulas to be able to say exactly what will result from any given combination of forces. The law of gravitation converted the chaos of forty centuries of astronomical observations into a cosmos, but chemistry is still without a Newton. The astronomer can calculate with great accuracy the forces acting between two planets in conjunction and what would be their movements in consequence; the physicist can do the same for two magnets, but the chemist has no measure of the forces acting between two elements, in fact, he cannot even tell in many cases whether there will be any reaction when he puts them together under new conditions.

The astonishing progress of physics during the last half century, resulting in the transformation of modern life through new methods for the utilization of heat, light and electricity, is chiefly due to the use of the greatest of all scientific generalizations, the law of the conversion of energy.   But although this forms the basis of chemistry as much as of physics, chemists have had to get along without its aid because there was no known way of applying it to chemical phenomena in general.   The physicist starting from a few well-established fundamental principles makes use, in drawing deductions from them, of the most powerful intellectual tool in the hands of man, but the chemist is confined to the slower process of inductive reasoning from multitudinous observations, of which very few are capable of expression in quantitative form so as to be utilizable mathematically.   Physics and chemistry have not been on speaking terms, for they talked different languages.   It was largely due to Willard Gibbs and others working along the line he indicated that they are being brought together, and the wedded sciences have already proved fruitful.   The new science, physical chemistry, in which the methods of physics are applied to the problems of chemistry, has within the few years of its existence made very rapid progress and has already solved many old puzzles and brought to light many new truths.   We are not yet in sight of any fundamental principles which shall bring together all the complicated phenomena of chemistry, but we owe to Willard Gibbs the first step toward accomplishing this by drawing from the laws of thermodynamics rules explaining a great variety of chemical reactions. When we realize the deplorable condition of chemistry as a purely empirical science with its unwieldy accumulation of facts, we can appreciate what a service to the science has been his genius for generalization and mathematical deduction.

To devote's one life to abstract studies in which the world at large can see no practical value requires not only an exceptional tenacity of purpose and the sacrifice of personal aims on the part of the individual, but also that he be exceptionally situated in order that his mind may be free from cares and distractions which would interfere with the necessary concentration and continuity of thought. Willard Gibbs was the right man in the right place. His life, training and circumstances were the best possible for the perfect development of his peculiar genius. He had the best education that America and Europe could give him, and a permanent position in Yale University which required of him merely the teaching of four or five advanced students in his own field of work. Although he received little support from the college, he inherited a modest competence, sufficient to provide for his quiet tastes and keep him from uncongenial occupations. For his research he required no large and expensive laboratory. The only apparatus he needed was pencil and paper, and a small upper room in the corner of the Sloane Physical Laboratory was his workshop. Here until late at night he continued year after year his solitary search for truth for its own sake, without any of those external stimuli such as the hope of fame or fortune or the pressure of necessity which most men need to spur them to such arduous exertion.

Four hundred paces north of this on High Street stands a plain square brick house with the two wooden Ionic pillars characteristic of many New Haven houses. Here in his sister's family he made his home and between these two points he walked daily with as much regularity as Kant at Königsburg. Except for his student years in Europe and occasional summer vacations in the mountains, his life was practically confined to this narrow range.

Josiah Willard Gibbs was the fifth to bear that name which

started from the marriage, in 1747, of Henry Gibbs with Katherine, daughter of the Honorable Josiah Willard, Secretary of the Province of Massachusetts. The grandfather of Henry Gibbs, Robert Gibbs, fourth son of Sir Henry Gibbs of Honington, Warwickshire, came to Boston about 1658.

Professor Gibbs inherited both his scholarly tastes and his disposition from his father, Josiah Willard Gibbs, a distinguished philologian, who was Professor of Sacred Literature in Yale Divinity School from 1824 to 1861. He was born in Salem, Massachusetts, in 1790, and was graduated from Yale in 1809, his father, grandfather and great-grandfather having been graduates of Harvard. What is said of him is quite as descriptive of his greater son. "The elder Professor Gibbs was remarkable among his contemporaries for profound scholarship, for unusual modesty and for the conscientious and painstaking accuracy which characterized all his published work." He married Mary Anna Van Cleve, the daughter of John Van Cleve of Princeton, New Jersey, and the great-great-granddaughter of Rev. Jonathan Dickinson (Y. C., 1706), the first President of the College of New Jersey.

Until 1846, Professor Gibbs occupied the house of President Day on Crown Street near College Street, and there all his children were born. The President meantime lived on the Campus in a house belonging to the College. When he retired from the Presidency he took possession again of his own house, and Professor Gibbs built on High Street.

His fourth child and only son, the subject of this sketch, was born February 11, 1839. An attack of scarlet fever when he was two years old left him with a somewhat delicate constitution, which was the cause of much anxiety to his parents and required of him through life a careful attention to health and regular habits.

He owed his preparation for college to the Hopkins Grammar School, of New Haven, and he generously repaid his obligation to this school by serving as one of its trustees for twenty-two years until his death. For seventeen years he was Secretary and Treasurer of the Hopkins School, and was diligent and efficient in the management of its financial affairs.

In 1854 he entered Yale College, where he distinguished himself by his proficiency in Latin and Mathematics, and maintained high standing in all his classes. In his Sophomore year he took the Berkeley Premium for Latin Composition; in his Junior year the Bristed Scholarship, the Third Prize for Latin Examination and the Berkeley Premium again; in his Senior year the Clark Scholarship, the De Forest Mathematical Prize and Latin Oration. He was also elected for excellence in scholarship to the Phi Beta Kappa Society.

After his graduation from Yale College in 1858, he remained for five years in New Haven, doing graduate work in physics and mathematics, for which he received the degree of M.A. in 1861 and Ph.D. in 1863. He was then made tutor in Latin and "Natural Philosophy," but the task of keeping large classes of Sophomores in order and getting hard work out of them was not one for which such a shy and modest young man was suited, and after three years of somewhat discouraging effort, he went abroad to continue his studies in mathematical physics. He had lost his father in 1861, three years after graduation.

His first winter was spent in Paris, and in 1867 he went to Berlin to study under Magnus. The winter of 1868–69 was spent in Heidelberg under Helmholtz and Kirchhoff, and in March he went to the Riviera for a few weeks and returned to America in June, merely passing through Paris on the way. Most of all his teachers he was influenced by Clausius, the great German physicist, and one of the founders of the science of thermodynamics. In this field, by extending the fundamental laws of heat and mechanical energy discovered by Sadi Carnot and Clausius to the most varied departments of physics and chemistry, Gibbs made his chief contributions to human knowledge. He expressed his admiration for Clausius in an obituary notice contributed to the American Academy of Science and Art. Clausius' conception of entropy was by him raised to the rank one of the most important of physical properties, and at the head of his principal paper, like a scriptural text, appears the law of Clausius: "The entropy of the world tends to a maximum."

In July, 1871, two years after his return to America, he was elected Professor of Mathematical Physics at Yale, a position which he held to the time of his death thirty-two years later.

It was at first an empty honor, for the university to which he was attached was slow to recognize his genius. For the first ten years of his professorship he received no salary whatever and little more than half the regular salary for several years thereafter. The most important service that a university can do to the world is the early recognition and encouragement of men of exceptional ability who are willing to devote their lives to the extension of human knowledge, yet this is the service most likely to be neglected. Yale has no name upon her roll of honor that stands for more originality and profundity in science than that of Gibbs, but it is a mere chance that it was not lost to her. When the Johns Hopkins University was started, Gibbs was invited to join its faculty, and, as the story goes, had already written a letter of acceptance intending to mail it the next morning, but Professor Thatcher happening to call on him that evening he mentioned what he had done and referred to the envelope on the mantelpiece before them. His friend begged him to hold it for a few days, and then hurried out to urge upon the authorities of the university the importance of retaining Gibbs in the institution. Some hasty councils were held, a small salary promised and Gibbs, gratified by this unexpected token of appreciation, was glad to agree to remain in New Haven. This intervention Professor Rowland of the Johns Hopkins was accustomed to call "the greatest crime of the century," believing that Gibbs would have found greater scope for his powers and would have exerted a wider influence in a university having a larger corps of graduate students than Yale had at that time. But it is hard to conceive of Gibbs in any other environment than that of Yale, and it is doubtful if his peculiar genius would have thrived elsewhere.

In 1873, when he was thirty-four years old, he published his first paper, a discussion of the methods for the geometrical representation of the thermodynamical properties of bodies. The most common of such graphical methods is the volume-pressure diagram, as in the indicator cards for testing the efficiency of steam-engines. In this the pressure of a gas is measured on one line and its volume on a line at right angles to the first. A point upon this diagram gives the state of the gas in regard to pressure and volume, a line represents any change of state, and the areas included measure the amount of work done on it in producing the change. But of course such a diagram on a plane surface in two dimensions cannot always clearly show the effects of changes in other physical properties, as, for example, temperature. For this a solid model in three dimensions is necessary, and the direct representation of more than three such variables is impossible because we cannot geometrically construct models of more than three dimensions. But Gibbs showed that by choosing volume, energy and entropy as the three physical properties of a body to be represented by the rectangular coördinates, a geometrical surface is formed which gives a complete graphical representation of all the relations between volume, temperature, pressure, energy and entropy for all states of a body, whether single or a mixture of different states.

The value of such graphical methods lies in the fact that they give at a glance a clear and definite conception of complex relations, such as cannot be obtained, at least by the ordinary mind, from the study of a table of figures or an algebraic formula. A mass of experimental data, very incomprehensible in themselves and even apparently improbable becomes quite clear on being plotted upon a diagram, and new points of interest become apparent, and promising lines of research are suggested. The use of geometrical representations, many of which originated with Gibbs, has been of great value in the development of the science of physical chemistry.

American scientists took little notice of "Gibbs' thermodynamical surface" as it is called, but in England it attracted the attention of Clerk Maxwell who in his *Theory of Heat* devotes considerable space to it, and constructed with his own hands a plaster of Paris model of such a surface for water in its three states of ice, liquid and vapor. A cast of this was sent to Gibbs, who was much pleased at this mark of appreciation from such a high authority, although he personally took little interest in the construction of such models, for to his mind they were superfluous. He did not think in mathematical formulas like Maxwell or in mechanical models like Kelvin, but seemed to have some peculiar method of his own for conceiving complex relations between quantities. The model is yet preserved in the Sloane Laboratory of Yale, the original in the Cavendish Laboratory of Cambridge. Students, who knew the story of plaster surface and Gibbs' extreme modesty, used to take a secret delight in asking questions about it. He would reply that "it came from Europe," and, further pressed, that it was "made in England."

In 1876 and 1878, Professor Gibbs published in two parts in the *Transactions* of the Connecticut Academy of Arts and Sciences a paper entitled, "On the Equilibrium of Heterogeneous Substances," to which may be accurately applied the much abused term "an epoch-making work," for it laid the foundation of the new science of physical chemistry. It was a triumph of creative intellect, rarely equaled in the history of science for originality, completeness and vigor of demonstration. It often happens in science that certain discoveries are, as it were, "in the air," and it is almost a matter of chance which individual catches them and by first putting them into concrete form, gets the whole credit for having originated them. The way of the new idea is usually so throughly prepared by the gradual development of current thought that its coming in some form is inevitable. America would certainly have been discovered within a few years if Columbus had failed, and the world would not have been long without the steam-engine if Watt had never lived. But Professor Gibbs' work in physical chemistry was not the product of such a general trend of thought. The materials of the new science had not been collected. He laid down laws for phenomena that had not then been observed, and gave in advance solutions to problems that had never been formulated. It is a signal refutation of the theory of Bacon that science can only progress by the slow accumulation of miscellaneous facts, from which in the course of time could be drawn general laws. On the contrary, it has been found that a science develops the most rapidly when, even in its infancy, there is a definite theory capable, to use Gibbs' phrase, of "giving shape to research."

As has been said, Professor Gibbs had no direct forerunner; it is also true that he had no immediate followers. For over ten years this paper was almost completely neglected, and it was not until some of the laws he enunciated had been independently discovered by European chemists, that attention was drawn to it, not by himself to establish a barren claim to priority, but by others because in his work these empirical laws were to be found more succinctly expressed, and also logically connected in a complete and consistent system of general principles.

The paper "On the Equilibrium of Heterogeneous Substances" was translated into German by Ostwald in 1892, sixteen years after the publication of the first part, and put into French by Le Chatelier in 1899; in both instances for the expressed purpose of promoting the development of the science of physical chemistry in which they were the teachers. Ostwald introduces the paper with these words:

"The contents of this work are to-day of immediate importance and the interest it arouses is by no means historical. For, of the almost boundless wealth of results which it contains, or to which it points the way, only a small part has, up to the present time, been made fruitful. Untouched treasures in the greatest variety and of the greatest importance to the theoretical as well as to the experimental investigator still lie within its pages."

Le Chatelier uses much the same language:

"Gibbs was able by a truly extraordinary effort of the scientific imagination and logical power to posit all the principles of the new science and to foresee all its ulterior applications. . . . To Gibbs belongs the honor of having fused the two sciences into one, chemical mechanics, of having constituted a completely defined body of principles, to which additions may be made in the future, but from which the progress of the science can take nothing away.

"His method, like that of Newton, Fresnel and Ampère, consists in starting with a small number of first principles or hypotheses,

and searching out all the necessary consequences of those principles, without ever introducing in the course of the reasoning any
new hypotheses or relaxing the rigor of the reasoning."

Since most readers will be obliged to form their opinion of the
value of Gibbs' work upon authority instead of personal judgment
it may be useful to quote a third estimate, that given by Professor
Larmor in the article on "Energetics," in the supplementary
volumes of the *Encyclopædia Britannica:*

"This monumental memoir made a clean sweep of the subject,
and workers in the modern experimental science returned to it
again and again to find their empirical principles forecasted in
the light of pure theory, and to derive fresh inspiration for new
departures."

That Gibbs' paper was so long neglected, and is even at the
present day not studied by many chemists, is due chiefly to two
causes: first, it is exceedingly abstract, complex and difficult to
comprehend, and, second, being published in the *Transactions* of
the Connecticut Academy of Arts and Sciences, it was not readily
accessible to all who might have found it profitable. This memoir,
which is likely to be more studied a hundred years from now than
it is to-day, is to be found among papers on subjects of such local
and transitory interest as the winds of New Haven and plans for
a bridge, never built, between New York City and Blackwell's
Island. Still we must remember that the service which the Connecticut Academy rendered him no other agency stood ready to
render or could have rendered as well, under conditions permitting
the careful elaboration and printing of the work, and for this the
Academy deserves the hearty thanks of all friends of science. All
of his work has now been made available by the publication, in
1906, of *The Scientific Papers of J. Willard Gibbs*, in two volumes
by Longmans Green & Co.

It will not be out of place to relate here an incident of his student
days at the University of Berlin, the humor of which did not
escape him then and which has certainly lost none of that quality
since. The conversation took place at a social gathering to which
he had been invited.

Professor X: "Sie haben eine Akademie der Wissenschaften in New Haven, nicht wahr?" (You have an Academy of Science in New Haven, have you not?)

Gibbs (innocently): "Ja wohl! Davon bin ich Mitglied." (Yes indeed. I am a member of it.)

Professor X: "Ach! so. Die Mitgliedershaft wird wohl ziemlich ausgebreitet sein." (The membership must be rather extensive.)

American scientists are much given to complaining that their work does not receive due recognition in Europe. This is doubtless true of the ordinary run of scientific papers, but this case, like some others, shows that really important work may be better appreciated abroad than at home. If American chemists had begun research twenty-five years ago on the lines indicated by Gibbs, they would have led the world in the development of physical chemistry, which now they, in imitation of European scientists, have recently taken up. Yale graduates who went abroad to study chemistry were sometimes first set to study the work of Gibbs whom they had never known at college.

But at the time when it was published there were few chemists in this country sufficiently familiar with higher mathematics to understand and utilize Gibbs' work. As we have seen, chemistry differed from physics in having no general laws capable of mathematical expression, and the chemist got along very well in his work if he knew arithmetic as far as percentage, so that he could calculate his analyses. It was not likely then that he would take the trouble to master a mathematical paper covering 300 pages and including over 700 equations, in which only a few simple chemicals such as salt, water, sulphur and hydriodic acid, are mentioned by way of illustration. But now as Le Chatelier says, "the algebraist with his formulas has drawn the attention of the chemists with their crucibles and conquered their contempt for integrals."

It is difficult to convey to the lay reader any clear idea of the contents of the paper "On the Equilibrium of Heterogeneous Substances." Perhaps some insight may be afforded by using the words of the Dutch chemist, Bakhuis Roozeboom, who was one of the first to realize the importance of the work. He says that it deals with "the sociology of chemistry." Previously chemists had been absorbed in the recognition of chemical substances as individuals and in studying their transformations, but Gibbs discusses their behavior in the presence of each other. He shows under what conditions of temperature and pressure different substances, and the same substances in different states, can exist together and what effect changes of these conditions will have upon the composition of such mixtures. Chemists used to confine their attention as much as possible to those reactions that went in one direction and resulted in a practically complete change into new compounds. They regarded incomplete and reversible reactions with the same aversion as pre-Darwinian botanists did, varieties which did not fit into their system of classification. Now chemists find the most interesting and most common reactions are those that proceed only partially in one direction when they are checked by the opposite tendency and an equilibrium established. The study of the effect of the conditions, such as temperature, pressure and relative amount of the components, upon such an equilibrium is one of the most fruitful lines of investigation now being carried on.

The best known of the formulas of this paper is that called " Gibbs' Phase Rule." It is usually expressed in this form:

$$F = C + 2 - P.$$

Where P denotes the number of phases (or distinct and separable masses of matter, such as chemical elements or compounds or solutions or mixtures of gases), C denotes the number of components (or chemical substances forming the constituents) and F denotes the number of degrees of freedom (or the number of the three variable factors, temperature, pressure and volume, which must be arbitrarily fixed in order to define the condition of the system). For example, let us take water alone, in which case $C = 1$. If we have water only in the form of a gas (steam or vapor), therefore in one phase, $P = 1$; therefore $F = 2$, that is, we must give two of the variables, say, the pressure and the temperature, before we can know the third, the volume. If we have water in contact with its vapor, we have two phases $P=2$, and therefore $F=1$, that is, if any one of the three conditions are decided upon, the other two must follow. When we consider water, ice and vapor altogether $P=3$, and therefore $F=0$, that is, none of the variable conditions can be chosen arbitrarily, for water, ice and vapor can exist together at only one temperature (nearly $0°$ Centigrade) and one pressure (4.6 millimeters of mercury). If the temperature is lowered, all the water freezes; if the temperature is raised, all the ice melts; in any event one of the phases disappears.

By the use then of this simple little arithmetical rule involving after the determination of the factors only the addition and sub-traction of numbers usually less than three, the behavior of the most complicated mixtures under all possible changes of condition is made known when once a few data are obtained by experiment, and it has found application in many widely diverse fields of science and industry. The reader who is sufficiently interested in the subject to follow it further is referred to the two books on the Phase Rule by Bancroft and by Findlay. The Dutch chemists were the first to make use of Gibbs' work, and Roozeboom, Van der Waals, Van't Hoff, Schreinemakers and others have within the last few years by the aid of the Phase Rule and other laws of equilibrium immensely increased our knowledge of such difficult matters as solutions, alloys and crystallizations. As examples of its practical applications may be mentioned its use in the study of sedimentary deposits, the metallurgy of iron and the igneous rocks. The Stassfurt salt deposits which supply the world with potash for fertilizers are composed of a curious and complicated mixture of various sodium, potassium, magnesium and calcium salts in layers aggregating a thousand feet in thickness. Professor Van't Hoff and his pupils have been for the last eight years engaged upon this problem, and have worked out the conditions under which these strata were deposited by the evaporation of sea water in a land-locked sea. Iron has been most useful to man because it is really several metals in one. By the addition of minute quantities of carbon it can be changed from soft, malleable wrought-iron, to hard, brittle cast-iron, or to steel which can be tempered in

many different ways. But the cause of these remarkable changes
and the conditions by which they were produced were not understood until the application of the Phase Rule to the subject of the
iron carbides, and many disasters have occurred from unexpected
weaknesses in structural iron which in the future we shall be better
able to avoid. The igneous rocks, such as granite, basalt and
porphyry, which form the principal part of the earth so far as we
know it, are composed of mixed silicates which were too numerous
for the mineralogist to name and too complex for the chemist to
classify. Now, however, they are being studied very successfully,
and the geologist, being given by the use of the Phase Rule, the
conditions of heat and pressure under which they were formed, will
be able to explain more satisfactorily the building of the world.

I have devoted so much space to this paper of Gibbs as an
example of the effect of theory upon scientific research that it will
be necessary to dismiss briefly his later, and, in part, equally important work. Between 1881 and 1884, Professor Gibbs developed
and taught his system of Vector Analysis, a new algebraic method
of treatment of physical quantities, like force, momentum and
velocity, which have direction as well as magnitude and can therefore be represented by lines. This work is in many respects an
improvement on the Quaternions of Sir William Hamilton, which
has never been a favorite method of analysis with physicists. It
was printed in 1881–84 for private circulation among mathematicians by Professor Gibbs, but was published in more complete
form by his pupil, Dr. E. B. Wilson, only in 1901.

In 1886, Professor Gibbs as Vice-President of the Section of
Mathematics and Astronomy of the American Association for the
Advancement of Science, gave an address on "Multiple Algebra,"
a development of the methods of Grassman. An astronomical
paper on a new method for the determination by the employment of Vector Analysis of elliptic orbits from three complete observations was published by the National Academy of Science
three years later; reprinted by Buchholz; translated into German
and incorporated in the last edition of Klinkerfues's *Theoretische
Astronomie.*

He devoted much attention to the electromagnetic theory of light, originated by Clerk Maxwell, which he defended against the elastic ether theory by showing its adequacy for explaining the phenomena of refraction and dispersion of light. The discovery by Hertz of the electric waves now used in wireless telegraphy has since given experimental proof of the correctness of Maxwell's theory. Gibbs also made important contributions to the theory of galvanic cells, by which can be calculated the electromotive force due to differences in the concentration of the dilute solutions of the cells or in the pressure in the case of gas batteries.

His final work was on the *Elementary Principles of Statistical Mechanics* in which he attempts the gigantic task of applying mathematical methods to the study of the motions of very complex systems too minute and complicated for detailed observation, as, for example, the vibrations of the molecules of a solid due to heat. This work has not yet been sufficiently studied for its importance to be fully understood, for it was published in 1902, as one of the Yale Bicentennial volumes. It is thought that the intense application and protracted labor required for the preparation of this work hastened his death, which occurred after a few days' illness on April 28, 1903, at the age of sixty-four. He was never a strong man and, like Kant, it was only by great carefulness of his health, and severe restriction of his activities and diversions that he was able to accomplish so much original work.

He was of medium height and slight figure, with delicate features, and bright blue eyes that twinkled quizzically when he had got a student cornered. His hair and full beard at the time of his death were pure white. He was punctual at every appointment, fulfilling every duty imposed upon him, however uncongenial, with the utmost conscientiousness. Yale knew him as "the man who never made a mistake." At the meetings of the Yale Mathematical Club which he founded and invariably attended, he listened with patience and consideration even to the most amateurish efforts. He was always ready to give his time and attention to any student coming to him for assistance, and would devote the whole of the lecture hour and as much more as necessary to the explanation of any point, however simple, if he found that one of his pupils failed to understand it, even at a time when he refused an offer of five dollars an hour for doing outside work. His customary remark at the end of every demonstration was: "Is it proved?" He was once asked what he meant by this, and explained that different minds required different degrees and kinds of proof. That this is true to a much greater extent than he realized is shown by the fact that some students, not particularly apt in mathematics, found his lectures difficult or impossible to follow. This was due to his complete absorption in his subject and his failure to comprehend that others could not take as long steps as he could. The tendency of his mind toward generalization, in which lay his unique power, was shown by a remark frequently upon his lips, "The whole is simpler than its parts."

His lectures were conversational, though usually well prepared and straightforward, never twice alike, so students often took what was nominally the same course a second year. Occasionally if a new idea occurred to him in the course of a lecture, he would forget his students and work it out on the blackboard. He carried few notes to the class room, and those merely the chief formulas. If he forgot a step in writing out a demonstration, he would stand and softly whistle, occasionally darting nervously across the room to fix the radiator. On leaving the class room he was apt to come back two or three times to see if he had not forgotten something.

His students were never neglected because they were few or because they interrupted his research work. Except in the very first years his courses occupied on an average of seven hours a week, and they were always freshly prepared and original. Sometimes with a single student before him, in such a subject as the electromagnetic theory, he would sit for two hours at a time in his characteristic posture, his hands folded and forefingers touching, developing his own system and extending it into new fields.

To those who were prepared for them, his lectures were most inspiring on account of their clear and logical demonstrations, their comprehensiveness and their pertinent and graphic illustrations. One of his pupils, Prof. H. A. Bumstead, in a sketch of Willard Gibbs, published in the *American Journal of Science*, speaks of his lectures as follows:

"No necessary qualification to a statement was ever omitted, and on the other hand it seldom failed to receive the most general application of which it was capable. His students had ample opportunity to learn what may be regarded as known, what is guessed at, what a proof is and how far it goes. Though he disregarded many of the shibboleths of the mathematical rigorists, his logical processes were really of the most severe type; in power of deduction, of generalization, in insight into hidden relations, in critical acumen and in utter lack of prejudice, and in the philosophical breadth of his view of the object and aim of physics, he has had few superiors in the history of the science, and no student could come in contact with this severe and impartial mind without feeling profoundly its influence in all his future studies of nature. In personal character the same great qualities were apparent, unassuming in manner, genial and kindly in his intercourse with his fellow men, never showing impatience or irritation, devoid of personal ambition of the baser sort or of the slightest desire to exalt himself, he went far toward realizing the ideal of the unselfish Christian gentleman. In the minds of those who knew him, the greatness of his intellectual achievements will never overshadow the beauty and dignity of his life."

Perhaps Professor Gibbs would have been more successful as a teacher if he had followed the custom of university professors in making use of the labors of his students and working with them, but he never took them into his confidence, and he rarely let anyone know what he was engaged upon until his work was complete and ready for publication. His work was solitary; he had no need of the stimulus of conversation or correspondence with men interested in the same subjects. He left comparatively few notes, and these are brief and elliptical, for he carried his work in his head until well thought out. Even then he was reluctant to give it publicity.

One of his students captivated by his system of Vector Analysis, told him that he thought it could be thrown into a form that could be more widely useful and even introduced into sophomore mathematics. But Gibbs replied: "What is the good of that? It is complete as it is."

He had such confidence in the results of his theoretical deductions that he took little interest personally in their experimental verification, yet he was fertile in suggestions of profitable lines of research, and had a keen perception of practical difficulties which would be encountered. In his lectures he not infrequently would spend considerable time in describing the apparatus by which some crucial experiment might be performed. Though he was so exclusively occupied with the theoretical side of his subject, he was by no means wanting in mechanical ingenuity. As a boy his favorite amusement was the making of mechanical toys, and after leaving college and before entering on his professional work he devised and patented an automatic car-brake.

It must be noted also that all his work, even the most abstract, had a definite practical purpose. He studied mathematics for its usefulness in the interpretation of nature, never as a mere mental amusement nor for the exercise and display of intellectual power. As he once remarked in a discussion at the Mathematical Club, "A mathematician may say anything he pleases, but a physicist must be at least partially sane." In an address on "Values" on the occasion of the twenty-fifth anniversary of the founding of the club he said that the difference between the great man and the lesser men in science lies in their relative power of perceiving the important thing, which is not necessarily the hardest thing. The great man sees clearly what is most needed at the time and does that.

Conscientiousness, caution, modesty and unselfishness were the prominent features in his character. He was so careful to give due credit to the work of his predecessors that he often read into a paper much more than its author had thought of. He had a just appreciation of the value of his own discoveries, but shrank from any form of praise or publicity. In 1901 the Copley Medal of the Royal Society of London, which is awarded for the most important scientific work done in any country, was given to Willard Gibbs, but he deprecated the congratulations of his friends who had read the announcement, with the remark: "Better not say anything about it. Very likely it is an error." To a friend who spoke of seeing one of his letters on electromagnetic theory in *Nature* he said, "Oh, did they really publish it?" Professor Ostwald of Berlin tried to get him to come to Europe to be lionized, but he persistently refused.

Although the recognition of his achievements was so long delayed, yet before his death he had received honors from many parts of the world. Besides the Copley Medal of the Royal Society, he received the Rumford Medal of the American Academy of Science and Arts; he was awarded honorary doctorates from the universities of Erlangen, Princeton, Christiania and Williams College; he was elected to honorary or corresponding membership in the American Academy of Boston, the National Academy of Washington and the Royal Society of London, the Berlin Academy and the French Institute, as well as learned societies in Haarlem, Göttingen, London, Cambridge, Manchester, Amsterdam and Bavaria.

As an estimate of the character of Prof. Willard Gibbs, no more appropriate words can be used than those in which he has unconsciously revealed his own personality and ideals in paying a tribute to the character of a colleague. In his obituary sketch of Prof. Hubert Anson Newton, he concludes a discussion of his mathematical and astronomical work with these sentences:

"These papers show more than the type of mind of the author; they give no uncertain testimony concerning the character of the man. In all these papers we see a love of honest work; an aversion to shams, a distrust of rash generalizations and speculations based on uncertain premises. He was never anxious to add one more guess on doubtful matter in the hope of hitting the truths, or what pass as such for a time, but was always willing to take infinite pains in the most careful test of every theory. To these qualities was joined a modesty which forbade the pushing of his own claims; and he desired no reputation except the unsought tribute of competent judges."

In an exceedingly interesting series of articles on "Josiah Willard Gibbs and his Relation to Modern Science," published in the *Popular Science Monthly*, May, 1909 *et seq.*, Dr. Fielding H. Garrison defines the characteristics of his genius in the following language:

"Ostwald, in his interesting *Biologie des Naturforschers*, has divided men of science into two classes: The classicists (*Klassiker*), men like Newton, Lagrange, Gauss, Harvey, who, dealing with a limited number of ideas in their work, seek formal perfection and attain it, leaving no school of followers behind them, but only the effect of the work itself; and the romanticists (*Romantiker*), who like Liebig, Faraday, Darwin, Maxwell, are bold explorers in unknown fields, men fertile in ideas, leaving many followers and many loose ends of unfinished work which others complete. In the logical perfection of his work and in his unusual talent for developing a theme in the most comprehensive and exhaustive manner, Gibbs was emphatically the Klassiker. But in the scientific achievement of his early manhood he showed something of the spirit of the Romantiker also. His mathematical theory of chemical equilibrium was, far in advance of any experimental procedure known or contemplated at the time of its publication, and, although some of his predecessors, like James Thomson, Massieu, Horstmann, had come within sight of the new land and even skirted its shores, Gibbs, with the adventurous spirit of the true pioneer, not only conquered and explored it, but systematically surveyed it, living to see part of his territory occupied by a thriving band of workers, the physical chemists. Cayley, in his report on theoretical dynamics in 1857, expressed his conviction that the science of statics 'does not admit of much ulterior development.' The work of Gibbs has added to it the immense field of chemical equilibrium and wherever 'phases,' 'heterogeneous systems,' 'chemical and thermodynamic potentials,' or 'critical states' are mentioned he has left his impress upon modern scientific thought. It is not without reason then, that Ostwald has called this mathematician 'the founder of chemical energetics,' asserting that 'he has given new form and substance to chemistry for another century at least.'"

Simon Newcomb

SIMON NEWCOMB

ASTRONOMER

1835–1909

By Marcus Benjamin

"To him the wandering stars revealed
The secrets in their cradle sealed;
The far-off, frozen sphere that swings
Through ether, zoned with lucid rings;
The orb that rolls in dim eclipse
Wide wheeling, round its long ellipse,—
His name Urania writes with these,
And stamps it on her Pleiades."

THESE lines written by Oliver Wendell Holmes on one of Harvard's most eminent men of science apply with even greater force to Simon Newcomb, who by common consent had achieved the reputation of being the foremost astronomer of his time and easily succeeded to the honor of being the world's Nestor of Science on the death of Lord Kelvin. Sir Robert S. Ball, formerly Astronomer Royal of Ireland and now Director of the Astronomical Observatory in Cambridge, England, wrote of him: "Science has sustained one of the most severe blows of recent years. America has lost her most eminent man of science, and not since the death of Adams has the world been deprived of so illustrious an investigator in theoretical astronomy." He was, says the same writer, "the most conspicuous figure among the brilliant band of contemporary American astronomers."

Simon Newcomb was the sixth in descent from Simon Newcomb who was born in Massachusetts, in 1666, and died in Lebanon,

Connecticut, in 1745. His paternal ancestors moved to Canada in 1761, and in Wallace, Nova Scotia, on March 12, 1835, the famous astronomer was born. His father was John B. Newcomb, who followed the precarious occupation of a country school-teacher, seldom remaining in the same place for more than one or two years, and he is described by his son as being "the most rational and dispassionate of men." From his *Reminiscences* we learn that of his father's family none acquired "great wealth," held "a high official position," or did "anything to make his name live in history." Simon Newcomb's mother was Emily Prince, a descendant of a long-lived New England family, that was widely connected, and she included among her ancestors Elder William Brewster, who came over in the *Mayflower*.

The story of the courtship of these two is of special interest. In his search for her whom he believed would make him a fitting wife, John B. Newcomb had gone on a visit to Moncton, New Brunswick, and there attracted by the strains of music from a church, he entered the building and found a religious meeting in progress. His eye was at once arrested by the face and head of a young woman playing on a melodeon, who was leading the singing. He sat in such a position that he could carefully scan her face and movements. As he continued this study the conviction grew upon him that here was the object of his search. He soon made her acquaintance, paid her his addresses, and became her accepted suitor. He was fond of astronomy, and during the months of his courtship one of his favorite occupations was to take her out of an evening and show her the constellations. It is even said that among the day-dreams in which they indulged, one was that their first-born might be an astronomer.

Of his mother, Newcomb wrote: "She was the most profoundly and sincerely religious woman with whom I was ever acquainted, and my father always entertained and expressed the highest admiration for her mental gifts, to which he attributed whatever talents his children might have possessed." Her strength was unequal to her surroundings, and she died at the early age of thirty-seven years.

During his boyhood days, owing to the nature of his father's vocation, the movings of the family were frequent, although until he was four years of age Simon lived in the home of his paternal grandfather, about two miles from the village of Wallace. Here he was taught the alphabet by his aunts and he says, himself: "I was reading the Bible in class and beginning geography when I was six." In greater detail perhaps, he writes:

"I began to study arithmetic when I was five years old, and when six, I am told, I was very fond of doing sums. At twelve I was studying algebra, and about that time I began to teach. I remember that I was thirteen when I first took up Euclid. There was a copy of it among my father's works."

After the boy had grown to manhood his father wrote for him an account of his early life from which the following extract is taken:

"At fifteen you studied Euclid, and were enraptured with it. It is a little singular that all this time you never showed any self-esteem; or spoke of getting into employment at some future day, among the learned. The pleasure of intellectual exercise in demonstrating or analyzing a geometrical problem, or solving an algebraic equation, seemed to be your only object. Your almost intuitive knowledge of geography, navigation, and nautical matters in general caused me to think most ardently of writing to the Admiral at Halifax, to know if he would give you a place among the midshipmen of the navy; but my hope of seeing you a leading lawyer, and finally a judge on the bench, together with the possibility that your mother would not consent, and the possibility that you would not wish to go, deterred me."

Newcomb in his *Reminiscences* of this period writes:

"Among the books which profoundly influenced my mode of life and thought during the period embraced in the foregoing extracts were Fowler's *Phrenology* and Combe's *Constitution of Man*. It may appear strange to the reader if a system so completely exploded as that of phrenology should have any value as a mental discipline. Its real value consisted, not in what it taught about the position of the 'organs,' but in presenting a study of human nature, which, if not scientific in form, was truly so in spirit. I acquired the habit of looking on the characters and capabilities of men as the result of their organism."

Referring to the small collection of books in the possession of his paternal grandfather he says: "Among those purely literary were several volumes of the *Spectator* and *Roderick Random*. Of the former I read a good deal. Three mathematical books were in the collection, Hammond's *Algebra*, Simpson's *Euclid*, and Moore's *Navigator*." These works were literally absorbed by him, and he also mentions Mrs. Marcet's *Conversations on Natural Philosophy* and Lardner's *Popular Lectures on Science and Art*, as books that greatly interested him during this period of his youth.

His desire for learning had exhausted the slender resources of his paternal home and so at the age of sixteen, while on a visit to his grandparents, in Moncton, he went to study with one Doctor Foshay, who lived in the village of Salisbury, fifteen miles on the road to St. John. An agreement was made with the physician which read as follows:

"S. N. to live with the doctor, rendering him all the assistance in his power in preparing medicines, attending to business, and doing generally whatever might be required of him in the way of help. The Doctor, on his part, to supply S. N.'s bodily needs in food and clothing, and teach him medical botany and the botanic system of medicine. The contract to terminate when the other party should attain the age of twenty-one."

This contract so gladly made soon became unsatisfactory and young Newcomb found himself

"Physician, apothecary, chemist and druggist,
Girl about house and boy in the barn."

With greater exactness he says: "I cared for the horse, cut wood for the fire, searched field and forest for medicinal herbs, ordered other medicines from a druggist in St. John, kept the doctor's accounts, made his pills, and mixed his powders."

This unfortunately left little time for reading and study and soon he began to realize that his growing years were being wasted.

He therefore determined to run away. After careful preparation he chose September 13, 1853, as the day on which to leave. In a short letter addressed to the doctor, he wrote:

"When I came to live with you, it was agreed that you should make a physician of me. This agreement you have never shown the slightest intention of fulfilling since the first month I was with you. You have never taken me to see a patient, you have never given me any instruction or advice whatever. Beside this, you must know that your wife treats me in a manner that is no longer bearable. I therefore consider the agreement annulled from your failure to fulfill your part of it, and I am going off to make my own way in the world. When you read this, I shall be far away, and it is not likely that we shall ever meet again."

He successfully eluded pursuit and made his way to Salem, Massachusetts, where he found his father who "after the death of my mother had come to seek his fortune in the 'States.'" From Massachusetts they proceeded to the eastern part of Maryland, where at Massey's Cross Roads in Kent County, early in 1854, he began his independent career as a teacher of a country school. A year later he got "a somewhat better school at the pleasant little village of Sudlersville."

In the summer of 1854 he made his first visit to Washington, and "speculated upon the possible object of a queer old sandstone building, which seemed so different from anything else, and heard for the first time of the Smithsonian Institution." Books of all kinds, especially those on mathematics, were eagerly sought and quickly mastered. Study resulted in research and then came results, culminating in the preparation of a paper on "A New Demonstration of the Binomial Theorem" which he sent to Secretary Henry, asking if he deemed it worthy of publication. In replying Professor Henry pointed out its "lack of completeness and rigor" although one part of the work "was praised for its elegance." Newcomb says of Henry's letter that "while not so favorable as I might have expected, it was sufficiently so to encourage me in persevering."

A change of schools in 1856, brought him within an easy ride on horseback to the city of Washington where soon "the Smithsonian Library was one of the greatest attractions" and from which he began to borrow the works of the great masters. There for the first time he saw the four volumes of the *Mécanique Celeste* by Laplace, "the greatest treasure that my imagination had ever pictured." And then he called on the Secretary and told him of his ambitions. He says of this interview: "When I found Professor Henry he received me with characteristic urbanity, told me something of his own studies, and suggested that I might find something to do in the Coast Survey, but took no further steps at that time."

On leaving the Smithsonian he made his way to the office of the Coast Survey and there asked if a knowledge of physical astronomy was necessary to a position in that office. Other visits to Professor Henry followed, and at one of these he received a letter to Julius E. Hilgard, then assistant in charge of the Coast Survey office. He promptly availed himself of this opportunity and of his reception Newcomb wrote: "I found from my first interview with him that the denizens of the world of light were up to the most sanguine conceptions I ever could have formed."

Towards the close of the year he received a note from Mr. Hilgard saying that "he had been talking about me to Professor Winlock, superintendent of the *Nautical Almanac*, and that I might possibly get employment on that work." This possibility was not one that could be safely disregarded, and on the last day of December, 1856, he started for Cambridge where the office of the *Nautical Almanac* then was. At that time there was no vacancy on the staff but he had not long to wait, for he writes:

"I date my birth into the world of sweetness and light on one frosty morning in January, 1857, when I took my seat between two well-known mathematicians, before a blazing fire in the office of the *Nautical Almanac* at Cambridge, Mass. I had come on from Washington, armed with letters from Professor Henry and Mr. Hilgard, to seek a trial as an astronomical computer. The men beside me were Professor Joseph Winlock, the superintendent, and Mr. John D. Runkle, the senior assistant in the office."

From 1857 to 1861, Newcomb remained in Cambridge as

computer in the office of the *Nautical Almanac*. It may be said that this office was established near Harvard University so as to be able to profit by the technical knowledge of experts, especially that of Prof. Benjamin Peirce, then generally accepted as the leading mathematician of America. The office remained in Cambridge until 1866 when it was removed to Washington. Newcomb's idea of the work may be understood best perhaps by his own presentation of the subject. He says:

"Supply any man with the fundamental data of astronomy, the times at which stars and planets cross the meridian of a place, and other matters of this kind. He is informed that each of these bodies whose observations he is to use is attracted by all the others with a force which varies as the inverse square of their distance apart. From these data he is to weigh the bodies, predict their motion in all future time, compute their orbits, determine what changes of form and position these orbits will undergo through thousands of ages, and make maps showing exactly over what cities and towns on the surface of the earth an eclipse of the sun will pass fifty years hence, or over what regions it did pass thousands of years ago. A more hopeless problem than this could not be presented to the ordinary human intellect. The men who have done it are therefore in intellect the select few of the human race. The astronomical ephemeris is the last practical outcome of their productive genius."

Newcomb, gifted with that appreciation of opportunities that indicates the man of genius, was quick to realize the advantages of a closer relation to the University in Cambridge and therefore enrolled himself as a student of mathematics in the Lawrence Scientific School where he pursued studies in that and kindred branches of learning under the eminent Benjamin Peirce. He received the degree of Bachelor of Science in 1858, and thereafter for three years was continued on the rolls of the University as a resident graduate.

The eclipse of the sun that occurred in 1860 was total in certain parts of British America, and it had fallen to Newcomb to compute the path of the shadow and the times of crossing certain points in it for the records of the office of the *Nautical Almanac*. It was therefore but natural that he should be selected to accompany the party sent to Saskatchewan by the *Almanac* office and in his *Reminiscences* he described with much interest the trip to the then far-away northwest. The expedition failed of success for "the weather was hopeless. We saw the darkness of the eclipse and nothing more." He consoled himself, however, with the following thought:

"It was much easier to go back and tell of the clouds than it would have been to say that the telescope got disarranged at the critical moment so that the observations failed."

In 1861 he learned of a vacancy in the select corps of professors of mathematics in the U. S. Navy, and in August, 1861, he made formal application for an appointment to the Hon. Gideon Welles, then Secretary of the Navy. His letter was brief and concluded with:

"I would respectfully refer you to Commander Charles Henry Davis, U. S. N., Professor Benjamin Peirce, of Harvard University, Dr. Benjamin A. Gould, of Cambridge, and Professor Joseph Henry, Secretary of the Smithsonian Institution, for any information respecting me which will enable you to judge of the propriety of my appointment."

Great was his satisfaction when a month later he found in the post-office "a very large official envelope containing my commission duly signed by Abraham Lincoln, President of the United States." He promptly reported to Washington where he was sent to the Naval Observatory and was assigned to work on the transit instrument. With this appointment his greater life-work began, in the prosecution of which he continued until within a very few days of the end of his life.

It is a far cry from that long-ago Naval Observatory with its primitive facilities to the now excellent equipment and attractive building on the observatory grounds on the hills northwest of Washington. Newcomb has described the work as follows:

"The custom was that one of us should come on every clear evening, make observations as long as he chose, and then go home. The transit instrument was at one end of the building and the mural circle, in charge of Professor Hubbard, at the other. He was weak in health, and unable to do much continuous work of

any kind, especially the hard work of observing. He and I
arranged to observe on the same nights; but I soon found that there
was no concerted plan between the two sets of observers. The
instruments were old-fashioned ones, of which mine could determine only the right ascension of a star and his only its declination;
hence to completely determine the position of a celestial body,
observations must be made on the same object with both instruments. But I soon found that there was no concert of action of
this kind. Hubbard, on the mural circle, had his plan of work;
Yarnell and myself, on the transit, had ours. When either Hubbard or myself got tired, we could 'vote it cloudy' and go out for
a plate of oysters at a neighboring restaurant."

He soon found that "no system of work of the first order of
importance could be initiated until the instrumental equipment
was greatly improved." The clocks, perfection in which is almost
at the bottom of good work, were quite unfit for use; the other
instruments were antiquated and defective in many particulars.
Slowly, however, the pressing needs were supplied and new instruments, notably a great transit circle, were obtained through the
indefatigable zeal of James M. Gilliss, who was in charge of the
observatory. Meanwhile the task of editing, explaining, and preparing for the press the new series of observations made by himself
and his colleague with the old transit instrument, devolved on him.
In 1863, in consequence of the death of Prof. J. S. Hubbard of
the professorial corps, Newcomb was given charge of the mural
circle. Of this new undertaking he says: "I soon became conscious
of the fact, which no one had previously taken much account of,
that upon the plan of each man reducing his own observations,
not only was there an entire lack of homogeneity in the work, but
the more work one did at night the more he had to do by day."
That he possessed the confidence of his superior is evident, for on
presenting the case to Superintendent Gilliss that official quickly
appreciated the fact that work done with the instruments should
be regarded as that of the observatory, and reduced on a uniform
plan, instead of being considered as the property of the individual
who happened to make it. Newcomb adds: "Thus was introduced the first step toward a proper official system."

The new transit circle arrived in October, 1865, and to his great delight, Newcomb was also given charge of it. Then it was that he began the work of determining the error in the right ascension of stars which he believed had crept into the modern observations made in Greenwich, Paris, and Washington and which prevented stars that were on opposite quarters of the heavens from agreeing. For more than three years this undertaking occupied his close attention, and in 1869 he found after working up his observations that the error he had suspected in the adopted positions of the stars was real. This investigation was conspicuously valuable in developing the fact that very difficult mathematical investigations were needed to unravel one of the greatest mysteries of astronomy, that of the moon's motion. Before, however, passing to the consideration of his scientific work more in detail it should be mentioned that he continued at the observatory until 1877, when he became senior professor of mathematics in the U. S. Navy with the relative rank of captain.

The year 1877 was perhaps the most important one in Newcomb's life. With all the strength of his powerful intellect, with all the accumulated experience that constitutes wisdom, with the prosperity that comes with success, and with an appointment that placed him at the head of a great scientific bureau he was indeed at the very zenith of his career. On September 15, 1877, he was assigned to the charge of the *Nautical Almanac* office, and of this appointment he says: "the change was one of the happiest in my life." He adds:

"I was now in a position of recognized responsibility, where my recommendations met with respect due to that responsibility, where I could make plans with the assurance of being able to carry them out, and where the countless annoyances of being looked upon as an important factor in work where there was no chance of my being such would no longer exist. Practically I had complete control of the work of the office, and was thus, metaphorically speaking, able to work with untied hands."

He found the office in a rather dilapidated old dwelling-house, not very far away from the observatory, in one of those doubtful regions on the border line between a slum and the lowest order of respectability. All of the computers did their work at their homes. He promptly hired an office in the top of the Corcoran Building, then just completed, and there he gathered around him his various assistants. He began his work with a careful examination of the relation of prices to work, making an estimate of the time probably necessary to do each job. On the staff were several able and eminent professors at various universities and schools, who were being paid at high professional prices. Soon he found it possible to concentrate all the work in Washington, thereby effecting a reduction in the expenses of the office. "These economies went on increasing year by year, and every dollar that was saved went into the work of making the tables necessary for the future use of the *Ephemeris*."

The program of work which he laid out included a discussion of all the observations of value on the positions of the sun, moon, and planets, and incidentally on the bright fixed stars made at the leading observatories of the world from the year 1750 on, and this work is described more in detail later in this sketch. Another valuable undertaking was the compilation of the formulæ for the perturbation of the various planets by each other.

For twenty years he continued in charge of this office, and as each passing year went on its way with its record of results it carried with it the gratifying assurances that the work under his supervision was more and more surely reaching its successful culmination. When the day for his actual retirement came he left the office with the satisfaction of knowing that his work had gained the appreciation of his colleagues at home and abroad, for no honors such as were conferred upon him had ever come to an American scientist.

The plaudit "well done, good and faithful servant" was surely his. Director Maurice Loewy who was long in charge of the observatory in Paris wrote:

"His activity has embraced the most diverse branches of astronomy. Not only has he given a great scope to the intellectual movement of this country, but he has also contributed in a very successful manner to elevate the level of the civilization of our age, enriching the domain of science with beautiful and durable conquests."

While a young man in Cambridge, Newcomb determined to devote his life to the prosecution of exact astronomy, and the first problem which he took up was that of the zone of those minor planets, called asteroids, which revolve between the orbits of Mars and Jupiter. This investigation, published in 1860, under the title *On the Secular Variations and Mutual Relations of the Orbits of the Asteroids* showed that the orbits of these bodies "had never passed through any common point of intersection" and hence were not fragments of a larger body that had met with some catastrophe as had been generally believed. "The whole trend of thought and research since that time," says Newcomb, "has been towards the conclusion that no such cataclysm as that looked for ever occurred, and that the group of smaller planets had been composed of separate bodies since the solar system came into existence."

His own statement of "the great problem of exact astronomy" to which he gave so much of his life and thought is as follows:

"It is well known that we shall at least come very near the truth when we say that the planets revolve around the sun, and the satellites around their primaries according to the law of gravitation. We may regard all these bodies as projected into space, and thus moving according to laws similar to that which governs the motion of a stone thrown from the hand. If two bodies alone were concerned, say the sun and a planet, the orbit of the lesser around the greater would be an ellipse, which would never change its form, size, or position. That the orbits of the planets and asteroids do change, and that they are not exact ellipses, is due to their attraction upon each other. The question is, do these mutual attractions completely explain all the motions down to the last degree of refinement? Does any world move otherwise than as it is attracted by other worlds?

"Two different lines of research must be brought to bear on the question thus presented. We must first know by the most exact and refined observations that the astronomer can make exactly how a heavenly body does move. Its position, or, as we cannot directly measure distance, its direction from us, must be determined as precisely as possible from time to time. Its course has been mapped out for it in advance by tables which are published in the *Astronomical Ephemeris*, and we may express its position by its deviation from these tables. Then comes in the mathematical problem how it ought to move under the attraction of all other heavenly bodies that can influence its motion. The results must then be compared, in order to see to what conclusion we may be led."

It is not easy to understand the obstacles that had to be overcome in a series of investigations in which in the solution of so complex a problem as that Newcomb undertook. The general treatment is indicated by Bostwick [1] in the following statement:

"If the universe consisted of but two bodies—say, the sun and a planet—the motion would be simplicity itself; the planet would describe an exact ellipse about the sun, and this orbit would never change in form, size, or position. With the addition of only one more body, the problem at once becomes so much more difficult as to be practically insoluble; indeed, the 'problem of the three bodies' has been attacked by astronomers for years without the discovery of any general formula to express the resulting motions. For the actually existing system of many planets with their satellites and countless asteroids, only an approximation is possible. The actual motions as observed and measured from year to year are most complex. Can these be completely accounted for by the mutual attractions of the bodies, according to the law of gravitation? Its two elements are, of course, the mapping out of the lines in which the bodies concerned actually do move and the calculations of the orbits in which they ought to move, if the accepted laws of planetary motion are true. The first involves the study of thousands of observations made during long years by different men in far distant lands, the discussion of their probable errors, and their reduction to a common standard. The latter requires the use of the most refined methods of mathematical analysis; it is as Newcomb says, 'of a complexity beyond the powers of ordinary conception.' "

The practical impossibility of ever completing this remarkable series of studies is almost obvious, for in magnitude that task is

[1] A. E. Bostwick, *American Review of Reviews*, August, 1909.

one probably not exceeded by any ever before attempted by an astronomer, and yet Newcomb persisted, although in many cases he was obliged to confine himself to a correction of the reductions already made and published. The number of meridian observations on the sun, Mercury, Venus, and Mars alone numbered 62,030, and these were contributed by the observatories at Greenwich, Paris, Königsberg, Pulkowa, Cape of Good Hope, and elsewhere. Says Newcomb: "The job was one with which I do not think any astronomical one ever attempted by a single person could compare in extent."

It was this elaborate task of "bringing this great problem of the solar system well-nigh to completeness of solution" that constituted Newcomb's life-work and in connection with which his name will go down in history. It involved "an almost complete reconstruction of the theories of the motions of the bodies of the solar system" and "at its foundation the complete revision of the so-called constants of astronomy." Such is the testimony of his successor in the office of the *Nautical Almanac*, who further adds:

"The distance of the earth from the sun; the displacement of the earth in its orbit by the attraction of the moon; the displacement of the stars due to the motion of the earth combined with the motion of light, which involves the velocity of light and space; the yearly precession of the equinoxes; the obliquity of the ecliptic; the dimensions and the masses of the planets; all had to be worked into a homogeneous system to be used as a basis for the tables of the sun and planets."

The moon early attracted his attention and it held him until the end. Almost his very first observations at the Naval Observatory in Washington "showed that the moon seemed to be falling a little behind her predicted motion." He soon found that other astronomers had found similar "inequalities" and therefore he determined to ascertain the cause of this phenomenon. He studied the records of other astronomers and after satisfying himself that the error had occurred prior to 1750, he searched the old records of Europe and in Paris, and in Pulkowa found evidence that traced the error back to before the year 1675, which in the elapsed time had with slight accretions amounted to sufficient to vitiate in a marked degree the records of astronomy. The compilation necessary to correct this error required years to perform, and although the corrections were promptly applied to work in progress it was not until 1878 that he was able to publish his *Reductions and Discussion of the Moon before* 1750.

Later when release came to him from official duties he returned to that subject and with the aid of a grant from the Carnegie Institution given him in 1903 and later, he devoted his leisure to a further investigation of this subject, culminating in a memoir on *The Motion of the Moon,* the final words of which were dictated by him after he had been stricken with the fatal illness that stretched him upon a bed of suffering and from which he never arose.

The sun and the moon and the planets yielded their secrets to the call of his mighty intellect, and science has profited to the benefit of humanity in consequence of the life of Simon Newcomb.

As Newcomb grew in reputation his advice was sought for many purposes, and his knowledge taken advantage of not only by our government but also by those abroad. Of these experiences, therefore, brief mention must be made.

In 1869 he was one of the party sent to Des Moines, Iowa, to observe the solar eclipse that passed across the United States in that year. He prepared the detailed set of instructions issued by the Naval Observatory to observers in towns at each edge of the shadow-path to note the short duration of totality. He was also a member of the party sent to Gibraltar to observe the eclipse that occurred in December, 1870. The day of the eclipse was cloudy so that the observations made were not of very great value. He made the trip from England to Gibraltar as the guest of the English official party, and among other guests was Prof. John Tyndall.

Of this period he wrote: "My continued presence on the observatory staff led to my taking part in two of the great movements of the next ten years, the construction and inauguration of the great telescope and the observations of the transit of Venus."

Concerning the first of these events Newcomb has told pleasantly in his *Reminiscences* of its origin. At a dinner party where several Senators were present the mortifying statement was made that there was no large telescope in Washington. This fact so interested Senator Hamlin of Maine that provision was made almost immediately by Congress for the construction of a suitable instrument. The necessary money was appropriated and to Newcomb was assigned the duty of negotiating the contracts, and later of supervising the construction of the object-glass. The great 26-inch lens was made by Alvan Clark and Sons, and on November 10, 1873, the first observations made with it,—those on the satellites of Neptune,—were begun. It is interesting to add that the famous discovery of the satellites of Mars by Asaph Hall in August, 1877, was made with this instrument. According to Newcomb: "The success of the Washington telescope excited such interest the world over as to give a new impetus to the construction of such instruments." Pleased with their success the Clarks were ready to undertake much larger instruments, and it may be said that a 30-inch telescope for the Pulkowa Observatory in Russia, the 36-inch telescope of the Lick Observatory in California, and, finally, the 40-inch of the Yerkes Observatory in Williams' Bay, Wisconsin, were the outcome of the movement.

A description of the second event will occupy but a few words. In 1871 Newcomb was appointed secretary of the commission that was created by Congress for the purpose of observing the transit of Venus on December 9, 1874, and under whose direction the expeditions sent by the United States government were organized. He also had much to do with equipping the expeditions that were sent to observe the transit in 1882, and he took charge of the party that went to Cape of Good Hope. His comment on the occasion is as follows: "The sky on the day of the transit was simply perfect. Notwithstanding the intensity of the sun's rays, the atmosphere was so steady that I have never seen the sun to better advantage. So all our observations were successful."

Early in 1874, the announcement was made that James Lick, of San Francisco, had transferred his fortune to a board of trustees in order to carry out certain public benefactions, one of which was the procuring of the greatest and most powerful telescope that had ever been made. Newcomb was soon consulted in regard to this interesting proposition, and in December, 1874, he was invited to visit the European workshops as an agent of the Lick trustees. This duty he promptly accepted, and after failure to negotiate satisfactory arrangements abroad, he finally advised that the making of the great 36-inch lens be given to Clark and Sons. From its inception, therefore, until its inauguration, Newcomb was the principal scientific adviser of the trustees of the Lick Observatory, and recommended for their consideration, Edward S. Holden, who was chosen their first director.

Of almost identical nature was his relation to the construction of the 30-inch object-glass for the Pulkowa telescope. In 1878, Otto Struve, the director of that observatory, began correspondence with Newcomb concerning the building of a large refracting telescope. Struve came to the United States on Newcomb's suggestion in 1879, and together they visited the workshops of the Clarks in Cambridge. After due consideration Struve decided to place the contract for making the object-glass with the American firm, and thereafter, until its completion, Newcomb was frequently consulted in regard to it. In 1887, in appreciation of this work, the Emperor of Russia ordered Newcomb's portrait to be painted and placed in the Government gallery of famous astronomers in Pulkowa. Two years later Newcomb received a rare vase of jasper on a pedestal of black marble, six and a half feet high, which "in recognition of these deserts, His Majesty, the Emperor, graciously sends as a present for you from the observatory of Pulkowa."

In 1884 he was invited to accept the professorship of mathematics and astronomy in the Johns Hopkins University, which place he held until 1893, when he resigned, but again returned to that chair in 1898, and two years later was made emeritus. In reference to his work it has been said that "no American would have been more worthy of succeeding Sylvester. As an astronomer his name has long shone with a lustre which fills with pride every American breast." Johns Hopkins was keenly appreciative of his services to that university, and in 1901 Newcomb was one of the two to receive the first award of the Sylvester prize. This prize is a handsome bronze medallion of the late Professor Sylvester framed in oak. In making the award President Gilman said: "The second copy of this tablet is now offered to Professor Simon Newcomb, a distinguished astronomer, who has been a friend of the University from its inception, and who guided the mathematical department for many years."

When it was decided to hold a World's Fair in St. Louis in commemoration of the purchase of Louisiana, an International Congress of Arts and Science was advocated by a distinguished group of educators and scientists, who on the acceptance of their plan at once recommended "that Simon Newcomb be named for President." In his history of the congress, Doctor Rogers says: "The choice for president of the Congress fell without debate to the dean of American scientific circles, whose eminent services to the government of the United States and whose recognized position in foreign and domestic scientific circles made him particularly fitted to preside over such an international gathering of the leading scientists of the world."

Of his remarkable success in securing the presence of the greatest men in the world in every domain of science there is abundant testimony. Nor is there need to discuss the work of the congress here, for the eight octavo volumes published after the event tell the story with exactness. Space, however, may be given to the opening words with which on the theme of "The Evolution of the Scientific Investigator," Newcomb at the very culmination of his splendid career opened the congress in the presence of perhaps the most distinguished audience ever gathered in the new world,—an audience which indeed testified by their presence to the homage which they proudly rendered to him whom they recognized as the world's first scientist. He said:

"As we look at the assemblage gathered in this hall, comprising so many names of widest renown in every branch of learning,—we might almost say in every field of human endeavor,—the first inquiry suggested must be after the object of our meeting. The answer is, that our purpose corresponds to the eminence of the assemblage. We aim at nothing less than a survey of the realm of knowledge, as comprehensive as is permitted by the limitations of time and space. The organizers of our Congress have honored me with the charge of presenting such preliminary view of its field as may make clear the spirit of our undertaking."

It must be remembered always that Newcomb's great work was on the mathematical astronomy of the solar system, involving as it did the preparation of the most exact possible tables of the motions of all the planets. These researches were published by the Nautical Almanac Office in eight quarto volumes entitled *Astronomical Papers of the American Ephemeris*. But this was by no manner of means all; for a volume at least would be necessary to merely mention his other very many addresses, memoirs, and papers. The titles of 376 of these have been carefully collected by Dr. R. C. Archibald and were published in 1905. Concerning these Prof. Arthur Cayley, formerly president of the Royal Astronomical Society of Great Britain, has said: "Professor Newcomb's writings exhibit, all of them, a combination on the one hand of mathematical skill and power, and on the other of good hard work, devoted to the furtherance of astronomical science."

During the years of his active connection with Johns Hopkins University, he was properly editor-in-chief of the *American Journal of Mathematics*, and during the rest of the time—from the foundation of the journal in 1878 to 1884, and subsequent to 1900—he was an associate editor. His literary activity was very great and but few important works of reference have been published without articles from his pen. He was one of the contributors to Johnson's *Cyclopedia*, and became the "astronomical mathematical editor" of that work for its edition published in 1900, as the *Universal Cyclopedia*. He wrote a number of articles, including that on Astronomy, for the tenth edition of the *Encyclopædia Britannica*, and was one of the "associate and advising editors" of the *Encyclopædia Americana*, and he was an associate editor of the *Dictionary of Psychology and Philosophy*. His magazine articles contributed to the *Atlantic, Popular Science Monthly,*

Harpers, North American Review, Forum, and other similar journals were many and valuable.

In book form he should be credited with the following works, many of which have passed through several editions and at least one, his *Popular Astronomy,* was republished in England and translated into the German, Russian, and Norwegian languages. The list includes *Popular Astronomy* (New York, 1878); *School Astronomy,* with Edward S. Holden (1879); *Briefer Course* (1883); *Elements of Astronomy* (1900); *Stars; A Study of the Universe,* translated into Dutch, Bohemian, and Japanese (1901); *Astronomy for Everybody* (1902); *Compendium of Spherical Astronomy* (1905) and *Side Lights on Astronomy* (1906); also a series of text-books comprising *Algebra* (1881); *Geometry* (1881); *Trigonometry and Logarithms* (1882); *School Algebra* (1882); *Analytic Geometry* (1884); *Essentials of Trigonometry* (1884); and *Calculus* (1887).

Of the text-books the following story is told concerning their origin: "One evening Professor Newcomb found his daughter Anita, now Mrs. McGee, poring over an algebra which he thought too abstruse for a beginner. 'Put it aside,' he said, 'I will write you something to study.' He began at once and wrote a lesson for her, and after this, wrote every evening her lesson for the next day. A complete algebra was the result. This was finally published, and a whole series of mathematical books followed."

Very early in life Professor Newcomb developed an interest in political economy and it was his habit to refer to astronomy as his "profession" and to political economy as his "recreation." A wise man knows the value of diverting his thoughts from his "profession" to his "recreation." At first the application of mathematics to public questions seems to have appealed to him most and he wrote on finance. Many of his earlier articles were published in such prominent reviews as the *North American* and the old *International;* some of these papers were anonymous. As years came to him, however, he broadened his views until he became an accepted authority in many branches of political economy. His opinions were highly valued and eagerly sought for, and in consequence they were given to the world in book form.

Professor Irving Fisher who fills so acceptably the chair of political economy in Yale University, has described with such skill Newcomb's contributions to political economy that I venture to include his brief analysis. He says:

"It is true that Newcomb sought not so much to add to economic science as to restate what was already known, but in so doing he struck out in many new paths. Perhaps his chief contribution was the distinction between a 'fund' and a 'flow' — , a 'fund' relating to a point of time and a 'flow' relating to a period of time. This distinction he applied especially to the societary circulation which he expressed in one equation between the circulation of money and the reverse flow of goods. He was apparently the first to state this equation and thereby to formulate accurately the so-called 'quantity theory of money.' He also applied the distinction between a 'flow' and a 'fund' to expose the fallacy of the wage-fund. The same distinction many of us have found extremely fruitful in the analysis of capital and income. Among other problems to the solution of which Professor Newcomb contributed may be mentioned the problem of the standard of deferred payments and the perennial problem of Labor and Capital. In general, Professor Newcomb was an advocate of *laissez faire*, but he distinguished sharply between the government policy of 'letting alone' and that of 'keeping out.'

"In Methodology Professor Newcomb maintained that Economics was a science and should be treated by scientific methods. One of the most stimulating discussions in his *Elements of Political Economy* is that concerning the nature of scientific method. He points out that a scientific law merely expresses what would happen under certain hypothetical conditions."

Of his writings on this subject the following are the more important: *A Critical Examination of our Financial Policy during the Rebellion* (New York, 1865); *The A. B. C. of Finance* (1877); *A Plain Man's Talk on the Labor Question* (1886); *Principles of Political Economy* (1886); and *The Problem of Economic Education* (1893).

As further evidence of his remarkable versatility may be mentioned his stories: *The Wreck of the Columbia* (1896); *The End of the World* (1903), which was translated into Japanese; and his novel *His Wisdom, the Defender* (1900); and finally *The Reminiscences of an Astronomer* (1903).

No American was ever more conspicuously honored than Simon Newcomb. Decorations, medals, and degrees were gladly conferred on him. The much prized red ribbon of the order of the Legion of Honor in the grade of "officier" was given him by the French government in 1896, and in 1907 he was advanced to the rank of "commandeur." The German Emperor made him a Knight in the Prussian order of Merit for Science and Art, and on his last visit to Europe, Professor Newcomb was received at luncheon by Emperor William. In 1874 he was awarded a gold medal by the Royal Astronomical Society of London, and in 1878 the great Huyghens gold medal was given to him by the Haarlem Society of Sciences under the auspices of the University of Leyden. This medal, it is interesting to add, is awarded biennially to the individual, who by his researches and discoveries or inventions during the previous twenty years, has, in the judgment of the Society distinguished himself in an exceptional manner in a particular branch of science. Although awarded every two years it is distributed among the various sciences, so that it is only once in twenty years that it is given to an astronomer. In 1890 he received the Copley medal from the Royal Society of London for his contributions to gravitational astronomy. This award is regarded as the most important of all those given by the Royal Society and ranks as the "blue ribbon" of Science in England. The first American recipient of this medal was Benjamin Franklin. Newcomb was the first to receive the Bruce gold medal awarded by the Astronomical Society of the Pacific. It was conferred on him in 1898 "as a recognition of services to astronomy."

The appreciation of his work by the Emperor of Russia in ordering in 1887 that his portrait be added to the gallery in Pulkowa, followed in 1888 by the gift of a jasper vase, as well as his award of the Sylvester prize of the Johns Hopkins University in 1901, have already been mentioned. To these tokens of recognition may be added the facts that in 1889 the Imperial University of Tokio, in Japan, officially presented him with two bronze vases of exquisite workmanship and design; also in 1895 he received the *Astronomical Journal* prize of $400 for the "most thorough discussion of the theory of the rotation of the earth, with reference to the recently discovered variation of latitude." And finally that the Imperial Academy of Sciences in St. Petersburg in 1897, gave him the Schubert prize of 900 roubles.

Universities gave him their highest degrees and he held the following honorary doctorates: George Washington, LL.D., 1874; Yale, LL.D., 1875; Leyden, Nat.Ph.D., 1875; Harvard, LL.D., 1884; Heidelberg, Ph.D., 1886; Columbia, LL.D., 1887; Edinburgh, LL.D., 1891; Padua, Phil.Nat.D., 1892; Dublin, Sc.D., 1892; Princeton, LL.D., 1896; Cambridge, Sc.D., 1896; Glasgow, LL.D., 1896; Oxford, D.C.L., 1899; Cracow, LL.D., 1900; Johns Hopkins, LL.D., 1902; Christiania, Math.D., 1902; and Toronto, LL.D., 1904. It may be added to this generous list of universities with which he was affiliated that he was always active in all matters that pertained to the progress of his own Harvard, the alumni of which testified to their appreciation of his interest by choosing him as one of their representatives on the Board of Overseers of that university, a place that he held at the time of his death.

In 1872 he was elected an associate member of the Royal Astronomical Society of London, and in 1877 he was made a foreign member of the Royal Society of London; holding also honorary fellowship in the similar societies in Edinburgh, 1881, Dublin, 1882, and Sydney, Australia, 1901. He held corresponding, associate or honorary membership in all of the great academies of science, including those in Sweden, 1875; Bavaria, 1876; Göttingen, 1888; Brussels, 1891; Rome, 1895; St. Petersburg, 1897; Amsterdam, 1898; Milan, 1899; Vienna and Berlin, 1904.

Conspicuous among the honors which tell of the appreciation of a man by his colleagues was the recognition received in 1887 by Newcomb in his election as one of the eight members of the council of the Astronomische Gesellschaft, an international astronomical society that meets once in two years.   In 1874 he was elected a corresponding member of the Institute of France and on June 17, 1895, was chosen one of the eight foreign associate members of the Academy of Science of the Institute of France, in succession to the illustrious Helmholtz.   This was the greatest honor that came to him; for indeed there is none higher, and since Franklin, Newcomb was the first native American to receive this greatest of all scientific honors.

In the United States his services to science likewise received conspicuous recognition.   In 1869 he was elected a member of the National Academy of Sciences which he served as vice-president in 1883–89 and as foreign secretary in 1903–09.   He was elected to the American Philosophical Society in 1878, and was its senior vice-president at the time of his death; and he was an associate fellow of the American Academy of Arts and Sciences.   Among the societies to which he was chosen president are the following: American Association for the Advancement of Science (1876), Society for Psychical Research (1885), Political Economy Club of America (1887), American Mathematical Society (1896), and Astronomical and Astrophysical Society of America (1899).   In his own home city he had been elected president of the Philosophical Society of Washington in 1879 and 1880, and again in 1909; and in 1907 of the Cosmos Club.

With wise judgment Newcomb in his will bequeathed to the United States for deposit and public exhibition in the National Museum, his foreign decorations, medals, prizes from scientific bodies, diplomas and certificates from universities and learned societies, so that for all time, they might testify to the recognition his genius had gained for him.   Merit is quickly appreciated in this great republic of ours, and to none does it yield its rewards more readily than to those who follow science.   Eloquent indeed are these silent evidences of recognition, for they will ever show that even the humblest may aspire to the greatest honors, if only he prove himself worthy.

Happy also was Newcomb in his home life.   In 1863 he married Mary Caroline Hassler, daughter of Dr. Charles A. Hassler of the U. S. Navy and granddaughter of F. R. Hassler, the first superintendent of the U. S. Coast Survey, and also great-grand-niece of David Rittenhouse of Philadelphia, famous as an astronomer in the early history of this country. And to their home in Washington—for that city was always their home—came many friends. Henry, with whom he "became very intimate," and other men of science were frequent visitors, but soon others came once, and then again, and so the circle grew. Men prominent in official life, like Garfield; statesmen, like Sumner; and officers high in the military service, like Sherman, were his friends. As his fame increased persons of distinction from all parts of the world when they visited Washington made it their pleasure to pay their respects to the astronomer. In his *Reminiscences* he tells how in the centennial year Dom Pedro d'Alcantara, then Emperor of Brazil, sought him, and in recent years the Hon. James Bryce, the present Ambassador from Great Britain, received his hospitality. But after all it was among the younger men that his influence was most beneficial. He was quick to recognize ability and equally quick to insist on its recognition. It was Holden, his "assistant on the great equatorial," who on his recommendation became the first Director of the Lick Observatory, and he refers to George W. Hill who was his subordinate on the *Nautical Almanac* as "the greatest master of mathematical astronomy during the last quarter of the nineteenth century." To his contemporaries he was always just and to his subordinates considerate.

He took his work seriously and he believed in telling the truth, that is, the absolute scientific truth, not what might have occurred or possibly what might have occurred, but absolutely what did occur as he saw it without any attempt at circumlocution or embellishing circumstances. The simple, plain, scientific statement of fact was all that he was willing to give, and it was what he demanded in return from those with whom he was associated. He had not much time for the trivial, and yet whatever he undertook no detail was ever disregarded as being insignificant. It seemed wise to the members of the Cosmos Club to place him in office as their president without the usual preliminary elections to the subordinate offices of manager and vice-president, and during the year of his incumbency he showed the utmost interest in the duties of the place, aiding materially in the progress of the Club by his many suggestions and excellent advice. His trips abroad were elaborately planned, and he always made careful preparation by reading volume after volume on the countries to be visited. A thorough study of his subject in the beginning led to a better appreciation of it afterwards.

Industry and persistency, combined with an intellect that enabled him to grasp the elements of a problem and conquer them, were the dominant traits of Newcomb's character. To these should be added the fact that he found his pleasure and recreation in pursuits that to many would have been hard work, but to him they were relaxation. Whatever came to him he did well and as genius may be defined as that quality of mind that develops its own environment then surely among the great men of the world, Newcomb was one of the very greatest.

Newcomb's last days were typical of his life, for they exhibited in a marked degree the characteristics of his genius. In the autumn of 1908 he returned from a trip abroad strengthened in mind and in body, eager to bring to a conclusion his great work on the *Motion of the Moon*, the completion of which had been so long deferred. A meeting of the Overseers of Harvard called him to Cambridge and on his return the symptoms of the fatal malady began to show themselves. Several visits to specialists in Baltimore failed to give him relief, but the disease was definitely diagnosed as cancer and located so as to make an operation impossible. When Newcomb was told that recovery could not be expected he asked to be brought home at once, and with that wonderful power of concentration, in moments of freedom from pain, he dictated the final words of his last contribution to science. On June 16 it was finished and then turned over to the printer. But the end was not yet, and for a month longer he continued to work preparing chapters for his biography and putting his business affairs in final shape.

And then on July 11, 1909, he passed away, and now he abides

"Where truth and joy and beauty ever are,
Beyond the sunset and the dying day,
Beyond the moonrise and the evening star."

As befitting his high rank of rear-admiral in the U. S. Navy he was given an official funeral, which was attended by President Taft and escorted by representatives of scientific bodies and the Ambassadors of France and Germany; they buried him in Arlington, where only those who have served their country are permitted to lie. Among the Nation's great dead he is at rest.

G Brown Goode

GEORGE BROWN GOODE

ZOÖLOGIST

1851–1896

BY DAVID STARR JORDAN

THE untimely death of George Brown Goode left a great break in the ranks of the scientific men of America. One of the most accurate and devoted of students, the ablest exponent of museum methods, a man of the most exalted personal character, Doctor Goode occupied a unique position in the development of American science.

George Brown Goode was born in New Albany, Indiana, on February 13, 1851, and died of pneumonia at his home on Lanier Heights in Washington City on September 6, 1896. According to Dr. Marcus Benjamin, to whom I am indebted for many of the details of this sketch:

"Doctor Goode was of Colonial descent. His family lived in Virginia, and he traced with pride his paternal line to John Goode, who came to that colony prior to 1660, and settled four miles from the present site of Richmond, on an estate which he named 'Whitby.' John Goode was one of the advisers of Bacon in 1676, in the first armed uprising of the Americans against the oppression of royal authority. On his mother's side he was descended from Jasper Crane, who came to New England before 1630, and afterwards settled near the present site of Newark, New Jersey. Doctor Goode's father was Francis Collier Goode, who married, in 1850, Sarah Woodruff Crane, and their distinguished son was born at the home of his maternal grandfather."

In 1857, Mr. Goode's parents moved to Amenia, in New York state, where the boy passed his early youth, and where he was prepared for college. In due time young Goode was matriculated in Wesleyan University in Middletown, Connecticut, where he graduated in 1870, at the too early age of nineteen.

The fixed curriculum of the college gave him little opportunity for the studies in which he was chiefly interested, and his standing in the conventional branches on which the higher education was then supposed to depend was not unusually high. He was, however, regarded as "a man exceptionally promising for work" in natural history.

Goode spent part of the year of 1870 in graduate work in Harvard, and there fell under the stimulating influence of the greatest of teachers of science, Louis Agassiz. Before the year was over he was recalled to Middletown to take charge of the Museum of Natural Science then just erected by Orange Judd. His work in Judd Hall was a prelude to his reorganization of the National Museum in Washington, an institution which will always show in its classification and arrangement the traces of his master hand.

In 1872, he first met Professor Baird in Eastport, Maine, and in 1873, while at the meeting of the American Association for the Advancement of Science, in Portland, Maine, he renewed this acquaintance. Professor Baird with his characteristic insight into the ambitions and possibilities of promising young men,— one of his notable qualities,—invited Goode to aid in the work of the newly organized Fish Commission. At that time Professor Baird was Assistant Secretary of the Smithsonian Institution, in charge of the National Museum, and also United States Fish Commissioner. The organizations were managed in similar fashion and all their activities directed to the same high ends. Very soon Goode was brought into the service of them both. In the summer he was employed by the Fish Commission in investigations and explorations along the Atlantic Coast. In the winter he divided his time between Wesleyan University and the National Museum, until the former institution was reluctantly compelled, in 1877, wholly to give him up. Till that date his only compensation for work done in Washington was found in duplicate specimens of fishes and other animals, which in turn were presented by him to the museum in Middletown.

Miss Lucy Baird writes (in a letter to Mr. T. D. A. Cockerell, who sends me this item): " From the time of their first meeting a warm personal attachment sprang up between them which deepened every year up to the time of my father's death. From the time when Mr. Goode became associated with the Museum work, my father's burdens in connection therewith became greatly lessened, as year by year, Mr. Goode's ability in that line developed. No cloud ever obscured their harmonious relations, I can recall but one difference between them and that was on an occasion when some idea had been carried out in connection with the Museum work,—an achievement in which they both felt a natural pride, each was determined that all the credit belonged to the other. They argued so strongly that they absolutely grew a little hot in discussing the matter. My father wished Mr. Goode to take all the credit, and Mr. Goode insisted that he had only developed what my father had created. . . . If my father," continues Miss Baird "had had no other title to the gratitude of the scientific world, it would have cause to remember him with gratitude for having afforded the facilities for the development of Mr. Goode's genius, though that, in time would have made itself known without aid."

In 1887 he became Assistant Secretary of the Smithsonian Institution, in charge of the National Museum. On the death of Professor Baird, he became for a time United States Fish Commissioner, holding the office without pay until a change in the law permitted the appointment of a separate salaried head. In his later years Mr. Goode devoted his whole energies to museum administration, a kind of work for which no one in the world has ever shown greater aptitude. Two important publications, *Museums of the Future* and *Principles of Museum Administration*, admirably embody his views and experiences in this regard. His appreciation of the importance of such work is characteristically shown in his dedication of an interesting genus of deep-sea fishes to "Ulysses Aldrovandi, of Bologna, the founder of the first natural history museum."

His interest in museum administration caused a large amount of "exposition work" to be intrusted to his hands. An exposition is a temporary museum with a distinctly educational purpose. It can be made a mere public fair on a large scale, or it can be made a source of public education. In Goode's hands an exhibition of material was always made to teach some lesson. He had charge, under Professor Baird, of the Smithsonian exhibits in the Centennial Exhibition of 1876, in Philadelphia. He served as United States Commissioner in the Fisheries Exhibition held in Berlin in 1880, and in London in 1883. He was a member of the Board of Management of the government exhibit in the World's Columbian Exposition of 1893, and also prepared the general plan of classification adopted for the Exposition. He was equally active in minor expositions held in New Orleans, Cincinnati, Louisville, Atlanta, and elsewhere. He was also concerned in the Columbian Historical Exposition held in Madrid 1892–93, and for part of the time acted as Commissioner-General for the United States. His services in that connection were recognized by the conferment of the order of Isabella the Catholic, with the rank of Commander. From the Fisheries Exposition in London he received a medal in honor of his services to the science of ichthyology.

Goode was always deeply interested in the historical and biographical side of science, and in the personality, the hopes, and the sorrows of those who preceded him in the study of fishes and other animals. This showed itself in sympathetic sketches of those who had to do with the beginnings of American science as well as with the dedication of new genera, to those who had done honor to themselves by honest work in times when good work was not easy, and was not valued by the world. Among these thus recognized by him was Thomas Harriott, of Roanoke (an associate of Raleigh), who published the first work in English on American natural history.

His interest in the biographical side of science led him to the scientific side of biography. From boyhood he was interested in genealogy. His own family records were published by him under

the title of *Virginia Cousins*. This has been regarded·as a model
genealogical monograph. Doctor Goode believed that the way
to do any piece of work is to do it thoroughly. While errors are
inseparable from all work in science, and no man can ever find
out the whole truth about anything yet whatever we really know
can be thrown into workmanlike shape. Nothing crude or incoherent in form at least, ever left Goode's pen.

Goode was one of the founders of the American Historical
Association, and a member of its executive council from 1889
till his death. He contributed to its *Proceedings*, in 1889, his
valuable paper on the "Origin of the National Scientific and
Educational Institutions of the United States." He was also a
member of the Southern Historical Society, organized in 1896.
Much of his leisure during his last two summers was given to the
preparation of the material that is used in the volume entitled
The Smithsonian Institution, 1846–96, which was his project, and
is a monument to his knowledge of science in this country during
the first half century of the existence of the Smithsonian Institution.

Goode was one of the founders of the Society of the Sons of
the American Revolution in the District of Columbia, and after
filling various offices was, in 1894, made President. He was also
Vice-President of the Society of the Sons of the Revolution, and
Lieutenant-Governor of the Society of Colonial Wars in the District of Columbia.

He was very prominent in the organization and conduct of
scientific societies, which he regarded as valuable agencies in the
spread of scientific knowledge. He had been President both of
the Philosophical Society and the Biological Society of Washington. He was elected to the American Association for the Advancement of Science in 1873, and to the National Academy of Sciences
in 1888. He was also a member of the Zoölogical Society of
London. His work in science was recognized in 1886 by the degree of Ph.D. from the University of Indiana, his native state.
It was the fortune of the present writer to accept as a thesis from
him the "Catalogue of the Fishes of the Bermudas," and to move
the granting of this degree. His relation to general culture and

executive work was recognized by Wesleyan University by the degree of LL.D. conferred in 1888.

The writer first met Mr. Goode in 1874, while he was engaged in work for the United States Fish Commission in Noank, Connecticut. He was then a young man of scholarly appearance, winning manners, and a very enthusiastic student of fishes. In figure he was of medium height, rather slender, and very active. His countenance was intellectual, and he seemed always to have a very definite idea of what he wished to do.

Our first meeting was in connection with an effort on his part to find the difference between the two genera of fishes called *Ceratacanthus* and *Alutera*. At this time I was greatly impressed with the accuracy and neatness of his work, and especially with his love of what may be called the literary side of science,—a side too often neglected by scientific men. He detested an inaccuracy, a misspelled name, or a slovenly record, as he would have despised any other vice. Indeed, in all his work and relations, moral purity and scientific accuracy were one and the same thing. He had inherited or acquired "the Puritan conscience," and applied it not only to lapses of personal integrity, but to weaknesses and slovenliness of all sorts. Hence he became in Washington not only a power in scientific matters, but a source of moral strength to the community. His influence is felt in the Museum, not only in the wisdom of its organization, but in the personal character of its body of curators. The irresponsible life of Bohemia is not favorable to good work in science, and the men he chose as associates belong to another order.

As to Doctor Goode's moral influence and youthful characteristics the following extracts from a private letter of Prof. Otis T. Mason will be found valuable:

"Two characteristics of the man fixed themselves upon my mind indelibly: I found him to be intensely consciencious and I could see that he was a young man who not only wished to live a correct life himself, but abhorred the association of evil men.

"Another characteristic which forced itself upon me was his devotion to the museum side of scientific investigation. He wrote a beautiful hand, and on one occasion he told me that it was just as much the duty of a scientific investigator to write a good hand and spell his names correctly, so that there would be no mistake in the label, as it was for him to make his investigations accurately. You will find if you will look over some of the specimens which he marked at that time, beautiful numerals, clear and distinct, so that there is no mistaking one from the other.

"Again, I discovered the pedagogic feeling to be very strong in him, and the interests of the public no less than of the investigator were constantly before his mind. Indeed, there was nothing about Doctor Goode in his admirable management of the Museum in later years that did not make its appearance to some extent when he had the work to do with his own hands. The germ of our present discipline manifested itself in the discipline which he exerted over his own conduct when he was junior assistant instead of director.

"About the time that Doctor Goode came to the Museum, I undertook to arrange the ethnological collections. I can remember the delight which it gave him to consider a classification in which the activities of mankind were divided into genera and species subject to the laws of natural history, of evolution, and geographic surroundings. The development of the Department of Arts and Industries has been the result of these early studies."

Doctor Goode had a wonderful power of analyzing the relations or contents of any group of activities, or of any objects of study. This showed itself notably in his two catalogues of collections illustrating the animal resources of the United States. These catalogues were written with reference to the arrangement of material for the exhibits of the Smithsonian Institution and the United States Fish Commission at the Centennial Exhibition at Philadelphia.

Doctor Gill says, in his admirable biographical sketch:

"It was the ability that was manifested in these catalogues and the work incidental to their preparation that especially arrested the attention of Professor Baird, and marked the author as one well adapted for the direction of a great museum. For signal success in such direction special qualifications are requisite. Only some of them are a mind well trained in analytical as well as synthetic methods, an artistic sense, critical ability, and multifarious knowledge, but above all the knowledge of men and how to deal with them.   Perhaps no one has ever combined, in more harmonious proportions, such qualifications than G. Brown Goode.   In him the National Museum of the United States and the world at large have lost one of the greatest of museum administrators."

The most striking character of Doctor Goode's scientific papers was perhaps their scholarly accuracy and good taste.   He never wrote a paper carelessly.   He was never engaged in any controversy, and he rarely made a statement which had later to be withdrawn.   Yet no one was more ready to acknowledge an error, if one were made, and none showed greater willingness to recognize the good work of others.   The literature even of the most out-of-the-way branch of zoölogical research had a great fascination for him, and he found in bibliography and in the records of the past workers in science a charm scarcely inferior to that of original observation and research.   In his later years administrative duties occupied more and more of his time, restricting the opportunities for his own studies.   He seemed, however, to have as great delight in the encouragement he could give to the work of others.

The great work of his life—*Oceanic Ichthyology*—was, however, written during the period of his directorship of the National Museum, and published but a month before his death.   Almost simultaneous with this were other important publications of the National Museum, which were his also in a sense, for they would never have been undertaken except for his urgent wish and encouragement.   If a personal word may be pardoned, *The Fishes of North and Middle America* (of Jordan and Evermann) which closely followed *Oceanic Ichthyology*, would never have been written except for my friend's repeated insistence and generous help.

In the earlier days of the scientific activities of the Smithsonian Institution, there was scarcely a young naturalist of serious purposes in the land who had not in some way received help and encouragement from Professor Baird.   With equally unselfish effectiveness and lack of ostentation, Doctor Goode was also in different ways a source of aid and inspiration to all of his scientific contemporaries. The influence of the National Museum for good in the United States has been great in a degree far out of proportion to the sums of money it has had to expend. It has not been a Washington institution, but its influence has been national.

The first recorded scientific paper of Doctor Goode is a note on the occurrence of the bill-fish in fresh water in the Connecticut River. The next is a critical discussion of the answers to the question "Do snakes swallow their young?" In this paper he shows that there is good reason to believe that in certain viviparous snakes, the young seek refuge in the stomach of the mother when frightened, and that they come out when the reason for their retreat has passed.

The first of the many technical and descriptive papers on fishes was the "Catalogue of the Fishes of the Bermudas," published in 1876. This is a model record of field observations and is one of the best of local catalogues. Doctor Goode retained his interest in this outpost of the great West Indian fauna, and from time to time recorded the various additions made to his first Bermudan catalogue.

After this followed a large number of papers on fishes, chiefly descriptions of species or monographs of groups. The descriptive papers were nearly all written in association with his excellent friend, Doctor Tarleton H. Bean, then Curator of Fishes in the National Museum.

In monographic work, Doctor Goode took the deepest interest, and he delighted especially in the collection of historic data concerning groups of species. The quaint or poetical features of such work were never overlooked by him. Notable among these monographs are those of the Menhaden, the Trunk-fishes, and the Swordfishes.

The economic side of science also interested him more and more. That scientific knowledge could add to human wealth or comfort was no reproach in his eyes. In his notable monograph of the Menhaden, the economic value as food or manure of this plebeian fish received the careful attention which he had given to the problems of pure science.

Doctor Goode's power in organizing and coördinating practical investigations was shown in his monumental work on the American fisheries for the Tenth Census in 1880. The preparation of the record of the fisheries and associated aquatic industries was placed in his hands, by Francis A. Walker, Superintendent of the Census. Under Doctor Goode's direction skilled investigators were sent to every part of the coast and inland waters of the country. A general survey of the aquatic resources, actual and possible, of the United States was attempted, and statistics of every kind were secured on a grand scale. His directions to field agents, still unpublished, were models in their way, and no possible source of information was neglected by him. The results of all these special reports were received and condensed by Doctor Goode into seven large quarto volumes, with a great number of plates. The first section of the *Natural History of Aquatic Animals* was a contribution of the greatest value. Although the information it gives was obtained from many sources, through various hands, it was so coördinated and unified that it forms a harmonious treatise, while at the same time the individual helpers are fully recognized.

All these works, according to Doctor Goode, belong to Lamb's category of "books which are not books." His expressed ambition to write a book not of this kind, one that people would buy and read, found actuality at last. In 1888, appeared his *American Fishes*, a popular treatise on the game and food-fishes of North America, a work without a rival because of its readableness, its scientific accuracy, and the excellence of its text. The work is notable for its quotations, which include almost all the bright things which have been said about fishes by poets and anglers and philosophers from the time of Aristotle to Izaak Walton and Thoreau. In this book more than in any other Doctor Goode shows himself a literary artist. The love of fine expression which might have made a poet of him was developed rather in the collection of the bright words and charming verse of others than in the production of poetry of his own. While limiting himself in this volume to fragments of prose and verse in praise of fishes and their haunts, it is evident that these treasures were brought forth from a mind well stored with riches of many fields of literature.

The most important of Doctor's Goode scientific studies had relation to the fishes of the deep sea. In all this work he was associated with Doctor Bean, and the studies of many years were brought together in the splendid summary of all that is known of the fishes of the ocean depths and the open sea. This forms two large quarto volumes—text and atlas—published under the name of *Oceanic Ichthyology*, shortly before Doctor Goode's death. The exploration of the deep sea has been mostly undertaken within the last twenty years. The monumental work of the *Challenger*, under the direction of the British government, has laid the foundation of our knowledge of its fauna. The *Travailleur* and the *Talisman*, under French auspices, and the *Investigator*, under direction of the government of India, have added greatly to our stock of information. The great work of Goode and Bean includes the results of these and of various minor expeditions, while through the collections of the *Albatross*, the *Blake* and the *Fish Hawk* they have made great additions to the knowledge of the subject. Indeed, the work of the *Albatross* in deep-sea exploration is second in importance only to that of the *Challenger*. In the work of the exact discrimination of genera and species, this work shows a distinct advance over all other treatises on the abyssal fishes. The fact of the existence of definite though large faunal areas in the deep seas was first recognized by Doctor Goode, and has been carefully worked out in a memoir still unpublished. In *Oceanic Ichthyology* and the minor papers preceding it, Goode and Bean had made known numerous new forms of deep-sea fishes, naming in the last-mentioned work alone one hundred and fifty-six new species and fifty-five new genera belonging to the abyssal fauna of the Atlantic.

But Doctor Goode's interest and sympathy were not confined to the branch of science in which he was a master. He had a broad acquaintance with general natural history, with crustaceans, reptiles, birds, and mammals. On all these groups he published occasional notes. Doctor Gill tells us that "the flowering plants also enlisted much of his attention, and his excursions into the fields and woods were enlivened by a knowledge of the objects he met with." "Anthropology," Doctor Gill continues, "naturally secured a due proportion of his regards, and, indeed, his catalogues truly embraced the outlines of a system of the science."

Doctor Goode was, as already stated, always very greatly interested in bibliography. No work to him was ever tedious, if it were possible to make it accurate. He had well under way the catalogues of the writings of many American naturalists, among others those of Doctor Gill and the present writer. Two of these are already published under the Smithsonian Institution as *Bulletins* of the United States National Museum, being numbers of a series of "Bibliographies of American Naturalists." The first contained the writings of Spencer Fullerton Baird (1883). Another is devoted to Charles Girard (1891), who was an associate of Professor Baird, though for his later years resident in Paris. A bibliography of the English ornithologist, Philip Lutley Sclater (1896), has been issued since Doctor Goode's death.

Doctor Gill tells us that "a gigantic work in the same line had been projected by him and most of the material collected; it was no less than a complete bibliography of Ichthyology, including the names of all genera and species published as new. Whether this can be completed by another hand remains to be seen. While the work is a great desideratum, very few would be willing to undertake it or even arrange the matter already collected for publication. In no way may Ichthyology, at least, more feel the loss of Goode than in the loss of the complete bibliography."

Doctor Goode was married on November 27, 1877, to Sarah Lamson Ford Judd, daughter of Orange Judd, the well-known publisher, and the founder of Orange Judd Hall at Wesleyan University, in which Doctor Goode's career as a museum administrator began. The married life of Doctor and Mrs. Goode was a very happy one; the wife and four children are still living.

As to personal qualities of Doctor Goode, I cannot do better than to quote the following words of two of his warmest friends. Doctor S. P. Langley wrote: "I have never known a more perfectly true, sincere and loyal character than Doctor Goode's; or a man who with better judgment of other men, or greater ability in moulding their purposes to his own, used these powers to such uniformly disinterested ends, so that he could maintain the discipline of a great establishment like the National Museum, while retaining the personal affection of every subordinate." "His disposition," says Doctor Theodore Gill, "was a bright and sunny one, and he ingratiated himself in the affections of his friends in a marked degree. He had a hearty way of meeting intimates, and a caressing cast of the arm over the shoulder of such an one often followed sympathetic intercourse. But in spite of his gentleness, firmness and vigor in action became manifest when occasion called for them."

Of all American naturalists, Doctor Goode was the most methodical, the most conscientious, and, in his way, the most artistic. And of them all no one was more beloved by his fellows. Neither in his life nor after death was ever an unkind word said of him.

Henry A. Rowland.

HENRY AUGUSTUS ROWLAND

PHYSICIST

1848–1901

By Ira Remsen

SOME persons are interesting on account of their ancestors, and some ancestors are interesting on account of their offspring. While it appears that some of the forbears of the subject of this sketch were interesting in their own right it is certain that they are interesting to the world at large chiefly because of their relationship to the distinguished physicist, Henry A. Rowland. It may help us to learn of what stock he sprang. His paternal great-grandfather, Rev. David S. Rowland, was a graduate of Yale and pastor of the First Congregational Church at Windsor, Connecticut. The son of David S. was named Henry Augustus. He was a graduate of Dartmouth College and succeeded his father as pastor of the church at Windsor, Connecticut. Of him it is said, "He was a man of sense and worth, who did not hesitate to speak what he regarded as the truth with freedom and plainness."

Next came the father of the physicist. He also received the name Henry Augustus. His biographer states that he was an "ardent, resolute, almost impetuous boy, a leader of sports on land and on water, his irrepressible spirits breaking out in his intercourse with his friends and companions, and in spite of every restraint, in laughter and frolic." "He was from very early years familiar with the gun and the fishing-rod, and all kinds of wood-craft and country sports." He was graduated from Yale in 1823, became a clergyman, and successively had charges at Fayetteville, South Carolina, New York, Honesdale, Pennsylvania, and Newark, New Jersey. The evidence is clear that he was a man of unusual ability, of the highest character, of high spirits, and of great moral courage. He married Harriet Hayes of New York, a gentle lady of sweet character and good mind. She lived to the age of 81, while her husband died in the fifty-fifth year of his age.

It was at Honesdale, Pennsylvania, in 1848, that the next Henry Augustus Rowland was born. Here he lived until 1855, when the family moved to Newark, New Jersey. He attended the Newark Academy. Mr. S. A. Farrand under whose teaching he came writes in regard to him:

"Henry A. Rowland entered the classical department of the Newark Academy in September, 1861, and began his preparation for the academic course in college. I remember him as a rather quiet boy of winning personality. He did well in all his studies excepting Latin, with which he found difficulty from the beginning. This was surprising, for he was a bright, willing boy, showing indications of unusual ability and yet was constantly dragging in this study. After a year of this experience I took him from his class in Latin and for some months heard him recite alone, in order to get a better opportunity to study his mental action and discover, if possible, his difficulty. I found no lack of ability, but so strong an aversion to Latin, while at the same time finding pleasure in other studies, that he could not control his mind and force it to do good work upon the repugnant task.

"I advised his mother to let Henry drop the distasteful study and to direct his education along those lines so distinctly marked in his nature. But this was before scientific studies had won their present prominence in our colleges. Classical traditions were strong in the family, his father, grandfather,[1] and great-grand-father having been graduates of Yale, and clergymen. His mother had no other thought than that Henry, with his superior ability, would follow in the succession and keep up the traditions of the family. For him to turn away from this and give himself to scientific studies seemed like throwing away her boy, and was not to be considered. He must continue his classical studies, and he would certainly grow to like them. He did continue them for a year or two more, during which time Mrs. Rowland and I had several conferences concerning the matter. Henry's dislike increased and was intensified by the addition of Greek to his studies. I had a deep sympathy with him, for he was struggling

[1] His grandfather was in fact a graduate of Dartmouth.

manfully to do that which to him was impossible. Finally, I said to his mother that my convictions were so strong that his educational development should proceed in different lines, that if he must continue his classical studies I preferred that he should do so in some other school.

"Mrs. Rowland decided to make one more effort, failing in which she would follow my advice. Henry was accordingly sent to Phillips Academy, Andover, Mass., where, after a brief period of torture with Latin and Greek, he was permitted to drop them, greatly to his delight and my own.

"From that moment he was happy, and continued to rise and shine with a clear and still clearer light."

In a letter to his mother written at Andover, he says: "I am not lazy at all now and am more punctual than most of the other boys." But the aversion to the study of ancient languages continued and after one year spent in the effort he was allowed to enter the Rensselaer Polytechnic Institute at Troy, New York. Here the atmosphere was more congenial. Soon after the year's work had begun, he wrote: "I am getting along finely and like it first rate. We study Algebra, Geometry, and French and, as I said before, are going to commence Drawing on Thursday." This was in 1865. Next year he wrote: "We have descriptive Geometry and Chemistry now besides Drawing. We are quite busy, but still have lots of fun snow-balling every afternoon before and after Chemistry." That science did not claim all his attention is evident from this passage taken from a letter written in 1867: "I am now reading Prescott's *Philip Second of Spain,* and have nearly got through the first volume. It is very interesting." But the ruling passion appears in the next sentence: "My steam engine is getting along finely but I do not have much time to work on it." Shortly after this he wrote: "I am going to read a paper on steam illustrated by experiments as soon as I can get the apparatus prepared. We are very busy and I have not been able even to look at my tools yet."

After three years spent at Troy, during which time he evidently did excellent work in most of his studies he decided for some reason that is not clear to go to the Sheffield Scientific School and take the course in Mechanical Engineering. Apparently he was not admitted to the regular course but was admitted as a special student in Chemistry. A very interesting letter written by him to his mother in 1868, soon after his arrival at New Haven, has been preserved. This is so significant that the principal part of it is here given:

"You probably all think that I am careless about the future but there is no one who thinks more about it than I do, and this is the reason why I do not like to talk about it. I feel as if it was my duty and vocation to be an investigator in science and I felt something like a Jonah when I came here to study mechanical engineering. I *know* I am best fitted for it and it is only a question of dollars that decided me. Besides that I have such a liking for experiment that I cannot think it was given to me to be a torment all my life as it would be if I did anything else. As to the practical part of it, I can only say that what *other* people have done *I* can do and other people have made their living by it (or something similar) and therefore I can do it."

Of his work at New Haven, Prof. George J. Brush writes:

"While here he showed himself to be an exceedingly intelligent and persistent student, interested not only in the regular course in analytical and general chemistry, but in many subjects not included in the course. Professor Johnson, with whom I have just been conversing about Rowland, recalls R's great enthusiasm in making metallic lithium by electrolysis. We saw in him a man of unusual ability and great promise, but his stay here was too brief for us to gain anything more than this general impression."

He spent only one year at New Haven and then returned to Troy. In 1870, he received the degree of Civil Engineer. He was now out in the world. What next? The only thing that offered itself was a job at surveying, and at this he went. During the next year an opportunity presented itself to him of going to California. In a letter written June, 1871, he says, in regard to this: "There is nothing I should like better if I had time to devote to a year of pleasure, but I have other work before me." From the autumn of 1871 to the summer of 1872, he taught chemistry and perhaps also physics at Wooster, Ohio, and in the autumn of 1872 he returned to Troy to teach physics. He seems to have enjoyed his experience at Wooster for he writes soon after his arrival at Troy: "I got away from Wooster all right and those who were most concerned seemed to be sorry to lose me. Nearly all my class came to see me before I left which was quite encouraging. I felt quite sorry to leave them but it was necessary." He was now only 24 years old, and it may be imagined that he did not find the work at Troy altogether easy. To his mother he writes: "I have been here 8 days now and am beginning to get used to it. There are 65 students under my instruction and I have to keep a pretty tight rein on them. They are very much inclined to cut up and I shall have to be pretty strict with them and not let them commence."

It will be of interest to learn what Rowland had been doing in the way of invention and investigation previous to the time of his appointment to the position at Troy. His tastes began to show themselves very early in his life. When only three years of age he made a model of a clock from an old raisin box. In his fourteenth year he made an electric machine out of an old bottle, and also Leyden jars to work with it. At the same time, further, he invented a method of making electromagnets by winding bare wire with layers of paper. In a note-book kept by him I find the following records:

"February, 1863: Uncle Forsyth gave me some money and I bought four cells of a galvanic battery (Bunsen cells). I had previously made some out of zinc and copper plates. Made motor etc. to go by it."

"November, 1864: Made shock machine."

"January, 1865: Made furnace to melt iron or manganese. Made manganese."

"July, 1865: Made large electric motor."

"October, 1865: Made astatic galvanometer. Needle hung by a new method."

"November, 1865: Made electrometer. Also polariscope by reflection from black glass."

"May, 1866: Made Ruhmkorff coil giving one-third inch sparks by winding iron wires wide apart with paper between. Made vacuum tubes by boiling mercury in tubes and sealing them up while boiling."

"June, 1866: Obtained a law that the mechanical equivalent of electricity is equal to its quantity multiplied by its intensity."

A note added in 1900, reads:

"By 'intensity' I meant tension or potential. Therefore the above is correct."

"February, 1868: Made very delicate astatic galvanometer. Used it for magnetic permeability experiments."

"September, 1868: Invented dynamo armature. The first continuous current armature ever made."

While in his seventeenth year, in the early autumn of 1865, Rowland wrote a letter to *The Scientific American* and much to his surprise this was printed. He says of it: "I wrote it as a kind of joke and did not expect them to publish it." This was his first appearance in print. Six years later he sent another paper to *The Scientific American*—this time a serious one. It was a criticism of an invention which was in conflict with the law of the Conservation of Energy. In this communication he displayed those qualities of mind which appeared in all his later work. Just after he returned to the Rensselaer Polytechnic Institute he published an article on "Illustrations of Resonances and Actions of a Similar Nature." This appeared in the *Journal of the Franklin Institute*.

No attempt will be made in this article to give a complete account of Rowland's scientific work, but it is necessary to refer to his most important contributions. One of his early experiences was discouraging, but out of it came encouragement. He had been for some time engaged in a research on the magnetic permeability and the maximum magnetization of iron, steel, and nickel, when he brought his results together and sent the article to a well-known American scientific journal for publication. He writes to his sister June 9, 1873: "I have just sent off the results of my experiments to the publisher and expect considerable from it; not, however, filthy lucre, but good, substantial reputation."

The article was rejected by the editor of the American journal and again rejected after revision. The fault was not with the article, for, when it was sent to Clerk Maxwell, in England, the highest authority, its value was at once recognized, and it was sent to *The Philosophical Magazine* for immediate publication. It appeared in that journal in August, 1873, and through it Rowland became favorably known to the scientific world. Professor Mendenhall has said of it: "It has always seemed to me that when consideration is given to his age, his training, and the conditions under which his work was done, this early paper gives a better measure of Rowland's genius than almost any performance of his riper years." It was this work that led to his selection in 1875 to be the first professor of physics in the Johns Hopkins University. The story has been well told by President Gilman in his *The Launching of a University*. The main point is this, that after a talk with General Michie, who was then professor of physics in the United States Military Academy, Mr. Gilman telegraphed to Rowland to meet him at West Point. Mr. Gilman says: "He came at once, and we walked up and down Kosciusko's Garden, talking over his plans and ours. He told me in detail of his correspondence with Maxwell, and I think he showed me the letters received from him. At any rate, it was obvious that I was in confidential relations with a young man of rare intellectual powers and of uncommon aptitude for experimental science. When I reported the facts to the trustees in Baltimore they said at once, 'Engage that young man and take him with you to Europe, where he may follow the leaders in his science and be ready for a professorship.' And so we did. His subsequent career is well known."

Rowland decided to go to Berlin to get in contact with the great physicist Helmholtz. Helmholtz was not at first inclined to receive the young American into his laboratory, but Rowland told him of an experiment he wanted to perform, and described the method he proposed to follow, and he was admitted. The object of the experiment was to learn whether any magnetic effect is produced when an electrically charged body is set in rapid motion. Rowland showed that there is an effect and the result is of fundamental importance to electrical theory. Maxwell, who was fond of versifying, writes in regard to this experiment:

"The mounted disk of ebonite
     Has whirled before nor whirled in vain,
  Rowland of Troy, that doughty knight,
     Convection currents did obtain,
  In such a disk, of power to wheedle
  From its loved north the subtle needle.

Other less skilful experimenters have failed to get the effect described by Rowland but, finally, after his death, it was shown beyond a question that he was right. He never for a moment doubted it.

At the end of the year spent in Europe, Rowland came to Baltimore to make preparations for the opening of the university in the autumn of 1876. It was some time in the summer that he made his first visit to the city that was to be his home for the next twenty-five years—the rest of his life. On this occasion, the writer, who had been appointed professor of chemistry on the same day that Rowland had been appointed professor of physics, also visited Baltimore, and the two who were to be so long and so intimately associated met for the first time. We spent a few very hot days in talking over plans with President Gilman. It was arranged that Rowland was to have for his laboratory some back rooms of the two dwelling-houses which were to serve as the temporary seat of the Johns Hopkins University. He said, "All I want is the back kitchen and a solid pier built up from the ground." He got in fact a number of small rooms but they were a sorry lot. Such changes as he asked for were made. While in Europe he had ordered apparatus freely—the best that could be had—not for lecture experiments, but for scientific work of the greatest refinement and importance. The equipment of the "laboratory" was all that could be desired—all that was desired by the man who was to work in it, who was to make the kitchen and the "back building" famous.

I remember that first meeting very clearly. The impression

that Rowland made on me was not favorable. Knowing that, in the natural course of things, we were to be thrown much together, I could not help wondering whether this was to be a pleasant or an unpleasant experience. I had my doubts. We were both, in those days, somewhat high-strung. It soon became evident that we should not always agree, and that between us there were likely to be heated conversations, but let me say at once that in a short time we came to know each other as well as two men can know each other, and for twenty-five years we were intimate, most intimate, friends. We understood each other and were ready to make such allowances as must always be made between friends if friendship is to continue. Strangers and casual acquaintances had a wrong conception of Rowland. This is easily understood. He was apt to put his worst foot forward. He made no attempt to conciliate—rather the contrary. It took time to get over this first impression, but those who knew him best learned that he had many most attractive traits of character. He was a staunch friend, incapable of anything mean. He was absolutely sincere. He was generous and affectionate. He had the highest ideals and tried earnestly to attain them. On the other hand, he despised sham and, whenever he detected it he did not hesitate to express his opinion in strong language—not always strictly parliamentary. Indeed it must be said that he appeared to derive a certain amount of pleasure from this kind of activity, and he no doubt often gave offense by it. He was a merciless critic, and no doubt the world offered him abundant opportunity for the exercise of his powers.

But let us now return to Baltimore where Rowland began work on the foundations of the Johns Hopkins University in the autumn of 1876. The little faculty of the University at that time felt that the best thing they could do was to lay emphasis on graduate work and especially on research. Rowland had this in mind in ordering apparatus in Europe, and in a short time he had probably the best collection of apparatus for research in America. It should be said here that the policy of the faculty was, in fact, the policy of President Gilman. We all agreed. To some of us, probably to all the younger members, the President said repeatedly, "Do your best work whatever it may be," and no body of workers could have been more free to work out their own salvation. The atmosphere was exactly suited to Rowland. He could not brook restraint. He had to do things in his own way. He was not fitted for the ordinary routine duties of a professor. He was an investigator, and to the work of investigation he turned at once.

He soon devised a method for the redetermination of the Mechanical Equivalent of Heat. This fundamental constant had been determined by others. Rumford laid the foundation for the work in observations made in boring cannon in the ordnance foundry at Munich, Bavaria. His attention was arrested by the well-known fact that the metal became hot in consequence of the friction caused by the boring. He then attempted to determine the amount of heat produced by a certain amount of work, or in other words to determine the relation between the amount of work done and the amount of heat evolved. Joule of Manchester, much later, took up this problem and with the aid of more refined apparatus and methods obtained a much more satisfactory result. Rowland used a modification of the method of Rumford. He obtained a figure for the Mechanical Equivalent of Heat that differed somewhat from those obtained by his predecessors and for twenty-five years this has stood the test of criticism. While he was engaged in the work he received a visit from a well-known chemist. After Rowland had explained what he was doing the visitor asked this question: "Suppose you should find that you get the same result as Joule, will you consider that you have wasted your time?" To which Rowland replied, "No. If my result should be the same as Joule's, that will prove that Joule was right."

I wish I had a picture of the surroundings in which this important work was carried on. The original back kitchen was not adequate. It happened that the university had come into possession of a small old building on a near street. This had been used as a grocery store. In the rear was a most disreputable looking room, dirty, small, dilapidated. Here the delicate apparatus was set up and here the experiments were carried on day by day, and it is certain that the work could not have been done better if it had been done in a palatial laboratory. The remark made by Garfield that "Mark Hopkins at one end of a log was a good enough college for him" might be appropriately modified to suit this case, "Rowland in a back kitchen is a good enough physical laboratory for the highest type of work."

The research on the Mechanical Equivalent of Heat was published in full by the American Academy of Arts and Sciences, the expense of publication being met by a fund established by Rumford, and in this connection it may be noted that this same American Academy awarded the Rumford prize to Rowland. Later, in 1881, the article describing his results was crowned as a prize essay by the Venetian Institute.

In 1881 Rowland was appointed a delegate of the United States to the International Electrical Congress that met at Paris. Realizing the importance of the accurate measurement of electrical quantities he made a thorough study of the fundamental quantity, the ohm. This work was afterward repeated and extended at the request of the United States Government. The results are of great important and are generally accepted.

Perhaps the best known achievement of Rowland is the concave grating. In order to study light from different sources it is necessary to analyze it. This is most readily accomplished by means of a prism. As is well known when sunlight is allowed to pass through a prism it emerges in the form of a spectrum. The white light of the sun is thus shown to be made up of lights of different colors—the well-known colors of the solar spectrum. Now every light has its own characteristic spectrum, and by observing the spectrum much can be learned in regard to the nature of the source of the light. By such observations, for example, it is possible to tell what chemical elements occur in the atmosphere of the sun and of the fixed stars. Light can be analyzed also by allowing it to fall upon a surface upon which a large number of parallel lines have been ruled very close together. Such plates are called diffraction gratings. Rowland felt that much progress could be made in this line of work if only larger and more satisfactory gratings could be made, and he set himself to work at this problem. In order to get good gratings a screw as nearly perfect as possible must be made. But to make such a screw is an extremely difficult matter. By a simple and ingenious device the difficulties were largely overcome and, with the aid of the historic screw which resulted, gratings far superior to any that had previously been known were made. By the motion of the screw the plate which rested upon it was moved slowly and regularly forward while a diamond point moved across its surface. The first gratings made were plane, but soon it occurred to the inventor that, if the lines should be ruled upon a concave surface, it would be possible to photograph spectra directly without the use of prisms and lenses and with much better results in every way. I happened to be with Rowland when the idea of the concave grating occurred to him. We were on our way from Baltimore to Washington to attend a meeting of the National Academy of Sciences. He was very quiet and we sat together almost the whole way without a word passing between us. This, however, was not unusual. We talked when we wanted to and, as often happened, we didn't want to. Well, in this instance I think I noticed that my friend was brooding more intently than usual. Just before we reached Washington he threw up his hands and said, "It will work. I'm sure of it." These words were not addressed to me but to space. I naturally wanted to know what he was talking about, but at first he could not bring himself to explain. Presently, however, he told me that he intended to go back at once to Baltimore to make preparations for ruling gratings on concave plates. He was positive he could do it and he saw at once the great advantages of this form of apparatus. My recollection is that he gave up the meeting of the National Academy and returned on the next train to Baltimore. At all events, it was not long before the first concave grating was ready for use and Rowland's maps of the solar spectrum in course of preparation. In a notice of his work recently written by a leading English physicist reference is made to the maps in these words: "The beautiful maps issued at a later date by Rowland,   . . .

are striking evidences of the value of the grating; the additions to our knowledge arising from this one discovery are already enormous; much has been achieved which, without it, would have been impossible."

When he went to Paris in 1881 he took some of his photographs and gratings with him. In a letter to President Gilman, Professor John Trowbridge of Harvard gives an interesting account of Rowland's reception. A part of that letter should be quoted here:

"Rowland invited Mascart, Sir W. Thomson, Wiedemann, Rossetti, and Kohlrausch to his room at the Hotel Continental in Paris, and showed them his photographs and gratings. It is needless to say that they were astonished. Mascart kept muttering *'Superbe'*—*'Magnifique.'* The Germans spread their palms and looked as if they wished they had ventral fins and tails to express their sentiments. Sir W. Thomson evidently knew very little about the subject, and maintained a wholesome reticence, but looked his admiration for he knows a good thing when he sees it, and also had the look that he could express himself upon the whole subject in fifteen minutes, when he got back to Glasgow.

"In England, Rowland's success was better appreciated, if possible, than in Paris. He read a paper before a very full meeting of the Physical Society—De la Rive, Professor Dewar of Cambridge Professor Clifton of Oxford, Professor Adams (of Leverrier fame), Professor Carey Foster, Hilger, the optician, Professor Guthrie, and other noted men being present. I was delighted to see his success. The English men of science were actually dumbfounded. Rowland spoke extremely well, for he was full of his subject, and his dry humor was much appreciated by his English audience. When he said that he could do as much in an hour as had hitherto been accomplished in three years, there was a sigh of astonishment and then cries of 'Hear! Hear!' Professor Dewar arose and said: 'We have heard from Professor Rowland that he can do as much in an hour as has been done hitherto in three years. I struggle with a very mixed feeling of elation and depression: elation for the wonderful gain to science; and depression for myself, for I have been at work for three years in mapping the ultra violet.' De la Rive asked how many lines could be ruled by Rowland. The latter replied: 'I have ruled 43,000 to the inch, and I can rule 1,000,000 to the inch, but what would be the use? No one would ever know that I had really done it.' Laughter greeted this sally. The young American was like the Yosemite,

Niagara, Pullman palace car—far ahead of anything in England. Professor Clifton referred in glowing terms to the wonderful instrument that had been put into the hands of physicists, and spoke of the beautiful geometrical demonstrations of Rowland   Professor Dewar said that Johns Hopkins University had done great things for science, and that greater achievements would be expected of it. Captain Abney wrote a letter which Rowland ought to show you, for, after having been read at the meeting, it was given to him."

What about Rowland as a teacher? It has already been said that he was not well fitted for the routine work of a routine professor. He would not have made a good college professor. This is not intended as a reflection upon the good college professor who in my opinion is a very good and useful man. Nor is it intended as a reflection upon Rowland. He was cut out for other work. In one sense he was one of the best and most successful teachers ever connected with the Johns Hopkins University. No teacher of physics in this country has ever trained as many men who have risen to places of importance and influence. He cared little for those who had not the desire to learn. That was the first condition to be satisfied. He cared little for the dullard or the clumsy. He could tell whether the student he was dealing with had anything in him. If he had not, he would not "waste his time over him" as he expressed it. But let him show promise and there could be no better guide and friend than Rowland. All his students respected him. Of course they did. His assistants also. They could not help it. Sometimes he was a little harsh in his treatment of his assistants, but they knew that at heart their chief was true and they always stood loyally by him in spite of occasional provocations. He owed much to his assistants and he was always ready to acknowledge his debt. They relieved him of many duties that were distasteful to him and, although he was the director of the laboratory, much of the work of directing fell to their hands. And they did not murmur, for they knew that in this way they were contributing to the success of his work.

He lectured regularly on such subjects as he thought ought to be presented to the students, and often in these lectures made valuable suggestions for researches. One of them being taken up led to the discovery of the Hall "effect." The student who did this work is now Professor Hall of Harvard. He did not follow up his students and they did not therefore acquire the bad habit of relying upon him for daily advice. On the contrary, he would give them just enough suggestion to get them started and then, to use his own words, "neglected them" so that they were obliged to cultivate self-reliance or fail. The treatment was not adapted to the weak but was admirably suited to the strong. One of his most distinguished students writes:

"Even of the more advanced students only those who were able to brook severe and searching criticism reaped the full benefit of being under him; but he contributed that which, in a university, is above all teaching of routine, the spectacle of scientific work thoroughly done and the example of a lofty ideal."

His lectures were not eloquent. Words did not come freely to him. There was a lack of finish and elegance in his talks, but, on the other hand, he could say forcibly and clearly what he wanted to say. There could be no doubt as to his meaning. Whatever subject he happened to be lecturing upon the subject that was uppermost in his mind at the time would be sure to come to the front. For example, he once undertook to build a sail-boat and became much interested in water-waves, and the part they play in determining the speed of a boat. It is said that during this period there were daily references to water-waves in his lectures, and, occasionally, as he told me, when, for one reason or another, he was not well prepared on his subject proper he would take up the hour by discussing the subject of sail-boats in a scientific way— no doubt to the advantage of his hearers. In some of his few addresses of a semi-public character there are passages that deserve to be remembered. Generally speaking these addresses made an unusually strong impression. Let me quote from one. He says:

"But for myself, I value in a scientific mind most of all that love of truth, that care in its pursuit, and that humility of mind which makes the possibility of error always present more than any other quality. This is the mind which has built up modern science to its present perfection, which has laid one stone upon the other with such care that it to-day offers to the world the most complete monument to human reason. This is the mind which is destined to govern the world in the future and to solve the problems pertaining to politics and humanity as well as to inanimate nature.

"It is the only mind which appreciates the imperfections of the human reason and is thus careful to guard against them. It is the only mind that values the truth as it should be valued and ignores all personal feeling in its pursuit. And this is the mind the physical laboratory is built to cultivate."

This passage is thoroughly characteristic of Rowland in form and substance. He felt, and felt intensely as usual, that natural science was the only subject really worthy of study except in so far as study of other subjects might contribute to the advancement of science. He retained to the end his abhorrence of the ancient languages and would not listen to arguments in their favor. He could not understand how anyone could spend his life in studying them. He could not understand how their study could be of the slightest benefit to the world. He was entirely sincere in this. He was incapable of insincerity. It must be acknowledged that this was his blind side. But why complain? A man who has the keenness of vision possessed by Rowland can afford to have a blind side, and the world can afford to be blind to the imperfection.

Though the man has been revealed to some extent in what has already been said, there are some traits which have not been touched upon. He was tall and lithe and quick in motion. His head would attract attention anywhere on account of the size of the brain above the ears and the size and strength of the lower jaw. Withal it was a head of refinement. His face had an intent expression which was increased by his near-sightedness. Probably his expression would have been described as severe by those who did not know him well. It was a masterful expression and was therefore a true index of his character.

In 1890 he married Miss Henrietta Harrison of Baltimore. The marriage was an unusually happy one. Of the three children of this marriage two are boys and one a girl. It is perhaps too early to speak with confidence of the future of these children. The older son, named Henry, seems to have inherited his father's tastes. Whether he has inherited the mental power and the strength that are necessary to make another Rowland, no one can tell.

Outside of the laboratory he had many interests. He was devoted to his family, and was very happy in the home circle. The depth of his affection was evident to those who knew him well, and it was evident to many who did not know him well and who considered him cold and austere. His conduct seemed incongruous. The matter becomes clear, however, if we take the only correct view of it. He was undoubtedly capable of all the finer feelings. His affection was true and deep, but he was extremely critical and he could, of course, easily find something to criticise. Having found it he expressed his opinion vigorously and with little regard for the feeling of his victim. As has been said before in this article he was apt to put his worst foot forward, and many did not wait or did not have the opportunity to see the other and better one. He had many friends, but few intimates. A friend, Professor Mendenhall, who has written an admirable account of Rowland says:

"His criticisms of the work of others were keen and merciless, and sometimes there remained a sting of which he himself had not the slightest suspicion. 'I would not have done it for the world,' he once said to me after being told that his pitiless criticism of a scientific paper had wounded the feelings of its author. As a matter of fact he was warm-hearted and generous, and his occasionally seeming otherwise was due to the complete separation, in his own mind, of the product and the personality of the author. He possessed that rare power, habit in his case, of seeing himself, not as others see him, but as he saw others. He looked at himself and his own work exactly as if he had been another person, and this gave rise to a frankness of expression regarding his own performance which sometimes impressed strangers unpleasantly, but which, to his friends, was one of his most charming qualities."

He read a good deal. In early life history interested him very much. He was fond of poetry in some forms, but he confined his attention to a few authors. In his later years, however, he became more and more absorbed in scientific subjects, and his interest in general literature became less. He retained, however, his fondness for music. He rarely failed to attend the concerts of the Boston Symphony Orchestra. Classical music was his principal hobby in this line. This is hard to understand in view of the fact that he had not a musical ear. He could not whistle nor hum the simplest air in tune.

Rowland inherited a love of sports from his father. His specialties were fishing, sailing, and horseback riding. The only kind of fishing that appealed to him was trout-fishing. I have had abundant opportunity to become acquainted with his skill, for summer after summer we have gone off together in pursuit of this delightful fish and of the joys of nature that its pursuit brings with it. His tackle was always in good trim, and he seemed to have an instinct that guided him aright while I was bungling along in the ordinary human way. He could cast a fly most enticingly. He never failed to get more and bigger fish than I, unless, as sometimes happened the fish were guilty of contributory negligence. In short, Rowland as a fisherman showed the same traits as Rowland the physicist,—intelligence, skill, patience, perseverance. It is further of interest to note that those fishing trips always brought the memory of his father clearly back to him. Some of the tackle he used had been used by his father, and often he found occasion to quote his father's counsel in matters pertaining to the art of fishing.

After his marriage, the fishing trips were given up and sailing took its place. He had practiced this art early and was passionately fond of it throughout life. He had a small sloop built in Baltimore according to his own design. It was taken from Baltimore to Mt. Desert with the aid of a professional skipper. In this boat that had accommodations for only two, he and I have cruised up and down the coast of Maine from Rockland to Eastport in all sorts of weather. We did all the work, prepared our own meals as far as they were prepared, and made our own beds as far as they were made. He had the reputation of being a reckless sailor and the people of Mt. Desert expected him to get in trouble. But he never did. In my opinion, and no one had as good opportunity to judge, he was a skilful and careful sailor. He knew what his boat could do, and he never took chances, when I was with him at least, and we never got into trouble.

He had learned sailing without much aid from others, and was singularly ignorant of the technical terms. He told me that he could never remember which was starboard and which port. I had acquired this elementary knowledge and was rather proud to be able to tell him. Whereupon he put an "S" on one side of the cockpit and a "P" on the other. But in spite of this constant reminder I am quite sure that with his eyes shut he could not have told which side "S" was on. And so with pennants. He never provided himself with them, because, as he said, "I don't know how to use them." Another peculiarity is the fact that his boat never had a name. He spoke of her as the "Spectrum," but that name did not appear on her. The essential thing to him was the boat. The boat was just as good without as with a name, and he got just as much fun out of the sailing without a knowledge of the lingo and the frills as with.

I have left the riding to the last, though it played a more important part in his life than either fishing or sailing. He took up riding after he came to Baltimore and never became as expert at it as at these. He was not graceful in his movements and was not a graceful rider. He seemed, however, to catch the essentials and soon he was known as a fearless and skilful rider. He joined the hunting club of Baltimore and for years rarely missed a meet. On one occasion in the early period of his history as a rider, he entered himself and horse as a competitor in a "gentleman's steeple chase." It was a difficult race. He won. I drove him out and back. His success gave him great satisfaction. As he was near-sighted and always wore eye-glasses he sometimes got into difficulty in riding through woods, but neither he nor his horse was ever seriously hurt. His passion for riding after the hounds is well illustrated by an experience he had in England of which Professor Trowbridge tells in the letter already referred to: "I introduced Rowland to a fox-hunting gentleman, an old acquaintance of mine, and I imagine Rowland got enough of English fox-hunting, for on my return from Birmingham, one evening, I found him stretched on the bed, a symphony in brown and red mud, his once glossy hat crushed into nothingness, his top-boots, once so new, a mass of Warwickshire mud. He dryly remarked that he guessed there wouldn't be any trouble about getting his hunting-suit through the custom-house now. He came very near breaking his neck, having been thrown on his head before he 'could calculate his orbit,' as he remarked." In the last years of his life he rode regularly though not after the hounds. He felt the importance of outdoor exercise for his health, and fortunately he enjoyed it. He did not care to ride in the park or along the broad frequented roads. Cross-country was his preference. At one period I rode with him daily, and learned more about riding than I had learned in all my previous existence. He had his doubts as to my ability to do some of the things he wanted to do. It must be confessed that I had my own doubts. Once we were flying along through the woods when with little warning we came upon what appeared to me a preternaturally and unnecessarily wide ditch. Without a moment's hesitation his horse made the leap. Mine followed and by good fortune I retained my seat and looked comfortable on the other side. Rowland turned to me and said simply: "Remsen, my respect for you has gone up." On another occasion my horse refused a fence which his had taken nicely. I tried it a second time without success and was about to give it up when Rowland called out: "Don't spoil the horse. *Make* him take it." He took it—in time.

One of his greatest pleasures in life was his annual visit to his country home at Seal Harbor, Mt. Desert, Maine. Some years ago he bought a small piece of ground on a rocky hill with a magnificent view and on it he built a comfortable, modest house. Here he went every summer with his family, and spent most of his time out of doors either sailing or walking, though he was not over fond of walking unless he wanted to get somewhere. For twelve or more years he knew that he had an incurable disease and that his life could not be a long one. This was one reason, perhaps the principal one, why he gave so much time to exercise in the open air. This led him also to read a good deal on medical subjects, and especially on anything pertaining to his own malady. We often talked of this, but I never heard him repine. He accepted his fate cheerfully though he felt keenly the fact that his family would not be adequately provided for, and this caused him during the last few years of his life to give much time to working out a beautiful and important system of telegraphy. The Rowland octoplex printing telegraph has since became widely known and is in use in some places. By this system it is possible to send simultaneously four messages in both directions over a single wire and have them appear printed. The sending is accomplished by means of an apparatus that looks and works like an ordinary type-writer. It is a wonderful machine. At the last Paris Exhibition it won the Grand Prix.

In politics he was too radical to be effective. His ideals were so high as to be practically unattainable. Consequently he was entirely out of sympathy with the existing order of things. He took every opportunity to tell those in high positions what he thought of them. I remember being at a dinner party one evening, at which the late Mr. James G. Blaine and Rowland were present. Now in the mind of Rowland, the idea of protection of industries was as a red, extremely red, flag to an active bull. In this particular case Mr. Blaine represented the obnoxious idea and Rowland straightway charged upon him in dead earnest. If the object of his antipathy had responded in kind, the scene would have been exciting in the highest degree. But he did not. I do not remember how it happened, but in a few minutes the atmosphere was clear and the company began to breathe freely again. When the party broke up Blaine walked away with his arm thrown over Rowland's shoulders. A little later Rowland said to me: "That Blaine strikes me as a pretty good fellow."

In matters pertaining to religion he was philosophic, not emotional. He accepted the underlying principles of the Christian religion and in general his life was in conformity therewith. He lived correctly not because he feared punishment hereafter, not because he had been commanded to, but because he clearly saw that this was the right thing to do. He was as free from anything that could fairly be called sin as anyone I have ever known.

Rowland received many honors from learned societies and universities at home and abroad. He was Honorary Member of the Royal Society of London, of the Royal Society of Edinburgh, of the Royal Academy of Sciences, Berlin, of the Cambridge Philosophical Society, of the Physical Society of London; Corresponding Member of the Royal Society of Göttingen, of the Academy of Sciences in Paris; Foreign Member of the Royal Swedish Academy of Stockholm; Associate Fellow of the American Academy of Arts and Sciences; Member of the National Academy of Sciences; and a member of nine other learned societies. He was awarded the Rumford Medal of the American Academy in 1884, the Matteucci Medal in 1897. He received the Honorary Degree of Ph.D. from Johns Hopkins in 1880—the only time this degree has been conferred *honoris causa* by Johns Hopkins—and the degree of LL.D. from Yale, in 1895, and from Princeton in 1896. He was made an officer of the Legion of Honor in 1896.

W. K. Brooks

WILLIAM KEITH BROOKS

ZOÖLOGIST

1848–1908

By E. A. Andrews

In the history of zoölogy in America the advent of Louis Agassiz may be taken to mark a transition period from the days of the great pioneers, Audubon, Wilson and others, who revealed the marvels of wild life in a new country, to the present epoch of intensive investigation of problems common to life the world over.

Of those who came in the footsteps of Agassiz was William Keith Brooks who in the field of marine zoölogy added to the pioneer work of explorer his own philosophical treatment of the most fundamental problems of life and linked the past thought of the fathers of zoölogy to the methods of investigation not possible until now. In the words of a great living zoölogist and president of a great University, "He was the wisest of American zoölogists" and "the greatest American zoölogist, at least from the viewpoint of philosophical thinking." In his life we find much of his greatness due to Nature,—to what was innate in him and much to Nurture,—to what his opportunities brought him.

William Keith Brooks was born in Cleveland, Ohio, March 25, 1848, the second of a family of four boys, and he enjoyed the helpful home life found in a relatively new country where his father, Oliver Allen Brooks, was one of the early merchants, having come to Cleveland from Burlington, Vermont, in 1835.

His mother, a refined and gentle woman, who was Ellenora Bradbury Kingsley, the second of three daughters, the only children of the Reverend Phinheas Kingsley, of Rutland, Vermont, died when the boy was but fourteen years old, yet we may ascribe to her one of the most powerful elements that made him develop as he did. Not only was she "a lady of rare qualities and keenly sympathetic with her children's dispositions" so that she trained him in his early years of greatest plasticity in the love of truth that led him to freedom, but, it may well be that some of his best traits came from the maternal side by direct inheritance. For William Keith was not the only son with appreciation of the ideal and the beautiful. The oldest, Oliver Kingsley Brooks, early showed an aptitude for art and was one of the first students and a very proficient one in the Cleveland School of Art. The youngest, Edward, has shown artistic ability of a high order, achieving a reputation as an original designer of furniture and household decorations. The subject of this sketch did not take instruction in drawing till his studies in zoölogy led him to the need of illustrations, when he received instruction from his brother Oliver, nevertheless in later life so successful was he in making ink drawings of the marine creatures he knew so well that a Baltimore artist judged his success in life to be largely due to his artistic skill. This taste for drawing came by inheritance from their mother, and as an index of clear mental images this was no mean gift. Both the parents of William Keith Brooks came from Vermont, and the following account will show a sturdy New England ancestry.

Prior to 1634 Thomas Brooks came from England to America and settled first in Watertown and then in Concord, Massachusetts. John Kingsley came from Hampshire, in England, and settled in Dorchester, Massachusetts, in, or before, 1638. From these two early settlers came the families that united as the parents of William Keith Brooks.

It will but emphasize his puritanical origin to enumerate the ancestors whose biblical names recall ideals and training of long ago. On the Brooks side the line of descent from Thomas Brooks ran through Joshua, through Noah, through a second Joshua the son of Noah, and through a third Joshua, who all lived in Concord, Massachusetts. Their simple useful lives contained little prophecy of the time when, in 1907, their descendant, one William Keith Brooks, LL.D., sought relief from the tedium of

WILLIAM KEITH BROOKS 429

too constant attendance upon the meetings of an International Zoölogical Congress to take a *trolley* trip from Boston to Concord!

A fourth Joshua Brooks served at the battle of Concord, but lived at Lincoln, now a part of Concord, Massachusetts. His son, the fifth and last Joshua Brooks, removed from Lincoln to Burlington, Vermont, and it was his son, Oliver Allen Brooks, who removed to Cleveland, Ohio, after the family had been but so short a time outside the bounds of Massachusetts.

On the mother's side the line of descent ran from John Kingsley through Eldad who lived in Dorchester, Massachusetts, and then through three men, John, Amos, and Isaiah Kingsley, who represented the family for some one hundred years at Windham, Connecticut. The next in descent, Phinheas, the son of Isaiah Kingsley, removed when ten years old, with his father, to Vermont. But here again the family remained but one generation in this state, for the second Phinheas Kingsley removed to Ohio.

Thus on one side seven, and on the other six, generations lived in Massachusetts and in Connecticut ill a brief sojourn in Vermont led them on to Ohio where Ellenora Bradbury Kingsley and Oliver Allen Brooks became the parents of William Keith Brooks.

In dearth of facts one may speculate that some of the excellencies that were given birth in him may have been due to summation of ancestral traits handed on by the Keith family, for may it not be significant that not only was the grandmother of William Keith Brooks on his mother's side a Parnel Keith, who was born in 1786, in Massachusetts, and lived to the age of 82 years, but his grandmother on the paternal side was a Melinda Keith, of Pittsford, Vermont, born in 1787. It was this name, "Keith," that was to be singled out by his best friend and helper, his wife, the "woman who understood," as a poet has it, for his special personal name.

The boy was educated in the Public Schools of Cleveland, attending a grammar school known as the Eagle Street School, and after that going to the Central High School, when fifteen, for at least three years. Here his rank was from 80 to 100, with highest standing in Latin, Rhetoric, English Composition, and Botany. The Principal and the Vice-Principal of the school were then Dr. Theodore Sterling and Sidney A. Norton, and in talking over the influences that had molded his life, Professor Brooks, when fifty years old, emphasized his debt of gratitude to the earnest and broad-minded teachers in the Public Schools of Cleveland.

But powerful as were the home influences and the school training there seems to have been an innate searching for truth that led the quiet, reticent, "shy," gentle, thoughtful child to make original observation and to look at many things from unusual points of view. He was not satisfied with the obvious or conventional explanation: his mind was unusual. Thus to a teacher who asked him, "If the third of six, be three, what would the fourth of twenty be?" he replied, "Five"—for, said he, "I don't see that altering the value of six alters the value of twenty."

His interest in natural history was that of the normal child, an interest in actions and in life and not in the collection of curious objects. But while he was no born naturalist in the sense that some are, who early learn to hoard up "specimens," he was fond of observing birds, and a back-yard pond as well as home-made aquaria served for delightful observations that left a lasting impress.

Passenger pigeons were then plentiful, myriads darkening the sky, and stray ones came to the pond to drink. Then there were the aquatic insects and snails with marvelous transformation and developments. The fundamental nature of reflex and mechanical acts in living things was indelibly learned by the sight of a dragon-fly that, though reduced by accident to little but head, still continued to eat what was set before it, though the food passed at once into empty air.

His father was a practical man who believed in all kinds of wholesome recreation for his boys, but was not himself given to scientific interests. In the neighborhood, however, were boys who collected insects, fossils, the then common Indian remains, shells and other objects. In fact in the yard of the Tuttle boys, their father had built them a frame structure they called the

"Museum" and the "Laboratory," and in it they did simple chemical and electrical "stunts" and kept their collections. Some of these older boys helped make the artificial pond in Brooks' yard and went there to sail their hand-long "yachts." All who had any bent toward natural history owed a lasting debt to the old-fashioned, all-round naturalist and leading physician, Dr. Kirtland, who had a real knowledge of the habits and lives of birds, bees, fishes and of flowers and was never tired of stimulating and aiding any youngster who showed a real interest in such things. They all loved and reverenced him, though some might make forays upon the fossil-collections in his barn.

One whom he must have looked up to in natural history interest, as friend of his elder brother, and also, by chance, his Sunday School teacher at St. Paul's Episcopal Church, was Albert H. Tuttle, now Professor of Biology in the University of Virginia. From his attendance upon this church and his docile and conscientious learning of Sunday School verses he stored up an acquaintance with the forms of theology that abided with him, though he rebelled at the pressure of society that would too early force upon his own children dogmas he wished them to judge when matured.

For good physical reasons the boy was not given to violent athletic sports, though winning a prize for excellence in calisthenics, since he had a most perfect harmony of nerve and muscle and a strong sense of form, rhythm, and spacial relations.

He early read the works of Charles Darwin and gained an abiding conviction of the impregnable nature of the evidence for evolution and of the wide reach of the principle of natural selection. It should not be forgotten that this was in a period when to many good people the names of Darwin and Huxley were as Apollyon, and even amongst zoölogists the new views were as yet not universally accepted and their leader in America, Louis Agassiz, in 1863, believed that naturalists were pursuing a phantom in their search for material gradations amongst animals and transmutations of lower into higher forms.

In the fall of 1866 his father consented and the studious youth went to Hobart College, Geneva, New York, and here a most potent influence acted to fashion the ultimate philosophy of his life. Eagerly seizing the opportunities offered by the college library he read and pondered the works of Bishop Berkeley with results that came to the surface in later life. Hobart thus became a formative force that he acknowledges in the dedication of his life-work in philosophic thought, his *Foundations of Zoölogy*, in the words: "To Hobart College; where I learned to study, and, I hope, to profit by, but not to blindly follow, the writings of that great thinker on the principles of science, George Berkeley, I have, by permission, dedicated this book."

While the environment given him by Hobart was so potent, it was brief in extent of time, for at the end of the sophomore year he left Hobart and entered Williams College, Williamstown, Massachusetts, where he graduated in 1870. At Williams College he took active interest in the famous Lyceum of Natural History that sent an expedition across South America. He was marked amongst his fellows as an unusual individual, was known as "the philosopher" and became the center of interest as the man with a microscope. In his room assembled those who appreciated his ability to lead in the intellectual interpretations of nature and to make her facts clear and of absorbing interest. A noted zoölogist, who as lower classman was once in Brooks' room tells an anecdote that shows Brooks' peculiar originality. It might be called an application of the microtome method and runs as follows: Wishing to demonstrate a cross-section of a human hair and finding it impossible to cut one thin enough, Brooks shaved his face and then engaged the boys in talk till such time as he thought his beard grown a little, when shaving again he got the desired slices in the lather.

At Williams, Sanborn Tenney taught Botany and Zoölogy and Brooks stood high in his natural history studies but also in Greek and especially in mathematics, and when he graduated at the age of 22 he was undecided which of these abstract studies he should follow.

He was an independent and thorough scholar, but took no

interest in prizes and marks; preferring to apply himself deeply to topics that interested him even if night work should force him to miss morning exercises. On graduating he was elected to Phi Beta Kappa.

Returning to Cleveland his future became a perplexing problem. Postgraduate work was not then in vogue and every young man who had obtained the A.B. degree was expected to enter a profession or begin self-support. But Brooks desired a higher education, and satisfaction of his mental rather than of his physical self. His step-mother did not favor further studies and at one time Brooks entered his father's counting-house, but the tedium of routine that had no immediate ideal in view for him was not to his nature and he gave it up after inventing a simple calculating contrivance that is said to have been used with satisfaction and practical benefit.

The only means to his goal seemed then, as so often now, the life of a teacher, and for three years, 1870-73, he taught as one of the Masters in the De Veaux College, a school for boys at Niagara, New York. Here he practiced the art of simple exposition that made his subsequent university lectures so unusual. Being free to enjoy the woods along the rapids and to contemplate the majesty of the falls he was in an environment stimulating to thought and aspirations.

But from this stepping-stone the young man who would be a zoölogist must go to Louis Agassiz, to gain the best training the country had to offer to the investigator of life. In 1873 Brooks was one of those fortunate ones who shared contact with the remarkable enthusiasm of Agassiz, the Master, in the well conceived but inadequately matured experiment, the Summer School on the Island of Penikese, in Buzzards Bay. The anatomy of fishes and the vitality of the ancient creature, Limulus, were impressed upon Brooks. Brooks was not daunted by the confusion due to the incomplete state of the buildings, but got directly at the essentials. With characteristic optimism he was found dissecting a shark in his wash-basin on his bed as a table. In the second year of the School, in 1874, Brooks with other great pupils of the lamented Master went again to Penikese to nurture the new conception of a summer school for teachers, both men and women.

At Cambridge the museum of Agassiz was of less value to him than the contact with McCrady whose work on the jellyfish of Charleston, South Carolina, and whose philosophical discussions alike roused in him keen response. In Boston, aided by Alpheus Hyatt, who gained for him the position of Assistant in the Boston Society of Natural History for the years 1874 and 1875, he learned the collections of mollusk shells by heart and could pick them out in the dark.

A fellow zoölogist, who was a good friend of Brooks through forty years, recalling the striking quality of Brooks' work as a student and his impressive earnestness, says that: "His mind was ever on the problems of his work."

When, on June 30, 1875, he received the degree of Doctor of Philosophy from Harvard College, he had already begun to publish natural history articles in popular magazines and brief reports of his own discoveries in anatomy and embryology of marine animals. Two of his earliest communications were presented in 1874 and 1875 at the Hartford and the Detroit Meetings of the American Association for the Advancement of Science.

He was recognized as a man of great promise and as in those days there was but little real university work on this side of the Atlantic it was natural for his friends to wish that he might study abroad. Indeed, Prof. E. S. Morse had urged upon Brooks' father that he be sent to Europe, but the kind and indulgent parent had to realize that the project was one that could not be financed.

That year of 1875 was one of the great moment in the life of Doctor Brooks; in it he gained his first real insight into research work at the seaside, and in it he aided in a successful Summer School for teachers. The latter was at his home in Cleveland, the former in the laboratory of Alexander Agassiz at Newport, Rhode Island.

In Cleveland the Kirtland Natural History Society was chosen as godfather to the new project in which Brooks was a leading spirit, but there was some opposition and lack of financial support till Andrew J. Rickoff, Superintendent of Public Schools, urged the use of the Central High School Buildings, during vacation, as all the three projectors, Albert H. Tuttle, Theo. S. Comstock, and William K. Brooks, were formerly pupils of that school. The school started with but three pupils, school-teachers, all women, from Indianapolis; but soon, after unexpected and most generous pecuniary aid from Leonard Case, twenty-five enthusiastic teachers attended the lectures, excursions and laboratory meetings. In Brooks' "splendid work of that summer," as Comstock has recently recalled it, we see the characteristic faith and confidence that led him to success even when at first, from lack of buildings, he thought they must hold field sessions only or use Doctor Kirtland's barn, relying upon "enthusiasm and contact with nature to somehow work out results," or when there were but three pupils, to say "three teachers well trained, means the sowing of seed which shall yield a harvest none can measure."

Going then to Newport he began his memorable research on the transparent marine animal Salpa. Meantime he eked out his resources by instructing some lads from New York in the mysteries of marine life which he knew so well how to make vivid and full of meaning.

As this was the beginning of an interest which with characteristic persistence he kept vividly burning till his death, his work on Salpa may well receive more extended notice here. When in 1908 his eyesight made it difficult for him to longer use the high powers of the microscope he rejoiced that he had what he thought his last piece of observational work so far finished that a summer of writing would make his completed drawings ready for the printer. This last monograph on the embryology of Salpa remains unfinished, as cruel sickness robbed him of that summer of writing.

But his first investigations on Salpa came to pass because Salpa was abundant in the clear waters of Newport and Alexander Agassiz suggested he should study them. So clear and translucent are these organisms that Brooks was able to make out the anatomy of the live animals by patient microscopic study without dissection.

He found the accepted views of great European authorities were not correct, that they had not seen all there was to be seen and had hence made false inferences. Though he says "this was my first effort in the field of Marine Zoölogy" the results were of great importance.

To understand his interest in Salpa and the peculiar way his mind worked upon its problems we must recall first that it is one of the quiet bag-like creatures, the Tunicates, whose embryology had shown them to be essentially like, and hence in the new views, blood relations of, the Vertebrates: and second that it was first in Salpa that the remarkable phenomenon of "alternation of generations" had been extended to animals.

So great was the interest in Europe in those problems centering in the Tunicates that Brooks defends his first publication of his results without all his evidence in illustrations, by the remark that students of Salpa were finding new facts so rapidly that one who held back his discoveries till his illustrations should be printed might well find his discoveries no longer new.

It was the poet-naturalist Chamisso who in voyaging around the world with Kotzebue, deduced for Salpa, in 1814, the phenomenon of "alternation of generations." This was universally accepted and Salpa was described as having two generations or different successive individuals with different modes of reproduction in each life-cycle. That is, there were solitary Salpas and chain Salpas found in the water, and the solitary ones were seen to make the chains of individuals by a budding or a non-sexual process. The individuals of the chains, however, had eggs and sperm and gave birth to solitary Salpas having a true sexual origin, but themselves again sexless. Thus there was said to be an alternation of sexless and of hermaphrodite individuals and a sequence of non-sexual and of sexual modes of generation.

Brooks found the same facts but, in addition, the real origin of the eggs—not in the chains but in the solitary individuals, which not only budded forth the chains but put an egg into each individual of the chain.

Hence he claimed then that there was no true alternation of

sexless with hermaphrodite states. For the eggs found in the chains which produce sperm and are therefore males, are not produced by these chains but are produced by the solitary Salpas and put into the male chains to be carried and nursed by them.

The life-cycle he held was thus but an alternation of females and budded out males. While "alternation of generation" did exist in some animals, it did not in Salpa where the phenomenon was first described,—a paradox such as Brooks was ever fond of.

By careful microscopic observation Brooks added new facts to the known anatomy of Salpa, and by keen interpretation boldly opposed the received opinions of the leading zoölogists. Later when the refinement of technique made it possible, he reëxamined and reiterated his views and was led on to many years of patient toil upon various problems of anatomy and of embryology in Salpa and its allies. Much of this work appeared in his great monograph, the *Genus Salpa*, 1893, in which he devoted some 303 quarto pages and 46 plates to his facts and theories.

In 1876 we find Brooks again at the laboratory of Alexander Agassiz, and now ready to dedicate himself at the age of 28 to the service of the fortunate school or institution that would prize him as a man who, having profited by the best training in zoölogy his country could give, had both successfully initiated a summer school after the ideals of Agassiz, and had made discoveries which he illuminated with the point of view of a genius.

It was not the old college, rich in traditions but hampered by customs and fears, but the new foundation laid by Daniel Coit Gilman, with its motto "*Veritas vos liberabit*"; that drew to it the rare spirits who were to embody its ideals. The opening of the Johns Hopkins University with Professor Huxley's address, February 22, 1876, was doubtless a welcome event to Doctor Brooks, the philosophical zoölogist. Twenty Fellowships, each yielding $500, were to be awarded to men who could develop research: of 152 applicants, 107 were deemed eligible and referred to specialists for election. Brooks was one of the twenty chosen.

But even when President Gilman was still in California and wrote East for advice as to the best man in America to hold the chair of zoölogy in the new University to be formed in Baltimore, Brooks was the man recommended strongly.

Preliminary preparations for Natural History work were made by Dr. Philip R. Uhler, Associate in Natural History, but he did but pave the way; the coming of Huxley's ideals in the mind of Prof. Henry Newell Martin, established the courses of instruction in Biology and in Physiology, but in the organization of the new work Brooks was at once made Associate in Natural History or in Biology, and he gave independent lectures on the anatomy of Invertebrates from January to the end of the year, 1877, for graduate students, while assisting Professor Martin in the first General Biology course in April and May of 1877. It is significant that Brooks also gave sixteen public lectures on "The Theories of Biology." In a sense the methods of this laboratory became a mingling of the ideals of Huxley and of Agassiz, the former translated by Martin, the latter by Brooks.

Later on we find him lecturing on embryology, comparative anatomy and osteology and upon morphological problems of more and more special nature with increasing remoteness from the needs of the beginner in zoölogy to whom, however, he gave some of his lectures and personal supervision down even to 1907. But his main influence was with the graduate students whom he trained, as Associate in Zoölogy, Associate Professor in Comparative Anatomy, Associate Professor of Morphology, Professor of Animal Morphology (in 1891), Head of the Biological Laboratory after the resignation of Professor Martin in 1893, Professor of Zoölogy, and Henry Walters Professor of Zoölogy, as the title changed from time to time. The Johns Hopkins University thus became his mental home, his stimulating environment for more than half his lifetime, through all the productive years from 1876 to his death in 1908.

To comprehend his unfolding here, we must recall both what he brought to the University and what the University held for him. What he seemed when he first came has been recently recalled by one of the very few here who marked him then, Prof. Basil L. Gildersleeve, who says:

"The very first lecture I heard him deliver, when he came here a young man, revealed to me at once his uncompromising demand of scientific evidence and his marvellous power of generalization. His popular talks, simple in their form as simple could be, opened vistas of startling significance to those who had learned to think at all. His thoughts did not so much wander through eternity as explore eternity with a measuring rod. To outsiders like myself who were not familiar with the patient process of his scientific research, the word 'genius' seemed to explain everything. He seemed to us one of those rarely gifted beings, in whom child-like sensitiveness is paired with immediate insight, nay, is one with it."

What opportunity the Johns Hopkins gave this gifted being cannot be realized, nor his life-work estimated without due emphasis upon the marine laboratory which he created and of which he was the Director.

He thus outlines his policy in one of his reports as Director:

"In natural science the policy of the University is to promote the study of life, rather than to accumulate specimens; and since natural laws are best studied in their simplest manifestations, much attention has been given to the investigations of the simplest forms of life, with confidence that this will ultimately contribute to a clearer insight into all vital phenomena . . . the ocean is now as it has been in all stages of the earth's history, the home of life."

And the gain he had from his contact with the sea is indicated in these lines taken from a manuscript headed:

"The Gastrula Stage. What does it mean?" "For many years it was my good fortune to spend my summer months upon our southern sea coast, studying with a microscope the steps in the wonderful process of evolution, or unfolding of animals from their eggs, and the memory of the time which was thus spent will always be the most vivid and suggestive impression of my life."

Coming to Baltimore, a city at the head of the Chesapeake Bay, with his experiences at Penikese and Newport, and his own successes in the Summer School of Cleveland fresh in mind, it was necessary that Brooks should turn to the Chesapeake Bay to make his environment supply his needs.

Accordingly, we find him in the spring of 1878 making a preliminary survey in search of a suitable spot for a Summer School in which to study the problems of life in the sea. Unfortunately the low sandy shores and reputed unwholesomeness of the mouth of the Bay offered but poor substitutes for the cold rocky shores of Newport, but he, as ever, made the best use of what was available. With a small sum granted by the University in 1878, he opened the first session of the "Chesapeake Zoölogical Laboratory," at Fort Wool, Virginia.

An artificial heap of stones, making an island of six acres extent, covered by fortifications and twenty miles from the ocean, was indeed a strange location for a marine laboratory, but lying in the Bay, three miles from one shore and one and a half from the other it had the advantage of some fifteen miles of tide-water sweeping by back and forth; though, to be sure, communication with the mainland was not always convenient. Here some seven workers made up the tentative laboratory that was in session eight weeks, and here Brooks had the opportunity to study the ancient animal forms Lingula and Amphioxus.

Though with but crude and scanty apparatus and relying upon occasional brief aid of tugboats for dredging expeditions, the party did good work which was published with the financial aid of citizens of Baltimore, Shoemaker, Garret, Pratt, Uhler, Gilman, Martin and others, as *The Scientific Results of the Chesapeake Zoölogical Laboratory.*

The history of the laboratory henceforth is Brooks' history, and we cannot refrain from recounting its annual periods of activity. In the second year, 1879, Crisfield, Maryland, the great oyster center, was selected in order that Brooks might aid the Maryland Fish Commission in the study of the oyster. Some eleven members of the laboratory lived there, having three barges as their laboratory, from June 25 to August 8, when even their enthusiastic endurance was forced to yield to the native mosquito, whom the inhabitants endured only by making "smudges" in the street and by moving over into the houses on the lee side. Returning then to Fort Wool, the second session was completed September 15.

But it was patent that the fauna of the Chesapeake Bay would not furnish the material needed for the problems Brooks was keen to study: the well-known richness of the fauna of Beaufort, North Carolina, drew him thither. With an annual appropriation of $1,000, and some $4,500 for a steam launch, built for him at Bristol, Rhode Island, and for other apparatus, Brooks in 1880 took a party of six to this rather remote village where they opened their laboratory from April 23 to September 30, more than five months of the year, in the residence known as the Gibbs house and bearing the distinction of being "built of cypress and put together with copper nails."

The success of this venture brought back a party of twelve in 1881, but some of these were students just finishing college work, drawn by this year's announcement that there would be an "Elementary seaside school" with fees of $25, and board and lodging available from $20 to $30 per month, and daily lectures by Dr. W. K. Brooks and Dr. S. F. Clarke. This session lasted from May 2 to the end of August.

Again in 1882, Brooks made one of a party of eight at Beaufort, from May 1 to the end of September. Seven months of the year at the sea-shore laboratory and the rest in the laboratory in Baltimore!

However, being appointed by the Governor, Oyster Commissioner, Brooks was obliged in 1883 to remain in the Chesapeake and opened the laboratory at Hampton, Virginia, occupying part of the new machine shop of the Hampton Institute from May 1 to October 1. This proved an unfavorable location for the forms of life that Doctor Brooks was interested in, though the visiting Englishman, William Bateson, there enjoyed 'the opportunity to add to his famous studies of the problematical worm Balanoglossus. It was there also that the equipment of the laboratory was enlarged by the purchase of a fast sloop yacht which, though black enough as to paint, mingled with its usefulness something of the traits of a white elephant, for its racing spars and deep center board were difficult to manage.

With both sloop and steam launch ten students returned again to Beaufort in 1884, when the laboratory was opened June 1 to September 19, though the illness of Doctor Brooks obliged him to return after a month and to leave the laboratory in the care of Dr. H. W. Conn. But the next year Doctor Brooks was again there with eleven students for the fifteen weeks from May 23 to September 15.

These hot summer days at Beaufort were free from convention, and some may recall their earnest leader in his room absorbed in microscopic study, clad in a drying bathing suit that was not of ideal fit.

In all his work Doctor Brooks avoided indirectness and paraphernalia, and did much with his own hands that might have been relegated to a subordinate. He became a licensed pilot to run the steam launch in and out of Beaufort Inlet and later took the risks of acting as pilot to the schooner from Baltimore on the voyage now to be described, though her keel scraped the bar in the trough of the ground-swell.

Rich as were the results of all these years of work at Beaufort, the fauna there did not satisfy all the demands of one devoted to the fundamental problems of the lower animals that make and dwell amidst coral islands. To such tropical life Brooks now made a daring journey. Starting May 10, 1886, from the wharf in Baltimore, in a small Bay schooner that was chartered by the day, the party of seven after head winds and various mishaps and a stop at Beaufort to take on laboratory furniture, did not reach their destination, Green Turtle Cay, Abaco, Bahama Islands, till June 2. Here they spent a memorable month of rare experience, and some lingered on till later. Of this voyage Doctor Brooks wrote to the *Baltimore Sun:*

"We had been shut up for nineteen days in a little schooner, smaller than those in which Columbus made his first voyage, in a hold which did not allow us to stand erect, with no floor except a few rough boards laid on the ballast of broken stone."

But immediately he says:

"We had found an endless source of pleasure and profit in the examination of the marine animals which drifted by us in the floating sargassum of the Gulf Stream, and we had seen for ourselves what we had so often read, that the ocean is the home of animal life, and that the life of the land is as nothing when compared with the boundless wealth of living things in mid-ocean."

In search of better opportunity to study the problems of floating life in the ocean, Doctor Brooks made a second expedition to the Bahamas in 1887, and established a laboratory for twelve students some three miles from Nassau, on the island of New Providence, from March 1 to July 1. But the steady growth in value of the marine laboratory, was destined to a rude shock following the financial losses to the Johns Hopkins University that made retrenchment necessary in all directions. After ten successful sessions the "Chesapeake Zoölogical Laboratory" was suspended, and its outfit dispersed.

Doctor Brooks, however, turned to the United States Fish Commission for aid and becoming Naturalist in charge of the Station at Woods Holl, Massachusetts, continued his work there with some of his students in the summer months of 1888; while in 1889 and 1890 they also were somewhat aided by the same Government bureau. But in 1891 the University was again able to promote his researches and sent him with some fourteen others to Jamaica, West Indies, May 26 to September 1. Here he established a successful laboratory at Port Henderson, on the shore of the harbor opposite Kingston and Port Royal. Though he hoped that the English plan for a Columbus Marine Station might aid him in future years, that plan did not materialize and henceforth Professor Brooks' energies were more given to work in Baltimore upon material that was obtained for him and less to personal study in new marine laboratories.

In 1892 he sent three of his students to investigate the edge of the great submerged table-land which borders the Gulf Stream on the east and they studied at Alice Town, North Bimini, while in 1893 others went back to Port Henderson, Jamaica, as did others again in 1896. Meantime Brooks took some six students to Beaufort again in 1894 and sent four there in 1895. Finally in 1897 a party of twelve in charge of Prof. James Ellis Humphrey spent two months at Port Antonio, Jamaica, with the lamentable loss from yellow fever of their leader as well as of the talented zoölogist, Dr. Franklin Storey Conant.

Since then the establishment by the Government of a permanent laboratory at Beaufort and of the Carnegie Station on the Dry Tortugas, have given facilities which Brooks was not slow to utilize for his own work and that of his students.

From this long recital we should learn that Brooks' "Chesapeake Zoölogical Laboratory" evolved to fit the conditions and was never crystallized nor hampered by rule or tradition; it was a free organism, choosing its own environment, and even dropped its outgrown name in 1891, to become the "Marine Laboratory."

Through the history of this laboratory as through the history of the university of which it was a part, ran a vein of good management which makes it remarkable for the great results achieved by little financial outlay, but with great labors of love and enthusiasm.

The researches carried on by Professor Brooks were the natural outcome of the above experience at the seaside or rather the problems he was interested in, led him to select the above environment. Beginning his publications with observations upon the embryology of mollusks, he long continued to make new discoveries in that group of animals, publishing several monographs upon marine and fresh-water mollusks, upon the squid and upon the molluscoidea. He was early interested in the Polyzoa and fresh-water sponges about Cleveland. The Marine Crustacea with their clear-cut problems of homology and of metamerism necessarily appealed to his mind, and his discoveries in this group, his works on "Lucifer," the "Stomatopods," and the "Macrura," are amongst the most valuable and well known of his contributions to knowledge. But amongst the still lower forms of life, the Hydroids and jellyfish, he found his love of beauty of form most satisfied. A monograph of American jellyfish in progress many years was never completed though the long years of patient work and remarkable pen drawings were largely given the light in many important publications. His work on Salpa as previously related bore upon the problem of Vertebrate origin, but most of his work dealt exclusively with the fundamental problem of animal morphology as represented in non-vertebrate groups. Yet he at one time lectured upon anthropology and when visiting Nassau he seized the opportunity to study the remains of the Indians who welcomed Columbus and whose tragic fate deeply impressed him. But with the exception of this monograph upon the "Lucayan Indians" most of his new facts were gathered outside the field of Vertebrate groups.

His work contains much thought, and he can scarce be called a prolific writer of small papers. It would be difficult to enumerate many more than 150 titles in the thirty years of most active work from 1876–1906.

But besides these technical papers he had meanwhile contributed many popular articles as well as theories, essays, and reviews. As early as 1877, his *Provisional Hypothesis of Pangenesis* was a bold and thoughtful attempt to make more acceptable the Pangenesis of Darwin, and his book *Heredity* in 1883 elaborated the like view that variations are handed down chiefly through the males. These views modified his conceptions of the place of woman in society and yet it was characteristic of his balance of mind that he wished to submit his theoretic conclusions to the test of experiment and thus to find out how far woman could profit by sharing the higher education of men.

Some of his most deeply and well-thought-out essays and lectures were brought together in book form in his *Foundations of Zoölogy* (Macmillan Co., 1899 and 1907), which must ever remain his chief contribution to philosophical thought. The work preëminently expresses his remarkable balance of mind; part of his purpose was "to show to them who think with Berkeley," that "it is a hard thing to suppose, that right deductions from true principles should ever end in consequences which cannot be maintained or made consistent"; that, "in my opinion, there is nothing in the prevalence of mechanical conceptions of life, and of mind, or in the unlimited extension of these conceptions, to show that this hard thing to suppose is true." And some of his point of view is paraphrased by an English reviewer as follows:

"But supposing the mechanical conception of life to be established, and admitting that the argument from contrivance would thereby lose its force, the attempted proof of the existence of a designer would not on that account be supplanted by disproof. Further, whatever the scientific account of nature may ultimately be, it can throw no light upon the primal cause or final purpose of the whole or of any part. Science tells us what takes place, and how it takes place, she discovers the succession of events and gives us a reasonable confidence in the steadfastness of that succession, but she refuses to admit any necessity therefor, and as to any cause that lies behind the veil of the physical universe, she remains for ever dumb."

But Professor Brooks was no mere dreamer and theorist holding himself aloof from the practical needs of his fellow-beings. His opportunities for carrying on his own researches did not lead him to neglect doing his best for his pupils and for the community in which he lived; and his best was to show them his ideals and to let practical execution develop their own powers. In 1879 he took part in a course of elementary teaching in Biology for teachers in Baltimore, giving fifteen Saturday morning lectures with three times as much laboratory work in which he was aided by Dr. S. F. Clarke. The fifteen teachers who applied, and six of them were women, were led to study such animals as amœba, hydra, sponge, starfish, sea-urchin, earthworm, leech, crawfish, crab, grasshopper, mussel, oyster, and squid.

The laboratory directions he drew up were sought for and used by Prof. Alpheus Hyatt in his work with teachers in the Boston Society of Natural History, and also by Walter Faxon in his work with undergraduates at the Museum of Comparative Zoölogy at Harvard, so that Brooks finally in 1882 made a book, his *Handbook of Invertebrate Zoölogy*, which was a most valuable and original text-book to aid the student at the sea-shore. He also took part in 1882 in an attempt to aid the employees of the Baltimore and

Ohio Railroad, giving a lecture "Upon some methods of locomotion in animals" in which after clearly describing the locomotion of several non-vertebrates he led to a brief exposition of the principles of natural selections and ended with the application that each to succeed should *"make yourselves a little different from your neighbors"* and that the one lesson which natural science teaches is "whatsoever thy hand findeth to do, do it with thy might."

His wish to aid the community also found expression in the establishment of a public aquarium in Druid Hill Park, but the time was hardly ripe and so the aquarium became a blacksmith shop.

But to the practical man Brooks gave the greatest boon in his work upon the oyster industry of Maryland. Finding in 1878 new and remarkable scientific facts regarding the American oyster he entered upon a thorough study of the problems of the oyster industries that meant so much to the state of his adoption. Realizing that the oyster was peculiarly adapted to reclaim for mankind the waste material swept into the Chesapeake by the rivers that drain so vast an area and carry off the wealth of the soil, and that the methods of fishing were primitive and wasteful, while legislation favored a few he pointed out in his Report as Oyster Commissioner what principles should be followed out, what legislation enacted, in order to greatly enrich the whole community. Though his recommendations were then rejected as being too ideal for the times, yet by lectures and discussions and by his popular book *The Oyster* published in 1891, and revised in 1905, he so kept the matter in the public eye that in 1906, legislation in the right direction was finally obtained and the future wealth of the state will be derived in part from his scientific beliefs and keen foresight. So deeply did the success of the oyster industry impress itself upon Professor Brooks that from 1882 he lived always in the eager hope of practical realization from his application of sound judgment upon extensive scientific observations. In fact when urged strongly to head the zoölogical department of a new university in the north, his desire to see the oyster industry restored to prosperity by the application of science to the welfare of the community was no small determining factor in keeping him in Baltimore. From this interest in practical work arose the labors of his pupils in studying and advancing the oyster industries of New England, New Jersey, Oregon, Louisiana, the Carolinas, and Maryland.

But to appreciate the labors of Professor Brooks both in practical and in theoretical knowledge we must know of his great physical handicaps. Born with heart anatomy incomplete from the standpoint of the average man, Brooks well knew his limitations in effort. At college, he believed death would overtake him at any time with exertion that his fellows might find of no harm. On his fortieth birthday he congratulated himself to have brought it so far, since at birth he was given but a few days of life as his probable fate. No insurance company would take his risk and soon or later the strain upon the internal adjustments of his organism must prove too great. Yet when overcome by death, November 12, 1908, after months of painful sickness, Professor Brooks had completed more than sixty years of life with a congenital heart defect said to be rarely carried to manhood. His colored drawings of stomatopods made in the heat of the Dry Tortugas in 1906, show no trembling of the hand but the old love of form and of color. Amongst his ancestors were seven who exceeded three score and ten; that Professor Brooks' life fell short is no wonder.

He was fond of pipe and cigars and at times chewed tobacco to relieve some suppressed irritation and produce the necessary quiet. He was by no means one who saved himself in work or who was careful of exposure and of diet, so that in his life of rough living at the shore he repeatedly was the prey to fevers and diseases as well as subject to many of the minor ills of the flesh which he bore with a fortitude that might to strangers seem indifference.

Deeply interesting but baffling must be the association in this man of such an incomplete and partly embryonic machinery of life with great balance and equalization of mental traits and the perennial spirit of child faith. But here is a special case of the intricate problem of mind and body whose answer we shall lack till, as Professor Brooks used to say, "we find out."

In personal appearance Professor Brooks was not tall, short in the limbs, of abundant flesh but of refined and small boning. With long, straight hair, he was conspicuous at Harvard and in his first years in Baltimore for his rich brown beard that added to his appearance of reserve force and emphasized the keen beauty of his seeing eyes. To the young student he seemed something sphinx-like.

The portrait by Thomas C. Corner, presented by some fifty of his pupils on his fiftieth birthday, represents him as they knew him, sedentary in habit, deliberate in all motions, rather careless of appearance, and long rapt in meditations to be broken by an individual uplift of the eye when about to express some matured thought or long-delayed answer.

His habits in work were evidently imposed by his physique and by his circumstances of life. After a day of lectures and laboratory work he might spend the evening with his family and later, when the household was at rest, write and study far on into the night with his feet wrapped warmly to gain the needed conditions for intense brain activity. In vacation time he might work all day or all night with his microscope, or rise early and work with intervals of short sleep. In his last years he found night work no longer possible and then turned to music to console and cheer his lonely evenings, repeating on a mechanical piano his favorites, such as the Fifth Symphony, the Overture to Tannhäuser and some fugues of Bach.

In his lectures he did not use notes, and made blackboard drawings with great care and symmetry. By imagining himself in the place of the phenomenon he wished to describe, he often made vivid and lasting impressions as in acting out the homologies of front and hind limbs, or in conceiving himself incased in rubber to make the locomotor organs of a squid, or clothed in the germ layer of a chick embryo. Prof. W. H. Howel has said of Brooks' lectures, "but the clearness, the orderliness, and the attractiveness with which he could present a subject was really unrivaled, as far as my experience goes. He seemed to have such a complete control of his mental processes, he thought so well and so clearly and expressed his thoughts in such appropriate language, that every student with a spark of interest in the subject was delighted; it was a treat to hear him lecture."

His methods were always extremely simple and direct, and he believed in doing himself what he wanted to have done well. In the laboratory he laboriously cut endless sections, sharpening his own microtome knife, and made so little use of others' aid that his chief researches are peculiarly his own in all their execution. Electric bells and speaking-tubes were not often used, and his resonant enheartening voice as he summoned the janitor seems still to pervade his work place.

In reading technical works and in preparing lectures he often wrote abstracts with pen copies of illustrations in cheap note-books, $5\frac{1}{2}$x$8\frac{1}{2}$ inches, folding lengthwise and convenient to carry in the pocket. Often these were written only on one side of the page, but later reversed and used again for some different topic. Rarely were dates given to MSS. and drawings, for time was of lesser moment to him than the ideas with which he grouped his materials in his own mind. He made no lists of his own works and no attempts to use clerical aid.

But it should not be inferred that he was too wedded to old-time simplicity. He soon learned to write his manuscripts on the type-writer, with characteristic deliberateness and continuousness. And though long preferring the direct and simple styles of microscope adjustment he used for his later Salpa work Zeiss's most refined apparatus and was proud to prepare series of sections of extreme fineness.

Professor Brooks found time for wide reading and was fond of the best in literature and careful in his own writings to seek for expression in simple English. His library contained well-worn favorites, but he was anything but a collector of books. For the pet dog that chewed his Shakspere he had but praise as showing good taste, but the pup that destroyed cheap novels was a rascal.

He was ever fond of a good joke, and took delight in an anecdote of unexpected and subtle turn. Though so devoted to his work as to be shut off from much social life, he was very fond of his friends and neighbors and glad to converse when he had a topic to develop or a congenial companion to listen to, but was often absorbed and so lacking in small talk as to seem unapproachable.

The topics of the day had peculiar aspects to him. In the Japanese War it was the unfortunate people of Manchuria who greatly excited his sympathy. The subject that interested him deeply was part of him and came to the surface in place of mere commonplaces; when giving lectures on the oyster problem he could talk of nothing else; when wrestling with philosophical problems he might give to his first met friend such sayings as "the term 'supernatural' is due to a misconception of nature, nature is everything that is."

Professor Brooks' anger rarely came to the surface, but he had strong natural likes and dislikes which underwent unexpected change as evidence accumulated. Bad politics, speciousness, and dishonesty and oppression aroused his long-continued animosity. He never forgave the superior officer who would defraud the state by having him sign receipt for wages in excess of what he received.

He had full sympathy for servants and those of restricted education and did many a deed of kindness known to few. In the period of his own greatest relief from poverty and acme of academic renown he was found bringing daily bottles of milk from his country home that the motherless children of the faithful laboratory servant might share his own advantages.

His sympathies extended beyond his fellow-man to animals and even to the plants he grew and tended as companions rather than as specimens. For long years his close companion and friend was the grand St. Bernard dog, "Tige," whom Professor James of Harvard has referred to as "that noble dog." Following his master from college life to Baltimore and through many of his wanderings by the shore this constant comrade falling prey to some heart disease was truly mourned and never forgotten, though other dog friends, many and varied, later came in his stead.

Professor Brooks was preëminently suited for the happy domestic life he led as he could ignore the petty frictions of daily life and though absorbed in his work yet rule with wisdom and firmness in all that concerned the actualities of existence. In his earliest days at Johns Hopkins he and some others who made the nucleus of the biological department took up their abode at "Brightside," a boarding house on the shore of Lake Rowland a few miles from the city. This led to his marriage, June 13, 1878, to Amelia Katharine, daughter of Edward T. Schultz and Susan Rebecca, daughter of David E. Martin. In after years he made his home permanently at "Brightside" since the owner, Mrs. Posey, bequeathed this most beautiful estate to her favorite niece, Mrs. Brooks.

So it came to pass that after years of struggle in a city home where even his most ingenious lamp hot-water apparatus would not make his favorite plants thrive in the window-case, Professor Brooks gained space and light in the country and was even able to have a diminutive greenhouse for the objects of his experiments and of his horticultural relaxation.

Happy as he was with his great trees and self-reared plants, it is well to recall that there were shadows to the bright cloud which many another would not have lived under so cheerfully. But he bravely suppressed natural revolt at extra family burdens laid upon him and by aid of his excellent business instincts was enabled to remove debts, enlarge and perfect the property while carrying out his ideals for his children. Recalling his own hard won university education he sent his son, Charles Edward Brooks, to the Johns Hopkins University, where he received the A.B. degree in 1900, and the Ph.D. degree in mathematics, in 1904. His daughter, Menetta W. Brooks, he also sent through Vassar College.

His determination to give his children this higher education ran counter to a year of needed rest and change in Europe, and he worked on till it became too late.

In his trips to the sea his family went also if anywise possible, and when absent from them Professor Brooks' anxiety made direct inroads upon his health. Through the long years of Mrs. Brooks' invalidism, Professor Brooks had grievous burdens of love to bear, and his devotion was most pathetic. She died in the spring of 1901.

His son being born in 1879, and his daughter in 1881, Professor Brooks' great pride in and love for his children and his devotion to his wife were well-known and potent elements in the life of most of his students who in the evening readings at Professor Brooks' house were taken so generously into its elevating influence.

A review of the names of the sixty men who came together at the end of 1908 to do honor to the memory of their late master would show that no small part of the work of Professor William Keith Brooks had been to train and influence many of the leaders in zoölogy. As Dr. A. G. Mayer has well said, "The spirit of his simple faith in research he has passed on to those whose lives were enriched by knowing him and who now follow where he led in the study of Science."

His influence over his pupils was peculiar—they recognized him as a leader in ideals while fully aware of his faults. One writes: "No man ever worked in a more single-minded and lofty spirit." Another says: "Like all great teachers he knew that the primary purpose of teaching is inspiration and illumination and that information is only of secondary importance." A third has pictured his influence as follows: "But Brooks' particular influence was due chiefly, I imagine, to the fact that all of us recognized in him a certain independence and profundity of thought. He was interested in the large problems of Biology. Concerning these problems he thought continually and deeply and along lines of his own. Those who were brought into close association with him, as students, appreciated this fact and at once accepted him as an intellectual guide and master. Matters of laboratory technique they might have to acquire from other sources, but from him they obtained the stimulus to real thinking."

Many of us might subscribe to the statement of one that "there are few men to whom I feel so much beholden," and very many are voiced in the words of another: "I owe Dr. Brooks a large debt of gratitude for what he did for me. I have often wondered why he let me do some of the things I did without any protest. Maybe he felt that sense would come after a while."

His contact with his pupils was not only in the laboratory and lecture-rooms but in the unconventional months at the seaside and in the intimacy of his evening reading at his home where the students were welcomed to his family circle and enjoyed Brooks' exposition of technical papers, philosophical writings, travels of naturalists, or even Kingsley's *Water Babies* and a poem of Hood.

Professor Brooks was not given to self-seeking and canvassing for academic preferments and honors, but his worth was not without recognition. Very early, when but thirty-six years old, he was elected member of the National Academy. Williams College in 1893, and Hobart in 1899, and the University of Pennsylvania in 1906, bestowed upon him the honorary LL.D. degree.

He was chosen a member of the American Philosophical Society in 1886, and of the Academy of Natural Sciences in 1887. He was a member of the Boston Society of Natural History, the American Academy of Arts and Sciences, the Maryland Academy of Arts and Sciences, and the American Society of Zoölogists while a fellow of the American Association for the Advancement of Science and of the Royal Microscopical Society. He was editor of the quarto series of *Memoirs* from the Biological Laboratory published by the Johns Hopkins University, and one of the editors of the *Journal of Experimental Zoölogy* and of the *Studies from the Biological Laboratory of the Johns Hopkins University*. He was Lowell Lecturer in 1901, and gave one of the chief addresses in 1907 before the International Zoölogical Congress in Boston.

For his scientific discoveries on the oyster he was awarded, in 1883, the medal of the Société d'Acclimatation of Paris and for his work on the stomatopods of the *Challenger* Expedition received a Challenger Medal. He also received a medal for an address at the St. Louis Exposition of 1904.

If in reviewing the life of this man who has been called "a sublimely simple man of rare and subtle culture" we ask what qualities of mind and character and what training have guided his contributions to the advance of science in America we must first clearly realize that in him the inborn overcame the obstacles of his experience however important may have been the circumstances of his life in shaping his self-expression. If with Professor Brooks we speak of inherent properties as nature and of superinduced changes of experience as nurture, in the life of Brooks we must emphasize the great importance of his nature; the childlike excellencies and deep thought-power given him from his origin while on the other hand the value of his nurture should not be overlooked. One of his early companions has recently said: "In all his training at home, in school and at college he was rigidly surrounded with influences adverse to original research or to scientific study." But we must not forget the formative power of his mother's influence, his church and school training, his college life and contact with great naturalists and later his rich opportunities at the Johns Hopkins and its seaside laboratories.

His talents were inborn and overcame obstacles and assimilated opportunities; but other opportunities might have made a very different result. His life was reactive to environment, but the environment acted as a stimulus and he reacted after his kind and was not passively molded by circumstances.

When all is said, William Keith Brooks was able to leave his mark on the development of science in America not so much by any "mystery" of "genius" as by stubborn labor, conscientious application to duty, by pertinacity of purpose, by concentration of his forces upon what he could do, by wisely seizing opportunities for self-expression, by living much in the ideal world so that he was not crushed by the weight of daily burdens and above all by being able to keep much of his child spirit even to the end.

INDEX

Philadelphia, Centennial Exhibition, *1876*, 278, 336, 394, 397
Physical chemistry, science of, 344, 349, 350
Physics, progress of, 343; *see also* Gibbs, Josiah Willard
Pictet, Prof. Adolphe, 10, 14
Pierpont, John, 96
Pike, Capt. Nicholas, 61
Plan of Creation, lectures by J. L. R. Agassiz, 156
Playfair, John, 98
Plotus anhinga, *see* Snake-bird
Poland, King of, 21
Polydactyle Horses, by O. C. Marsh, 299
Polynesian Archipelago, exploration of, 238; *see also* Wilkes Exploring Expedition
Port Antonio, Jamaica, 444
Port Henderson, West Indies, laboratory at, 443
Porpoise, The, see Wilkes Exploring Expedition
Porter, Rev. Noah, 92
Potato introduced into France, 50
Pourtalès, Louis François, Count de, 163
Prévost, Constant, 254
Priestley, Dr. Joseph, 96
Prussia, King of, 152, 156, 157
Pteranodontia, *see* Pterodactyls
Pterodactyls, 301
Pterosauria, *see* Pterodactyls
Pulkowa, observatory at, 376, 378, 379; *also* 384
Putnam, Frederick Ward, 335

Quadrupeds of America, by Audubon and Bachman, 82, 84
Quaternions of Sir William Hamilton, 356

Race problem, Wyman's views on, 191
Radiation, experiments on, 34
Rainbow trout, 274; *see also* Food-fishes
Raleigh, Sir Walter, 313, 394
Rattlesnake, The, 198
Red Cloud Agency, 294
Relief, The, see Wilkes Exploring Expedition
Rennel, James, 97

Reptilia and Amphibia, publications on, by E. D. Cope, 328, 329
Researches among the Fossil Fishes, by J. L. R. Agassiz, 153, 154
Respiration of Turtles, by Mitchell and Morehouse, 177
Review of North American Birds, by S. F. Baird, 272
Rhynchosporeæ, North American, by Asa Gray, 215
Rickoff, Andrew J., 435
Ridgeway, Robert, 272
Rittenhouse, David, 95, 130, 387
Ritter, Heinrich, 114
Robins, Benjamin, 18
Robison, John, 99
Roemer, (Breslau), 291
Rogers, Prof. William B., 193, 308
Roozeboom, Bakhuis, 353, 355
Rose, Gustav, 114, 244 *note*
Rose, Heinrich, 114
Rothrock, Dr. J. T., 183 *note*, 221
Rowland, Henry Augustus, birth and education, 406; distaste for classics, 406, 420; teacher of chemistry and physics, 408; early inventions, 409; professor at Johns Hopkins, 411; sent abroad, 411; meeting with Dr. Ira Remsen, 412; laboratory equipment, 412; personal qualities, 413, 418, 421; research work, 415; concave grating, 415, 416; relations with students, 418; marriage, 420; love of music and sports, 422; fatal malady, 424; invention of octoplex printing telegraph, 425; attitude toward politics and religion, 425; honors, 426
Royal Institution, London, 9, 43
Rozier, Ferdinand, 74 '
Rumford, Benjamin Thompson, Count, birth and early education, 10; life as student and teacher, 12; marriage, 14; introduction to Gov. Wentworth and results, 15; rôle of landed proprietor, 15; sent to England, 15; becomes member of Colonial Office, 17; enters British army, 19; devises new code of marine signals and plans a frigate, 19; elected Fellow of Royal Society, 19; becomes Secretary for Georgia and Under Secretary

080923